THE
HISTORY OF COMMODITY
FUTURES TRADING
AND ITS REGULATION

Jerry W. Markham

PRAEGER

New York
Westport, Connecticut
London

Library of Congress Cataloging-in-Publication Data

Markham, Jerry W.
   The history of commodity futures trading and
its regulation.

   Bibliography: p.
   Includes index.
   1. Commodity exchanges – United States – History.
2. Commodity exchanges – Law and legislation –
United States – History.   I. Title.
HG6049.M37   1986   332.64′4   86-25246
ISBN 0-275-92313-4

Library of Congress Catalog Card Number: 86-25246
ISBN: 0-275-92313-4

First published in 1987

Praeger Publishers, 521 Fifth Avenue, New York, NY 10175
A division of Greenwood Press, Inc.

Printed in the United States of America

The paper used in this book complies with the Permanent
Paper Standard issued by the National Information Standards
Organization (Z39.48-1984).

10 9 8 7 6 5 4 3 2 1

To Mollie, Sean, and Marcia

CONTENTS

ABBREVIATIONS

ACLI   ACLI International Commodity Services Inc.

AITC   American International Trading Company

Amex   American Stock Exchange

BVN   bullion value demand promissory note

CBOE   Chicago Board Options Exchange, Inc.

CEA   Commodity Exchange Authority

CFTC   Commodity Futures Trading Commission

CREEP   Committee to Re-Elect the President

EFP   exchange of futures for physical

FCM   futures commission merchant

FDIC   Federal Deposit Insurance Corporation

FTC   Federal Trade Commission

GNMA   Government National Mortgage Association

ICCH   International Commodity Clearing House

INTEX   International Futures Exchange, Inc.

LIFFE	London International Financial Futures Exchange
LME	London Metal Exchange
NASD	National Association of Securities Dealers
NFA	National Futures Association
PIK	payment in kind
SEC	Securities and Exchange Commission
Simex	Singapore International Monetary Exchange
SIPC	Security Investors Protection Corporation

PREFACE

Until recently, the commodity futures industry has been a little-known and much misunderstood part of the financial community. Its trading practices were little understood by anyone except for the most arcane specialists. The creation of the so-called financial futures (e.g., futures contracts on stock indexes) has done much to lift this screen of obscurity. Today, much of Wall Street and many major financial institutions are heavily involved, directly or indirectly, in the futures industry.

Because of the large leverage inherent in futures contracts, and the attending temptation for abuse that such leverage permits in fast-moving markets, commodity futures trading has a long history of federal regulatory efforts. Those efforts were designed to tame the "wheat kings" and their successors who have sought to manipulate and commit fraud in these markets. The first efforts to establish federal regulation began in the late nineteenth century and continues today. In the interim, numerous statutory requirements have been adopted, commissions created, cases brought, and rules adopted, generally with little success. In recent years, however, federal regulation has become more pervasive and has become an integral part of this industry, which has for years styled itself as the last true bastion of free enterprise, unrestrained by burdensome federal regulations. This book examines that evolutionary process.

Specifically, Part I of this book traces the beginnings of futures trading in the United States. It describes the problems that engendered calls for federal regulation, and it traces the history of that regulation. Part II of the book describes the operations of the Commodity Futures Trading Commission, the federal regulatory agency now charged with responsibility for regulating commodity futures trading. Part II also discusses the internal turmoil at that agency that hampered its operations in the early stages, and it describes the operating structures and problems encountered by the

Commission. Part III is a review of the instruments regulated by the federal government, such as futures contracts, leverage contracts, and options. It also discusses the problems associated with "hybrid" instruments that do not fall completely within any of those categories.

This book is not intended to be a definitive history of commodity futures trading. That work is yet to be written. Rather, it seeks to trace the history of the efforts to establish governmental controls in these markets and the problems encountered by federal regulators. Those problems involved some mundane issues but also included global concerns such as participation and possible manipulation of markets by foreign governments such as, for example, the Soviet Union. Finally, this book is not intended to be a treatise on the law of commodity futures regulation. It is a history and, for that reason, I have eschewed long citations or involved analysis of regulations.

ACKNOWLEDGMENTS

I would like to express my thanks to Joan Creigh. She was able to find, almost instantly, the most obscure government reports and sources, from which I obtained much of the information upon which this book is based. Her efforts substantially eased the research burden.

I also particularly want to express my appreciation to Eva Spencer, head of the word processing department in the Washington office of Rogers & Wells. She spent many long hours typing and revising the manuscript. Eva, who was my secretary at the Commodity Futures Trading Commission, made the writing task a much simpler one, and certainly a less tiring process for the author.

Finally, I would like to thank Karen Seegren, who cheerfully prepared the bibliography and the index, two difficult and thankless tasks.

PART I
THE BEGINNINGS

1
THE BEGINNINGS

The origins of futures trading is obscure, but the Futures Industry Association has traced its sources back to 2000 B.C., "when the merchants of what is now Bahrein Island took goods on consignment for barter in India." The Chicago Board of Trade asserts that such trading also existed in Greco-Roman times. Feudal landowners in seventeenth century Japan also traded commodity futures in the form of rice "tickets" or warehouse receipts on their production.[1]

Whatever the ultimate origins of futures trading, it seems clear that its immediate predecessor was the "to arrive" contract widely used in Europe by the eighteenth century. This was simply a contract for the purchase of goods upon their arrival. For example, ship cargoes were often sold before their arrival in port on a "to arrive" basis.

The "to arrive" contract also filled an important need in the grain trade in the United States, which had expanded rapidly during the nineteenth century. This was because grain prices during the early stages of American development were subject to a seemingly endless cycle of boom and bust. At the end of the crop year, farmers would flood the market with grain, and prices would drop drastically. Grain would then be left to rot, or simply be dumped, as prices became so low that transporting it to market became a losing proposition. Later in the year, shortages would develop and prices would rise as dramatically as they had fallen. Consequently, buyers and sellers sought to provide for their needs by contracting for the delivery of quantities and grades of grain at an agreed-upon price and delivery date in the future, depending on when the grain would be needed and when it was available. This was accomplished through "to arrive" or forward contracts.

Soon a practice developed whereby these "to arrive" contracts were themselves bought and sold in anticipation of changes in market prices.

Indeed, by 1859 the "to arrive" contract had become a medium for trading, and speculation, as well as for the actual purchase and sale of grain. This was later replaced by a standardized "futures contract" on the Chicago Board of Trade, the first organized commodity exchange in the United States for futures trading.[2]

Founded in 1848, the Chicago Board of Trade initially served as an exchange for all types of commodity trading, including grain, beef and pork, lumber, salt, hides, high wines, alcohol, fish, coal, wood, lead, wool, stone, brick, and various kinds of produce. The Board of Trade provided a market place for farmers to transport their crops to sell and grading facilities for the grain upon delivery.

Initially, the membership fee for the Chicago Board of Trade was $5, and its rules were limited in number and scope. In 1859, however, the Chicago Board received a charter from the Illinois legislature, which remains in effect today. It authorized the Chicago Board of Trade to establish rules, to enter arbitration awards and to appoint inspectors of grains. The Arbitration Committee authorized by the legislature heard all business disputes among members that they wished to submit to that Committee. An Appeals Committee was formed to review the awards of the Arbitration Committee. The exchange also imposed disciplinary authority over its members, and various committees were established for such matters as adopting rules and resolving membership issues.[3]

At first, futures contracts in this market were privately negotiated between traders acting outside the regular marketplace as well as on the floor. But in 1864, the Chicago Board of Trade officially recognized this trading, and established rules for trading began taking place in the "pits" on the premises of the Chicago Board of Trade.[4] Thereafter, in 1873, the Chicago Board of Trade adopted trading hours designed to ensure that competition was concentrated on the floor of the Exchange. Trades conducted after hours were not recognized as legal and binding commitments— a system that is encompassed within the federal statutory scheme that now regulates the futures markets.[5]

This early effort by the Chicago Board of Trade, however, did not accomplish the goal of limiting trading on its floor. The Chicago Open Board of Trade, a competitor to the Chicago Board of Trade, began futures trading in 1877 as an alternative to the Board of Trade.[6] Trading in futures was also conducted by curb trading, which was simply trading conducted off the floor of the Chicago Board of Trade, often on a convenient street corner. As one writer described this curb market, which in effect allowed extended trading hours in commodities beyond those of the Chicago Board of Trade:

> They are the hardest worked race of beings on the face of the earth. They get up at sunrise, bolt their steak and rolls, and rush down to the "first

board," which meets at a well-known corner between 8 and 11 o'clock. At 11 the "second board" met at the Board of Trade rooms, but buyers and sellers waited for the New York dispatches, which were due about noon. Early in the afternoon the "third board" congregated on the corner before mentioned (called Gamblers' corner by some unregenerate rascal), ... The "fourth board" met on the sidewalk opposite the Tremont House an hour later, and trading continued until 9 o'clock, when the overworked grain traders went home for a few hours' sleep.[7]

By 1868, futures contracts had become standardized on the Chicago Board of Trade, and speculation became the focus of trading there. Abuses were rampant. It was charged at one point that hardly a month elapsed without a corner on the marketplace. For example, in 1868, it was reported that there were three corners in wheat, two in corn, one in oats, one attempted corner in rye, and another threatened in pork. Things had not improved by 1874, when there was almost a corner a month during the latter half of the year. In 1878 there was a squeeze in May wheat, a corner on July wheat, and a squeeze on December wheat. A corner on other markets occurred in almost every month of the year in 1881. In 1882 there were four corners, and defaults on contracts occurred in wheat in April, June, July, and August. There was a corn corner in August, a lard corner in September, and a ribs corner in October. In 1887 the "Kershaw failure" occurred in the wheat market. A squeeze was also run in May wheat. In 1902 an oats corner was conducted on the Chicago Board of Trade, and the John W. Gates corner was attempted in 1905 in the wheat market, but it failed.

One of the big "plungers" in the Chicago wheat was Benjamin P. Hutchinson. Hutchinson (or "old Hutch," as he was called by his biographer) first began his operations in the wheat pit around 1864. In 1866 he was given credit for the first significant corner in the wheat pit, a singular honor. Hutchinson dominated the Chicago market until the early 1890s. But other manipulators vied for the title of "Wheat King" in their cornering operations. One such trader was E. L. Harper, known as "Crazy Harper," a former sewing machine salesman. In 1887 Harper attempted a wheat corner in competition with various other groups, including a mysterious syndicate from California. But Harper was routed by the bears, and it was reported that some 19 firms failed as a result. It was also later discovered that Harper had used a bank where he worked to finance his trading by an elaborate check kiting scheme. He was given a 10-year prison sentence.

Another well-known aspirant for the title of "Wheat King" was Joe Leiter. A Harvard graduate, Leiter began his famous attempt to corner wheat on the Chicago Board of Trade in 1897. It appeared at first that Leiter had cornered the December wheat contract. But his corner was broken when P. D. Armour, the largest short, hired a fleet of boats to bring grain into Chicago. Led by a flotilla of tugboats, Armour's ships broke through the ice on the Great Lakes and delivered to Leiter some 10 million bushels of wheat. Undaunted, Leiter continued to buy, but a river of wheat poured into Chicago from all sections of the country. Finally, the corner collapsed in "a pit of frantic brokers fighting like madmen." Leiter and his family lost several million dollars, and he was indefinitely suspended from the Chicago Board of Trade.[8]

Another great plunger was James A. Patten, who conducted numerous cotton corners, the most famous of which occurred in 1909.[9] One other notorious trader was "King Jack," whose real name was William Sturges. King Jack attempted to corner the corn market in 1874. For a time, he had control of the marketplace, but only a few months later he was himself trapped in another corner. Sturges refused to pay up his obligations, defying the board of directors of the Chicago Board of Trade in the process. Later, Sturges was expelled, but after protracted litigation he was reinstated to membership.

The Chicago Board of Trade sought to prevent these practices by various resolutions. In 1874 the Illinois legislature passed an anti-corner statute. But these efforts were not successful. Numerous states also passed statutes prohibiting gambling in futures contracts, many of which still remain on the books. These laws prohibited futures trading where there was no intent to take or make delivery. But the courts held that pro forma assertions of intent with respect to delivery were sufficient to preclude application of these statutes.

The great market operators were legends in their own time. Indeed, it was said that children often aspired to be the Wheat King rather than president. By the turn of the century, speculation on the grain exchanges had also become a widespread practice by many ambitious businessmen. One such individual, John Anderson Truman, became wealthy as a result of his speculations in wheat futures at the Kansas City Board of Trade. In 1901, however, in a single grain transaction, he lost some $40,000 or more, causing him to drastically cut family expenses. This included the termination of his son's college education, who was later to lament that, "I never got a university education. You can feel the lack of it when you sit here. . . . It is a shortcoming." John's son, Harry, also had to give up his "beloved piano lessons." As will be discussed below, Harry's annoyance with futures trading became known to the grain exchanges when he became the thirty-third president of the United States.[10]

THE GOLD CORNER

The development of commodity futures trading occurred on the East Coast during the mid-1860s in gold. The New York Gold Exchange was established in 1864 to handle the gold trading business there. By 1866 it had 437 members and 117 associates, many of whom were also members of the New York Stock Exchange.

During the Civil War, the price of gold rose and fell with Union victories and defeats, particularly after the suspension of specie payment by New York banks in 1861. It was then that Congress began its first effort to regulate commodities speculation by prohibiting futures trading in gold; it prohibited all contracts in gold coin or bullion that were to be delivered at any date subsequent to the making of the initial contracts, and all short sales in gold and bullion. But that legislation was repealed only a few weeks after its adoption, after it proved unsuccessful in stabilizing prices.

In 1869 Black Friday occurred on the New York gold market. This was the climax of Jay Gould's and Jim Fisk's famous effort to corner the gold market. Gould and Fisk had recognized that the supply of gold outside the U.S. Treasury was limited, and they attempted to keep the Treasury Department from selling gold in any unusual amounts. They did so by arguing that, in keeping the price of gold high, they were helping the farmer by making his crops worth more in gold. As a result, the supply of gold was restricted by the government, and its price rose.

The "Gold Pool," which Gould and Fisk had established to carry out this corner, was broken when President Grant ordered his Secretary of the Treasury to sell gold and to buy bonds. When this news reached the Gold Room on Wall Street, the price of gold collapsed, destroying the corner attempt. The results were described as follows:

> Operators old at the game lost their heads and dashed hatless and crazed through the streets, eyes bloodshot and brains afire; the crowd in New Street became a mob. The price of gold plunged downward thirty points. Transactions, amounting to over four hundred million dollars, could not be cleared by the Gold Exchange Bank, and clearances were suspended for a month, and gold dealings for a week.[11]

OTHER EARLY EXCHANGES

The Milwaukee Chamber of Commerce was organized in 1858 to serve as a mechanism for the trading of grain. In 1861 the New York Commercial Association was organized as an exchange for commodity trading. It changed its name to the New York Produce Exchange in 1868. The Merchant Exchange of St. Louis was organized in 1876, and began trading in futures by 1882. Other exchanges were also organized during the period of 1869 to 1890. These included the Duluth Board of Trade, the Minneapolis Chamber of Commerce, and the Kansas City Board of Trade, where John Truman engaged in his speculations.

After the turn of the century, the Omaha Grain Exchange, the San Francisco Chamber of Commerce, the Seattle Grain Exchange, and the Portland Grain Exchange were formed to conduct trading in commodities. The New York Coffee Exchange, which had been formed in 1882, initially traded futures contracts in coffee. But, in December 1914, it also added a contract for sugar on the exchange. Still later, it consolidated with the New York Cocoa Exchange.

Another New York exchange, the New York Cotton Exchange, was also established in the late 1800s. Among its founding fathers were the Lehman brothers, who had formed a cotton trading business in Montgomery, Alabama, during the Civil War. After the Civil War, they moved their cotton trading operations to New York. Later, the Lehman brothers branched out into trading other commodities and still later became investment bankers, fathering the famous investment banking firm, Lehman Brothers. Herbert H. Lehman, a member of this family, became governor and later senator of New York.

PRIVILEGES: THE FIRST COMMODITY OPTIONS

Trading on the Chicago Board of Trade expanded during the Civil War, and board members began protecting their contracts by dealing in "privileges." For a small fee the purchaser of an option was thus given an option or "privilege" to purchase or buy grain at a fixed price. These contracts are also referred to as "puts" and "calls." Normally such options were valid only for the following marketing day, although the terms could vary.

In 1865 the Chicago Board of Trade sought to prohibit "privilege" trading, because it was widely thought that such trading was simply gambling. This prohibition was not effective, because trading could still occur under the Board of Trade's prohibition. The only sanction was that the Board would not enforce the obligations. In 1874 the Illinois legislature banned options trading and false rumors that were designed to influence commodity prices. Subsequent legal interpretations of this legislation, however, substantially clouded its actual prohibitions.

In 1876 and 1877, the Board of Trade passed additional resolutions designed to stop privilege trading. The 1877 resolution stated that a member transferring a privilege to an "innocent party" would be deemed guilty of fraud. But this prohibition was also not effective. Still later, the Board did bring actions against persons trading in puts and calls, and it suspended three members. The exchange also began a massive investigation to determine the extent of privilege trading. In the course of that investigation, the Board of Trade summoned more than thirty of its members to testify under oath about their trading in prohibited privileges. Some fifty other members were also questioned, and private detectives were employed. It was reported in the press that the investigation had implicated half the members of the Board. No substantive disciplinary action was taken, however, and the suspensions of the three members previously disciplined for options trading were lifted.

In order to avoid the exchange's prohibitions against puts and calls, the contracts were modified and designated as "indemnity of sale or purchase." Under this guise, options continued until 1910. In that year, the exchange was investigated by the federal government. Its directors then voted to abolish trading in indemnities. But a few months later, that restriction was rescinded by a vote of the exchange's membership.[12] Option trading then flourished once again until, as described below, the federal government intervened.

BUCKET SHOPS

Another serious problem in the early years of futures trading was the "bucket shops" that made their appearance on LaSalle Street in Chicago in the 1880s. Essentially, a bucket shop is an establishment where bets can be made on current prices for commodities.[13] The bets are not executed as contracts on any exchange, but rather are placed on the bucket shop's books, just as would be done by a bookie, who offsets his bets by his own resources. Such resources were often sadly lacking, as discovered by successful wagerers when they came to collect their winnings. The bucket shops became so popular that gambling in grain came to be viewed as a national pastime at the turn of the century.

The Chicago Board of Trade sought to stop the bucket shops, whose reputations and tactics were impugning the integrity of its marketplace (as well as posing a threat of competition to the Exchange), by cutting off access to its market quotations, upon which the bucket shop operations were wholly dependent for their operations. Commission houses also began discontinuing the posting of quotations on office blackboards. Nevertheless, the bucket shops continued to thrive. This was due in part to competition from other exchanges which fostered the bucket shops

> The Consolidated Exchange, the second largest stock exchange in New York City and at one time the most powerful rival of the New York Stock Exchange, came to be regarded as a den of bucketeers. The Chicago Open Board of Trade, the "Little Board" in Chicago, was captured by bucketeers in order to obtain commodity market quotations.[14]

By the late 1880s, legislation had also been adopted in several states against bucket shops. But the Board of Trade's right to withhold quotations was subjected to a welter of conflicting court decisions, and the bucket shops continued to operate. Later, after many years of tangled legal maneuvers, the Board of Trade obtained a spectacular victory in the U.S. Supreme Court against C. C. Christie of Kansas City, the "Bucketshop King," through a decision handed down by the Court in 1905.[15] The Board also prosecuted its members for engaging in bucket shop activities, once again using detectives and undercover methods. A series of expulsions resulted, and 281 persons in Illinois were indicted for violating anti-bucket shop legislation in that state.

FEDERAL LEGISLATIVE EFFORTS

The "populist revolt" that occurred during the 1890s was occasioned in large measure by the erratic price changes in agricultural commodities that were impoverishing the farmers.[16] It was thought by the farmers—who were represented by the Grange movement—that the Chicago Board of Trade was responsible for the volatility of prices that often precluded farmers from being assured of a reasonable price for their crops. As a result of this farm movement, Congress began introducing legislation in the 1880s that was designed to supplement existing state prohibition against trading and gambling in futures, as well as bucket shops.

Between 1880 and 1920 there were some 200 bills introduced in Congress to regulate futures and options trading. For example, in 1883 a bill was introduced to prohibit the use of the mails in connection with futures trading. In 1887 bills were introduced to prohibit and punish persons dealing in futures. None of these bills were reported out of committee. In 1890 the so-called Butterworth Bill sought to tax dealers in options and futures. It was reported out of committee, but it did not come up for a vote on the floor.

In 1891 and 1892 several bills sought to prohibit futures trading, and from these evolved the Hatch Bill, which proposed to levy a prohibitive tax on all futures trading in grain and cotton. The bill was passed in the house by a vote of 167 to 46, and later by the Senate with some amendments. It was then reported out of conference, but the House did not have time to vote on the amendments approved by the conference, and a vote to suspend the rules, which would have allowed timely consideration, failed. The bill was introduced in the next Congress but was not passed. If adopted, the Hatch bill would have required dealers in options and futures to pay the sum of $2,000 annually, plus a fee of 20¢ for each bushel of grain traded. It was estimated that this bill would have cost the industry close to the unheard of figure of $2.5 million, just to continue their business.

In 1908 another series of proposals to legislate futures trading began. In the 60th Congress (1907-1909), 25 bills were introduced, which were designed to prohibit futures trading. In 1909 an attempt was made in

Congress to tax bucket shops, but it failed. An effort was also made to ban from interstate commerce all activities involving cotton futures contracts, but this too was defeated. Seventeen other bills were introduced in the 61st Congress and 42 in the following Congress.

At regular intervals through 1905 to 1921, congressional committees also investigated and reinvestigated the grain trade. For example, in 1910 hearings were conducted on bills for the prevention of dealing in futures on boards of trade. The Chicago Board of Trade and other exchanges successfully fought the bill. In doing so, they drew heavily on the decision of the Supreme Court in the anti-bucketing case, where Justice Holmes accepted the concept of futures trading.[17] This became a familiar source for the Board of Trade in defending speculation, as well as its oft-repeated reminder that there are no speculative grain markets in Russia.

In 1908 a report of the Commissioner of Corporations was published on the cotton exchanges, in response to a House resolution. As a result of that report, legislation was adopted in 1914 that was entitled the Cotton Futures Act. That act did not, however, broadly regulate cotton futures trading, but established a commercial difference system for pricing and the use of federal standards for the grading of cotton. Other legislation included the Grain Standards Act and the Warehouse Act, which also sought to standardize conditions on the delivery and storage of commodities subject to futures contracts.

WORLD WAR I AND THE FTC STUDY

In 1917 Germany's unrestricted submarine warfare, the U.S. declaration of war in April, as well as a shipping shortage led to a frenzy of speculative trading in commodities. Legislation was later enacted to control prices, and it was not until July 15, 1920, that the Chicago Board of Trade resumed wheat trading, although futures trading did continue in other commodities. At the time that trading in wheat futures resumed, prices immediately dropped precipitously (by some 57 percent) in an "orgy of gambling operations" that drove prices far below the cost of production.

This price drop was the result of a "great bear raid" maintained for nearly 10 consecutive months in the face of record export demand. When the raid began, the December futures contract on the Chicago Board of Trade opened at $2.75 per bushel. Before it ended, the price of cash wheat had fallen to $.85 a bushel.

Problems were also encountered before the outbreak of World War I in the cotton market, where violent price fluctuations were occurring on the strength of war rumors. To lessen the effects of those price swings, limitations on daily price movements were imposed for the first time.[18] That effort came too late for some speculators, including H. L. Hunt, the eccentric oil billionaire, whose flair for gambling led him to become the richest man in the world. According to family legend, H. L. had learned to read commodity quotations before he was three years old, and he closely followed his father's successful futures trading. In 1917, however, H. L. lost everything when he sold short on the cotton futures market and prices skyrocketed. Undaunted, he was able to recover from this financial setback through his fabled poker-playing abilities, and he later achieved great wealth through his operations in the Texas oil fields. As will be discussed below, H. L. Hunt's sons, Nelson Bunker and Herbert, were also to achieve national notoriety in the 1970s from their own futures speculations in soybeans and silver.[19]

The disruptions in the wheat market resulted in a massive study of the grain industry by the Federal Trade Commission (FTC). Several volumes of that study were completed on September 15, 1920. The study delved into every aspect of commodity trading, hedging, and market practices. Among other things, it noted that one of the most important functions of the exchanges was collecting, recording, and distributing quotations and market information.

The FTC study found that the grain exchanges were undoubtedly affected by a national public interest, and it closely examined futures trading in grain. It examined a variety of practices, including the development of private wire systems, job lot trading (trading in small increments), the use of cross trades, the practice of trading against customer orders, the bucketing of orders, and the use of "give-ups." The FTC study also examined the role of hedging and speculation in the futures markets.

THE FUTURES TRADING ACT

The sharp drop in prices that occurred at the end of World War I set the stage for federal legislation. This legislation, the first attempt at comprehensive federal regulation of futures trading, was the Futures Trading Act of 1921. The essence of the statute was to authorize the Secretary of Agriculture to designate exchanges that met certain minimum qualifications as "contract markets." To accomplish this goal, the Grain Futures Act imposed a prohibitive tax of 20¢ per bushel on options and on grain futures contracts that were not traded on exchanges approved by the government.

It was thought that, by placing the exchanges under the supervision of the Secretary of Agriculture, bucket shops could be eliminated. Thus, "the men who buy under the present bucket shop system will not have any place to buy unless they do business through a contract market"; the "bucket shop is wiped out in this bill, because a bucket shop is not a contract market."[20]

It was noted by one of the sponsors of this legislation, Senator Capper, that the plan of the Grain Futures Act was to correct only the evils in futures and options trading. He stressed that the legislation did "not concern itself at all with the sale or purchase of actual grain, either for present or future delivery. The entire business of buying and selling the actual grain, sometimes called 'cash' or 'spot' business, is expressly excluded. It deals only with the 'future' or 'pit' transaction, in which the transfer of actual grain is not contemplated."[21]

It was noted in Congress that "bear raids" by manipulators were occurring every year, shortly before or immediately following the harvest, and that this was playing "directly into the hands of European importers, who are enabled to buy millions of bushels of wheat in the futures market at a reduced price, which they later exchange for cash wheat."[22]

Senator Capper also described particular abuses. In one instance, an individual had embezzled funds to use for trading on the Chicago Board of Trade in an amount exceeding $1 million. In another case, a state bank had to be closed because of an embezzlement that was used to finance futures trading in Chicago. In another small town, a prominent citizen, the bank president, had become a fugitive from justice at age 72, after embezzling $150,000 of a depositor's funds to use for trading on the Chicago Board of Trade. He conducted that trading through a secret chamber in the bank with direct wire connections to the Chicago brokerage houses. Senator Capper's list also went on to describe "a constant stream of suicides," by strychnine and other means, that followed losses on the markets. Senator Capper also stated that a bookkeeper in a grain operator's office had told him that the country "would be shocked if it knew how many women were 'playing the market'."

Senator Capper further charged that the Chicago Board of Trade was a "gambling hell," that it was the "world's greatest gambling house": "Monte Carlo or the Casino at Habana are not to be compared with it."[23] Sixty years later John H. Stassen, counsel for the Chicago Board of Trade, noted with respect to these remarks that "these populist politicians were marvelous orators, of course. What they lacked in economics, they certainly made up for in elocution."[24]

Despite its altruistic goals, the Futures Trading Act was declared unconstitutional in 1922 by the Supreme Court in *Hill v. Wallace*.[25] The Court held that the statute was an unconstitutional exercise of the congressional taxing power. This did not, however, slow congressional interest in imposing regulatory controls. Only two weeks after the Supreme Court declared the act unconstitutional, new legislation was introduced. This legislation was based on Congress's authority to regulate interstate commerce. Otherwise, it was substantially identical to the 1921 legislation that was held unconstitutional.

One week after its introduction, hearings were held in the House on this new legislation over a five-day period. In that brief time, and based on its prior hearings, Congress found that transactions in grain involving options and futures are "affected with a national public interest," that their prices are quoted in the United States and foreign countries and form a basis for determining the prices of products for producers and consumers. It also found that transactions in options and futures are extremely susceptible to speculation, manipulation, and control, and that sudden and unreasonable fluctuations in the grain prices often occur. It found that such fluctuations were an obstruction to and a burden on interstate commerce.

With respect to the Supreme Court's decision declaring the Futures Trading Act of 1921 to be unconstitutional, the House report to the new legislation noted,

> on the 15th day of May, 1921, May contracts were selling in Chicago at $1.48; the next day after the decision of the Supreme Court, . . . [in *Hill v. Wallace*] Chicago newspapers carried headlines announcing that wheat had advanced 4 cents a bushel as a result of the restrictions being taken off the exchanges. It is also admitted that wheat declined from that time on until the 31st day of May, when May contracts had declined to $1.16 a bushel, or a total decline of 32 cents a bushel in 15 days. Attention might be called to the fact that this happened at a time when the visible supply of the world's wheat had not increased and that there was no favorable crop report issued from any source to change the price of wheat. Also attention has been called to the fact that this condition was most manifest on the Chicago exchange, where there was evidently a straight-out manipulation of the market.[26]

The Chicago Board of Trade responded predictably to these conclusions. Its supporters charged that these price fluctuations were the result of misinformation in Department of Agriculture reports. It was noted that the Board of Trade had been in business for 73 years and, despite panic and prosperity and peace and war, it had never closed its doors on a single business day. The exchange's defenders also pointed out that a joint conference committee on grain exchange practices (made up of representatives of the exchanges, the farmer's elevator movement, and the U.S. grain growers) had been formed in the last year to cure the problems and concerns involving the grain exchanges and cooperative elevator concerns. Apparently it was thought that this would be an alternative preferable to legislation. Supporters of the exchanges also argued that the government could stop manipulation through its Sherman Act antitrust powers, and it was urged that this "radical" legislation not be adopted.

Notwithstanding this opposition, the Grain Futures Act was adopted by Congress in 1922. In making its determination that interstate commerce was affected by grain exchanges, the statute adopted much of the vituperative language contained in the above House report, that is, in finding that prices are extremely susceptible to speculation and manipulation. This section of the bill was carried forward into more recent legislation, until the futures exchanges convinced Congress in 1982 to remove it from the federal statute books.[27]

The Grain Futures Act established, as did its predecessor, a licensing system that required commodity exchanges to be designated by the federal government as "contract markets." The Grain Futures Act also sought to prevent price manipulation by requiring exchanges to act to prevent such conduct. Although this act, as will be discussed below, was subsequently replaced by the Commodity Exchange Act of 1936, it nonetheless forms the core of the current regulatory scheme. That is, Congress still seeks to regulate futures trading by subjecting it to the requirement that such transactions be conducted on a "contract market," licensed by the federal government.[28]

The Grain Futures Act authorized the Secretary of Agriculture to designate a board of trade as a contract market under certain conditions. This included a requirement that the exchange be located at a terminal market where the grain was sold that was subject to its futures contracts; that the exchange maintain records of its transactions; that it allow representatives of the Department of Justice and the Department of Agriculture to inspect its books and records; that the exchange take steps to prevent its members from disseminating false and misleading crop or market information; and that the exchange establish procedures to prevent manipulation of prices and corners.

The Grain Futures Act also established a Commission composed of the Secretary of Agriculture, the Secretary of Commerce, and the Attorney General, who was authorized to suspend or revoke the registration of an exchange as a contract market if it did not meet the above standards. In addition, persons violating the statute could be barred from trading on a contract market. The Secretary of Agriculture was also authorized to make investigations and to publish reports on the work of boards of trade and marketing, but he could not disclose the business transactions or trade secrets of any persons or the names of customers, except under limited circumstances.

To carry out the provisions of the act, the Secretary of Agriculture established the Grain Futures Administration within the Department of Agriculture. The Grain Futures Administration was responsible for day-to-day regulation under the Grain Futures Act. It initially maintained only a small staff in Washington. Its field headquarters was in Chicago, where it maintained a "considerable force" for the purpose of gathering daily reports from traders. Offices with a small staff were also maintained in Minneapolis and Kansas City.

As an early effort to maintain surveillance over the futures markets, the Grain Futures Administration required daily reports to be made to it by clearing members of each exchange. These reports, however, did not allow a review of individual market operators who were clearing their trades through the clearing member. Accordingly, the Grain Futures Administration also required the clearing members to report daily the market position of its customers exceeding a designated amount. Once such an account was of such a large size it was called a "special account." The Grain Futures Administration complained, however, that it had only one auditor and that, while the Chicago Board of Trade members were willing to make their records available for inspection, the one auditor was unable to make any kind of meaningful check.

In 1923 the Grain Futures Administration also complained that, after it had adopted its rules requiring daily reports and access to the records of traders, "propaganda" immediately developed from within the exchanges that the Grain Futures Administration was responsible for the decline in the price of wheat. The exchange community contended that the new regulations had decreased the volume of trading by frightening away bullish speculative buyers who did not want their business transactions known. The Grain Futures Administration responded that no satisfactory explanation was given by those responsible for this "propaganda" as to why the price of corn rose under the same laws and Administration.

In 1927, however, the Grain Futures Administration suspended its requirement of daily reports for large traders, because of continuing charges that its reports were keeping large bullish speculators from operating in the wheat market and were thereby depressing prices. It suspended reporting requirements from February 26, 1927, until November 1, 1927. It then determined that its reports did not have the effect of discouraging bullish speculators.

This still did not stop industry criticism. In October 1932, the Secretary of Agriculture therefore once again suspended reporting requirements. Thereafter, wheat prices went down instead of up. Indeed, they reached record lows. It was then discovered that the large speculative traders, instead of remaining out of the grain futures market as a result of reporting requirements, were operating principally on the short side of the market during the period that the reports were suspended.

The Grain Futures Administration also maintained an observer on the floor of the Chicago Board of Trade throughout its sessions. Although members complained when the observer entered the pits, the Administration found this necessary in order to obtain a true picture of the trading operations, particularly on days when price fluctuations were unreasonably wide.

OTHER GRAIN FUTURES ADMINISTRATION ACTIVITIES

In 1925 the Grain Futures Administration investigated delivery practices on the Chicago Board of Trade, including a practice of "passing" delivery notices in order to close a position. In one such instance a delivery notice was passed by seventeen firms. The Grain Futures Administration also examined "flashes" from the trading floor (reports of occurrences on the floor, such as who was buying or selling in large amounts). It found that many of these wire flashes were misleading because the persons making the statements did not possess all of the facts, and the quantities mentioned in these flashes were often at variance with the actual amount traded. The firms or persons mentioned in the flashes were also not notified of their contents, precluding them from correcting erroneous information. This practice was brought to the attention of the Chicago Board of Trade. The exchange thereafter adopted a rule prohibiting members from using the names of individuals, firms, or corporations, and from stating definite quantities as having been bought or sold unless based on substantiated facts.

Other false reports were also disseminated. For example, in September 1930, a spurious telegram was sent regarding the financial difficulties of the Canadian wheat pool. The telegram was sent over the signature of a prominent Winnipeg grain firm, and its contents were disseminated widely through many commission houses. The authenticity of the message was denied before the opening, but prices were still weak. The Winnipeg Grain Exchange offered a reward of $1,000 for the identity of the person sending the telegram, but no one came forward to claim the reward. The Grain Futures Administration concluded that this "incident vividly demonstrates the need of an adequate exchange system of censorship of the crop and market information disseminated over the private telegraph wires of futures commission houses."[29]

The Grain Futures Administration also encountered problems in crop reports. It was found that statements were often misleading, creating fear rather than describing actual damage. Those reports were also often vague. In one instance a crop expert stated that he found black rust in every wheat field he entered between Detroit and Grand Forks, North Dakota. The writer did not state, however, how many fields he entered between those two points, a distance of some 95 miles and covering hundreds of farms.

Concern was also expressed over information about crop conditions abroad, which predictably had a significant effect on U.S. prices. Reports were often conflicting and inaccurate. The Grain Futures Administration found, for example, that

> Last spring gossip was circulated referring to financial failures in certain parts of Europe as a result of the drastic decline in wheat prices. This caused a flurry in the market. An investigation revealed that the report was very much magnified and misleading and that the failures involved wheat as to the value of only about $25,000. This item, however, originated in a foreign country and it was not within our power to exact any penalty under the grain futures act.

News of crop damage due to diseases and insect pests have given the greatest annoyance. Many of these reports are so framed as to be just within the law. To remedy this situation plans are now being considered for a closer supervision of news items of this character so as to prevent the circulation of reports of crop damage unless they can be fully supported.[30]

The Administration noted that its role was one of investigation and that actual regulation was conducted by the exchanges. When it found violations it reported them to the officials of the contract markets, and they were responsible for correcting them. The Grain Futures Administration illustrated this role by a market situation where there were about eight times as many contracts as there was corn available on the market to satisfy the contracts. At that time, one-third of the open interest was in the hands of a single trader, an amount in excess of the quantity of corn available. The Grain Futures Administration brought this to the attention of the president of the Chicago Board of Trade, and he took the necessary precautions to ensure that the firm holding the long contracts made no effort to force, on the last day, a price above the commercial value of the corn.

The Secretary of Agriculture published a report on trading in grain futures during the calendar year 1923. The report was in response to a Senate resolution and was occasioned by irregular price movements in the wheat futures market on the Chicago Board of Trade. The Senate resolution had sought to determine whether there were efforts on the Chicago Board of Trade to "bear the market" (whether the market was being depressed by the short selling of professional traders or speculators). The secretary's report was unable to determine that that was the case. The secretary did find that prices rose from $1.05 to $1.25 per bushel and then declined to $1.15 during a three- to four-month period. Thereafter, an irregular advance began again, followed by another downturn. It was found that about 30 percent of all transactions in wheat futures on the Chicago Board of Trade were "scratch trades," which were transactions that were opened and liquidated on the same day at the same price, so that there was no profit or loss. Such transactions were exempt from a sales tax payable on all other trades. The investigation also found several large traders in the market but did not conclude that any of them had manipulated the market.

In 1926, in response to another Senate resolution, the Secretary of Agriculture issued a second report on subsequent price fluctuations in wheat futures. The Department initially met opposition trying to obtain information from various clearing members, although the majority of the members of the Chicago Board of Trade had been fully cooperative. After complaining to the exchange of this lack of cooperation, the reports were promptly supplied by the clearing members. It was then discovered that certain traders had scattered their positions in various accounts in order to avoid reporting requirements. It was also found that the majority of the days during which there were wide and erratic price fluctuations were days on which one or more large traders bought or sold more than 2 million bushels of wheat. In fact, eight traders had accumulated positions of 2 million bushels or more. These large speculative operations were determined to be important price making factors, and it was stated that regulation was needed to limit excessive speculative transactions. The secretary concluded, however, that there was no concerted action for the deliberate purpose of manipulating the market. Nevertheless, it was found that the erratic price fluctuations were largely artificial and were caused directly or indirectly by heavy trading on the part of a limited number of professional speculators.

It was also noted that these large-scale buying and selling operations completely disrupted the market and resulted in abnormal fluctuations that were felt in every large grain market in the world. During the period from July 8, 1924, to the end of January 1925, it was thus found that the price of May wheat advanced from $1.19 to $2.05, an unusual price advance during peace time. From the high of $2.05 there was a sharp price break in early February, and by February 11 the price had dropped to $1.77, bouncing back once again to $2.02. Then the market utterly collapsed to bottom at $1.36 on April 3. These violent and unusual price changes practically paralyzed the grain and milling business. Strong protests were made by growers and various associations and trade bodies. It was suggested by the Department of Agriculture that limitations be imposed on the size of positions and the amount of buying and selling that could be conducted during a day by speculative traders.

In response to the secretary's investigation, the exchanges, under the threat of losing their contract market license, adopted several reforms. This included establishing modern clearing systems by the Chicago Board of Trade; the adoption of rules that allowed the Board of Directors of each exchange to limit daily price fluctuations and market prices of grain during emergency periods; and the creation of a business conduct committee by each of the contract markets with broad disciplinary powers over the transactions of members in order to prevent manipulation and to generally supervise their conduct.

By 1925 the Grain Futures Administration had found no violations that warranted prosecution under the Grain Futures Act. Nevertheless, in 1926 and 1927 bills were introduced to preclude or limit futures trading, but they were not passed. The Grain Futures Administration did note that some traders were splitting their transactions so that they would not have to report them. It amended its regulations to prevent this conduct.

In 1926 the Grain Futures Administration claimed responsibility for preventing a very drastic decline in wheat prices, as a result of its efforts in urging the exchanges and large traders to limit heavy short selling. The agency, however, denied any interest in determining appropriate prices for products. Rather, it was seeking to prevent manipulation.

The Grain Futures Administration also found fraudulent schemes and devices designed to "mulct the credulous everywhere" by promising large profits with little risk. These schemes were conducted through transactions in options. In one case, the operators of such a program were indicted and convicted of mail fraud. This scheme was described as follows:

> Customers would pay the defendant through the so-called *Investors Daily Guide* $12.50 for an advance guaranty or a decline guaranty and $25 for a spread guaranty including both an advance and a decline in one contract. . . . The designated price above or below which the market might fluctuate with profit to the customer was determined by the proprietor of the *Investors Daily Guide* and, though supposed to be established with relation to the market price when the contract was issued, it was, in reality, placed so far above or below prevailing prices as to eliminate all probability of the markets fluctuating sufficiently during the contract period to return any profit to the patron.[31]

The Grain Futures Administration observed that trading in privileges (puts and calls) had become increasingly evident after the Supreme Court held their regulation to be unconstitutional under the 1921 legislation. Thus, as noted above, the Futures Trading Act had sought to stop trading in privileges in grain by a prohibitive tax, but the decision of the Supreme Court in *Hill v. Wallace* held the statute unconstitutional in certain respects. It did not, however, specifically determine whether the tax on options was also unconstitutional. Several years later, in *Trusler v. Crooks*,[32] the Supreme Court held that that section of the 1921 legislation was also unconstitutional, and privilege trading resumed. Some exchanges, however, such as the Winnipeg Grain Exchange and New York Cotton Exchange, still prohibited members from trading in privileges, and state laws prohibited many of these transactions. The Chicago Board of Trade apparently was allowing, at least tacitly, this trading to occur in large volume. Accordingly, the Grain Futures Administration undertook an investigation into options trading, and subsequently published a report on the methods and use of such instruments.[33]

The Grain Futures Administration also discovered that the all-Russian Textile Syndicate was trading on the Chicago Board of Trade in large amounts over a four-day period in 1930. The syndicate was shorting the market and forcing prices down by sales that were ordered by Moscow. The sales were for almost 8 million bushels of grain. This was some 11 percent of the total sales on the Chicago Board of Trade during those days. During this period wheat prices declined sharply.

In response to this development, the Chicago Board of Trade passed a resolution that stated that it was the Board's conclusion that the selling of futures upon the exchange by any foreign government is a new development of commerce of seriously objectionable character and must be brought to an end. It was later concluded, however, by a committee of the House of Representatives that the selling by the Soviet government was not intended to depress the price of wheat. Rather, it was found that the Soviets could not contract forward for their wheat, because they had been off the market for many years and had no established grades. Consequently, all they could do was load their wheat onto vessels, ship it to market, and sell it for whatever it would bring on the open market. Had it been broadcast that they were doing that, however, prices would have quickly dropped, and the Soviets would have received less for their grain. It was for that reason that they were hedging their grain on the Chicago market.[34]

The Grain Futures Administration recommended to Congress that it be given authority to impose limitations on holdings by traders who were trading for speculative purposes. It noted that it had found a great many cases where prices had moved in line with heavy concentrated trading of a purely speculative character. In 1931 bills were introduced in Congress to allow speculative limits to be established, but they were pending in committee on the adjournment of the 71st Congress. Nevertheless, industry claims were made that traders were transferring their transactions to the Winnipeg Grain Exchange to avoid the possibility of being limited in the size of their positions. A Royal Canadian Commission, however, later found that this had not been the case.

In 1933 the Grain Futures Administration once again called for legislation on position limits, noting that one individual speculator had held approximately 14 percent of the aggregate open commitments in a major wheat future on the world's largest grain futures market. But such legislation was not adopted until 1936.

2

THE CREATION
OF THE COMMODITY
EXCHANGE ACT

THE CUTTEN CASE

One of the most flagrant abusers of the grain markets was Arthur Cutten, a trader on the Chicago Board of Trade who the government described as "perhaps the greatest grain speculator this country ever knew." In 1924 Cutten squeezed the price of wheat to a historical high of over $2. In the process, he beat the "Great Bear," Jesse Livermore, out of some $3 million.[1]

Cutten was later charged by the government with failing to report the size of the positions he controlled, as required by the Grain Futures Act, so that he could manipulate the price of grain. It was found that he operated through numerous accounts, and that he held contracts for a substantial amount of available wheat supplies. Cutten had tried to counter these charges through a series of articles he co-authored in the *Saturday Evening Post*. There, he attempted to portray himself as a misunderstood businessman fighting for the ideals of America and freedom from government regulation.[2] His publicity efforts, however, quickly collapsed when he was subsequently indicted for tax evasion.

Cutten was nevertheless to play a prominent role in subsequent congressional hearings on a need for additional legislation to regulate futures trading. The Supreme Court had held in *Wallace v. Cutten*[3] that the Secretary of Agriculture could not deny Cutten trading privileges on contract markets because the act did not apply to persons who had manipulated the market in the past; rather, it applied only to a person who *is* manipulating commodity prices. As a result, the Grain Futures Act was weakened.

Equally notorious were the activities of Thomas M. Howell, who, like Cutten, was charged with concealing his trading through numerous accounts. At one point, Howell held all of the corn available for delivery in Chicago and 94 percent of the corn in the entire United States, much of which he shipped to Canada as a means to squeeze corn prices on the Chicago Board of Trade. The government's case against Howell was dismissed on the same grounds as those in the Cutten decision. A private antitrust suit against Howell was also unsuccessful.

The Grain Futures Administration found itself hampered in other respects. For example, the Commission administering the Grain Futures Act (the Attorney General, the Secretary of Commerce, and the Secretary of Agriculture) dismissed a complaint brought by the Grain Futures Administration against a group of traders who were taking customer orders into their own accounts and, with the accommodation of a third party, confirming the order to their customers at prices they themselves set, but within the range of prices occurring on the floor during the period they were holding the orders. The Commission concluded that, while such conduct may be fraudulent, it was not manipulative conduct that could be remedied under the Grain Futures Act.

THE GREAT DEPRESSION

The stock market crash in 1929 also had serious repercussions for the commodities markets. Commodity prices began to drop precipitously, and efforts were undertaken by the federal government to stabilize those prices. To that end, in May 1929, President Hoover established a Federal Farm Board, which was required to minimize speculation in commodities and to prevent or control surpluses. On November 17, 1930, the Farm Board established the Grain Stabilization Corporation. It sought to stabilize wheat prices by buying large amounts of wheat in the open market. Wheat prices were then depressed as a result of the worldwide economic situation and an oversupply of wheat.

The operations of the Grain Stabilization Corporation initially had the effect of holding U.S. wheat prices above European prices. The purchasing program established such a large surplus that it became a threat to the market, which then began depressing prices. It also began engaging in commodity futures transactions, which Congressman Hugo Black sought unsuccessfully to stop.

In any event, government efforts to stabilize prices were unsuccessful because it could not limit supplies, and Arthur Cutten was able to crow, "I told you so" because he had contended that the government could not control prices. Later, in Congress, it was noted that while the Federal Farm Board was spending millions of dollars in trying to sustain wheat prices, Cutten was a constant short seller, selling more than 73 million bushels of grain on the futures markets.

Grain prices continued their decline, and the Chicago Board of Trade was closed on the bank holiday declared by President Roosevelt (from March 4 to March 15, 1933). Thereafter, volume increased and prices rose, but then they sensationally collapsed on July 19 and 20, 1932. The Chicago Board of Trade was closed for two days following this drastic decline, with the exception of a 15-minute session on July 22 to permit buyers of indemnities to exercise their privileges. Following the reopening of the market on July 24, 1932, the Board of Trade adopted rules that limited the amount of daily price fluctuations in commodities (i.e., when commodity prices moved the amount stated in these "price limit" rules trading in that future had to stop). Trading in privileges was also suspended by the exchange, and reporting requirements were reinstated.

Thereafter, the Grain Futures Administration conducted an investigation to determine what caused the sharp price decline. It was found that the debacle resulted principally from activities of not more than ten traders who controlled fifteen speculative accounts. A large portion of their tremendous holdings were suddenly dumped on the market. At first this was for the purpose of taking profits, but it compelled the liquidation of large accounts that were inadequately margined. The Grain Futures Administration concluded that this "economic catastrophe" again demonstrated the need for position limits to avoid concentration by a few large accounts.

On March 20, 1934, the president approved a Code of Fair Competition for grain exchanges under the National Industrial Recovery Act that was designed to stop improper practices in the trading of futures contracts. This code was the result of some eight months of negotiations on the part of the exchanges and government representatives from the Grain Futures Administration. It required the exchanges and the members to enforce and maintain minimum margins. It also required the exchanges to maintain limitations on fluctuations in the price of futures and to prohibit options trading.

The collapse of grain prices and the ensuing depression eventually led to a presidential call for expanded regulatory controls over both the securities and commodity exchanges. The president's message, which was delivered to Congress on February 9, 1934, stated that

> The exchanges in many parts of the country which deal in securities and commodities conduct, of course, a national business because their customers live in every part of the country. The managers of these exchanges have, it is true, often taken steps to correct certain obvious abuses. We must be certain that abuses are eliminated and to this end a broad policy of national regulation is required.
>
> It is my belief that exchanges for dealing in securities and commodities are necessary and of definite value to our commercial and agricultural life. Nevertheless, it should be our national policy to restrict, as far as possible, the use of these exchanges for purely speculative operations.

I therefore recommend to the Congress the enactment of legislation providing for the regulation by the Federal Government of the operations of exchanges dealing in securities and commodities for the protection of investors, for the safeguarding of values, and so far as it may be possible, for the elimination of unnecessary, unwise, and destructive speculation.[4]

In another letter, this one addressed to the chairman of the House Committee on Interstate and Foreign Commerce, dated March 26, 1934, the president noted that the people of the United States believed that "unregulated speculation in securities and in commodities was one of the most important contributing factors in the artificial and unwarranted 'boom' which had so much to do with the terrible conditions of the years following 1929."[5]

Because securities and commodity exchanges were regulated by separate committees of Congress, they received different congressional treatment. Transactions in securities thus became subject to the regulation of the Securities and Exchange Commission (SEC), under the Securities Act of 1933, the Securities Exchange Act of 1934, and other acts later adopted. The commodity legislation resulting from the market collapses that led to the Great Depression was not enacted until 1936, and the commodity exchanges were subjected to the regulation of a separate Commodity Exchange Commission. That legislation, however, was substantially the same as that passed by the House in 1934, too late to receive final consideration by the Senate prior to the adjournment of the 73rd Congress. This gave faith to the opponents of the Commodity Exchange Act, but a sharp drop in cotton future prices of nearly 200 points in March 1935 undercut the efforts of the opponents of this legislation, because it was found by Congress that there was no satisfactory explanation for that price drop and no "ready means by which any agency of the Government could ascertain the true facts. . . ."[6]

It was found by Congress in enacting the Commodity Exchange Act that, since the passage of the Securities Exchange Act of 1934, there had been an increasing tendency on the part of professional speculators to transfer the activities from the securities markets to the commodity markets. Congress was also concerned with the "speculative orgies" that were occurring on the grain exchanges. It was charged that the price American farmers received for their grain was "dominated and controlled by the gambling price manipulations on the Chicago Board of Trade." It was also noted in Congress that organized agriculture had sought legislation for years that would curb excessive speculation on the grain exchanges and that the Grain Futures Administration had repeatedly pointed out the problems to American grain producers that were being caused by "relentless grain gamblers." It was also stated that the Grain Futures Act had been "almost a complete failure. It has no teeth. Under the present Act the grain exchanges were supposed to regulate themselves. This they have not done."

It was further charged in the Senate debates that brokerage firms commonly used margin monies deposited by small speculators to extend credit to large preferred speculators, often trading on the opposite side of the market. It was noted that, in such instances, "the small traders furnish[ed] the capital for margin requirements not only for themselves but oftentimes for the very operators who take the opposite side in order to fleece them as lambs." There had also been a recent failure in Chicago of a futures commission merchant that resulted in a loss of almost $1 million in margin funds. It was noted that the depositors of the margins were only general creditors in the bankruptcy proceeding.[7]

Cutten was also a target. It was charged that he had "ruined more farmers in this country than any other single man. If you could gather together all the bones of the people he has caused to die an economic death, they would form a triumphal arch from Chicago to New York, where he went for bigger gambling operations through which he could safely ride."[8] It was also stated on the floor of the Senate that when "business was lagging in the outlying offices of Chicago commission firms, a whisper that Cutten was buying wheat would cause orders to start rolling from all over the country."[9] He was identified as always being on the buying side of the market, when, in fact, he was short millions of bushels.

Senator Capper, one of the strongest supporters of the Commodity Exchange Act of 1936, asserted on the floor of the House that wheat growers in the United States had for years been injured by "bear raids" and "May squeezes" conducted by "vicious short selling on a huge scale at the hands of big manipulators who virtually have been in control of the board of trade and have used it unscrupulously to accomplish their ends." He stated that the Board of Trade had become "one of the world's great gambling places." Senator Connelly also charged that Patton, "the great wheat king," had furnished the most "thrilling"—if not the most sordid— chapter in the Chicago wheat pit in past years by mastering the entire wheat market.[10]

This is not to suggest that there was no opposition to this legislation. To the contrary, the opponents of the act were vociferous. As a minority report from the committee on Agriculture stated with reference to this legislation: "This is not American. This is Russian. Only the cellars of Petrograd and the mines of Siberia are missing." The Act was referred to as "more Soviet legislation."[11]

In considering this legislation, Congress was given a report prepared from information obtained by the Department of Agriculture concerning the background of individuals trading futures contracts. It was found that these traders included 6 dead men, 18 undertakers, 2 butlers, 5 chauffeurs, 6 janitors, 12 candy store proprietors, 1 clam digger, some 25 assorted clergymen, 1 dilettante, one individual who "just fizzles around," one "ostrich feather," 1 duck raiser, 1 fiduciary, 1 knife sharpener, 32 laborers, 19 manicurists, 523 physicians, 112 dentists, 397 attorneys, 4 mayors, 3 police chiefs, 3 Senators, 8 judges, 23 government employees (including 7 Internal Revenue agents), 1 ambassador, 1 former governor, 1 professional gambler, 1 retired pugilist, 104 secretaries and stenographers, 36 students, 1 underwear company president, 1 spinster, 4 unemployed widows, and 11 other widows. Among the greatest concentration of traders were found to be 1,025 housewives and 530 unemployed individuals.

The "fundamental purpose" of the Commodity Exchange Act of 1936 was to "insure fair practice and honest dealing on the commodity exchanges, and to provide some measure of control over those forms of speculative activity which so often disrupt the markets to the damage of producers and consumers and even the exchanges themselves."[12] But the Commodity Exchange Act, as adopted in 1936, was narrow in its scope. It only applied to agriculture commodities that were then the subject of commodity futures trading, so that grains, butter, eggs, potatoes, rice, and cotton were regulated. No provision was made for adding new commodities that would in the future become subject to futures trading. Rather, the inclusion of new commodities into the regulatory scheme required amendments to the statute.

To carry out the regulatory functions required by the Commodity Exchange Act, as adopted, Congress created the Commodity Exchange Commission, which comprised the Secretaries of Agriculture and Commerce and the Attorney General. The Secretary of Agriculture was given day-to-day regulatory authority over these markets, and on July 31, 1936, he formed the Commodity Exchange Administration, as an agency within the Department of Agriculture, to carry out those functions. That agency, which was later renamed the Commodity Exchange Authority (CEA), replaced the Grain Futures Administration.

The Commodity Exchange Act prohibited manipulation, although it did not define that term or provide any guidance as to how this economic "crime" could be committed. The act also sought to curb excessive speculation by providing for the adoption of "position limits" to restrict the size of positions held by speculators. The act further sought to stop the practices so heavily criticized in the hearings and debates, such as offsetting customer orders, misleading statements, wash trading, fictitious sales, and accommodation trades.

The act also established registration requirements for brokerage firms, which are identified in the commodity futures industry as "futures commission merchants" (FCMs). Customer margins were finally required to be held in trust by FCMs. It was thought that these requirements would eliminate from the market persons unfit to deal with customers.

The commodity option scandals that had long been experienced in the commodities markets also led the Congress to prohibit the trading of commodity options on the commodities in which futures trading was then being conducted. It did not, however, prohibit options trading on other commodities.

THE COMMODITY EXCHANGE ADMINISTRATION

The CEA was created in 1936 and became the principal regulator of futures trading in the United States until 1974, when the present regulatory scheme was adopted.[13] The CEA viewed the statute under which it regulated as follows:

> the Commodity Exchange Act is not a guaranty of high prices for agricultural products, nor an assurance of a ready market for them at all times. It simply provides a measure of restraint over fraudulent and manipulative practices, and facilitates the maintenance of fair and honest farm-commodity exchanges.[14]

Under the new legislation the CEA promptly designated the following exchanges as contract markets:

Chicago Board of Trade
Chicago Mercantile Exchange
Chicago Open Board of Trade
Duluth Board of Trade
Kansas City Board of Trade
Los Angeles Grain Exchange
Milwaukee Grain and Stock Exchange
Minneapolis Chamber of Commerce
New Orleans Cotton Exchange
New York Cotton Exchange
New York Mercantile Exchange
New York Produce Exchange
New York Wool Top Exchange
Portland Grain Exchange
St. Louis Merchants Exchange
San Francisco Chamber of Commerce
Seattle Grain Exchange

By August 20, 1937, some 900 futures commission merchants and 665 floor brokers had also been registered. Like its predecessor, the CEA maintained close contact with the exchanges. A member of the field staff of the CEA attended all meetings of the Business Conduct Committees of those exchanges.

The CEA almost immediately encountered its first market emergency when it appeared that there was congestion in the September 1937 corn future contract, which ultimately resulted in the suspension of trading in that future by the Chicago Board of Trade. After the suspension, the directors of the Board of Trade established a settlement price for corn for the traders still holding positions. It was later found by the CEA that one trader on the long side and two on the short side had dominated the September future. Indeed, the principal long traders controlled some 74 percent of all the open commitments on the long side, while the two principal shorts held nearly 29 percent of all open commitments on the short side. In the words of the CEA, "the result was a stubborn struggle between the opposing interests. They refused to settle their contracts except on profitable terms."[15]

Corn futures trading also encountered problems in the December 1936 contract. The CEA issued a call that required long traders to identify their trading and positions in that market. Those reports showed that one firm had an excessively large position. The Business Conduct Committee of the Chicago Board of Trade thereupon asked the firm holding that position to refrain from adding to its open contracts and to liquidate 30 percent of its open contracts. As a consequence, the December futures were closed out in a satisfactory manner and without erratic price changes.

Congestion was found, however, in rye and corn in the May 1936 contracts, but problems were avoided here as well, when one speculator at the request of the exchange liquidated his position. The CEA conducted another investigation into potato prices to see if these were being manipulated downward on the Chicago Mercantile Exchange. The investigation revealed no evidence of any effort on the part of any group to force the price of potatoes down. Instead, it was found that there was a very small volume of trading in potato futures on the Chicago Mercantile Exchange, especially compared with the broader volume in the spot market, and that the volume of trading was insufficient to affect the large off-exchange market.

The CEA also encountered problems in false crop reports and market information. For example, one report predicted the largest wheat crop ever in a producing state, while Department of Agriculture estimates were approximately half that amount. Another report issued nationwide, by a firm that stood to benefit, inaccurately reported on damage done by black rust to the wheat crop. In still another instance, misleading information was sent out concerning an unsubstantiated report on a large purchase of grain for export. In the latter instance, the report was found to have been purely a mistake.

Position limits were established by the CEA that restricted the size of positions that speculators could hold in grain futures to two million bushels. The CEA identified the considerations that went into determining such limits as follows:

> The purpose of such limitations is to eliminate drastic price changes brought about by the operations of large speculators. Too rigid limitations would, however, probably bring about the very conditions desired to be remedied for they would restrict speculation within such narrow limits as to accentuate price changes. Moreover, unreasonably low limitations might dislocate the machinery of the futures market to such an extent as to jeopardize its entire value for hedging purposes. It is therefore of the utmost importance that limitations should be established only after the most thorough investigation and when every aspect of the effect of such limitations has been contemplated.[16]

The CEA informally urged the exchanges to adopt minimum margin requirements for speculative traders, if they had not already done so. The CEA pointed out that while the Commodity Exchange Act contained no authority to require the adoption of minimum margin rules, such rules "tended to insure fair competition between commission firms and would tend to protect customers who, in the absence of substantial margin requirements, might be inclined to take a larger position in the market than their means would justify."[17] Several exchanges agreed with these arguments and adopted minimum margin rules.

From its inception, the CEA conducted detailed examinations of the books and records of futures commission merchants to determine if segregation requirements were met. The total number of examinations completed between September 1, 1937, and August 31, 1938, was 654. Those examinations revealed that over 100 firms were undersegregated in amounts totaling over $750,000. In another case, that of Burke & Co., an undersegregation of $60,000 was found. This firm was placed in bankruptcy, but commodity customer claims were given preferences in the distribution of funds segregated for their benefit; they participated as common creditors for the balance of their claims. As a result, customers received about 46 percent of their claims, while general creditors received only about 28.5 percent. This was the first criminal case under the Commodity Exchange Act and the first case in which the segregation provisions were given a priority in bankruptcy proceedings.

Another early issue involved so-called discretionary accounts (accounts of customers whose trading was controlled by a third person). The CEA was concerned with counselors who solicited the management of commodity accounts among the general public and received remuneration for directing trading for the account. It found that these counselors frequently obtained accounts on the basis of misleading statements and misrepresentations of fact in which extraordinary profits were promised. It was also discovered that the overwhelming majority of the accounts they managed were unprofitable and were operated in a manner that misled their owners.

In its investigation, the CEA found some 4,488 discretionary accounts being traded. Those accounts were controlled by some 3,257 individuals. Of these, approximately 600 were managed by so-called professional commodity counselors. It was also found that many counselors engaged in unethically and socially undesirable practices, such as allocating orders among customers hours or even days after the trades had been executed. This allowed the trader to determine which customers, including himself, would receive profitable trades. Another fraudulent practice involved closing out profitable trades in customer accounts, while unprofitable trades were held open without the knowledge of the owners. This led the owner of the account to believe that the account was profitable when, in fact, it was losing money.

Officials from the leading commodity exchanges met in Washington on August 1, 1938, to consider what rules were necessary to meet these discretionary account problems. Thereafter, every contract market represented at the conference adopted amendments to the rules to prevent such practices.

The CEA maintained surveillance over market letters and advisory reports on commodity prices that were issued by most brokerage firms. This was because they were found to have a substantial but short-lived effect on commodity prices. The CEA noted that on numerous occasions, inaccurate or misleading statements were called to the attention of brokerage houses, and they invariably corrected such reports.

The CEA also conducted an investigation into large trading by foreign interests in U.S. futures markets. It found that the volume of transactions executed on domestic futures markets far surpassed that of foreign markets and that some foreign interests had found it advantageous to utilize U.S. markets for hedging and other purposes. It was concluded, however, that the total volume of transactions on U.S. markets by foreign interests was relatively unimportant. Speculative holdings in wheat, for example, were less than 2 percent owned by foreign interests. It was further concluded that speculation by large U.S. traders in foreign markets was not great.

A review was also made of the number of deliveries made on futures contracts. It was found that only a small number of futures contracts were actually the subject of a delivery. The CEA noted that even hedgers seek delivery only rarely because most dealers preferred to contract for specific qualities to meet their individual needs.

The CEA also uncovered the so-called Buchhalter plan launched by William C. Durant and Joseph Buchhalter of New York City. These two individuals traded through the firm of H. W. Armstrong & Co. The plan was described as follows:

The method of trading under the Buchhalter plan was the execution of grain futures orders on the Chicago Board of Trade through power of attorney which put the customer's account in spread positions between futures. If either side of the spread showed a profit of 1 cent the profit was taken, but the position was reestablished so that further profits could be taken if the market continued to move in the same direction. As a result, however, large unrealized losses accumulated on the other side of the spread.

Administration accountants and investigators found that purchase and sales statements were sent by H. W. Armstrong & Co. to customers to show the realized profits on the closed trades and that frequently checks were sent to the customers although the accounts had unrealized losses on the open trades greatly in excess of the unrealized profits. Under this scheme of trading customers were led to believe that they were assured weekly or monthly "incomes," the amount depending entirely upon the amount of the original "investment".[18]

A complaint was issued by the Secretary of Agriculture against Armstrong & Co., Durant, Buchhalter, and others. The Secretary of Agriculture later entered an order denying trading privileges on all contract markets to H. W. Armstrong & Co., Joseph Buchhalter, and others.

The CEA also became involved in a battle that began initially with a quarrel between the Chicago Board of Trade and the Cargill Grain Co., one of the largest grain firms in the United States. Cargill had been required by the Chicago Board of Trade to liquidate a part of its long position in September corn. It thereafter was expelled from membership on the Chicago Board of Trade. Cargill then filed a complaint with the CEA, alleging that the Chicago Board of Trade had violated the Commodity Exchange Act by this expulsion. In 1940 the Commodity Exchange Commission dismissed the Cargill complaint, finding that the Board of Trade did have reason to believe that a manipulation and corner were threatened because of the market operations of Cargill.

The Secretary of Agriculture thereafter brought charges against Cargill, alleging that it had engaged in wash sales and that it manipulated the December corn future on the Chicago Board of Trade by short selling to the extent of about 10 million bushels, while at the same time it was operating a corner in the 1937 September corn future. It was charged that these manipulations created an artificial price. On March 6, 1940, an order was issued by the Secretary of Agriculture denying trading privileges to Cargill until further notice.

Cargill did re-enter the market later. It was charged with manipulating the price of oat futures in 1951 and 1952, and was barred from trading futures contracts on that commodity. Subsequently, 23 years later, Cargill was found to have manipulated the May 1963 wheat contract on the Chicago Board of Trade. In that instance, Cargill held 62 percent of the open long interest in the May contract, as well as the principal available deliverable supplies, creating an artificial price. Sanctions were suspended by the Secretary of Agriculture, however, because it took some eight years to conclude the case.

Returning to the pre-World War II era, congestion developed on three occasions in 1939 in the cotton market: "a few traders control[led] such a large percentage of the open contracts that prices may be unduly influenced by the operations of those traders or where, toward the end of the life of a future, delay of liquidation by longs may cause the maturing future to advance in relation to more distant months and relative to prices of a cash commodity."[19] It was found that large numbers of speculators were seeking to take advantage of price disparities, but that there was no evidence of collusion.

In 1939 Stanley W. Gongoll of Minneapolis and eight of his affiliated companies were charged by the Secretary of Agriculture with unlawfully acting as futures commission merchants and with failing properly to account for customer funds. This led to the bankruptcy of Gongoll, and his indictment under charges of grand larceny and embezzlement. Gongoll had burned a large part of the records of his transactions, but the records that were recovered indicated that he had had more than 3,000 customers, and that the losses they had suffered had been as much as 3 million dollars. Gongoll was sentenced to prison for 10 years under state law. In another case, D. W. Kohler was charged with illegally trading in options contracts, which were banned by the Commodity Exchange Act of 1936. He pleaded guilty and was fined $25 and court costs. This case involved solicitation and orders for privilege transactions to be executed on the Winnipeg Grain Exchange.

In examining the operations of H. O. Bedford & Co. of El Paso, Texas, the CEA found that it was operating a bucket shop and misappropriating customer funds. Bedford, a principal in the firm, was sentenced in state court to three years in the penitentiary. Similarly, N. J. Larimer & Co. of Wenatchee, Washington, was found to have been operating a bucket shop, and the principal there was given an indeterminate sentence, with a maximum penalty of 15 years. Other bucket shops were also discovered.

It was noted in 1939 by the CEA that there were some fifteen commodities that were not regulated by the Commodity Exchange Act of 1936, but which were the subject of futures trading. They were cheese, cocoa, coffee, cottonseed meal and oil, frozen eggs, hides, lard, molasses, peanuts, provisions (ribs and bellies), soybeans, sugar, and tallow. The CEA stated that

> While detailed information as to the practices and the character of futures trading in the uncontrolled commodities is not available, it is safe to assume, on the basis of complaints received from time to time, that the

same need exists for Federal supervision of futures trading in all unregulated agricultural products as in the 14 commodities now covered by the act. Manipulation, fictitious transactions, and excessive speculation are relatively just as harmful in one group of commodities as in the other.[20]

It was also noted by the CEA that, despite the fact that trading commodity futures had been a recognized marketing practice for nearly 100 years and had later developed into a trade having an average annual value of more than 23 billion dollars, there had been no comprehensive study made of its value in the social structure. It recommended that such a study be conducted. Unfortunately, although limited efforts have been undertaken, no comprehensive study has been made even yet.

3
THE WAR YEARS
AND BEYOND

By 1940 the effects of the European war were being felt in U.S. commodity markets. Wheat, corn, and cotton were in acute demand in Europe, even though they were surplus crops in the United States. It was noted by the CEA that

> The outstanding importance of American futures markets among those of the world magnifies the dangers which might develop were foreign traders to indulge in manipulative tactics. Such traders would be outside of the jurisdiction of the Administration and could only be denied trading privileges on American markets. None of the criminal provisions of the law could be applied to them. The Administration therefore maintained a constant vigilance over the trading operations of foreign individuals and concerns.[1]

As a part of its surveillance, the CEA once again conducted investigations of transactions by foreigners in the grain and cotton markets, but it was found that long holdings of large foreign accounts totaled only a small percentage of the open interest on the Chicago Board of Trade and there were no short positions. In cotton, however, foreign interests held about 15 percent of the open contracts in New York. A subsequent investigation also found only a small amount of foreign cotton was hedged in U.S. markets and that it did not constitute a burden on them.

The closing of the markets in Antwerp and Roubaix-Turcoing in September 1939 left the New York Wool Top Market as the only remaining wool top futures market in the world. Wool tops were used for worsted wool, and trading volume drastically increased and prices rose rapidly as war demand for this product soared, causing speculative interest to increase. As a temporary protective measure against further price disturbances from war developments, the Secretary of Agriculture, in May 1940, requested all contract markets trading in grain futures to prohibit further trading at prices below those prevailing at the close of the market on that date. Just before this order, prices on the Chicago Wheat Market had fallen when Germany began its invasion of France. In May 1941, the Secretary of Agriculture also asked the exchanges to consider other steps to discourage speculation on the commodity exchanges as a part of the national defense effort. This request met with little affirmative response from the exchanges.

Nevertheless, unlike the outbreak of World War I, the attack on Pearl Harbor did not result in serious price disturbances, due in large measure to several precautionary measures that had been taken to prevent panic trading. This included increased margin requirements and narrower price fluctuation limits, and close checks on market positions and floor trading practices. The CEA, on the evening of Sunday, December 7, 1941, thus called the major exchanges and their officials and asked their boards of directors to meet the next day to take whatever action was necessary. Some commodities hit their price limits, and the CEA asked the exchanges to prohibit trading the next day at prices above the closing prices on the previous day in those commodities. On the following day there was trading in some of the commodities under the limits, and the ceilings were taken off those commodities. Ceilings were kept on butter, eggs, and soybeans for several days, all of which lessened the shock of the war news. Later, trading was effectively suspended in lard, soybeans, cottonseed meal, and soybean meal as a result of a shortage of supplies relative to war needs. Soybean oil, butter, and tallow also stopped trading, and there was virtually no trading in corn. Nevertheless, there were large numbers of open contracts and cotton, and even wool tops continued as a futures market. It was later found, however, that the wool top market was dominated by two large wool top makers who also handled customer orders. The CEA concluded that their activities gave them information about the market that was otherwise unobtainable.

In order to help control speculation on the part of small traders who were attracted to the market by war news and "speculative fever," the CEA recommended that the exchanges increase their margins, which most of them did. The CEA stated that

> Although the Commodity Exchange Act does not grant authority to fix margins, the problem was considered when the law was amended in 1936. Proper margin rules can help to prevent the entrance into the markets of irresponsible traders, and undesirable speculative forces; and can minimize unwarranted switching of speculative accounts from one commodity or market to another.[2]

The CEA began making investigations for the Navy Department to determine the composition of commercial houses and the nature of their trading, as well as to determine whether there were concentrated holdings or unwarranted speculative activity that could affect commodities. In addition, at the request of the Treasury Department, the CEA gathered material on the trading in commodity futures by foreign nationals using blocked funds. Several surveys were also undertaken for the Office of Price Administration.

World War II did not stop the CEA's anti-fraud prosecutions. In 1944, for example, General Foods Corp. and Daniel Rice and others were charged with manipulating and attempting to corner the rye futures markets. A suspension of General Foods' trading privileges for 30 days was ordered by the CEA, but the Seventh Circuit Court of Appeals later set that sanction aside.

Several cases were also brought against brokerage firms who had undersegregated customer funds or who had allegedly bucketed such funds. In the case of Arthur J. Flynn, for example, customers complained to the state district attorney in Greenfield, Massachusetts, that they had turned over funds to Flynn to participate in the operation of a commodity futures pool but were unable to collect their profits. An investigation conducted by the CEA disclosed that Flynn had been running a confidence game in which customers in three states had invested more than $100,000 in cash in securities with him. It was found that Flynn's trading was negligible, that he had sent confirmations of purchase and sales to customers for contracts that were not executed on any contract market, and that he had rendered monthly statements of "profits," which he actually paid in some instances from capital invested by other customers. Flynn was placed into bankruptcy and later pleaded guilty to ten counts of larceny and was imprisoned.

In a case involving W. G. Edwards Company of Rapid City, North Dakota, the CEA found that a FCM, in order to increase its profits, had entered into a plan whereby it charged the usual rate of commission, as fixed by the exchanges, but in addition confirmed the trades of customers as a principal at a price of one-eighth of a cent or more under or over the price at which the order was executed, thereby obtaining additional compensation for its services as broker. This was done through the firm's "error" account or by simply bucketing the trades. Although the CEA concluded that the broker had not intended to defraud its customers—the firm's legal advisers had approved of this plan—the firm's trading privileges were suspended.

The most common violation found by the CEA involved the practice of taking the opposite side of a customer's order without the customer's prior consent. It was noted that violations of this nature frequently resulted in poorer execution prices than if the order were competitively executed on the floor of the exchange. Charges were brought against various firms and individuals, and they were suspended from trading.

Another widespread abuse that was discovered by the CEA was known as "giving a name." This practice was in the nature of an arrangement between brokers to take customer orders into their own accounts instead of executing them openly on the floor of the exchange. Over 46,000 separate transactions were examined to find the extent of this abuse, and about 1,200 questionable trades were found. Specific cases were discussed in detail with brokers and officials of the Chicago Board of Trade. As a result, more stringent trading rules were adopted by the exchanges to prevent this practice.

THE POSTWAR YEARS

Cotton was one of the few important agricultural commodities that was not placed under price ceilings during World War II. Until the end of 1944 the cotton markets were, nevertheless, relatively free from erratic price movements. Early in 1946, however, the market situation began to change. Price ceilings on raw cotton were proposed but then abandoned, and margin rates in cotton futures were raised to a high level and then suddenly lowered by the exchanges, when the Price Control Act expired on June 30, 1946. The market then became the target of speculative activity. The extension of the Price Control Act did not alleviate that pressure. The Federal Reserve Board also decided independently to increase margins on securities transactions from 75 to 100 percent. This had the effect of driving securities speculators into the commodity markets.

The subsequent price rise in cotton during the third quarter of 1946 and its collapse in October "constituted one of the most rapid and extensive price movements in the history of the cotton markets."[3] On October 18, 1946, the cotton markets were thus flooded with a wave of liquidation orders which forced them to close. It was found that the price break was accelerated by the forced liquidation of many thinly margined accounts, the collapse of two large accounts, and the unwarranted extension of credit to others. It was noted by the CEA that many new speculative accounts had been attracted to the markets by small margin requirements, and speculators were caught overextended when prices dropped. In fact, nearly one-third of the speculators in the market on the eve of the price break were completely "washed out" of their positions. Over 80 percent of these speculators were small traders. The CEA, nevertheless, found no manipulation or effort to "break" the cotton market. Selling was evenly distributed and the activity of foreign accounts was negligible.

The CEA later stated that its efforts to curb excessive speculation had been seriously hampered because of inadequate margin requirements for speculative traders. Most margins were 10 to 15 percent or less of the market price. The CEA found that these small cash requirements had furnished an unusual inducement to speculators, but that financially weak traders were unequipped to maintain themselves in fast-moving markets. It found that the hasty entrance and exits of such speculators contributed to the acceleration of price increases and the deepening of price declines.

The CEA asserted that the margin problem also extended into grain futures, as well as to cotton. Significant speculative interest was focused on the Chicago wheat market in February and March of 1947, where margins were 8 to 12 percent of the price of the wheat underlying the futures contracts. Many small traders were forced to cover their short positions as prices fluctuated. In March 1947, the CEA asked the exchanges to increase their margin requirements for grain to 25 percent of the cost of those commodities. Some of the exchanges complied, but the Chicago Board of Trade adopted only token increases. Later, all of the exchanges reduced their margin when prices started declining again. Thereafter, on September 15, 1947, with prices rising once again, the CEA requested the exchanges to increase their margin requirements to 33⅓ percent of commodity prices. The exchanges refused to comply with the request; although they did place into effect sliding-scale margin increases that the CEA deemed inadequate. On October 6, 1947, the Commodity Exchange Commission, by direction of President Truman, requested all grain futures exchanges to increase their minimum initial margin requirements to not less than 33⅓ percent. The exchanges agreed to that request, and the volume of speculative trading in wheat and corn declined sharply.

In December 1946, the CEA investigated butter prices on the New York Mercantile Exchange. Based on that investigation, the Dairymen's League Cooperative Association of New York was indicted for manipulating the price of spot butter in interstate commerce as a means of maintaining fluid milk prices, which were linked to butter prices. In order to maintain butter prices, the League purchased over 600,000 pounds of butter in a six-day period. The Dairymen's League and four of its officers later pleaded guilty and were fined $29,000.

In 1946 the CEA charged that Rueben L. McGuigan had described himself as a commodity trading advisor and that he had mailed numerous circulars and sent collect telegrams urging the purchase and sale of commodities. It was found that these activities had affected prices in the futures contracts they referenced and that the respondent had benefited from those price changes by secret futures positions he maintained in accounts in his wife's maiden name and in fictitious names. He was suspended from further trading.

The CEA was questioned by Congress in 1946 on what efforts it was undertaking to coordinate its activities with the SEC. The CEA's response was that it had found nothing to report to the SEC, because most of the entities it dealt with were partnerships and not corporations whose securities would be of interest to the SEC. The CEA also stated that there was a restriction in the Commodity Exchange Act that prevented it from calling to the attention of the SEC apparent violations of the federal securities laws, namely, that the CEA was prohibited from disclosing the names of traders. The CEA stated that, in any event, it had observed no such violations.

In 1948 the CEA discovered that a large number of traders were maintaining offsetting long and short positions in the same futures of the same commodity and the same market. It was found that these transactions were for the apparent purpose of deception, including the creation of false impression of market activity, the avoidance of delivery of futures contracts, the deception of customers as to the true condition of their accounts, and the avoidance of income tax liability. To safeguard against this activity, a new regulation was adopted by the CEA, which prohibited the holding open of both sides of a speculator's offsetting positions in the same future after the trades had been completed. CEA regulations were later tightened additionally to require competitive executions on the floors of the exchanges. The CEA stated that it was a "cardinal principle" of exchange trading that purchases and sales be openly and competitively executed on the floor by "open outcry." The CEA did find, however, that there were legitimate reasons in certain circumstances for noncompetitive executions, as in the transfer of a trader's contracts from one FCM to another "involving no change of ownership, or in the exchange of futures contracts in connection with cash commodity transactions."[4]

An investigation of the wool top market disclosed that a large break in prices was the result of the sale of the position of two large speculators that were hastily sold out. In another investigation, it was found that a practice of "stopping" had been employed on the New York and New Orleans cotton exchanges (i.e., it was found that large numbers of orders were being offset before the opening and before the close by mutual agreement between brokers to trade with each other). The "stopping" orders had been given for execution at the opening of the market or at the close. When these orders were received, the brokers would mutually agree on their execution and would execute the orders at prices approximating the average official opening prices.

It was noted that this practice expedited and allowed the execution of orders that otherwise might not have been executed. Nevertheless, the CEA concluded that it was a form of offsetting prohibited by the Commodity Exchange Act. The CEA stated that it is generally assumed by the trading public that all orders on commodity exchanges are competitively executed and that any exception to the general rule of auction trading should be specifically provided for, so that the customer will know in what manner his transaction is being executed. The CEA suggested to the exchanges that they revise their rules to authorize average price trading. This would remove the CEA's legal objections. Thereafter, exchange rules were adopted to authorize this practice.[5]

In February 1949, a large break in grain prices occurred. In the morning session on February 8, a wave of liquidations swept the Chicago grain market. It was found by the CEA that small traders were concentrated on the long side of the market and that the heavy liquidation of their accounts when prices dropped was a major factor in the continuing sudden drop in prices. The CEA concluded that this was a result of inadequately financed commodity accounts permitted by low margin requirements. The CEA stated that its

> investigation of the grain markets of February 8 and 9 tells much the same story found by other investigations of commodity price breaks. When people enter a speculative market with only a small part of the total value of the commodity put up as margin, the tendency is to acquire the largest position possible with the funds at hand. With any considerable decline in prices, traders of limited financial resources are forced to withdraw from the market—or be sold out. When this happens to a substantial number of traders a further sharp break in prices is the inevitable result.[6]

Thereafter, a report was completed by the Commodity Exchange Authority analyzing speculative trading in grain futures. The report was concerned primarily with the trading behavior of small speculators and the results of their trading. It was found that the great majority of speculators lost money in the grain futures market. Of the 8,782 speculators whose operations were analyzed, 6,598 had net losses, compared with 2,184 who had net profits. In other words, there were three times as many loss traders as profit traders. The losses of speculators were approximately six times their net profits—there were 12 million dollars in losses compared with about 2 million in profits. It was found that the high loss ratios were due largely to the characteristic of small speculators to hesitate in closing out loss positions. It was determined that small speculators had a clear tendency to take their profits and let their losses run, which is exactly the opposite course of an astute trader. It was also found that amateur traders were more likely to be long than short in the futures market.[7]

THE KOREAN WAR

In 1949 and 1950, increased speculative trading of an almost "frenzied" character occurred in commodity futures as a result of the outbreak of the Korean war. A congested market situation in the October egg future on the Chicago Mercantile Exchange resulted in suspension of trading there.

The speculative operations examined by the CEA included soybean futures, where speculative holdings were found to far outweigh the needs of hedgers. It was also found, once again, that margin requirements were low, enabling traders to finance speculative transactions with relatively small down payments. It was concluded that this was a contributing factor in the upsurge of speculative activity and attendant price rises. The CEA stated that

> A speculator who purchased just before the Korean episode and deposited the minimum margin could have "cashed in" five weeks later on July 28 with an approximate 450 percent profit on lard, 300 percent on cottonseed oil, 300 percent on soybeans, 150 percent on cotton or wool tops, and a comparatively modest 100 percent on the relatively sluggish wheat futures.[8]

As the result of these agriculture price increases, President Truman, on April 26, 1951, requested Congress to extend the Defense Production Act of 1950 and to add a provision to its terms that would authorize federal control of margins. President Truman had previously charged in 1947, in the first broadcast ever to be televised from the White House, that "gambling in grain" was the cause of high food prices and that grain prices "should not be subject to the greed of speculators who gamble on what may lie ahead in our commodity markets."

A congressional committee also began an investigation of the commodity price fluctuations arising from the Korean War, and of rumors that members of the Truman administration were profiting from commodity futures, trading as insiders. Sensing a political scandal, a Senate subcommittee began an investigation, and Harold Stassen, then a serious contender for the Republican presidential nomination, charged that eleven administration officials had made more than 4 million dollars in commodity speculation since the outbreak of the Korean conflict. Congress then passed a joint resolution requiring the CEA to publish the names of speculators in the market. President Truman signed the resolution, only to learn that his close friend and personal physician, General Graham, had been speculating in the commodity markets and had made over $6,000 in a few months' time. It was also found that a special assistant to the Secretary of the Army, in three years of commodity speculation, had made almost $1 million. He denied that inside information had played any part in his success, but he resigned after it was charged by Harold Stassen that the official's "sense of right and wrong is not fully developed."[9]

Thereafter, the leading commodity exchanges announced increases in their speculative margin rates, which led to the defeat of the margin provisions of the Defense Production Act. This defeat came notwithstanding Senator Humphrey's charge that the president should be given full authority to "crack down" on commodity speculation, which the Senator contended was adding billions of dollars to the cost of the defense program.[10] In early 1951, a general ceiling price regulation was also imposed by the Office of Price Stabilization. But futures trading prices were not directly affected in most instances, because they did not approach the levels at which the ceilings applied.

On August 10, 1950, only a few months after the invasion of South Korea, the CEA reported that a "Chinese group" was trading in the market and causing prices to soar; it was found that there was very sizable trading by customers with Chinese names and in some instances with Hong Kong addresses. It never became clear whether the Chinese were Nationalists or Communists. But the president of the Chicago Board denied published reports "that a virtual corner of soybeans by 'Chinese Nationalists interests had been instrumental in causing prices to soar from $2.20 to $3.45 a bushel.' "[11]

There were in fact thirty-one accounts with Chinese names holding some 3 million bushels. Also, a number of large-scale traders came into the market with Chinese names. All of the accounts were speculative. One account also increased its position to over 2.5 million bushels. It was found that this account was a Hong Kong merchant and that the purchase was distributed among the accounts of fourteen of its customers. Each of these fourteen individuals held positions just one contract below the CEA's reporting requirements, and the accounts took delivery of some 2 million bushels of soybeans. It was found that the circumstances surrounding these accounts pointed to common control of possible common ownership (*i.e.,* to the accounts of the Hong Kong commission firm). It was ultimately found that there were some forty-nine speculative accounts with Chinese names or Chinese connections.[12]

EGGS, RYE, AND OTHER PROBLEMS

An investigation by the CEA also disclosed that speculative operations had distorted egg futures prices in October 1949, which as noted above, caused the Chicago Mercantile Exchange to suspend trading. It was found that a small number of traders had a large portion of the long contracts in the October egg future. As delivery date approached, the two largest traders maintained their long positions. This resulted in a tight market situation because the shorts were experiencing difficulty in obtaining supplies. The Chicago Mercantile Exchange restricted trading in the October eggs to liquidation only and increased minimum maintenance margins. Later, it suspended all trading in that future and fixed a settlement price on the eggs subject to delivery. It was found that the largest speculator, and one of its customers, had transmitted buy orders into two other large speculators' accounts, suggesting they were operating in tandem. Those traders together held over 70 percent of the total long commitments in the October egg future.[13] Criminal charges were brought against Great Western Food Distributors, Nathaniel Hess, and others. Great Western was also subsequently suspended from trading futures, as the result of a prior corner in eggs it effected in 1947, and that sanction was upheld by the Seventh Circuit.

These were only the first of a series of cases brought by the CEA charging manipulation of egg prices. For example, it was charged that G. H. Miller & Co. and others had manipulated egg future prices in 1952. The court of appeals found that the traders there had cornered the market, and that they had the "shorts on their knees and at their mercy." Manipulation cases in eggs were also brought by the CEA in 1956, 1958, 1961, and 1964. A massive case was also brought against David Henner, a floor broker on the Chicago Mercantile Exchange. He was charged with manipulating 1968 shell egg future prices by bidding the price up at the close of the trading period. He was suspended from trading for thirty days as the result of this conduct.

In another investigation, the CEA sought to determine the percentage of orders in cottonseed oil futures entered by outside customers that met in the ring (i.e., how frequently were customer orders to buy and customer orders to sell matched against each other?). The CEA was seeking to ascertain what percentage of customer orders were matched against floor traders and local members trading for themselves. It was found that customer orders to buy and sell met each other in approximately 38 percent of the contracts executed. The rest were executed by trading with local members and floor traders engaged primarily in scalping operations. It was also found that this floor trading activity was in the hands of a relatively small number of floor traders, and that a small minority of brokers were prearranging orders noncompetitively on a "considerable scale."[14]

The CEA also focused on other floor trading practices on the commodity exchanges. It found there was a marked decline in "job lot" trading. Trading in grain futures historically has been conducted in round lot contracts, which in most grains is a unit of 5,000 bushels. A small proportion was conducted in job lots of 1,000 bushels or 2,000 bushels. It was found that this job lot trading had decreased following the war.

By 1952 the CEA had begun to place increased importance on the enforcement of its limits on individual speculators. It noted that, with the imposition of these limits, so-called market leaders could not build speculative lines of more than 2 to 3 percent in open contracts, making it more difficult to achieve a dominating position and narrowing the field for manipulative and corning operations. It was also found that the position limits set by the CEA were generally followed by traders. In thirteen instances reviewed by the CEA, when speculators exceeded limits in grains and cotton, most involved small amounts that were due to carelessness or bookkeeping errors and were reduced immediately when the trader was put on notice. It was concluded that speculative limits did not decrease the general interest in soybean futures trading, nor did they diminish the liquidity of the market. In fact, the level of soybean futures trading had increased after the imposition of limits. It was also found that large-scale speculative trading affected prices.

The rye market on the Chicago Board of Trade was another "notorious" center for speculative abuses. The market was controlled by a small group of clubby traders, and it was said "one had to be of the right religion to trade rye." The rye crop was small, and the market was, therefore, susceptible to manipulation. There were also constant rumors of dominant positions held by one name trader or another, most often Daniel Rice. Rice had previously been charged, along with the General Foods Corp., with attempting to corner the rye futures market in 1944, but he too was exonerated by the Seventh Circuit of any wrongdoing in that caper. Interest waned in the rye market in the early 1960s, ending the problems in that contract that had continually plagued the Business Conduct Committee of the Chicago Board of Trade.[15]

Problems were also encountered during the early postwar years in commodities that were not subject to regulation by the CEA. For example, although the government had never won an antitrust suit previously against the commodity exchanges, the Federal Trade Commission nevertheless charged the Coffee Exchange (now the Coffee, Cocoa, and Sugar Exchange) in 1954 with having violated Section 5 of the Federal Trade Commission Act. That statute prohibits unfair methods of competition and unfair deceptive acts or practices. The coffee exchange did not trade commodities that were regulated under the Commodity Exchange Act, but the FTC charged that the "S" contract on the Coffee Exchange was an unreasonable restraint of trade that hindered and restrained competition among its members. It contended that the terms of the contract were so restrictive that it resulted in a very thin market—creating a possibility that at delivery time the supply would be insufficient to meet demands of buyers and thereby causing adverse price movements. The Coffee Exchange entered into a consent decree pursuant to which it changed its contract, that is, it broadened its terms to permit futures trading in coffee that covered approximately 70 percent of the world's coffee crop.

In 1955 a study was conducted of coffee prices for a Senate subcommittee created for that purpose. It was noted that no limits were imposed by the New York Coffee and Sugar Exchange on speculative trading. It too found that the Coffee "S" Contract was only restrictive in nature and that the thin market resulting from this was subject to manipulation and wide price swings. The subcommittee recommended that a better contract be established, but suggested that further consideration of whether coffee should be added to the commodities regulated under the Commodity Exchange Act be suspended until the Federal Trade Commission's action was resolved (it was then still pending) and other events were studied to determine whether regulation was needed. The Senate Committee on Agriculture, however, recommended in 1954 that coffee futures be added to the act. This did not occur until 1974.[16]

In the regulated commodities, the CEA brought charges of manipulation of the soybean market in 1954 against Landon Butler and the Black Gin Company. The Continental Grain Company was also charged with manipulating wheat futures in 1955, and it was suspended from trading wheat and corn futures for 90 days.

Later, the CEA reported that it was observing "group action" by traders attempting to manipulate the markets, and it noted the difficulty of proving collusion or common understanding between the members of such groups.[17] The CEA cautioned that this group trading technique could threaten market stability to the point that it would be unable to preserve the integrity of the market. In apparent response to such concerns, the CEA was given authority to subpoena witnesses. This was done by incorporating provisions of the Interstate Commerce Act into the Commodity Exchange Act. The CEA also noted that it depended heavily on the exchanges to punish violators, particularly for small infractions. It was this approach, as discussed below, that led to charges that the CEA was merely a tool of the industry. The CEA's ability was also called into question by the fact that it was not until 1953 that any court of appeals upheld a CEA order suspending any individual's trading privileges for violating the manipulation prohibitions in the Commodity Exchange Act.

Futures trading in onions was brought under the Commodity Exchange Act in 1955, and a manipulation case was brought by the CEA, charging that Vincent Kosuga and others had manipulated onion prices in 1955 and 1956. Onions had long been the subject of extreme price fluctuations even before the advent of futures trading. Nevertheless, there were efforts in Congress to ban it, which eventually succeeded. The CEA took a neutral position, stating that it did not believe that prohibiting futures trading in onions would by any means be a panacea with respect to preventing the wide price fluctuations in onions that occurred even before futures trading in onions began. The Department of Agriculture also noted elsewhere that the perishable nature of onions had precluded the regulatory scheme under the Commodity Exchange Act from preventing the wide seasonal price swings traditional in the marketing of onions.

Nevertheless, Public Law 85-839 was enacted on August 28, 1958, to ban onion futures trading.[18] The Chicago Mercantile Exchange brought an action to declare the statute unconstitutional. The law was upheld by the courts, however, and the exchange suspended all trading in onion futures and ordered all open contracts settled on the basis of prior closing prices.

Volkart Brothers and certain of its officials were charged by the CEA with manipulating the price of the October 1957 cotton futures contract on the New York and New Orleans cotton exchanges. It was found that Volkart held most of the long open interest on these exchanges, as well as much of the available deliverable supplies. The Fifth Circuit Court of Appeals, however, dismissed the case because it was not shown that the short traders used due diligence in converting uncertified cotton to certified stock in order to meet their delivery obligations. In another action, it was charged by the CEA that Murlas Brothers Commodities Inc., a brokerage firm, and others had manipulated potato future prices on the New York Mercantile Exchange. The respondents were suspended from trading for their own accounts for a period of 60 days for this conduct. Also, in 1962, it was charged that Internatio (wool) and Albert Aladjen had manipulated the May 1962 wool futures contract on the New York Cotton Exchange. The respondents were suspended from trading for 20 days.

In 1963 the CEA reported on two cases that it had brought recently involving different brokers who were trading for customers who had died. In another case, a trader was charged with wash trading, a violation of the Commodity Exchange Act. While contesting the case, he invited the manager of the CEA's Chicago office to accompany him to the trading pit to watch him wash trade while the case was pending. The CEA noted before Congress that it was powerless to do anything but bring another complaint against him.

4

THE SALAD OIL DEBACLE
AND MARKET TURMOIL
IN THE 1970s

In 1963 one of the most notorious financial scandals of modern American history exploded onto the nation's headlines. It involved the mysterious disappearance of some 1.6 billion pounds of salad oil and losses in excess of $200 million by investors and financial institutions. Its source was Anthony DeAngelis, an overweight, 240-pound man who was known to the trade as the "salad oil king," and to his friends as Tino. A high school dropout, DeAngelis began his business in hog butchering and later became a principal player in the New York meat business, a business that expanded rapidly during World War II.

In 1949 DeAngelis began running into a series of regulatory problems. Among other things, he was charged with cheating the federal school lunch program, and a company he controlled was the subject of an action by the SEC. Undaunted, DeAngelis jumped aboard the government's "food for peace" program. Operating through the Allied Crude Vegetable Oil Refining Corporation located in Bayonne, New Jersey, DeAngelis began competing through this small company with some of the giant corporations of America. He nevertheless became an almost immediate success. By the late 1950s, Allied was shipping more than 75 percent of the edible oils shipped overseas. Large quantities of the oil that DeAngelis shipped, however, began springing leaks, and "[b]efore long warehouses from Brazil to India were awash in rancid salad oil."[1]

DeAngelis, through Allied, also began using the American Express field warehousing services, a part of the American Express credit card company's empire. This business was designed to allow American Express to expand into the business of issuing warehouse receipts as collateral for bank loans. For that purpose, the field warehousing firm merely had to take over supervision of the customer company's storage facilities and ensure that the goods pledged for bank loans arrived and remained in the facilities. Allied's business with American Express expanded rapidly, and it was estimated that 80 percent of all the soybean oil in the country was flowing through Allied's Bayonne, New Jersey facilities.

Anonymous charges, however, were being made in 1960 that DeAngelis was using phantom oil in Allied's tanks, that there was water in DeAngelis' storage tanks rather than oil. The caller stated that one large tank contained

> a metal chamber of some kind which went from the top of the tank to the bottom of the tank. It was under the hole where you would normally drop a bomb (sampling device) to determine the quality of the content of the tank. Whenever we went to take inventory at that tank, he said, we would be dropping the bomb down this metal chamber which was filled with soybean oil but the balance of the tank had water in it.[2]

Despite these allegations, the American Field Warehousing inspectors were unable to find, at the time the allegation was made, any discrepancy.

DeAngelis' downfall came when he started buying soybean oil futures contracts in anticipation of closing a large deal with the Spanish government, a deal that aborted. DeAngelis then began a series of frantic efforts to postpone the losses that he subsequently suffered on the soybean futures contracts. In one case, he paid a brokerage firm, J. R. Williston Bean, for negotiable warehouse receipts with fraudulent American Field Warehousing receipts. In 1963 he also opened an account with Ira Haupt and Company of New York. By the end of August 1963, DeAngelis, through Allied, owned 79 percent of the cottonseed oil futures on the New York Produce Exchange and 20 percent of the soybean oil contracts on the Chicago Board of Trade. The contracts held by Allied had a paper value of some $160 million, but for each drop in one cent per pound in price, Allied would suffer a loss of over $13 million.

Finally, the whole DeAngelis empire collapsed when oil prices declined. Allied was forced into bankruptcy, and Wall Street began to face the consequences. The brokerage firms of Ira Haupt and Williston Bean were suspended for failing to meet their obligations. This was only the second time in the history of the New York Stock Exchange that a member firm had been so suspended. The New York Stock Exchange also contributed 9.5 million dollars to customers of Ira Haupt. The American Express Company placed its subsidiary into bankruptcy—a humiliating experience. The total losses for all creditors was some $200 million, including millions of dollars of losses caused by phony unauthorized receipts and receipts for nonexistent oil in the American Express warehouses. It was truly a scandal that touched almost all of Wall Street, and it shook the U.S. financial community to its core.

But the salad oil scandal received only passing comment from the

CEA. It claimed that because of its timely action in assuring that customer funds were segregated at the brokerage firms involved with the Allied Crude accounts, there were no losses of customer funds. The CEA did concede that the bankruptcy of Allied had caused a severe break in soybean oil and cottonseed oil prices and heavy losses in the vegetable oil industry and financial community. But it noted that the Allied scandal was the result of fraudulent warehouse receipts that were not registered with the exchanges and therefore were not eligible for, and were not used for, deliveries on futures contracts in the exchanges. The CEA also stated that these warehouse receipts were outside the jurisdiction of the Department of Agriculture and the CEA. It was charged, however, that the CEA had been "blasé" about DeAngelis' purchases, that it knew he was using dummy accounts for his trading, and that the CEA "had been exposed as lacking the will and the means to curb speculative abuses."[3]

SUGAR, WHEAT, AND OTHER COMMODITIES

Although it did not regulate futures trading in sugar, the CEA did conduct an investigation of that market in 1963, at the request of the Secretary of Agriculture, to determine what caused a then recent large increase in volume of trading and "spectacular" increases in the price of sugar. The report of the CEA found that excessive speculation in sugar futures on the New York Coffee and Sugar Exchange contributed materially to the sharp rise in prices and to their later sharp drop. But no evidence of manipulation was found.

In August and September 1963, sugar prices again rose sharply, and the CEA maintained close surveillance of sugar futures trading and instituted a program of required reports for this "runaway" market. Later, the supply situation in sugar diminished the likelihood of excessive speculation, and the reports were discontinued. The CEA, however, recommended to Congress that sugar futures trading be placed on the list of commodities subject to the Commodity Exchange Act. Congress declined to do so until 1974. Price breaks also occurred in other commodities, including congestion in the 1964 May wheat contract on the Chicago Board of Trade and the Minneapolis Grain Exchange. A sharp price increase also occurred in Maine potatoes on the New York exchange.

There was additional concern over the effects on prices of actual and projected sales of wheat to the Soviet Union, which occasioned a wave of buying by small traders in the Chicago soybean market. Trading operations in New York cotton and wool futures also required extensive investigations by the CEA, as well as questionable trading operations, and possible price manipulation, in shell egg futures on the Chicago markets and spot eggs in New York markets. Sanctions were imposed against long wool traders for manipulation. Flax seed futures were also investigated, along with trading practices in the potato futures market and the cottonseed oil futures markets.

As one of its principal regulatory tools, the CEA conducted what it termed "trade practice investigations" (comprehensive investigations of floor trading practices on the various exchanges). In one such trade practice investigation, some 4,300 transactions in grain were examined. The CEA found that a trading practice had developed in the market that had resulted in about 10 percent of the trading volume being wash trades. Despite their obvious importance, the CEA did not have the manpower to conduct more than a few such investigations.

In 1968, following criticism by the General Accounting Office that more trade practice investigations were needed, the CEA sought to conduct its trade practice investigations through more automated data processing systems. One such investigation involved job lot trading on the Chicago Board of Trade (trading in commodities for less than 5,000 bushels). This investigation disclosed a complete lack of competition in execution of customer job lot orders, resulting in customers being required to pay a premium on a purchase and to sell at a discount. There were also instances of wash sales and fictitious trading. As a result of this investigation, job lot trading on the Chicago Board of Trade was discontinued and complaints were issued against seven floor traders for wash and fictitious trading.

The General Accounting Office report criticizing the lack of Trade Practice Investigations by the CEA also stated that floor traders on commodity exchanges had special advantages over the trading public. It noted that a study by the SEC Commission of floor trading practices in the securities markets had resulted in adoption of plans designed to eliminate all such trading that was not beneficial to the market. It was suggested by the General Accounting Office that a study similar to the SEC's should be conducted by the CEA.

The CEA initially declined to do so, stating that the funds that would be needed for such a study could be better used elsewhere. It later conceded that such a study would be desirable, but that it must be recognized that there were basic differences between commodity and securities markets— securities markets use a specialist system designed to permit reasonable price continuity by evening out temporary disparities between public supply and demand. The commodity markets did not have such a specialist system, and floor trading was a necessary part of their operations.

A test study was, in fact, subsequently conducted by the CEA in floor trading in a potato futures contract on the New York Mercantile Exchange. It was found that day trading by floor traders represented a small, relatively stable percentage of trading and that short term intra-day price movements resulted principally from trading by the general public, as opposed to trading by floor traders. It was also found that, twice as often as not, floor traders were trading against price movements, which indicated to the CEA that their trading restricted, rather than accentuated, price movements. It concluded, therefore, that further study was not a high-priority matter.

In 1966 the CEA expressed its concern to the Chicago Board of Trade that margin levels were inadequate and recommended that they be raised in order to deter excessive speculation then occurring on the exchange. The Board of Trade made "small token increases," but not enough to curb the speculative fever, at least in the view of the CEA. It was further noted that a number of inadequately financed and poorly staffed firms had to be registered by the CEA as futures commission merchants because the law did not authorize the establishment of minimum financial requirements. It was also found that, in some instances, officials in firms being registered had histories with other law enforcement agencies, including prison records.

THE 1968 AMENDMENTS

In 1968, amendments were made to the Commodity Exchange Act that were designed to allow increased regulation by the CEA. The legislative history of these amendments reflected a deep animosity between the Agriculture Department and the industry it was regulating. It was charged, for example, by George L. Mehren, Assistant Secretary of Agriculture, before the U.S. House of Representatives that the legislation was needed because there were "documented abuses by the score—from petty thievery to operations of confidence men, to swindling. . . . "

The Secretary of Agriculture, through Mehren, sought authority to disapprove exchange rules and to bring additional commodities into the regulatory scheme as well as the authority to enjoin violators and to establish further protections for customer funds. Mehren noted before the House that the commodity futures industry had grown to some 17 million transactions per year, involving $75 billion in annual volume in regulated commodities alone. The assistant secretary stated that most trading being done on the exchanges was for speculation. He stated that "[s]peculation may not be evil, but neither is it 'a thing of beauty and a joy forever' as one academician last year testified."

The assistant secretary also pointed out various abuses, noting that, as one example, one of the largest speculators in history operated by persuading eight prominent brokerage firms to falsify their records in order to conceal his speculation. When apprehended, the speculator stated that, due to harassment and interference from the federal government, he would sell out his "long" position and return to Canada. In fact, he had a short position and was hoping that his announcement would depress prices and allow him to profit further.

In another case described by Mehren, a large company sold futures heavily in Chicago, with offsetting purchases on the Winnipeg Grain Exchange. The company then moved oats from Winnipeg to Chicago to depress Chicago prices in relation to Winnipeg, thereby ensuring a large profit on the position. The assistant secretary noted that another large speculator had lost heavily in a manipulative attempt, partially financed by warehouse receipts on soybeans. But it was discovered that the elevators, where the soybeans were purportedly held under the receipts, were empty when his creditors tried to redeem the receipts.

To correct such problems, the assistant secretary sought regulatory authority over futures trading in coffee, sugar, and livestock. On that score, he noted that the Federal Trade Commission had found that price fluctuations were frequent in these markets and that this was amplified by the failure of the New York Coffee and Sugar Exchange to institute proper safeguards, such as those followed by regulated exchanges. It was also stated that excessive and totally unregulated speculation in sugar futures stimulated the sugar price "explosions" of 1963, and "violent fluctuations" in the price of pork belly contracts that were generated by "speculation alone."

Mehren additionally pointed out that there were no fitness standards for futures commission merchants registered under the act—anyone who applied was granted a license. He noted, for example, that a Los Angeles bookie establishment had been charged with grand theft, but it nevertheless had been registered. The individual operating this FCM had also applied for and obtained membership in a leading commodity exchange under an assumed name, and thereafter defrauded his commodity customers by trading their funds in his own account in unregulated sugar futures. Upon discovery, he fled the country but was later apprehended.

The Department sought injunctive authority to stop abuses. Such actions were to be brought by the Attorney General, after the secretary determined there was a violation. The Department stated that this was the most vital of the amendments it was seeking, because the market was often damaged before the Department could complete protracted administrative proceedings and before a final order could be obtained. The assistant secretary noted that, in one case, two individuals associated with the salad oil swindle had opened their own firm and began churning out customer accounts. These two individuals had previously had their registration as securities broker-dealer revoked and had pleaded guilty to securities fraud in another case; they were also named in a land fraud case. The CEA, however, was powerless to stop them until after lengthy administrative proceedings and a criminal indictment. The secretary also sought cease-and-desist authority for minor violations. It was stated that this authority would also avoid the necessity of suspending the registration or trading of a large brokerage firm, which was the only remedy then available.[4]

Legislation was also sought to make persons liable for willfully aiding and abetting violations of the Commodity Exchange Act, as well as to expand the antifraud provisions of the act to cover all persons who handled customer orders. With respect to the latter, the Department cited an instance where an individual—who was not a member of an exchange or otherwise subject to the CEA's jurisdiction—placed "good trades" in his own account and "poor trades" in the customer accounts he controlled. Yet the individual was not subject to the antifraud provisions of the Commodity Exchange Act, as they were then written.

Reporting requirements were sought to be strengthened by requiring persons holding reportable futures positions to also report their cash transactions. Restrictions were requested to limit the types of investments that could be made with customer funds by brokerage firms, as well as a requirement that floor traders be required to register with the CEA, even if they were trading only for their own accounts. The Department sought further authority to approve exchange rules and to require exchanges to enforce their rules. The assistant secretary noted that a requirement that exchanges be required to enforce the rules appeared to be "redundant," but noted that a CEA trade practice investigation had revealed that an exchange was not enforcing the rules with respect to the matching of buying and selling orders of different customers, which was permitted only under established exchange procedures. It was found that exchange officials were not even familiar with the provisions of their rule, which set standards under which such matching could be done. The assistant secretary stated that "[t]his kind of 'self-regulation' cannot assure honest, open and efficient trading."[5]

The industry hotly contested the assistant secretary's charge that commodity futures trading was being abused. Two of the larger exchanges stated that his remarks were "exaggerated, intemperate and insulting," "a grotesque misrepresentation" of the industry, that Mehren had "gravely distorted the picture," and that his remarks amounted to "irresponsibility".[6] The Chicago Board of Trade's chairman, Robert Martin, later to become a commissioner of the Commodity Futures Trading Commission, also vehemently opposed the secretary's request for injunctive relief, asserting that this could interfere with market processes. He testified that there is a delicate balance in the commodities markets and that this balance was maintained by sensitivity to outside influences difficult for someone not familiar with the markets to realize. He stated that

> Because of this, use of the injunctive power as the Department [of Agriculture] has suggested it would be almost like making a surgical incision with a meat ax. Its use to affect market positions could not in any way be limited. It would necessarily affect thousands of contracts and millions of dollars of investment. Its impact could be felt the country over, from

the largest processor to small country elevators and individual farmers. And all of this could happen with no advance warning, no bond and no provision for compensating the losses of unsuspecting traders. Their losses would, in fact, be incalculable.[7]

Chairman Martin further argued that a judge would have difficulty understanding the complex commodity markets. He also leveled his sights on the CEA, noting that three of its six cases on manipulation had been reversed by the courts, suggesting that the CEA did not itself have the expertise to determine when violations were occurring.

The Chicago Mercantile Exchange, which for some unknown reason boasted that its building had been dedicated by Will Rogers in 1928, also warned against a "Russianization" of the futures markets by federal regulation, a theme that was carried for years in subsequent exchange advertisements. The Coffee and Sugar Exchange noted that sugar and most coffee were produced abroad, which meant that the producers, in any event, would be beyond the reach of the Department of Agriculture. It also argued that futures business would go abroad if the exchange was subject to regulation, particularly if the government was given control over margin requirements.

On the other hand, the National Grain Trade Council suggested that Congress examine the creation of a completely new independent regulatory agency, along the lines of the Securities and Exchange Commission, to regulate futures trading in all commodities. The SEC also participated in the hearings, through Philip A. Loomis, general counsel of the SEC at that time and later a commissioner. He conceded that the SEC's understanding of the commodities markets was "limited," but did express regulatory concern with securities brokers and dealers who also acted as commodity brokers, because the latter activity could threaten their securities activities in the event of financial difficulties. The SEC spoke in favor of allowing the Secretary of Agriculture to prescribe minimum financial requirements for futures commission merchants and supported the measures sought by the Department for injunctive relief.

The resulting 1968 amendments fell far short of the Department's ambitious proposals. For example, injunctive authority was not added to the statute.[8] The amendments were, nevertheless, significant. The provisions that were adopted included a broadening of the antifraud standard, the imposition of aiding and abetting liability, cease and desist authority, and a provision for the secretary to "non-disapprove" rules of the exchanges. In addition, livestock and livestock products futures contracts were added to the commodities regulated under the act, and the amendments increased criminal penalties and made several other changes.

The 1968 amendments also gave the CEA authority to establish minimum financial requirements for FCMs. The 1968 amendments implemented fitness requirements, and the CEA began individual checks on the fitness of persons registered with it. These included evaluating information from the Securities and Exchange Commission, the Office of the Inspector General, the FBI, and the General Services Administration.

THE 1970s: VIET NAM IN THE COMMODITIES MARKETS

The early 1970s saw charges—which were never proven—that manipulations and bear and bull raids were being conducted periodically in numerous unregulated commodity futures contracts such as coffee and sugar. But the CEA administrator, nevertheless, saw no "pressing" need to add new commodities to the Commodity Exchange Act.

In 1971 the CEA conducted six intensive investigations of possible price manipulation in the commodities it regulated, compared to an average of one investigation per year in prior years. The CEA also pointed out to Congress that trading volume had increased substantially in the early 1970s in both regulated and nonregulated commodities. It was found that customer complaints of mishandling of accounts by brokerage firm employees had increased sharply. The CEA was additionally confronted by the failure of brokerage firms as a result of the securities operations during Wall Street's "back office" crisis. In fact, the Chicago Board of Trade had threatened to close one of Wall Street's major brokerage houses, Hayden Stone, because of its apparent insolvency. A last-minute merger, however, allowed the firm to continue its operations.[9] Nevertheless, the CEA administrator saw no need for additional personnel. Instead, he informed Congress that broader use of automated data processing would also support control over the regulated commodities.

In the early 1970s, Congress became concerned about the "Great Grain Robbery," that the Soviets were using the Commodity Futures Markets as a means to manipulate prices and obtain large profits at the expense of American consumers.[10] It was thought the Soviets were secretly buying large futures positions, as well as large amounts of cash grain. The former would rise sharply in value upon the announcement of the Soviet cash grain purchases, allowing them to obtain substantial profits on the futures contracts, which then could be used to offset the purchase price of their previously purchased grain. The consumer, however, would pay higher prices for their grain products. Although these charges were never proven, they were of serious concern to Congress. It was also noted by the CEA that grain companies were making heavy uses of the markets to hedge their sales to the Soviets, which were totaling $1.2 billion in 1973.

Skyrocketing food prices also reached record levels in 1973. For example, soybean prices had increased by over $8 per bushel in a period of some five months. One congressman described public perception of the problem as "an opinion that there has to be somebody, some little publicized group that controls prices and is getting the money." Rising costs to consumers was described as a "near panic situation." Farmers were complaining that they were not receiving a large enough share of these high prices. It was thought that price fluctuations, which were extreme, were the result of the markets being manipulated and squeezed.[11] In fact, the CEA brought manipulation charges against J. R. Simplot and Peter J. Taggares, the potato barons of America, charging manipulation of the potato futures market on the Chicago Mercantile Exchange in 1971.

One of the largest problems encountered during this period was the sale of so-called naked options (options sold by a firm that did not own the underlying commodity or did not cover its position in the futures markets). The leader of these modern bucket shops was one Harold Goldstein, who opened an office on April 28, 1971, in Los Angeles, California, to sell options on commodity futures not regulated under the Commodity Exchange Act. In less than two years, he pyramided an $800 investment into a brokerage firm with over 100 branch offices worldwide and which sold over 175,000 options valued at some $70 to $85 million or more. Goldstein had maintained that his options were backed by a computerized program to buy futures contracts for every option. He claimed that he covered his obligations by matching positions on the futures markets. In fact, he covered his positions only during the first few months of operation but not thereafter, when the options were naked. Goldstein/Samuelson subsequently failed, when the SEC and state authorities brought actions charging that Goldstein was selling securities. Customer losses were estimated at some $85 million. Before his firm failed, however, numerous other firms followed his example, leaving thousands of defrauded customers who had been collectively fleeced of millions of more dollars.

In response to the naked options problems, the CEA called the heads of the exchanges into Washington. The CEA asserted that puts and calls trading had no economic justification and that it brought into the market small traders who really did not have the risk capital to do that type of trading. It was noted that sellers of puts and calls sold their product by claiming that a trader could not lose more than the amount of the premium paid, but in fact the premiums were so high it was virtually impossible for anyone to make a profit on puts and calls.

Because puts and calls were being sold on commodities that were not regulated under the Commodity Exchange Act, the CEA was virtually powerless to stop their spread. Yet, even after the Goldstein/Samuelson disaster, the CEA was not prepared to recommend additional legislation. However, it did adopt a regulation that prohibited futures commission merchants registered with it from trading puts and calls.

THE *DES MOINES REGISTER* ARTICLES

A series of articles by Clark Mollenhoff and others that were published in 1973 by the *Des Moines Register* contended that the $200 billion commodity futures industry had virtually no controls to protect small traders and the consuming public. One article stated that the CEA had turned the task of regulation over to the exchanges themselves, and that the exchanges were run in a "club-like atmosphere." It was charged that there were strong indications of rigged markets in eggs and meats and that this had cost consumers and commodities traders millions of dollars.

It was noted that the CEA had refused to ask for any greater authority or appropriations to regulate the markets fully. CEA administrator Alex Caldwell came under particular fire for his seeming indifference to the problems in the futures markets. It was also noted that his efforts to computerize the CEA's operations, in order to avoid staff increases, had failed because the computers had kicked out so many potential violations that they were useless.

The articles further charged that the exchanges were conducting "star chamber" proceedings against members where the members were barred from being represented by a lawyer or from subpoenaing witnesses necessary to prove their cases. A vice-president of the Chicago Board of Trade was also quoted as saying that the regulation of commodities was primitive in comparison to the securities industry.

It was further charged in the articles that the CEA did not conduct any investigations of wheat sales at the time of the huge export deal with the Soviet Union. This was despite reports that persons and companies had advance tips about the sales and had used that information to make large profits. It was elsewhere suggested that the closing price on the Kansas City Board of Trade had been raised in order to affect the USDA subsidy program in connection with the Soviet wheat sale.

The Commodity Exchange Commission was also criticized as being incapable of handling large-scale market abuses; one critic called it a "lethargic appendage of the Department of Agriculture which in modern times met only infrequently and acted with even less dispatch."[12] It was also claimed that penalties levied by the CEA, when invoked, were inadequate. The *Des Moines Register* articles also charged that the CEA had been criticized for its handling of the DeAngelis scandal by a secret internal report prepared by the inspector general of the Department of Agriculture. In fact, the inspector general's report was a damning indictment of the CEA, finding that

> CEA relied on exchanges to enforce their rules and to insure that all trades were executed competitively. Insufficient effort was made to determine whether trading rules were enforced even though the regulations

require that trading is to be done openly and competitively in the pit. Our examination of exchange records disclosed several instances of apparent abusive trading practices. We found evidence of direct and indirect bucketing of customer orders, accommodation trading, excessive trading between brokers executing customer and house account orders for the same firm, and matching customer orders. There were a significant number of trades between partners or members of the same firm. Although exchange rules do not prohibit this, there is no assurance that the trades were competitive and that the trades were not wash trading used to manipulate prices and deceive other traders. We noted a case where one spreading transaction between affiliated members exceeded 20 percent of the total volume of all transactions in the two futures. It did not appear that the transaction was executed competitively.

It was CEA policy not to review clearing house records for violations of day trading speculative limits. We found that the total trading on these reports exceeded the total trades reported to CEA for three traders.

We also found other suspected violations of trading rules which we believe indicate a lack of control, detection, and enforcement of rules governing the execution of customer orders. We found transactions involving trades where the same broker was on both sides of a trade and where trading between combinations of brokers appeared to be intentional. Also, a number of trades were made where associated members, acting as floor brokers executing customer orders for other clearing members, traded between themselves to an extent great enough to indicate that such trading was pre-arranged. Further, floor brokers executing orders for other clearing members successfully manipulated the orders and prices by executing similar orders for their own personal accounts which had a price movement effect and then executed clearing members orders.[13]

5

THE COMMODITY FUTURES
TRADING COMMISSION (CFTC)
ACT OF 1974

The next assault on the CEA occurred during its annual appropriations hearings. Normally these were lifeless affairs where only the most general and gentle of questions were directed to CEA officials. Following the *Des Moines Register* article, however, the CEA was required to respond directly to its charges and for the first time was required to justify its regulatory record. This was not the last hostile hearing, however, because Representative Neal Smith also held hearings through his subcommittee on Small Business Problems. It charged that allowing the exchanges to carry out self-regulation was like "putting the fox in charge of the henhouse."[1]

The House and Senate Agriculture Committees began efforts to establish new legislation. Specifically, the House Agriculture Committee held a hearing and appointed a special subcommittee to study and prepare any necessary legislation. Later, the Committee itself, as well as the Senate Committee on Agriculture, became involved, held extended hearings, and filed voluminous reports, all of which supported Congress' conclusion that strengthened regulation was needed.

The Senate Agriculture Committee thus stated that legislation was needed "to further the fundamental purpose of the Commodity Exchange Act in insuring fair practice and honest dealing on the commodity exchanges and providing a measure of control over those forms of speculative activity which often demoralize the markets to the injury of producers, consumers, and the exchanges themselves." It noted that, since the 1968 amendments to the Commodity Exchange Act, there had been a major shift to a market-oriented economy. It found that, as a result, "futures markets are playing an increasingly important role in the pricing and marketing of the nation's commodities," and that "in recent years, the consumer has become increasingly aware that futures markets have a direct effect on such matters as his grocery bill and the cost of his home." It was also found that the general public had been entering the futures markets in growing numbers, attracted by the wide price swings and the possibility of large profits.[2]

The Senate Committee further noted that many large and important futures markets were completely unregulated. This included coffee, sugar, cocoa, lumber, plywood, and precious metals, including the "highly sensitive" silver market, and markets in a number of foreign currencies. It was noted by the Senate Committee that discussions were under way to expand the futures markets to such things as home mortgages and ocean freight rates. The Committee stated:

> A person trading in one of the currently unregulated futures markets should receive the same protection afforded to those trading in the regulated markets. Whether a commodity is grown or mined, or whether it is produced in the United States or outside, makes little difference to those in this country who buy, sell, and process the commodity, or to the U.S. consumers whose prices are affected by the futures market in that commodity.[3]

The Committee found that additional regulatory tools were needed to ensure appropriate regulation. It concluded that the importance of futures trading to the general public and to the nation "equals" the importance of the securities markets, and that it was, therefore, time to establish a regulatory authority similar to the SEC to regulate commodity futures.

It was noted by Congress that the CEA had a "geriatric" problem, that its total number of employees had declined during a period when trading had soared, and that the CEA had been unable to secure personnel with the requisite futures backgrounds and professional skills to accomplish its regulation. In addition, the CEA had no independent legal staff, requiring it to draw on Agriculture Department attorneys servicing several other bodies within that department. It was also found that the CEA had only limited authority to impose penalties, that the issuance of a cease-and-desist order or suspension of a trader required as many as five levels of review within the Department, causing long delays. As a consequence, Congress concluded that existing federal oversight provided by the Commodity Exchange Act of 1936 was "weak," and that "the present regulatory activities of the Commodity Exchange Authority in the Department of Agriculture are totally inadequate to police the industry under the limited authority given them by the present law."[4]

The House Agriculture Committee additionally noted that new investments in commodity futures were being channeled from the securities markets because of their high leverage, low margin requirements, and volatile price action. It was found that, based on 1973 dollar volume, commodities trading far exceeded that of securities dealing, and that a price for a seat on the New York Stock Exchange was $95,000, while a seat on the Chicago Mercantile Exchange, the second largest domestic futures exchange, had recently traded at $112,500.

Congress found problems on the exchanges themselves. It concluded that self-regulation often did not work because tradition and self-interested members displaced the public interest. It was charged that owners of the exchanges manipulated and evaded the traditional rules for their own personal gain. In that connection, the House Committee traced the history and evolution of self-regulation in the commodities industry, noting that initially exchange standards were ideals rather than minimum requirements. Later, the courts began to look upon exchanges' self-regulation as a guarantee to the public that its members would not violate its code of conduct. It was found that the 1968 amendments, which allowed the government to disapprove contract market rules, had the unintended effect of weakening self-regulation, because the exchanges began reducing their regulatory scheme after court cases began holding that the failure to enforce exchange rules was a violation of the Commodity Exchange Act that would support suits for private litigants.

Congress discovered that the CEA had relied on the exchanges to enforce their rules and to ensure that all trades were executed competitively. But as noted above, the inspector general for the Department of Agriculture had examined exchange records and found numerous, apparently abusive trading practices, including bucketing of customers' orders, excessive trading between brokers, executing customer and house orders at the same time, and improper matching of customer orders. In one case, a spread transaction between affiliated members was found to have exceeded 20 percent of the total volume of all transactions in the two futures involved in the spread. It also appeared that these transactions were noncompetitive. Widespread pre-arranged trading was also found.

Congress also examined the 1972 grain sale to the Soviet Union. It was stated on the floor of the House:

> Our experiences with the Soviet wheat deal demonstrate the disastrous effects which unfair trading practices can have on farmers and consumers alike. Major grain exporting companies speculate freely on the commodities exchanges, and it appears their manipulation of the trading allowed them to buy wheat cheap and keep it secret from other traders. Later they sold it at higher prices to the Russians. We have all seen the results in high food prices and short grain supplies. Without new controls there is nothing to prevent foreign nations from manipulating commodity futures.[5]

Congress concluded that there was a real danger that futures markets could be squeezed or manipulated by foreign companies, "some of which have access to huge resources of foreign governments." It was stated:

They can buy at a fixed price from a grain dealer who in turn hedges his risk on our commodities markets.

By dealing with four or five companies simultaneously the way the Russians did, the foreign company can sometimes buy more of one commodity at a fixed price than could possibly be delivered. They can indirectly speculate in huge volumes on our market. The grain companies who sell to him would not know at the time they sign the contract for a fixed price the extent to which other dealers are also obligating themselves for the same kind of grain. This happened in the Russian grain deal. They bought 50 percent more wheat than they needed. Cargill said that although they assumed the Russians were negotiating with others, they had no idea they were buying the quantity of grain which they bought. Then they transferred the huge risk involved onto the backs of the unsuspecting American producers and processors. By overbuying their needs, they could later sell part of it at a much higher price and profit from a manipulation which would be prohibited for domestic traders.[6]

It was found that the CEA had, indeed, referred for investigation charges that the markets were being manipulated as the result of the Soviet grain sale to the Kansas City Board of Trade, which determined that there had been no manipulation. Later, however, the CEA completed its own investigation and found that the market had been manipulated on the close for several days, resulting in the payment of millions of dollars more in export subsidies. These charges were never proved in court.

The House Committee concluded:

Self-regulation is a commendable and noble concept and useful in such a complex atmosphere as that which surrounds futures trading. It cannot continue to function without a strong Federal regulatory umbrella over self-regulatory activities of the industry. Self-regulation cannot be permitted to be a barrier against public policy and the interests of the American public. Yet, with proper Federal supervisory authority, needed self-regulatory efforts of the exchanges can live a useful life into the 21st Century and, hopefully, beyond.[7]

Numerous other problems were found that needed to be addressed by the new legislation, including schemes that involved the systematic solicitation and bilking of unsophisticated customers in nonregulated futures contracts. It was also charged that consumer prices were being inflated because of excessive speculation and manipulative practices in futures trading. In that connection, it was noted that in 1973 when prices had skyrocketed, soybeans futures were largely concentrated in the hands of a relatively small number of processors and traders. Indeed, over 90 percent of all long contracts for July soybean futures on the Chicago Board of Trade were found to have been held by only four traders. It was also reported that 1973 cotton market prices had been affected by speculation—

one trader on the New York Cotton Exchange had held 67 percent of all long contracts for the month of October. Price distortions in corn futures were also cited.

Alex Caldwell, in a sharp turn around from earlier years, appeared in the hearings with his own laundry list of proposals to strengthen the Commodity Exchange Act. Among other things, he sought authority to allow the CEA to require amendments to be made in specific exchange rules; to regulate the content of advertising of brokerage firms; to provide for computerized floor trading on contract markets (but not to mandate it); to require a government-sponsored insurance or trust fund for customers such as the Federal Deposit Insurance Corporation (FDIC); and to bring all futures trading under federal regulation. Caldwell also sought to relieve the CEA of the authority and responsibility for investigating and prosecuting cash market price manipulations, unless they were related to the operations in a commodity futures market. He further sought to prohibit trading by floor brokers for their own account and for customers except when permitted by the regulatory agency. Similar restrictions were sought to be imposed on FCMs for trading for their own account and for customers. He sought injunctive authority, noting once again that it took months, and sometimes years, to stop practices that clearly were fraudulent.[8] The Department of Agriculture also sought to require the registration of commodity advisers and commodity pool operators in order to eliminate practices that had "enticed unsuspecting traders into the markets with, far too often, substantial loss of funds."[9]

The CEA sought legislation that would require contract markets to demonstrate that their contracts had an economic purpose; that would give them the authority to impose monetary penalties to require registration and fitness checks for all persons handling customer accounts; and that would allow the government to impose market controls where there was a market emergency. It also sought to require contract markets to establish a procedure for settlement of customer claims, with an appeal to the agency.

Other suggested changes included such things as: giving the government the authority to set margins and to restrict excessive speculation in commodity markets when speculative transactions exceeded 50 percent of the market in a particular commodity; requiring the establishment of an office to study market conditions and to provide information to the public; providing a civil remedy against a trader obtaining and profiting from inside information concerning proposed government action; and banning speculation or hedging in commodity futures by foreign governments or their agencies.

It was charged that as a result of low margin requirements set by the exchanges, "gamblers and amateur dabblers looking for quick riches" were coming into the commodity futures market in increasing numbers.[10] Attempts were therefore made on the floor to include authority in the government to regulate margins on futures trading. It was noted that the House Committee on Banking and Currency had reported a bill in the prior year to extend the Economic Stabilization Act that included a provision that would have granted the Secretary of Agriculture authority to set margins.

The exchanges, however, contended that margins in the commodity industry were for their protection. It was believed that if this power to set those margins was taken away from the exchanges, the exchanges could not properly protect themselves and disaster could come very quickly. Accordingly, Congress concluded that it should not put this authority in the hands of the federal government.

Legislation was enacted in 1974 as a result of the above concerns. The most important provision of this legislation, the Commodity Futures Trading Commission Act of 1974, was the creation of an independent five-member regulatory commission: the Commodity Futures Trading Commission (CFTC). Although the House bill had initially provided for a five part-time member commission composed of four public members and the Secretary of Agriculture or his designate, the Senate had voted for an independent full-time commission. The latter was accepted in conference.

The CFTC was established as an independent regulatory agency, composed of a chairman and four commissioners appointed by the President, by the advice and with the consent of the Senate. The legislation directed the president to establish and maintain a balanced commission with persons of demonstrated knowledge in futures trading, as well as persons with knowledge of the production processing and distribution of commodities regulated by the act. It was further required by Congress that not more than three members of the Commission be members of the same political party. Each commissioner's term was five years. The chairman of the agency was authorized to appoint the heads of its major administrative units, but such appointments were subject to approval of the entire Commission.

Congress established various provisions in the 1974 legislation designed to ensure the independence of the CFTC from the executive branch of government. This included a provision for the Commission to have a general counsel reporting directly to the Commission and serving as its legal adviser, and for the appointment of other attorneys to represent the Commission in court and in its disciplinary proceedings. Provision was made for an executive director to be appointed by the Commission, with the advice and consent of the Senate. In signing this legislation, however, President Ford objected to this provision, stating that it was unconstitutional in providing for a separate executive appointment, outside the White House, that would be subject to congressional approval. Consequently, as discussed below, the name of the executive director of the CFTC was never submitted to Congress for approval.

To further ensure its independence, the CFTC was authorized to employ investigators, special experts, administrative law judges, clerks, and other employees, as well as consultants and experts. The CFTC was granted authority to enter into contracts, including the authority to rent necessary space for its offices, authority that is not granted to many federal agencies. This was an expression of annoyance by Congress at an aborted attempt to move the SEC to Buzzard's Point, an isolated location in Washington where there was an empty building that no agency was willing to use. Provision was also made for the comptroller general to conduct reviews and audits of the CFTC and make reports thereon to Congress. The CFTC was required to furnish the comptroller with information regarding the operations of the CFTC and to provide access to its books and records.

Provision was made for a liaison with the Department of Agriculture. This was, in essence, a compromise of the House provision that would have made the Secretary of Agriculture or his designate a member of the Commission. The liaison office was to be established within the Department of Agriculture and to be staffed with employees of the CFTC. The Department of Agriculture was also to appoint a liaison officer to work with the CFTC and to maintain an office there.

Another housekeeping provision required the Commission to submit budget estimates requested by the president or the Office of Management and Budget to the House and Senate Appropriations Committee as well. Once again, President Ford objected to the constitutionality of this provision when he signed the legislation. Similar requirements were contained in the statute for legislative recommendations of the CFTC, as well as testimony and comments on legislation that were submitted by the CFTC to the president or the Office of Management and Budget.

With respect to options trading, the CFTC Act continued the ban on options tradings on commodities that were previously subject to regulation under the Commodity Exchange Act (the "previously regulated" commodities). The CFTC was given authority to permit trading in options in all other commodities under such terms and conditions as it determined to prescribe. The CFTC was required to issue regulations governing options trading on the previously nonregulated commodities within one year, except that it could obtain an extension of that limitation by notifying designated committees of Congress that it was unable to do so within that period, which it did.

A unique provision was included in this legislation, which authorized the CFTC to grant "reparations" (damages) to any person injured as the result of a violation of the Act by a person registered with the CFTC. Such claims were required to be filed within two years after the cause of action accrued. Reparations awards of the CFTC were made reviewable in a circuit court of appeals. In instances where the CFTC issued an award and no appeal was taken, the party receiving the award was allowed to have the award enforced in a district court, with provision made for attorney fees where the customer eventually received a favorable award. The order of the CFTC in such proceedings was stated to be "final and conclusive." There was no provision made for any *de novo* review in a district court and no opportunity for a jury trial.

Another significant feature of the legislation was its extension of jurisdiction. The CFTC was given "exclusive" jurisdiction over options and commodity futures contracts. It was stated, however, that this amendment was not intended to supersede or limit the jurisdiction of the SEC or other state or federal regulatory authorities or the jurisdiction conferred on the courts of the United States or any state. With respect to the exclusive jurisdiction of the CFTC, the Conference Committee also stated, however:

> Under the exclusive grant of jurisdiction to the Commission, the authority in the Commodity Exchange Act (and the regulations issued by the Commission) would preempt the field insofar as futures regulation is concerned. Therefore, if any substantive State law regulating futures trading was contrary to or inconsistent with Federal Law, the Federal Law would govern. In view of the broad grant of authority to the Commission to regulate the futures trading industry, the Conferees do not contemplate that there will be a need for any supplementary regulation by the States.[11]

In addition, the legislation stated that nothing in the Commodity Exchange Act

> shall be deemed to govern or in any way be applicable to transactions in foreign currency, security warrants, security rights, resales of installment loan contracts, repurchase options, government securities, or mortgages and mortgage purchase commitments, unless such transactions involve the sale thereof for future delivery conducted on a board of trade.[12]

This was the so-called Treasury amendment, which recognized that these types of commercial instruments should not be regulated by the CFTC as futures contracts, unless they were in fact traded on a futures exchange. It also reflects the fact that at the time the CFTC Act amendments were considered, there were proposals to trade futures contracts on at least some of these instruments. In fact, the International Monetary Market had already commenced trading on futures in foreign currency.

Commodity trading advisers and commodity pool operators were required to be registered under the new statute. The term *commodity trading adviser* was defined in essentially the same terms as securities investment advisers under the Investment Advisers Act of 1940. Exempted from the definition were banks, trust companies, newspaper reporters, lawyers, accountants, teachers, floor brokers, futures commission merchants, bona fide newspapers or other publications of general and regular circulation, contract markets, and any other persons specified by the CFTC. These exemptions, however, were available only if the advisory activities of such persons were solely incidental to the conduct of their business or profession. The term *commodity pool operator* was also defined. It was stated that such entities would include investment trusts, syndicates, and similar forms of enterprises who solicited and received funds from others by the sale of stock or otherwise for the purpose of trading in commodity futures contracts. Once again, the CFTC was allowed to specify persons who could be excluded from this requirement.

In addition, the legislation required "associated persons" to register with the new agency. These individuals were defined as employees of futures commission merchants who solicited or accepted customer orders (other than in a clerical capacity) or supervised persons so engaged. The CFTC was also authorized to specify appropriate standards for testing, training, experience, and qualifications of associated persons, futures commission merchants, and floor brokers.

In another provision, Congress directed the CFTC to determine within six months whether floor brokers should be permitted to trade for their own accounts or accounts in which they have trading discretion and also execute customer orders for futures contracts. If the CFTC concluded that such trading should be permitted, it was to specify the terms and conditions under which it could be conducted. In making these determinations, the CFTC was to consider the effect on liquidity of trading in the markets, and the CFTC was allowed to make separate determinations for different contract markets. It was directed to make similar determinations with respect to trading by futures commission merchants.

The CFTC was given broadened authority over contract markets. It was permitted to change or supplement delivery requirements of exchanges where they did not permit delivery of grades, locations, or quality, or where there were locational price differentials that presented a threat of price manipulation, market congestion, or abnormal commodity movements. In addition, contract markets were required to establish a fair and equitable procedure for arbitration of customer claims and grievances against members or employees of the contract market. It was required that such procedures be voluntary. The legislation further stated that such procedures could not result in compulsory payment, except as agreed between the parties. These protections were available only to "customers," which specifically excluded futures commission merchants and floor brokers.

The exchanges were required to submit their rules that related to the terms and conditions of futures contracts or related to trading requirements to the CFTC for approval. Such approval or disapproval was to be made by the CFTC within 30 days, unless it advised the contract market of its inability to make such a determination within that period of time. Exchanges were allowed by this legislation to adopt rules to meet emergency market situations. Such rules, however, were to be adopted only in conformity with the terms and conditions specified by the CFTC as an emergency, and such rules were only to be temporary. The CFTC was also allowed to exempt operational and administrative rules of the exchanges from the requirement that they be submitted to the CFTC for approval.

The CFTC was further authorized to alter or supplement the rules of a contract market if such a market refused to do so after request by the CFTC. This applied to specified contract market rules, including the terms and conditions of the contracts, the form or manner of execution, the financial responsibilities of members, methods of soliciting business, and the form and manner of handling and recording customer orders. The CFTC was specifically excluded, however, from approving or supplementing or changing contract market rules governing levels of margin.

The CFTC was given emergency authority over contract markets. When the CFTC determined that a market emergency existed, it was authorized to take such action as it believed necessary to maintain or restore orderly trading for liquidation of futures contracts. The term *emergency* was defined to include threatened or actual market manipulations and corners, acts of the United States or foreign governments affecting commodity prices, or any other major market disturbances that prevent the markets from accurately reflecting the forces of supply and demand.

With respect to the CFTC's emergency action authority, the Senate would have required a determination that the emergency itself would have a greater adverse impact on the market than the CFTC's proposed action. This provision, however, was deleted because, in the view of the Conference Committee, it might not be practicable for the CFTC to reach such a judgment. The Conference Committee stated, however, that it did not intend the CFTC's emergency powers to be used to prescribe a remedy more severe than the malady to be cured. It declared that the CFTC was to carefully exercise this power to use expert and impartial judgment.

The act specifically authorized the exchanges to discipline their members, including expelling them in accordance with their rules. Any such disciplinary action against a member was required to be reported to the CFTC. The CFTC was authorized to review the standards and procedures for disciplinary action and to review disciplinary decisions by exchanges. It was authorized to affirm, modify, set aside, or remand any exchange disciplinary action.

The CFTC Act amendments also provided that a contract market seeking designation as such was required to show that the transactions it sought to be designated were not contrary to the public interest. This was a Senate provision, which the Conference Committee adopted, concluding that it included a concept of an "economic purpose" test, which had been provided in the House bill. This economic purpose test, however, was subject to a "final test of the 'public interest.' "[13]

The CFTC was given injunctive authority, which the Department of

Agriculture had sought since 1968; although the legislation directed that no restraining orders were to be issued *ex parte*. The CFTC was authorized to bring such actions, but it was also authorized to request the attorney general to do so. Where the CFTC brought the action, it was to inform the attorney general of the suit and advise the Department of subsequent developments.

The CFTC was authorized to impose civil penalties of $100,000 for each violation of the Commodity Exchange Act. Specific provisions in the statute governed the manner in which the amount of the penalty was to be determined. For example, the CFTC was to consider, in the case of persons whose primary business involved commodity futures trading, the appropriateness of the penalty in light of the size of their business and their ability to continue in business and the gravity of the violation. The CFTC was also authorized to impose fines against exchanges that failed to enforce their rules. Penalties for manipulations were increased from $10,000 to $100,000.

Leverage transactions were brought within the ambit of the CFTC's jurisdiction. The amendment did not define leverage transactions, but simply referred to these contracts as a standardized contract commonly known to the trade as a margin account, margin contract, leverage account, or leverage contract. The CFTC's jurisdiction was extended only to leverage contracts in silver and gold bullion and coins. CFTC rules adopted under this grant of jurisdiction were meant to ensure the financial solvency of the transactions and to prevent manipulation or fraud. The CFTC was authorized to determine if leverage contracts were in fact futures contracts; if so, they were to be regulated as such. Such a determination would effectively have spelled their demise because they would have to be traded on a contract market.

Another section of the 1974 legislation provided for the creation of a national futures association. The legislation established a framework for such an association. It was, in effect, to be the equivalent of the National Association of Securities Dealers Inc., which governs the conduct of broker/dealers in the United States who are not members of contract markets. Among other things, the rules of such associations were required to be designed to prevent fraudulent and manipulative acts, to promote just and equitable principles of trade, and to protect the public interest. Provisions were required for discipline.

The new legislation prohibited "insider trading" by the CFTC or its employees, that is using "information acquired by virtue of the employment or position" in futures trading. The Conference Committee allowed Commission employees and Commissioners to purchase actual commodities in their farming or ranching operations and for their own consumption. None of these provisions, however, applied any insider information prohibition to other market participants, except where they acquired the information from a CFTC employee or commissioner. The limited scope of this prohibition was to be a problem that the CFTC was to grapple with in later years.

The amendments also addressed the CFTC's authority to establish position limits. The legislation authorized the CFTC to define the term *bona fide hedging* for purposes of exempting such trading from position limits. Previously, this definition had been set forth in the act itself. But it was too restrictive, as the result of new contracts being developed and expanded use of futures contracts. The House bill had authorized the CFTC to exempt arbitrage transactions. It defined the term *arbitrage* to mean the same as a spread or straddle. The Senate provision retained that exemption but limited the definition of arbitrage to domestic markets and authorized the CFTC to define international arbitrage. The Conference adopted the Senate provision because of an apparent concern that international arbitrage could have a broader definition than that encompassed by the Senate, as for example, the arbitraging of currencies between two countries.

The CFTC was authorized to conduct regular investigations of the futures markets and to furnish reports of its findings to the public. It was directed to cooperate with the Department of Agriculture and other federal agencies in their market investigations so as to avoid unnecessary duplication. The CFTC was prohibited from disclosing in such a report information that would separately disclose the business transactions of any persons and trade secrets or names of customers, except as provided in other provisions of the statute.

The CFTC was directed to submit to the Congress, by June 30, 1976, a report concerning the need for insurance for persons trading in commodity futures contracts who suffered losses as the result of the insolvency or financial failure of a futures commission merchant.[14] The CFTC was to report on the need for and (if there was a need) the form and nature of any legislation needed to effect such insurance. The CFTC was also directed to maintain research and information programs, and to determine the feasibility of trading by computer and the expanded use of modern information technology by commodity exchanges and the CFTC itself. It was directed to assist in the development of educational programs regarding futures trading.

The 1974 legislation addressed the need for the CFTC to assure competition in the futures markets. The legislation thus contained a provision requiring the CFTC, in issuing any orders or rules or regulations or approving contract market rules, to take into consideration the public interest to be protected by the antitrust laws. The CFTC was required to "endeavor" to take the least anticompetitive means of achieving the objectives of the Commodity Exchange Act. In this connection, the Conference Committee stated that this requirement was not intended to constitute a procedural roadblock to the CFTC in carrying out its duties, and that it was not required to conduct separate proceedings to consider antitrust and anticompetitive matters.

Finally, although not specifically required by the legislation, "time stamping" was addressed by Congress (i.e., whether the exact moment of execution in the pit should be identified on the order when it was executed). It was stated that most members of the Conference Committee favored the time stamping provision, but that Congress was concerned that it might not be technically possible to implement a time stamping procedure on the effective date of the act. The conferees urged the CFTC and the commodities industry to move quickly to develop a technically feasible approach to time stamping and to put it into effect at the earliest possible date. It was noted that time stamping would permit the CFTC to determine whether floor brokers traded ahead of their customers in order to get the best prices themselves and would allow the CFTC to assess the effect of floor traders on market prices when prices began moving.

As if all of these dramatic changes were not enough for the commodity futures industry, the commodity exchanges and the industry became the subject of actions by the Justice Department, which required them to discontinue the use of fixed commission rates. The fixing of these rates, it was thought by many, was the principal basis for the existence and continuation of the exchanges. The exchanges, however, agreed to unfix their common rates, an event that was shaking the securities industry at about the same time and which resulted in a broad restructuring of the securities industry.

6
THE CREATION
OF THE CFTC AND
ITS FIRST YEARS

The 1974 amendments to the Commodity Exchange Act became effective 120 days after their passage, on April 21, 1975. The CFTC commissioners, however, were not nominated until March 1975, and were not confirmed by the Senate until six days before the CFTC assumed all responsibility for regulating the commodity futures markets. The CFTC immediately assumed control over the existing CEA staff and hired additional staff and consultants. The agency initially worked out of the basement and cafeteria of the Department of Agriculture's offices in Washington. But within a short time it moved to the "Bender Building," a privately owned office building in the business district of Washington, D.C. There, the CFTC resided for approximately one year, until it moved to its present headquarters at the corner of 21st and K streets in northwest Washington, D.C.

The CFTC's first chairman was William T. Bagley, a senior partner in a California law firm. Bagley, a graduate of the University of California at Berkeley and the Boalt Hall School of Law, had previously served as a member of the California state assembly and had been in a close race for California state controller, a key position in California government. He was forty-seven years old. The other commissioners were Gary L. Seevers, a member of the President's Council of Economic Advisers; Read P. Dunn, Jr., the executive director of the International Institute for Cotton in Brussels, Belgium (Dunn had had broad international experience in commodities); Robert L. Martin, the former chairman of the Chicago Board of Trade, who had so vigorously opposed giving the CEA injunctive authority; and John Rainbolt, the CFTC's vice-chairman, a lawyer who had served as counsel to the House Agriculture Committee. Rainbolt drafted the 1974 amendments to the Commodity Exchange Act for the House Agriculture Committee.

The CFTC Commissioners quickly assembled a professional staff to supplement the CEA. It drew heavily on current and former staff members of the Securities and Exchange Commission. These included Tom Russo, Fred White, Ed Lyons, William Schief, and Richard Nathan. Howard Schneider, a partner in a large Wall Street law firm, was appointed as the CFTC's first general counsel. Beverly J. Splane became the executive director of the agency, a position that, as noted, was provided for by the statute and which required congressional approval that was never sought nor given. Other senior staff members included Mark J. Powers, a former staff member of the Chicago Mercantile Exchange and a leading author on the subject of commodity futures trading. He became the chief economist at the CFTC. Each of the commissioners also hired his or her own staff, consisting of an administrative assistant, an economist, and a legal assistant. Bagley also hired several individuals to serve in the chairman's office, including De Van Shumway, the former director of press relations for Richard Nixon's Committee to Re-Elect the President (CREEP), and Pamela Pecarich.

Several CEA staff members were given senior positions in the agency. These included Charles Robinson, who apparently was the only lawyer at the CEA, Donald Tendick, who was later to become the agency's executive director, Robert Clark, the director of the CEA's Chicago office, John Mielke and Blake Imel, two economists, and Britt Lenz in the CEA's Chicago office. CEA staff members also initially remained as directors of the New York and Kansas City regional offices that had been previously established by the CEA.

The CFTC was assisted in implementing the CFTC Act of 1974 by some 23 reports prepared by an Interagency Steering Committee, which was established by the Office of Management and Budget to facilitate the transfer of the administrative and enforcement provisions of the Commodity Exchange Act to the CFTC. These reports addressed, among other things, the need for regulation of leverage and options contracts, the establishment of limits on the amount of contracts that could be held by speculators in the newly regulated commodities, registration concerns, and several exchange regulatory issues.[1]

The CFTC began adopting rules almost immediately to implement its new authority. It proposed antifraud rules for options, leverage contracts, and foreign futures contracts; it established a guideline for contract markets to use in enforcing their rules; and it promulgated a guideline for the economic and public interest requirements contained in the legislation for new contract market designations. The CFTC also provisionally designated ten boards of trade as contract markets for fifty-three commodities. It adopted an interim emergency rule that permitted the exchanges to take emergency actions in the event of a market emergency, and it requested comments and issued interpretations concerning exchange arbitration procedures.

As another important first act, the CFTC adopted a rule that required contract markets to enforce certain of their rules already in effect. This rule was to be significant because contract market rules were required by the CFTC Act of 1974 to be approved by the CFTC. Through this rule, the CFTC avoided reviewing all of the rules of the exchanges already in existence. Indeed, to this day, the CFTC has not reviewed those rules. Rather, its review has been limited to amendments to existing rules and to new rules.

The CFTC nevertheless experienced, almost immediately, severe problems in approving exchange rules. It was soon flooded by a stream of new rule proposals and contract market designation applications. The CFTC simply did not have the staff to conduct a thorough review without causing long delays. It also compounded the problem by requiring the exchanges to submit all of their rules for review even if they were not covered by the Commodity Exchange Act; this requirement was imposed to ensure that the exchanges did not too narrowly construe the CFTC's rules review authority. Nevertheless, the CFTC did adopt a rule to narrow as much as possible the scope of the rules it required to be approved. But this effort met with little success in alleviating delays. As a result of continued complaints from the exchanges concerning the long delays, in 1982 Congress amended the Commodity Exchange Act to require approval by the CFTC within a minimum period of time, so that exchange rules could become effective more quickly.

These were all significant matters.[2] But the greatest part of the agency's time was spent in organizing itself and fighting battles within its own staff. Although this in-fighting might be dismissed as mere bickering among bureaucrats, in fact it did much to shape the entire regulatory structure of the CFTC.

One major conflagration concerned the integration of the CEA staff into the new CFTC structure. Many of the major policy positions had been filled by "outsiders," most of whom were completely unfamiliar with the commodity markets, although many of them were former Securities and Exchange Commission staff members. The CEA staff believed their experience and expertise were being slighted. Many of the newcomers, however, believed, rightly or wrongly, that the CEA had been discredited by Congress, and that it had not been an effective regulator. They therefore "tended to 'look down their noses' at the employees inherited from CEA."[3]

This battle was being fought at the same time as another fight between the lawyers and non-lawyers in the agency. Most of the CEA staff members were non-lawyers and they sided with (indeed they were recruited by) the new non-lawyer policymakers. But this battle was waged most effectively by the latter, who were deeply antagonistic toward lawyers. Intermingled with these battles were attempts to divide the general counsel's authority among various divisions that would also be independent of the executive director, as was the case at the Securities and Exchange Commission.[4]

Although the lawyer versus non-lawyer fights were never resolved (they more or less faded away), the CEA was eventually integrated into the new staff. Three divisions were also established. One was the Division of Trading and Markets, which was responsible for the day-to-day regulation of exchanges' financial responsibility requirements for registrants and for writing most of the agency's substantive rules. The Division of Enforcement was given responsibility for injunctive actions brought by the CFTC, the supervision of reparations proceedings, and the conduct of disciplinary proceedings against registrants and persons violating the Commodity Exchange Act. The Division of Economic Analysis was made responsible for large trader reporting and surveillance over trading activities in the markets. The general counsel's office still maintained a central role, defending cases brought against the CFTC and all appeals of the agency's decisions in the appellate courts. It also acted as the agency's adviser in administrative proceedings and sought (and this battle continued for years and is undoubtedly continuing today) to review all the recommendations and activities of the other divisions.

The executive director's office (the prime mover in the anti-lawyer campaign) sought to obtain primacy over the other divisions of the agency, including complete policy control over all recommendations to the CFTC and allocation of staff resources. This would have effectively eviscerated the Division of Trading and Markets and the Division of Enforcement. This war raged for some time at the senior levels of the CFTC; the executive director lost. The essential resolution of this latter struggle was that the Division of Trading and Markets was generally allowed to operate independently of the executive director and other divisions. The general counsel was allowed to review the Division's Trading and Markets recommendations, but it had no authority to veto them. If there is a difference between that Division and the general counsel, it is resolved before the Commission itself. In practice, the Division and the general counsel's office generally work out their differences before taking them to the Commission. A similar arrangement resulted with respect to the Division of Enforcement. The general counsel's office, however, fought long and hard to have a greater role. In effect, it sought to have the Division report to it with respect to its legal theories and recommended enforcement actions. This encroachment was vigorously fought, and the Division of Enforcement too achieved substantial independence. Nevertheless, the general counsel's office maintains a much more adversarial role with respect to the Enforcement Division's recommendations and enforcement activities.

The Division of Economic Analysis was where many of the former

CEA staff members were placed, and they, at first, fell within the domain of the executive director. As noted, this division maintained control over reporting requirements, and it conducted the day-to-day surveillance on the markets to see what large traders were in the markets and what problems were developing. It also reviews contract market applications. This Division now operates pretty much independently but, since it has no enforcement capacity, it serves more as a support and information service for the Commission and other divisions. It thereby avoids many of the confrontations that occur between the Division of Enforcement and the general counsel's office.

The general counsel's office also remained independent of the executive director. The executive director's office was thus largely taken out of the day-to-day regulation. Its role has been one of maintaining control over personnel and operations of the Commission, and directing resources. This, of course, is a significant and important task, but does not give the executive director's office much public visibility.

A press office was also established. Although it initially sought to give the agency some flair, its present role is to summarize actions undertaken by other divisions. Congressional liaison and other offices also were established, but their roles are generally narrowly circumscribed. There have also been various other "policy" staff members who have floated about the Commission at one time or another in one or another roles.

Early struggles at the CFTC also focused on the role of the regional offices established by the CEA. Early on, Bagley moved the old CEA offices in Chicago and New York to the Sears Tower in Chicago and the World Trade Center in New York. Bagley had been appalled when he discerned that the CEA's landlord in Chicago was the Chicago Board of Trade, which was where the CEA had kept its offices. The CFTC also established an office in California. The importance and the administration of the regional offices has changed in concept and perception several times. Today, the regional offices do not exercise policy roles. Rather, they work through one or another of the divisions. Nevertheless, the CFTC maintains an enforcement capacity in these offices. The Chicago office also, for years, maintained the registration system for the CFTC, which has now largely been assumed by the National Futures Association. The Chicago and New York offices are deeply involved in large trader reporting.

In its first year the CFTC adopted a number of housekeeping provisions. Privacy and Freedom of Information Act requirements were implemented, as well as rules of procedures for the CFTC's administrative proceedings. The CFTC's chairman also conducted a campaign called "open government" in which he sought to keep the CFTC's meetings as open as possible. In one well-publicized action, the chairman threw all of the CFTC's "confidential" rubber stamps into the Potomac River. The chairman also threatened "tough" enforcement.[5]

The CFTC created several advisory committees to advise it on key issues. These included an advisory committee on Commodity Futures Trading Professionals, a committee on Market Regulation, a committee on the Economic Role of Contract Markets, and a committee on Market Instruments. Later, reports were filed by these advisory committees, which made several recommendations concerning actions the CFTC should take.

The CFTC's advisory committee on Commodity Futures Trading Professionals made several recommendations. It recommended that commodity professionals be required to disclose to prospective clients the risks of futures trading and that brokers be required to pass a basic commodities examination as a condition for registration. It recommended that standards be adopted for professionals who advertised their trading performance as a means to induce customers to allow them to trade the customers' funds. It also recommended that the CFTC supervise the advertising practices of commodity trading advisers and that commodity pool operators as well as futures commission merchants be required to meet financial and segregation requirements. With one member dissenting, it recommended that the exchanges be allowed to set professional standards for floor brokers.

The CFTC's Advisory Committee on the Role of Contract Markets concluded that futures trading provides important economic benefits to the public by providing an institutional framework for competitive price discovery and for hedging. It recommended that the CFTC not deny a contract market designation unless it would be contrary to the public interest; it would have retained an economic purpose test in making that determination. It urged that contract terms and conditions be made more effective, stating that these were the most effective means for preventing market abuses; more so than regulatory action after an abuse had occurred. It also recommended that the terms and conditions of futures contracts mirror as closely as possible the marketing pattern of the cash commodity underlying the contract. It recommended that particular scrutiny be given delivery requirements so as to prevent congestion problems. It stated that the CFTC should not concern itself with proliferation of contracts, that is, market users should be free to decide which contract they wished to trade if there were several competing contracts. The committee further recommended that foreign traders be accorded access to U.S. futures markets, but that such access should be made conditional on disclosure of the foreign trader's activities under the CFTC's reporting requirements.

The advisory committee recommended that the CFTC shift its regulatory emphasis away from fixed speculative limits. This was because they provided little control over hedgers and virtually no control during delivery months. It recommended that they be supplanted by improved monitoring and surveillance programs. The CFTC did later drop speculative limit requirements for intra-day trading as the result of this recommendation. But the events in the silver market in 1979-1980, as described below, resulted in its placing renewed emphasis on position limits as a regulatory tool.

In the meantime, the CFTC sought to expand the definition of bona fide hedging, which would allow greater use of the markets by commercial operations. It requested public comment on the definition of international arbitrage in order to determine whether such transactions too should be exempted from position limits. Although these comments were requested in August 1975, no action has yet been taken.

The CFTC also sought comment on an issue left over from the CEA, whether accounts controlled by a futures commission merchant had to be aggregated for purposes of speculative limits. The CEA had previously concluded that all controlled accounts held by a futures commission merchant, including recommended trading programs, should be aggregated for purposes of position limits, even if the accounts were traded by separate employees of the firm. This meant, for example, that an account executive holding a power of attorney in the Dallas office of a firm who had never even spoken to, or knew the existence of, another account executive in the same firm's branch office in Maine with powers of attorney over entirely separate accounts, would have been required to aggregate their accounts for position limit purposes. This, of course, would have effectively prevented the brokerage firm from trading any large amount of discretionary accounts or from using the recommended trading programs that became popular in the 1970s: customers making certain minimum deposits would be given specialized trading recommendations (sometimes on the basis of computerized projections) which were not received by other customers.

Indeed, the FCM could have been placed in imminent danger of violating position limits at any time, since it would never know when these independent account executives were entering orders in the same market. Similarly, computerized trading programs of FCMs generating recommended trades would have required aggregation. Accordingly, the CFTC sought comment on these issues and later determined that aggregation was not required, if in fact there was separate control of accounts by employees.

The exclusive jurisdiction granted to the CFTC had the immediate effect of preempting the jurisdiction of the states and the SEC, which together had virtually stopped options firms from engaging in large-scale operations. The CFTC had been warned of this "regulatory gap" by one of the task force reports prepared by the Interagency Steering Committee. But it chose to ignore that report and adopted no immediate regulations for options trading, except for an antifraud rule of uncertain dimensions. One firm, the American Options Corporation in Salt Lake City, Utah, immediately sought to take advantage of that situation. Previously, as the consequence of prior abuses, it had been subject to strict regulations by the State Securities administrator in Utah. When the

CFTC came into existence, however, its exclusive jurisdiction pre-empted those restrictions.

The American Options Corporation seized on that factor and immediately began offering options on a widescale basis throughout the United States. It also expanded its business operations into California, where Harold Goldstein was reported to have shown up in its offices. The CFTC began an immediate investigation with almost its total enforcement staff, the director, and two employees assigned to him on a temporary basis from other parts of the Commission. Shortly afterward, the CFTC filed its first injunctive action, naming American Options Corporation and certain of its principals, all of whom consented to the relief sought.

But this was only the beginning. Options firms quickly sprang up in New York, California, and various cities, following the footsteps of the American Options Corporation. Sensing the dangers presented by these firms, John Schobel and another CFTC staff member recommended that options trading be suspended. The CFTC, however, determined to first examine the alternatives to regulate commodity options. It did not immediately adopt any proposals, however, other than the antifraud rule, and options firms continued to proliferate. Several other enforcement actions were then brought against companies such as J. S. Love and Associates Options Ltd. that were selling so-called London options. In fact, in many instances the options were not traded on London markets and were, therefore, simply "naked" options such as those sold by Harold Goldstein.

The CFTC did seek to require firms dealing in commodity options to register with it as commodity trading advisors and later as futures commission merchants, but this regulatory effort proved to be spectacularly unsuccessful, and the CFTC later proposed and adopted, as described below, stringent rules. But they came too late to save the CFTC from the greatest commodity options scandal of all.

It was discovered, after lengthy proceedings before federal courts around the country, that the owner of one of the largest of the firms that sprang up as the result of the CFTC preemption of state control was an escaped felon. By that time innumerable other boiler shops were also soon operating around the country, in numbers that were far beyond the abilities of the CFTC to control. Chairman Bagley asserted that these commodity options firms were "some of the worst lie-by-day, fly-by-night operations in the financial world."[6] The CFTC's Division of Enforcement also opened over 200 investigations, most of them involving options firms, and from mid-1976 to mid-1977, the CFTC spent $1.5 million and 50 staff-years of time on options matters. The CFTC simply could not prevent fraud in their trading. It therefore determined in 1978 to suspend options trading, with certain limited exceptions. Later, however, options were permitted to be traded on exchanges under a pilot program.

ARBITRATION AND OTHER RULES

As another of its first actions, the CFTC addressed the arbitration provisions in the new legislation. It concluded that the arbitration sought by Congress required customers to be advised of the fact that arbitration was voluntary before they signed an arbitration agreement, and the CFTC required customers to be given an opportunity to avoid arbitration after a dispute arose, so that the customer could seek reparations instead. Procedural standards of fairness were also established.

In addition, the CFTC attempted to lay to rest the Bernard Rosee arbitration case, which had been highlighted in the *Des Moines Register* articles that so harshly criticized the CEA. It was charged that Rosee had been unfairly treated in an arbitration conducted by the Chicago Board of Trade. Rosee petitioned the CFTC to investigate those charges and to bring administrative proceedings against the Chicago Board of Trade, and the CFTC directed its Division of Enforcement to conduct an investigation and to render a report. The Division recommended that the Commission deny Rosee's petition, finding no misconduct on its part or by CEA employees. The Division, however, suggested that the Chicago Board of Trade reopen its arbitration proceedings voluntarily, in view of substantial evidence discovered by the Division that the exchange's arbitration committee, which had rendered the decision that resulted in the revocation of Rosee's membership, was misled by evidence submitted in the proceeding.

Rules were also proposed to govern the standards by which commodity exchanges could discipline their members. Among other things, members subject to disciplinary proceedings were given the right to have attorneys represent them, eliminating the practice of many exchanges of excluding lawyers. Respondents in such proceedings were also entitled to a hearing on the record and to procedural due process.

In June 1977, the CFTC proposed, and later adopted, standards for reviewing disciplinary actions of exchanges. In brief, it established a *certiorari* process, rather than a right of appeal to the Commission. In other words, a person adversely affected by a contract market disciplinary proceeding could petition the Commission, but had no right to such review. It was in the discretion of the Commission to grant the petition.

SEC CONFLICT AND OTHER JURISDICTIONAL ISSUES

One of the most momentous occurrences in the CFTC's early existence was its conflict with the Securities and Exchange Commission (SEC). That dispute was to have long-range implications for both the securities and the commodities industries. The conflict arose when the CFTC approved a proposal by the Chicago Board of Trade to conduct trading in futures contracts on mortgage-backed certificates guaranteed by the Government National Mortgage Association (GNMA). Upon learning that the CFTC had approved this proposal, the SEC staff objected. Specifically, the director of its Division of Enforcement, Stanley Sporkin, advised Thomas Russo, the first director of the CFTC's Division of Trading and Markets, that the CFTC had no jurisdiction over GNMAs ("Ginnie Maes") because they were, in the view of the SEC, securities. When advised by Russo that the statute had been amended to give the CFTC exclusive jurisdiction over futures trading, even on GNMAs, the SEC's Enforcement director stated that "somebody must have been messing with the statute." The CFTC staff quickly assured him that it was Congress who had done the "messing." Nevertheless, the SEC staff continued to press this issue and lengthy correspondence was exchanged between the two agencies as to their relative jurisdictions.

The result was basically a standoff, except that the GMNA futures contracts were allowed to trade without interference from the SEC. That fact was not forgotten, however, in the SEC. It patiently waited for revenge, and several years later it approved options trading on Ginnie Maes on the Chicago Board Options Exchange, which was within the SEC's jurisdiction. Because these options would be in direct competition with the GNMAs futures contracts on the Chicago Board of Trade, the latter exchange sought to have their trading enjoined, contending that the SEC had no power to approve such options. The SEC lost that case in the Seventh Circuit.[7] As noted below, however, the chairmen of the SEC and CFTC reached a *modus vivendi* that Congress enacted into law and which resolved much of this conflict.

The CFTC also began asserting its exclusive jurisdiction in other areas. For example, in a speech to the North American Securities Administrators Conference in 1975 by CFTC vice-chairman John Rainbolt, the CFTC asserted that the states were preempted from any regulatory authority over transactions in commodity futures contracts and commodity options, but that they could bring fraud actions under their general antifraud or criminal laws or could themselves bring suit under the Commodity Exchange Act as *parens patriae* for their citizens. This, of course, led to widespread consternation among the various states. They were concerned that CFTC regulations would be inadequate to protect their citizens. To meet those concerns, and to facilitate coordination with the states, the CFTC created an Advisory Committee on State Jurisdiction and Responsibilities, composed of state securities administrators and the CFTC's general counsel.

The CFTC also issued a statement of policy concerning the doctrine of primary jurisdiction—whether antitrust and other cases among private litigants involving the commodity exchanges and commodity trading should be referred to the CFTC first for discussion. Two Supreme Court cases had directed that such matters be directed to the CEA.[8] The CFTC, however, took the position that the doctrine of primary jurisdiction should be applied only where important regulatory policy questions were raised in the litigation that fell within the responsibility of the CFTC. This, in the view of the CFTC, would not generally include fraud claims.

THE POTATO DEFAULT AND OTHER ACTIONS

In May 1976, the CFTC faced its first real crisis in the futures markets when defaults occurred in the Maine potato contract traded on the New York Mercantile Exchange.[9] After an extensive investigation, the CFTC brought manipulation charges against both the longs and shorts, charging that they had both sought to manipulate the market by controlling supplies and by staying in the market for delivery in a showdown that resulted in the defaults. The CFTC also brought an action against the exchange itself. The defaults were also the subject of extensive private litigation, some of which evidently reached the Supreme Court.

What occasioned the default was that, on the last trading day for the May contract, one trader raised his long positions by some 2,500 contracts, to a total of well over 4,000 contracts. When other traders hopped on the bandwagon, the result was an inadequate supply of Maine potatoes to cover the open long positions, a classic corner. The shorts then defaulted on 1,000 contracts that required them to deliver some 50 million pounds of potatoes. Such a default was virtually unprecedented, and it shocked the industry.[10]

In the words of the CFTC's chairman, the defaults were the result of a fatal game of "chicken" between the shorts, headed by the two western potato barons who had been the targets of the CEA for a 1970 potato manipulation (John R. Simplot of Boise, Idaho, and Peter J. Taggares of Othello, Washington) and the longs (who included Howard Collins of Oswego, New York). The CFTC charged that each side had attempted to manipulate prices in its own favor.

The CFTC's investigation in the case was massive. As in the Battle of the Bulge, noncombatants from all parts of the CFTC were assigned to the Enforcement Division to take testimony (some never having observed a deposition before) and to gather evidence. Remedial relief was obtained by the CFTC, but litigation continues even today.[11]

Problems persisted in the Maine Potato contract. In 1979, another market emergency occurred when a long position of the potato crop suffered "extensive pressure bruising," and 90 percent of potatoes tendered for delivery for the March 1979 contract did not meet contract specifications. Supplies were also uncertain for future contract months. The exchanges then took emergency action, voting to liquidate the positions.[12]

The CFTC also encountered emergencies in other markets. As the result of a number of disasters and political upheaval, coffee prices rose from 55¢ per pound to $1.50 by August 1976. The CFTC also discovered that two traders held 82 percent of the long open interest in the September 1976 Coffee "C" futures contracts on the New York Coffee and Sugar Exchange, at a time when deliverable stocks were low. The Exchange took emergency action by limiting trading to liquidation only. But there were four more market emergencies in coffee during 1977 in which liquidation-only trading was ordered. Still another market emergency occurred in coffee in 1979.

The CFTC began an investigation of the coffee traders using the market, focusing particularly on agents of Brazil and El Salvador, who, it was charged, were attempting to maintain artificially high coffee prices through a $100 million dollar commitment and by an elaborate trading scheme dubbed "Operation Central Park." The *New York Times* stated in a front page article that the life of a government regulator, presumably someone at the CFTC, had been threatened in connection with this investigation. The article also made a point of noting that the CFTC's former general counsel, Howard Schneider, was representing the Brazil entities and that he had addressed a letter to a CFTC investigator, Dennis Klejna (who later became the CFTC's Enforcement director) as "Dear Dennis."[13] It is unclear what that was supposed to imply, but at least some former staff attorneys appearing before the CFTC now take care to address CFTC staff officials formally by their last names in correspondence, even if they have known them for years, lest they too become targets of the *Times*.

Whatever the case, a manipulation action was later brought by the CFTC against an El Salvador company. The CFTC's complaint, filed in March 1979, charged Compania Salvadorena de Cafe S.A. of El Salvador and its general manager with manipulation of the July 1977 coffee "C" contract. Four other companies, including two brokerage firms, and five individuals were charged with aiding and abetting the manipulators. In 1983 a summary disposition was entered against Salvadorena's general manager, wherein he was found to have entered wash sales for over 470 coffee contracts and was fined $200,000 and prohibited from trading on U.S. contract markets. The successor to Compania Salvadorena was lightly sanctioned by being prohibited from speculative trading on U.S. markets.

Still another major issue that developed early in the CFTC's existence was the use of the commodity markets for so-called tax straddles. These trades, which were often pre-arranged to avoid any risk of economic loss, sought to establish losses on one side of the straddle in one tax year. An offsetting gain in the other side of the straddle was realized in the following year. The effect was to defer taxes for a year or to transform short-term gain into long-term gain. Although this device had been used by large speculators for many years, it became a popular tool for public investors in the 1970s.

The CFTC did not attack this practice as a tax scheme. Rather, it sought to preclude the use of fictitious and pre-arranged trades to accomplish tax goals. The Internal Revenue Service also became interested in this practice, and it issued various rulings that indicated such transactions would not be recognized, and in 1982 the Internal Revenue Code was changed to preclude further abuses. Today, there is no holding period for futures contracts. They are all taxed at an effective rate of about 32 percent, and open positions are marked to market at year's end, when the tax must be paid on them, even though they are not closed positions.

7
THE CFTC WRITES
THE RULEBOOK

NET CAPITAL

In October of 1976, the CFTC commenced one of its most significant regulatory reforms. This was a proposal, authored by Tom Russo and John Manley (respectively, the director and chief accountant for the Division of Trading and Markets), to upgrade minimum financial requirements for futures commission merchants. Simply stated, net capital requirements require brokerage firms to maintain an amount of liquid capital sufficient to meet customer demands. It is, in effect, a liquidity requirement designed to ensure that a brokerage firm does not let its financial position deteriorate to the point of endangering customer funds.

The contents of such rules are necessarily complex. For example, in valuing the assets of a firm, complex determinations must be made as to their liquidity. To illustrate, securities are a valuable asset with a market value that is generally readily determinable, but their value could change quickly before they could be sold. To reflect this possibility, their market value is given a "hair cut," that is, a percentage deduction to account for the risk of market fluctuation in values. Similarly, many receivables are not readily receivable. Therefore, they may be excluded in determining net capital.

The most significant reform adopted by the CFTC required futures commission merchants to be audited by independent financial accountants and that their financial statements be certified. Uncertified quarterly statements were also required. Previously, the CEA had relied on its own spot audits to assure the veracity of the financial statements it received semiannually.

Because of the complexity of net capital requirements, the CFTC simply did not have the staff to determine whether financial requirements were met by every firm every year. Consequently, this requirement, while imposing substantial cost on firms, was designed to ensure their continued financial integrity. The certification requirement, coupled with early warning requirements, is also designed to ensure that the CFTC is on early notice when a firm is in financial trouble, and steps can be undertaken to prevent or limit injury to customers.

ACCOUNT INSURANCE

In November 1976, as required by the 1974 amendments, the CFTC rendered a report to the Congress that addressed the need for legislation establishing insurance for owners of commodity futures accounts against loss by reason of the insolvency or financial failure of a futures commission merchant. In addressing this need, the CFTC considered, on a historical basis, losses in commodity accounts from 1938 to 1974. It also conducted a cost-benefit analysis that compared the ratio of commodity account losses to those in existing government-sponsored insurance programs. The commodity account loss ratios were substantially lower. It was also found that public confidence in the safety of their funds was sufficient, and that the cost-benefit ratios demonstrated that insurance protection was not cost effective. The CFTC therefore concluded that there was no need for legislative action.

Thereafter the Bankruptcy Act of 1978 was passed. It constituted a massive reform of the general bankruptcy laws and contained provisions governing the insolvency of a futures commission merchant. The primary protection for investors in commodity futures contracts is that their funds are kept in segregated trust accounts. It often happens, however, that a breach of such trust may occur—the broker could convert the funds, either to trade for its own account or to meet the margin calls of another customer. In such instances, the new Bankruptcy Code provisions provide for the equal sharing of all customers in any remaining segregated funds, that is, every customer will receive a pro rata share of the remaining customer funds, with some limited exemptions. These customers have a priority over all other creditors in such funds.

But the revision of the bankruptcy laws did not provide insurance protection. Rather, it provides only for an orderly means of establishing priorities for funds that are left after insolvency occurs and customer funds are misused. This, of course, does not provide the same protections that are found in the securities industry through the Security Investors Protection Corporation (SIPC). And, while the CFTC concluded that SIPC legislation was not needed, two large bankruptcies occurred in 1980 and 1981 that caused serious customer losses.

One of these proceedings, the first bankruptcy under the new Bankruptcy Act provisions and which involved Incomco, Inc., had its lighter moments. During the formation of a creditor's committee, a bankruptcy official suggested that a small creditor should be included on the committee, as well as large creditors. A volunteer from the large number of small creditors in the courtroom was then requested. As was reported in the *Wall Street Journal,* a spritely 82-year-old man "sporting a flowing white beard and wearing maroon pants, a red shirt and white tie," as well as a candy-striped cane, volunteered for service. When asked to identify himself, he stated that his name was Santa Claus. Thinking fast, the bankruptcy judge asked for some identification. Undaunted, the old man produced a driver's license and other identification that indeed identified him as Santa Claus.

Apparently foreseeing headlines in the next day's papers, the bankruptcy official asked the attorney forming the creditor's committee if Mr. Claus was acceptable to the committee or would he prefer another small creditor. The lawyer, taken aback, turned to Gary Stumpp, an attorney in the large Wall Street firm of Cadwalader, Wickersham, & Taft, who was also acting for a large creditor, and asked if there was not a movie about this sort of thing. Stumpp confirmed that there was such a movie, "Miracle on 34th Street." Recalling the outcome of the trial in that movie, the attorney then turned back to the bankruptcy official and stated that he would be proud to have Santa Claus appearing on the committee. According to the *Wall Street Journal,* an elated Santa Claus shouted to the creditors in the courtroom: "Don't worry. . . . You're all my partners now. Everything is going to be all right."[1] In fact, the customers did recover over 50 percent of their funds, which is not a bad outcome in a bankruptcy proceeding. In another bankruptcy proceeding involving Chicago Discount Commodity Brokers, Inc., the firm was short some $3 million in customer funds.

A subsequent bankruptcy by Volume Investors, Inc., a clearing member of the Commodity Exchange, Inc., involved a deficit in customer funds as the result of option trading. This gave rise, once again, to the question of whether account insurance is needed. On July 29, 1985, the CFTC held a public hearing regarding the Volume Investors' default. The default, which was caused by the effect of a rapid increase in price on some 12,000 naked gold options written by three Volume Investors customers, resulted in liabilities of $13.7 million to some 100 customers, $9.1 million to clearing organizations, and $1.4 million to other FCMs and general creditors. Volume had only some $10 million in assets to meet these obligations. Because the default occurred in the commodity options market during the course of the CFTC's pilot program on exchange-traded options (discussed below), it engendered heightened concern over the effectiveness of market protection mechanisms.

The CFTC's Division of Trading and Markets concluded that the Volume Investors default was caused by: (1) the low cost of acquiring short option positions, possibly fostering excessive accumulation of such positions; (2) the accumulation of option positions by three customers which, based on a market move of even $2.00 per ounce, would have exhausted the capital of the carrying firm in the event of a default (the price actually moved some $30 per ounce); (3) the failure of existing market surveillance techniques by both the carrying firm and the exchange to identify these concentrated positions as a financial risk and the lack of rules to require either their reduction or additional margin; (4) the failure of the carrying firm to cease to do new business once it was undercapitalized and to cease to meet margin calls once it was undersegregated, such that customers' money was used to fund the margin obligations of customers already in default; (5) the lack of preparedness of the exchange's clearing corporation to order and facilitate the suspension of operations of the carrying firm and the liquidation or transfer of positions; and (6) the lack of adequate mechanisms to identify the default promptly.

The Division's study also concluded, however, that the existing regulatory safeguards did operate to mitigate the effect of the default on customers and the exchange itself. In particular, the clearing house guarantees to the other side of the market effectively maintained market integrity. In addition, CFTC segregation requirements ensured that there were at least some funds available for the receiver to develop a plan of distribution to nondefaulting customers.

Nevertheless, the Division believed that the default underscored the need for additional customer and market protections in order to avoid similar occurrences in the future and to plug perceived regulatory "gaps" in the current structure. Accordingly, the Division recommended that the CFTC propose a number of amendments to the current regulatory system. In order to address the problem of concentration of positions, the Division recommended that the CFTC propose for public comment a regulation requiring FCMs to take a capital charge if positions in a particular commodity become concentrated to a certain extent in the accounts of a few customers and on one side of the market.

The Division also recommended that the Commission request the National Futures Association to conduct a study of the role that insurance could play in reducing the effect of defaults. In support of this recommendation, the Division issued a voluminous study assessing the history of commodity trading losses and the projected benefits of insurance funds in assisting the transfer of positions and the protection of customers. It stated the industry had changed substantially since the November 1976 CFTC recommendation against account insurance, suggesting that such insurance may now be appropriate. The Division also noted that since the 1976 study the number of commodity brokerage firm failures had increased, there had been some twenty-four failures in recent years, almost five a year, with higher average losses of almost $2 million per year. None of the firms were members of an exchange.

An enforcement action was brought against the Commodity Exchange Inc. for failing to prevent the Volume Investors' default. Numerous other cases were filed, and the exchange battled with investors over whether it should cover their losses.

The concentration rules proposed by the Division of Trading and Markets were draconian and would have caused serious problems for many firms. It was charged as being an overreaction to an admittedly serious, but not apocalyptic, event. The Chicago Board of Trade and the futures industry responded in kind. Brandishing a $1 million war chest, the Chicago Board of Trade threatened an all-out legal assault if the rules were adopted. At last report, the CFTC was reconsidering these proposals, and some form of compromise will hopefully result.

DUAL TRADING AND TIME STAMPING

Still another significant issue addressed by the CFTC in its early years concerned so-called dual trading requirements, that were to determine whether floor brokers or futures commission merchants could trade for their own accounts, as well as for the accounts of their customers. Under the 1974 legislation, the CFTC was directed to consider whether and under what conditions such dual trading should be permitted. The CFTC's advisory committee on Regulation of Contract Markets and Self-Regulatory Associations considered this issue, and a separate report (the Kane-Weinberg report) was prepared by two of its industry committee members.

After considering these reports, the CFTC determined not to ban this practice. Rather, it established regulations designed to ensure that abuses would be eliminated. This included prohibiting floor brokers and futures commission merchants from trading for their own accounts ahead of customers, from trading discretionary accounts, and from disclosing orders of customers to others except to the extent necessary for their effective execution (such knowledge could allow third parties to take advantage of a customer). Trading standards for futures commission merchants and introducing brokers were also established.

The CFTC's consideration of dual trading additionally focused on time stamping of customer orders in a manner that would allow an audit trail on a minute-to-minute basis. Under previous standards, customer orders had to be time stamped when received at a futures commission merchant's office and when received on the floor for execution. Time stamps were also required when the order was reported back to the futures commission merchant. This allowed a substantial audit trail capacity. It did not, however, provide the exact time of execution, because there was no requirement that the order be time stamped in the pit upon execution, and orders of floor traders were not time stamped at all. Such information could be obtained, in many cases, by a comparison of exchange "time and sales" reports, but to do so was laborious, and accuracy was not ensured.

Concern was expressed in Congress in 1974, as noted above, and later by the CFTC, that this provided opportunities for the mishandling of customer orders. It was thought that a to-the-minute execution time stamp would allow the market price in the pits to be compared with the time of the execution of the customer's order. It could then be determined whether the customer had a fair execution. The CFTC initially proposed to prohibit "dual trading" on those exchanges, which did not require time stamped executions. A great deal of industry opposition, however, was expressed against this proposal, because in active pits there was no technology available that would allow time stamping without interfering with trading. There was also an obvious concern that floor brokers would be held to greater liability in active pits, as when they missed filling an order because the transaction occurred on the opposite side of the pit or because the market was moving so fast that the trader was unable to execute an order at its limit price.

Because of industry opposition to such a requirement, and after a CFTC task force concluded that it was not feasible for all exchanges to time stamp trades in the pit, the CFTC in 1976 required contract markets, at a minimum, to establish a "bracketing" system. Under this procedure, color-coded order tickets were used that allowed a determination of the execution time within a half-hour period. This system was thought to be sufficiently flexible that it would not interfere with the broker's transactions and not cause a paperwork crisis that could affect the liquidity and effective operation of the commodity pits.[2] The CFTC asserted, however, that this was to be only an interim measure and that its goal was to require time stamping of trades within one minute of their execution.

In 1984 the CFTC once again proposed to amend its rules to require that transactions on the floor of the exchange be time stamped upon execution. The CFTC stated that such a system was needed to ensure that it would be able to develop a full trade sequence reconstruction, the so-called audit trail, that would allow the detection of trade abuses and prevent dual trading abuses. The CFTC noted that some contract markets did have one-minute timing systems, and it stated that those exchanges

> have much enhanced surveillance capabilities. In these systems, the time of trade execution to the nearest minute is recorded by or for the broker or trader. . . . This more precise data substantially aids market and trade practice surveillance by permitting exchange compliance staff to more readily determine whether a particular pattern of trading is suspicious, and thus whether further investigation is needed. In contrast, when the

30-minute bracket indicator (and for customer trades, the time stamps on the order ticket) is the only time reference available, in many instances a determination of whether trading is suspicious is not possible without the laborious and time-consuming reference to the underlying documents, such as the order tickets and trading cards.[3]

Finally, in January 1986, the CFTC announced the adoption of rules that would require a record of the execution time of orders in one-minute increments. The exchanges are required to comply with the rule by October 1, 1986. It was stated that this rule was needed to track the trading of exchange members for their own accounts on the floor, which involves up to 70 percent of all exchange transactions.

OTHER RULES

In February 1977, the CFTC announced a proposed plan for the comprehensive regulation of commodity pool operators. In brief, a commodity pool is a group of traders who have pooled their funds for trading commodity futures contracts. Such pools are managed and traded by an expert trader who is compensated by various means (generally, by a percentage of assets in the pool plus a performance fee). The supposed advantage of a commodity pool is that a person unfamiliar with commodity futures can receive the advantages of an expert, the commodity pool operator and/or its commodity trade adviser. At the same time, unlike other commodity traders, the participant in a commodity pool may have her risk of loss limited to the amount of her investment, since the commodity pool is a separate entity that screens the investor from liability for margin calls that exceed the amount of the funds already invested.

Because any pool of funds presents temptation, and because the risk of commodity futures trading is so great, the CFTC was concerned, as was Congress in 1974, that commodity pool operators be subject to regulations that ensure that they give customers all the appropriate disclosures and that safeguards are in effect to ensure the integrity of the pools. Accordingly, after reviewing the recommendations of its Advisory Committee on Commodity Futures Trading Professionals, the CFTC adopted regulations requiring a risk disclosure statement that sets forth conflicts of interest and relevant risks in simple terms, as well as disclosure requirements about the background and experience of professionals operating the pools. In addition, a provision was made for disclosure of "track" records, which are often used by professional operators to publicize their pools. The CFTC was concerned that any such trading records be accurate and be in a format that would not be subject to misleading interpretations. Requirements were also imposed on the handling of customer funds.

At the same time, the CFTC proposed, and later adopted, a scheme of regulation for commodity trading advisers. Here, too, the Commission was concerned that customers be given full disclosure before they invested funds with commodity trading advisers who were directing their accounts. The CFTC, in that regard, adopted a risk disclosure requirement similar in nature to that for commodity pool operators. This included boldface warnings of appropriate risks. Commodity trading advisers were also required to report conflicts of interest, and their track records were required to be set forth in a specified format. Full disclosures were also required as to fees charged to customers.

In September 1977, the CFTC proposed rules governing "standards of conduct for commodity professionals for the protection of customers." These "customer protection" rules would have ensured that customers were given the same protections they received under other federal regulatory schemes, such as the federal securities laws. Among other things, the rules contained a proposal for "suitability." This was a securities laws concept where, initially, brokers were required to "know" their customers. That is, it was a protection for the broker to ensure that it would receive funds from the customers sufficient to pay for their securities. In other words, it was a protection for the industry, rather than the customer, because the failure of a firm caused by a customer who did not have funds to pay for securities adversely affected everyone in the industry.

Later, "suitability" became part of the so-called shingle theory under the federal securities laws. Under this theory, brokers are viewed to be professionals with obligations to their customers. That is, like doctors and lawyers, they hang out their shingle and represent themselves to be professionals on whom customers can rely.

In the securities industry, suitability today is a standard whereby brokers may not recommend to a customer transactions that are unsuitable for the customer in light of the customer's investment needs and desires. No such standard had previously been adopted in the commodities industry. For one thing, in view of the highly speculative nature of such transactions, such a standard would impose considerable difficulty in application.

Another customer protection rule proposed by the CFTC concerned churning. This, too, is a securities-based concept, which prohibits a broker from excessively trading a customer's account, over which the broker has control, for the purpose of generating commissions. The difficulty in applying this standard to commodity futures trading is that commodity transactions are short-lived, unlike many securities transactions. The volatile nature of the market also encourages traders to make more rapid and numerous trades than in the securities industry. Indeed, it is not infrequent for securities investors to hold their securities for months or even years. In the commodity futures industry even a month is a long time to hold a position.

Still another proposed customer protection rule concerned unauthorized trading. The CFTC sought a flat prohibition against this practice, and it proposed to require written authorization from customers who gave trading discretion over their accounts to a commodity professional. It was thought that by requiring a formal document, it would be more difficult for a broker to claim informal discretionary authorization to enter trades.

In addition, the CFTC sought to impose supervision requirements. The CFTC was concerned that commodity professionals should be required to supervise their employees to stop fraudulent practices. Another proposal was to bar advertisements containing hypothetical, short-term, or selective track records, which could be used to mislead customers. Another rule was proposed to require futures commission merchants to give their customers a printed statement of the risks of futures trading, and still another rule sought to require brokerage firms to use due diligence in handling customer orders.

After considering comments on these proposals, the CFTC adopted only the proposals for risk disclosure statements by futures commission merchants, supervisory requirements, and the prohibition against unauthorized trading. In so doing, the CFTC stated that it was not adopting the other proposed rules, because their requirements were inherent in the statute and that adoption of the rules could unintentionally narrow the scope of existing standards. Later, the CFTC rejected any suitability requirements, which has been the center of industry opposition since the creation of the CFTC. But administrative law judges at the agency continue to state that there is such a requirement, and the CFTC recently sought to shove this hot potato onto the National Futures Association, directing it to determine if suitability requirements should be required. The CFTC also declined to adopt the churning rule on similar grounds, but in its cases it has regarded this conduct as fraudulent and has established standards for determining when churning has occurred and whether an account is controlled by the broker. But this still leaves much confusion as to the status of customer protection in the commodities industry.[4]

THE SOYBEAN AFFAIR

In April 1977, the CFTC faced another crisis. This one involved the Hunt family of Dallas, Texas, several members of which had taken large positions in the soybean market on the Chicago Board of Trade. The Hunt family was headed by Bunker and Herbert Hunt, two sons of H. L. Hunt, the oil magnate who had accumulated the world's largest fortune, after having lost everything in his own futures speculations.

In 1977 soybean prices had increased from about $6 to over $10 a bushel from the 1976 prices. This was attributed to a shortage in 1976 "old crop" soybeans. A similar run-up had occurred in 1973, prior to the creation of the CFTC, and was (as noted above) a matter of substantial concern to Congress when it was considering the need for the CFTC.

During April 6-8, 1977, the price of soybeans reached levels that were exceeded only by the record 1973 prices. The price gain for three days was 56¢ per bushel. This meant a three-day profit of $2800 for each contract held by a person with the right to buy soybeans under a futures contract from the Chicago Board of Trade. At that time, the Hunts held collectively over 4,500 contracts. This would have meant a profit for the Hunts of over $12 million during that three-day period alone. In fact, the Hunts' profits were much greater, because they had purchased their contracts earlier at even lower prices. Estimates of their total profits ranged as high as $95 million.

On April 21, 1977, soybean prices advanced 17¢, for a profit of almost $4,000,000 on the Hunt positions. At that time, Brazil announced that it was suspending soybean exports temporarily; this news came on top of announcements by China that it was buying large amounts of American soybeans. The rise in soybean prices then began spilling over into corn and wheat, and there was concern that the national economy was being seriously threatened by the inflationary effect of these price rises.

The CFTC's concern was not with the crop shortages. Rather, it was concerned that futures traders might seek to take advantage of tight supplies. The CFTC market surveillance staff, therefore, had carefully reviewed the trading that was occurring on the Chicago Board of Trade. In the course of that review, they discovered the large positions of various members of the Hunt family in soybeans future. Collectively, the Hunts' positions were far in excess of the CFTC's position limit of three million bushels of soybeans for speculators. It appeared to the CFTC that the Hunts were acting in concert in trading soybeans, and they were asked repeatedly to liquidate their position by the CFTC. But they refused to do so.

The Hunt positions were, indeed, large. The entire United States carryover inventory for the old crop soybeans covered by the Chicago Board of Trade contracts was estimated to be some 65 million bushels. The Hunts' contracts in various delivery months gave them the right to take delivery of over one-third of that entire projected supply. The Hunts also held soybean contracts for May delivery that amounted to almost eight million bushels of soybeans. The total stock of deliverable amounts of soybeans in Chicago was estimated to be only some 10 million bushels.

After the Hunts refused to reduce their positions voluntarily, the CFTC determined that it would bring an injunctive action to stop them. It filed that action on April 28, 1977. This began a pitched battle between the CFTC and the Hunts, which was fought up and down the federal courts in Chicago. After a trial conducted by CFTC attorneys Lloyd Kadish, Mike

Stewart, and others, and after skirmishes on several issues, the federal district court in Chicago concluded that the Hunts were acting in concert. The court found that Bunker Hunt had opened accounts for his son and daughters and had loaned them money to engage in the trading and had suggested that they begin such trading.

It was also found that Bunker's children, who were trading millions of bushels of soybeans, had never traded in the market before. Indeed, one of Bunker's daughters was a college student living in a sorority house at the University of Alabama. Bunker Hunt's son, a freshman residing in a fraternity house at the University of Tulsa, used a pay telephone to make collect calls to his father to discuss and carry out his trading. Bunker Hunt's daughters also asserted that they had decided to invest in soybean futures at a luncheon with each other in the Zodiac Room of Neiman-Marcus in Dallas. CFTC investigators discovered that the Zodiac Room was a tearoom where high fashion shows were held for the matrons of Dallas society.

It was also found that the Hunt brothers, Herbert and Bunker, consulted a climatologist to advise them on weather patterns that could affect soybean prices. A particularly damaging piece of information, which was discovered in the course of the CFTC's case, showed that the Hunts had actually totaled their own positions together on a daily basis. This established the CFTC's case that they were acting in concert in violation of CFTC position limits. Donald Tendick and Britt Lenz, former CEA staff members (Tendick later became the CFTC's executive director), thus testified that the Hunts' trading practices were remarkably similar and concerted.

The district court, however, refused to enjoin the Hunts, even though it found that they had acted together in violation of the CFTC's position limits. On appeal, the Seventh Circuit reversed the decision and ordered that the Hunts be enjoined from further violations. The Court of Appeals also indicated that the CFTC was authorized by its statute to seek to require the Hunts to disgorge their profits, although it noted the difficulty of proof in doing so.

The CFTC also instituted administrative proceedings against the Hunts to impose civil penalties and to determine whether they should be barred from trading commodity futures contracts in the future on U.S. markets. That action was subsequently settled, with the Hunts being subject to a civil penalty of $500,000. They also agreed to a prohibition against further violations of the Commission's position limit rules.

There was some interesting fallout from the Hunt decision. One of the nation's largest grain companies, Cook Industries, traded opposite to the Hunts in the soybean market. As a consequence of losses experienced in that trading, its two chief traders, Willard R. Sparks and Christopher R. Parrott, resigned, and that company was substantially destroyed. The

Hunts had warned Cook that it was on the wrong side of the market, but it continued its position.[5]

This was not the last experience that the CFTC was to have in the volatility of soybean prices. As will be discussed in a subsequent chapter, in 1980 and again in 1983, large price swings were encountered. In 1980, the grain embargo against the Soviet Union after the invasion of Afghanistan resulted in a closing of the soybean futures market for two days, as well as other grain markets. In 1983 it was found that a declining price trend in the grain markets was not inconsistent with fundamental supply-and-demand conditions for soybeans and that no evidence of price manipulation was apparent.

THE 1978 AMENDMENTS

The CFTC encountered widespread criticism as the result of its handling of the Hunt case, specifically its publication of their positions in the market. It was also harshly criticized for failing to take prompt action against the two traders, who held over 70 percent of the December 1976 coffee futures contract;[6] administrative backlogs in registrating applicants; and failing to conduct sufficient commodity trading practice investigations and audits. One senator also accused William Bagley, the agency's chairman, of being a "windbag,"[7] and it was stated that "the CFTC is perhaps the most poorly administered, misdirected Federal Commission in the U.S. Government, 'bar none.' "[8] Rosee also was complaining once again of his grievances with the Chicago Board of Trade, and the CFTC was criticized severely for the commodity option scandals that had engulfed the agency by this time. At the same time, a series of articles by Colleen Sullivan and Jerry Knight in the *Washington Post* were highly critical of the CFTC and its chairman. Among other things, these articles noted that the agency had become a revolving door for staff members who were leaving in droves to work in the industry or to represent industry participants before the Commission.

Another embarrassing criticism of the CFTC was contained in a report prepared for Congressman Jamie Whitten of Mississippi by the Surveys and Investigations Staff of the House Committee on Appropriations. It too found fault with the CFTC's management problems. It found that many civil service positions at the agency were "over graded" and that the CFTC had a disproportionate number of political appointees. The *Whitten Report* found, among other things, that drivers of CFTC officials were being paid over $35,000 per year for their services, and that the agency had paid over $45,000 for employee parking spaces. In addition, the report found that there had been a "flagrant" misuse of funds for consultants to avoid civil service hiring restrictions.

Cost and audit controls at the CFTC were found to be wanting or nonexistent. Abuses were also found in contract awards. For example, one former employee in the chairman's office was given two management consulting contracts, which in the aggregate exceeded the amount required for competitive bids. The *Whitten Report* stated that "[t]he Chairman has been quoted as acknowledging that the purchase orders were split purposely to remain below $10,000 in order to avoid the competition required when an award exceeds that amount." Favored treatment was found to have been given to another contractor, and the CFTC's general counsel refused to render a favorable legal opinion on another procurement contract. The *Whitten Report* found that, nevertheless, the executive assistant to the chairman was of the view that "if nobody was going to jail, CFTC should not concern itself with technicalities."[9]

Various federal agencies also saw that this criticism gave them an opportunity to poach on the jurisdiction of the CFTC. That opportunity was furthered by the fact that CFTC's existence was limited by a "sunset" provision in the Commodity Exchange Act: the agency would be terminated unless Congress determined to renew its charter by reauthorizing the Commission at periodic intervals.[10]

The first reauthorization process occurred in 1978. Lengthy hearings were held and voluminous reports filed, but the CFTC survived the process with its jurisdiction pretty much intact. Nevertheless, as noted, severe criticism was directed at the agency, and it was clear that its continuance forever as a federal agency was in no way guaranteed on the basis of its record during its first few years in existence.[11] The CFTC also faced serious political problems with the Carter administration and Congress. In that connection, one of its Commissioners, David Gartner, had recently been confirmed by the Senate. Shortly afterward, however, it was discovered by the press that Gartner's children had received some $72,000 in stock as gifts from Dwayne Andreas, the chairman of Archer, Daniel Midland, Co., one of the country's largest agribusinesses and a company trading in futures contracts. As such, it was subject to CFTC regulation. Although Gartner had disclosed this information during his confirmation process, it had passed unnoticed. After the press picked up the story, however, various senators, as well as President Carter and Vice-President Walter Mondale, who had been responsible for Gartner's appointment, requested Gartner's resignation. Gartner refused. Various proposals were then introduced in Congress to eliminate the CFTC or to restructure it so that Gartner could be removed from the Commission. Dismissal was also sought for CFTC's chairman, William Bagley, who had also fallen into congressional disfavor after the *Whitten Report*.[12] Those proposals came to naught, except that the statute was changed to allow the president to remove the chairman, who resigned before this could occur.

In defense of the CFTC, it faced a formidable task in imposing regulatory control over an industry that, heretofore, had been virtually un-regulated. The industry was proud of its efforts in resisting government regulation, proclaiming itself to be the last bastion of free enterprise, where market forces were the regulators, rather than government rules. Survival of the fittest was the watchword of the commodity pits and elsewhere in the industry. Many commodity traders did not willingly accept govern-mental regulation, whatever its goals. Indeed, there was, and is, a strong body of public opinion throughout the United States against "overregu-lation" and government interference with business.

This was also a time of education for the CFTC. Although there were many CEA employees at the CFTC, they had not exercised the type of regulatory control envisioned by Congress when it created the CFTC. The CFTC, understandably, was also reluctant to impose regulations that (in view of its limited experience) could unduly interfere with the commodities markets.[13] For example, the Commission sought to establish regulations for commodity options in a step-by-step process that would allow their trading, but eliminate abuses. Instead of suspending options trading en-tirely from the outset, the CFTC had thus sought to adopt only such regulations as would be necessary to stop fraudulent practices and eliminate persons from the industry who would engage in fraud. Those efforts were simply outstripped by the widespread fraud that developed almost over-night in the commodity options industry. Obviously, in hindsight, the CFTC should have immediately suspended options, but there were enormous pressures not to exercise such a heavy-handed regulatory role at that time.

The CFTC was also faced with the necessity of establishing itself among other regulatory agencies, such as the Securities and Exchange Commission and the Federal Reserve Board, with much longer experience in regulation. The greater experience of these agencies and their nearly complete control over the industries they regulated were in stark contrast to the unregulated and unyielding industry faced by the CFTC. When viewed in that light, a much more charitable view is possible of the CFTC's slowness in responding to the options issues and the criticism incurred in other areas where it seemed to act too hastily or harshly.

The options scandals were, nonetheless, a matter of obvious interest to Congress when it considered the CFTC's reauthorization in 1978. But the CFTC's suspension of commodity option trading in 1978, before the congressional hearings on its reauthorization, helped to defuse that issue. Congress simply amended the statute to reflect the CFTC's suspension of options trading. It also directed that the CFTC inform appropriate com-mittees of Congress before allowing commencement of widespread com-modity options trading.

The dispute before Congress on CFTC jurisdiction in the 1978 reau-thorization process was principally fought by the SEC. It was seeking to expand its jurisdiction to include the regulation of futures contracts, where the commodity underlying the futures contract was a security. The Chicago Board Options Exchange, Inc. (CBOE) supported the SEC. The SEC and the CBOE argued that options and futures contracts are functionally indistinguishable and that, because the SEC already had jurisdiction over options on equity securities, it should have jurisdiction over futures on securities as well. Predictably, the commodities exchanges and the CFTC opposed the CBOE and the SEC. They argued that futures are separate instruments that need to be regulated by a single entity, regardless of the nature of the underlying commodities.

The Treasury Department and the General Accounting Office also submitted proposals for allocating jurisdiction between the SEC and the CFTC, as well as to give the Treasury some authority over futures trading. The Government Accounting Office urged that the SEC be given authority over futures contracts on securities that were subject to the provisions of the Securities Act of 1933. The Treasury Department sought jurisdiction over futures contracts on government securities such as Treasury bills and GNMAs.

Congress rejected all of these proposals. But it did require the CFTC to "maintain communications" with the SEC, the Treasury, and the Federal Reserve Board, and to "take into consideration" the views of the two latter agencies in approving applications for trading in futures on government securities.

The states also weighed in during the congressional hearings, in their own effort to obtain greater jurisdiction. But the CFTC successfully argued that its exclusive jurisdiction should be maintained. Nevertheless, the states were given statutory authority by Congress to bring *parens patriae* actions on behalf of their citizens under the provisions of the Commodity Exchange Act. This gave the states regulatory authority. But at the same time, it ensured a uniformity of law.

There were other significant amendments added in 1978. One was designed to remove an obstruction to the development of the National Futures Association (NFA), an entity envisioned by the CFTC Act of 1974 to be a national self-regulatory body, modeled after that of the National Association of Securities Dealers Inc. (NASD) in the securities industry. It was believed by Congress that through the 1974 amendments this type of self-regulatory body would fill an important gap in self-regulation in the commodity industry as well, leading to the regulation of non-member firms.[14]

One problem that had been encountered after the 1974 act, and which had precluded the development of the NFA, was that there was no provision for mandatory membership. It was thought that if an organization imposed such a requirement without congressional authorization, it would be a breach of the antitrust laws. The 1978 amendments were designed to give that authorization, and to allow the NFA to take over the registration functions of the CFTC. Thereafter, the NFA went forward and is now functioning as a nationwide self-regulator.

Another amendment in 1978 sought to prevent the type of press conference that led to the disclosure of the Hunts' positions by the CFTC when it filed its soybean case. The Hunts had objected strenuously to this disclosure, because it told other members of the marketplace the size of the Hunts' position. The CFTC action was also designed to force the Hunts to liquidate their positions in a rapid manner. The sharks immediately began circling over at the Chicago Board of Trade, and prices dropped, to the Hunts' consternation. The 1978 amendments did not preclude the CFTC from disclosing a trader's position in court proceedings, but it did preclude public press conference type releases.

Another change, brought about by the options scandal, required fingerprinting of CFTC applicants for registration. Had such a system been in effect, it was thought, Lloyd Carr (a.k.a. Alan Abrahams) might have been discovered at an earlier date. Congress also authorized the CFTC to regulate all leverage contracts, going beyond the gold and silver authority previously given to the CFTC by the 1974 amendments. Numerous other amendments were also made to strengthen the agency.

8

FOREIGN TRADERS: SILVER, GRAIN, AND MORE PROBLEMS IN CONGRESS

SPECIAL CALLS

Another problem encountered by the CFTC in its early years involved its surveillance of the trading of individuals located outside the United States but who were trading in U.S. markets. Large traders on U.S. contract markets are required by the CFTC to file reports with the CFTC identifying their positions and background information about themselves.[1] Through this information, the CFTC, on a daily basis, can maintain effective surveillance over the marketplace. If there are unusual price movements, the CFTC is particularly interested in the identity of the participants. It may even have its staff contact traders to determine why the large participants have acquired such large positions and what their intentions are. When large speculators are observed in the market, the CFTC's concern is particularly heightened, and they will focus on those persons.

There is a gap in this surveillance procedure. Large foreign customers are not required to report their positions when they trade in an omnibus account through what is called a "foreign broker" (an entity that operates as an FCM abroad; foreign brokers are not required to register with the CFTC, as are domestic FCMs). As a consequence, while the CFTC could determine in its surveillance that a foreign broker is in the market, it will not normally be able to determine the identity and nature of the foreign broker's customers. To fill this gap, the CFTC has set up a requirement that subjected foreign traders to a "special call." Thus, while large foreign traders did not have to report on a daily basis, as do domestic traders, their foreign brokers were called on by the CFTC to supply relevant information at any time by a "special call."

A difficulty encountered by the CFTC with its special call procedure is that a foreign broker receiving a special call may decline to disclose the identities of its customers, because they may view such information to be confidential. Indeed, disclosure of their identity may be in violation of the laws of many foreign countries. The CFTC, however, is of the view that the confidentiality requirements of a foreign government cannot be a basis for restricting its surveillance over a foreign national's activities on U. S. markets. In the view of the CFTC, foreign traders voluntarily trade on U. S. markets. In so doing, they subject themselves to all of the CFTC's rules and regulations. If a foreign trader does not wish to submit to CFTC jurisdiction, including the requirement that the trader's identity be disclosed upon request, the foreign trader need only refrain from trading. The CFTC therefore gives little credence to foreign law conflict claims.

In *In the Matter of Wiscope S.A.*,[2] the Second Circuit reversed a determination of the CFTC that a foreign broker had failed properly to supply information in response to a special call. The Court of Appeals did so on the ground that the call was not properly authorized; it had been erroneously issued to an affiliate of the respondent. The court stated that the CFTC must cut "square corners" in issuing such special calls. Despite this setback, the CFTC continued to issue special calls and brought a number of proceedings in which it imposed sanctions against foreign brokers that refused to comply with them. Today such special calls are an accepted, albeit unloved, part of the CFTC's regulatory process.

MARCH 1979 WHEAT FUTURES CONTRACT

In March 1979, the CFTC faced another market emergency. This time the problem involved congestion in the March 1979 wheat future on the Chicago Board of Trade. Here, the CFTC acted promptly under its emergency powers and directed the Chicago Board of Trade to suspend all trading in the contract. In so doing, the CFTC found that a small number of speculative traders were maintaining potentially dominant positions in the contract, and that they were maintaining those positions even though the contract was about to expire. The combined positions of this small group of traders substantially exceeded the total quantity of wheat currently available for delivery in fulfillment of the Chicago Board of Trade contract. It was further found that there was a significant shortage of transportation and warehouse facilities that precluded bringing further supplies to the marketplace.

The Chicago Board of Trade immediately challenged the CFTC's action, contending that its declaration of a market emergency was arbitrary and capricious. The exchange sought preliminary injunctive relief in the Chicago Federal District Court against the CFTC. The district court enjoined the CFTC, but the Seventh Circuit Court of Appeals reversed, holding that this was a matter within the CFTC's discretion that was not judicially reviewable.[3]

This decision, of course, caused much consternation in the industry. It gave the CFTC carte blanche to act at any time the CFTC believed an emergency existed, and the criteria for an emergency would be purely within the discretion of the CFTC. Review would be unobtainable even where the CFTC was wrong. This gave the CFTC a powerful weapon. This decision also made clear, for the first time, that the judgments of the exchanges would be subordinated to that of the CFTC, notwithstanding the fact that the exchanges were much closer to the marketplace and had much greater experience than the CFTC and its commissioners.

The CFTC did not come off quite so well in another tiff with the Chicago Mercantile Exchange and the Chicago Board of Trade. Those two exchanges had expanded delivery months without seeking the prior approval of the CFTC. The CFTC obtained a temporary restraining order, but that injunction was subsequently dissolved, and the district court refused further relief, after it was shown that the CFTC had approved the same delivery months for a New York exchange. The CFTC, under its power to alter exchange rules, later ordered the Chicago exchanges to change their rules to provide that new cycles would not be added without first seeking CFTC approval, which made the litigation moot. This was the first time the CFTC had used that authority.

DEFERRED DELIVERY CONTRACTS

If the CFTC believed that the options suspension had rid it of fly-by-night operators, it was sadly mistaken. They simply shifted their operations to a "new" product. Under the Commodity Exchange Act, the CFTC was, in effect, excluded from regulating cash sales of commodities for "deferred shipment or delivery," a term that is not defined by the statute. Espying that language, the commodity option operators quickly changed their products into "deferred delivery" investments. In fact, these new products were commodity options or future contracts under a new name.

To stop this charade, the CFTC embarked on a new round of injunctive actions across the United States. It also formed a task force in Florida to combat these operations, an area where they were the most active. In California, the CFTC saw Harold Goldstein emerge once again in the form of a company called CoPetro Marketing Group Inc., which sold oil contracts to the general public. Goldstein sought to structure its contracts as deferred delivery contracts. By this time, Goldstein had become one of the most colorful characters in American finance. As noted, the original Goldstein/Samuelson debacle had led in large measure to the creation of the CFTC. Goldstein later appeared at a CFTC hearing, on leave from prison and under guard, to testify about the dangers and abuses of commodity options. When he was released, he immediately formed CoPetro.

The CFTC brought an action charging that Goldstein was in fact selling futures contracts. The courts upheld the CFTC in its determination, and the company was enjoined from further sales; it was also placed in bankruptcy. Following its demise, Harold moved into phony banking deals through a bank he had established in the Caribbean. Later, with federal agents closing in, Harold fled the country aboard a stolen 58-foot yacht, stealing someone's wife in the process. Apprehended on the high seas by the FBI and Bahamian police, Harold now faced several more years of rehabilitation. This was his third such trip into the "population," having also been convicted after his initial Goldstein/Samuelson problems in a gold scam.[4]

The incarceration of Harold Goldstein did not stop the CFTC's concern with off-exchange instruments. It found petroleum contracts being sold illegally, and some twenty-nine firms were jointly sued by the CFTC to stop those activities. It also brought suit against a firm conducting widespread operations in coal contracts, all of which were designed to avoid CFTC regulations under the cloak of deferred delivery contracts. Diamonds also became a popular medium for these disguised options contracts. Unlike its experience with commodity options, the CFTC generally prevailed quickly in the suits it brought, and effectively stopped these operations. This activity, however, once again demonstrated the susceptibility of options trading to fraud. It was also evidence of how popular these types of investment were to small investors who were willing to send an unknown firm several thousand dollars after a cold-call solicitation from an individual they had never seen before, all on the basis of promises of large profits.

Recognizing the market interest in options, the CFTC authorized the exchanges to conduct a pilot options program for trading in options. This program allowed a limited number of options to be traded on each exchange. It was thought that, if options trading were conducted on an exchange, they could be regulated as tightly as futures contracts, which have not experienced the widespread problems found in commodity options. The CFTC's pilot program imposed stringent requirements on the exchanges and tough disclosure requirements (requiring large boldface warnings in addition to those given to futures customers). To date, this program has been successful; although in 1985, the jump in gold option prices led to the Volume Investor's failure on the Commodity Exchange Inc., raising renewed questions as to the pitfalls of options trading.

TREASURY/FEDERAL RESERVE STUDY

In May 1979, the staffs of the Department of Treasury and the Federal Reserve Board issued a report of an investigation they had made into the expansion of trading in futures contracts on financial instruments. They were concerned with duplicative and overlapping financial futures contracts traded by the various exchanges. The staffs examined the possible inadequacy of deliverable supplies and the ability of the exchanges and the CFTC to maintain effective surveillance over the growing number of contract markets, particularly where duplicative contracts were traded simultaneously on several exchanges. They were also concerned with the plans of financial houses to expand their promotion of Treasury futures to a wide range of possibly less knowledgeable market participants. The staffs sought to determine whether financial futures contracts posed any appreciable threat to the effective performance of the cash market in Treasury securities. If so, they would have implications for the effective management of Treasury financing and Federal Reserve open-market operations.

When completed, the Treasury/Federal Reserve study constituted an in-depth review of the financial futures markets and their interrelationship with the cash markets in government securities. It reviewed hedging practices and speculative interests. It also reviewed the effect on the cash markets. The study made several recommendations to the CFTC for strengthening regulation. But it also recognized the beneficial nature of futures trading. This recognition gave a green light, in effect, to financial institutions to enter the futures markets, as did various banking regulations that allowed expanded use of futures contracts by banks. The report thus signaled an acceptance by the principal regulators of financial institutions that these instruments could be an important part of sophisticated programs in managing money and interest rate risks. The Treasury/Federal Reserve study paved the way for efforts that had already begun to allow institutions to participate in the marketplace.

One type of institution that found the commodity futures markets to be particularly attractive were mutual funds. These funds could use the futures markets to hedge interest rate risks through the trading of futures contracts on financial instruments. In addition (with the advent of so-called stock index futures) the funds, for example, could hedge against overall losses in their portfolio caused by a drop in the marketplace. This market risk could thereby be offset without selling an entire portfolio. The CFTC and the SEC have cooperated to broaden this market for these participants. For example, the SEC concluded that funds trading solely in financial futures need not register with it as investment companies or as investment advisers. Conversely, the CFTC took the position that mutual funds and certain other entities regulated by different bodies, that use the futures markets only for hedging, and with other limitations, need not register as commodity pool operators or as commodity trading advisers.

Other institutions also entered the market as they realized its benefits. These included savings and loans and other deposit organizations (trading for their own accounts as a means to hedge interest rates) as well as other institutions, such as insurance companies, with interest rate risks. The bank regulators also acted to authorize this trading. As a consequence, by the mid-1980s futures trading became more and more a Wall Street institution and less an agricultural preserve.

THE "SILVER CRISIS"

Much has already been written about the events in the silver market in 1979 and 1980. In brief, commencing in 1979, the price of silver increased from some $6 an ounce to a peak of some $50 an ounce in January 1980. Then, prices fell rapidly and, in March 1980, the so-called silver crisis emerged when the Hunt family of Dallas, Texas, failed to meet millions of dollars of margin calls at various brokerage firms.[5] The Securities and Exchange Commission and the CFTC subsequently filed massive reports about these events, and the effects that they had on the various brokerage firms involved. It was charged that the Hunts and others held market positions at one point with a value of over $9 billion.

After an investigation that lasted some five years, the CFTC also brought charges of manipulation against the Hunts and others, charging that they had conspired to manipulate the silver market. In addition, the CFTC imposed regulatory reforms, including a requirement that all exchanges adopt requirements imposing position limits on all futures contracts. It was thought that this would reduce concerns that large speculators could affect market prices.

The events in the silver market created other fallout. On April 7, 1984, Congressman George Hansen was convicted of violating the 1978 Ethics in Government Act for failing to disclose, in reports required to be filed by members of Congress, that over $100,000 in loans were made or guaranteed by Nelson Bunker Hunt to him and his wife, and that his wife made an $87,000 profit in two days of trading silver futures contracts during the price run-up in 1979. Hansen was also convicted of failing to disclose $135,000 in loans received from three other individuals, including a convicted bank swindler.

THE GRAIN EMBARGO

On January 4, 1980, as noted above, President Carter embargoed 17 million tons of grain that had already been sold to the Soviet Union. That action was taken in retaliation for the Soviet incursion into Afghanistan. Because this action was likely to result in pandemonium in the grain pits, the CFTC, in an emergency Sunday meeting, ordered the suspension of grain futures trading for two days.

The CFTC's action was supported by many market participants and was based on its view that the sudden shock to the market, and the uncertainty concerning the government's plans for compensating the grain companies affected by the embargo, would not allow the market to reflect supply and demand accurately. The CFTC noted that the embargo meant that roughly half a billion bushels of grain would not be delivered to the Soviet Union, causing severe pressure on prices, and margin calls of $400 million per day would go out each day the market traded to price limits. The CFTC stated, "[d]islocation of this magnitude, on very short notice, could have had adverse effects, not only on the market participants, but on banks and brokers as well."[6]

1982 AMENDMENTS

In 1982 Congress once again took up the reauthorization of the CFTC. A principal part of the amendments that resulted from this process was to enact the Shad-Johnson Accords, the jurisdictional agreement previously reached between the chairmen of the Securities and Exchange Commission and the CFTC. Under this agreement, as enacted, the SEC was given jurisdiction over options on securities, including GNMAs and certificates of deposit. It was also given jurisdiction over options or indexes of securities and options on foreign currency trading on any national securities exchange.

The CFTC, on the other hand, was given jurisdiction over all futures contracts. This included futures contracts on exempted securities (other than municipal securities) and on groups of securities, or indexes, as well as options on futures contracts on such indexes. In addition, futures contracts and options on futures contracts for the securities of individual corporations and municipal securities were not permitted. The CFTC was given exclusive jurisdiction over options on foreign currency, unless it was traded on a national securities exchange.

One battle in Congress over the 1982 amendments was whether the SEC should be given, in effect, a veto power over approval of stock index futures contracts by the CFTC. Congress concluded that stock index applications filed with the CFTC subsequent to December 1982 would be subject to SEC review. The SEC was also given, in effect, a veto power, if the contract did not meet certain specified minimum requirements, so that it could not be readily susceptible to manipulation. If the veto was exercised, then a provision was made for a hearing and judicial review was permitted.

Several other jurisdictional issues were also addressed in the 1982 amendments. One concerned the concurrent jurisdiction of the SEC and the CFTC over commodity pools, where interests in the pool were sold to the general public. The SEC had previously claimed that the sale of such interests were securities subject to its jurisdiction. The 1982 amendments endorsed that role for the SEC. It does not appear, however, that the Investment Company Act of 1940 would apply to a commodity futures pool, unless it was also investing in securities. But the Investment Company Act and the Investment Advisers Act of 1940 would apply to options on a security, options on stock indexes, and options on foreign currency where such options are traded on a national securities exchange.[7]

Another jurisdictional issue concerned the trading of off-exchange instruments. The CFTC proposed that the states be given "open season" on nonexchange instruments, such that they could bring the full panoply of their laws against such instruments. The states had sought even greater authority, protesting that they were hamstrung by the CFTC's exclusive jurisdiction and that their citizens were not receiving adequate protection. But the Congress adopted the "open season" concept proposed by the CFTC, and did not allow the broader regulation envisioned by the states over the commodity markets.

Still another jurisdictional issue concerned the CFTC's regulation of foreign futures contracts. Congress added additional authority in 1982 to allow the CFTC to adopt regulations to govern their offer and sale in the United States. The CFTC was specifically denied authority to review the terms of foreign futures contracts, and it was prohibited from regulating the conduct or rules of foreign boards of trade.

The 1982 amendments created a new category of registrant-introducing brokers. These are simply firms that introduce the business of their customers to a futures commission merchant, who carries those accounts and handles the money of the customers. Previously, such entities had operated as "agents" of futures commission merchants. Because of abuses and concern that the CFTC did not have adequate regulatory control, greater regulation was thought to be necessary.

Still another issue in the 1982 amendments was the regulation of leverage contracts. The CFTC had determined that such contracts should be regulated as futures contracts. Congress concluded, however, that the CFTC should quickly adopt a comprehensive regulatory scheme for leverage contracts. It also expressed concern with a CFTC-imposed moratorium on the entry of new leverage firms into that business, stating that such a moratorium was anticompetitive.

In addition, Congress addressed the issue of private rights of action. Although the Supreme Court had already concluded that there was an implied right of action inherent in the Commodity Exchange Act, the 1982 amendments made that right an express one. The amendments also established a two-year statute of limitations and limited the instances under which such actions could be brought; private actions can now be brought only for actual damages, eliminating a right to punitive damages. Restrictions were placed on the types of persons who could seek recovery and on actions brought against exchanges.

A highly political issue in the 1982 reauthorization process was whether there should be a "user fee" for transactions in commodity futures. It was thought that the operations of the CFTC could be financed by the "users" of the marketplace through such a fee. This proposal was met by strong industry opposition, however, and Congress did not adopt it.[8] Another provision, adopted in response to President Carter's grain embargo after the Afghanistan invasion, related to the sanctity of contracts. Under the amendment, the president was prohibited from embargoing grain already under contract. Such embargos can be prospective only.

Congress also added provisions in 1982 with respect to the regulation of contract markets. One such amendment allowed a limited right of review before a circuit court with respect to emergency market actions ordered by the CFTC. This provision was added as a result of industry opposition to the decision of the Seventh Circuit, which had virtually precluded judicial review of CFTC emergency actions. The new amendments allow CFTC actions to be stayed if the CFTC's action is arbitrary, capricious, an abuse of discretion, or otherwise not in accordance with law. Although this was a setback for the CFTC, Congress bolstered its authority in another area. It thus added a provision specifically authorizing the CFTC to set margins limits in a market emergency, a power that had long been sought by the CEA.

Congress acted to streamline the CFTC's rule review process. This was done by limiting the CFTC's review to the terms and conditions of commodity futures contracts; all other contract market rules could be implemented 10 days after their submission to the CFTC, unless the contract market requested review or the CFTC determined that further review was needed. Specific time limits and other requirements were imposed on the CFTC for the remaining rules reviewed by it. Contract market applications were also required to be acted on by the CFTC within stated periods of time.

The 1982 amendments broadened the authority of the CFTC to delegate its registration functions to the National Futures Association. In the 1978 amendments, the CFTC had been allowed to delegate its registration authority for associated persons to the NFA. The 1982 amendments allowed such delegation to be expanded to include all registrants. These amendments were significant. The CFTC had been overwhelmed by the large number of applications it processed, and the industry was completely frustrated with the long delays encountered in the registration process. The delegation to the NFA sought to resolve those concerns.

The Commodity Exchange Act was also amended in 1982 to allow the CFTC to begin a pilot program for exchange trading of agricultural options, which had been banned since at least 1936. This was designed to allow farmers to participate in the options markets and to receive the advantages of options trading.[9]

The 1982 amendments directed the CFTC and other government agencies to make several studies concerning futures trading. One such study was to be conducted by the Federal Reserve Board, the CFTC, the SEC, and the Treasury. This study was to examine the economic effect of options and futures trading, including its effect on capital formation. Another study by the CFTC was to review abuses of inside information on the commodity markets and to determine whether this was a problem that should be addressed by Congress and the agency. Still other studies were ordered, including a review by the CFTC of large traders in livestock.[10]

EXCHANGE LINKAGE

One of the most significant events occurring at the CFTC subsequent to the 1982 amendments was the authorization granted by the CFTC to the Chicago Mercantile Exchange to enter into a linkage with the Singapore International Monetary Exchange (Simex). This linkage reflected the fact that futures trading had become a worldwide financial industry. It also reflected a desire to allow trading through extended hours, even on a 24-hour basis. Extended trading hours would permit traders to cover their positions or respond immediately to world events at any time. For example, precious metal prices respond sharply to political events around the world, and traders could take immediate advantage of opportunities offered by such events whatever time they occur in any part of the world. Traders also want the opportunity to protect themselves rapidly should a political development occur after the close of trading on their own domestic market. Exchange linkages permit this extended trading day. Several other exchanges are also discussing worldwide linkages.

THE JOINT STUDY

Pursuant to the terms of the 1982 amendments to the Commodity Exchange Act, the CFTC, the SEC, the Federal Reserve Board, and the Department of Treasury concluded their study of the futures and options markets. The report concluded that the new financial futures and options markets serve a useful, economic purpose in allowing the hedging of economic risks. The study also found that financial futures and options markets do not have any measurable negative implications on the formation of capital. Indeed, it was found that they appeared to have enhanced liquidity in some cash markets. The study also concluded that, while financial futures regulated by the CFTC and options contracts regulated by the SEC differ in many important respects, they also have many common elements and both serve similar economic functions. It was also found that these markets are often closely interrelated and that close harmonization of federal regulation is needed.

The study further found that trading in functionally similar instruments under the respective jurisdictions of the Securities and Exchange Commission and CFTC had not resulted in any significant harm to public customers or to the underlying cash markets. It was noted, however, that some aberrations had resulted from arbitrage trading in index options and the securities in those indexes, and that further monitoring was needed. It was also found that the Securities and Exchange Commission and CFTC had adequate authority to regulate the markets.

INSIDE INFORMATION STUDY

In September 1984, the CFTC rendered its study on the nature, extent, and effects of futures trading by persons possessing material inside information. The study concluded that there are persons who possess material inside information that could affect the regulatory environment for futures trading. For example, it was found that government officials and officials connected with self-regulatory organizations possessed information and advance knowledge of factors that could affect market prices. It was also found that persons executing customer orders possessed inside information from such orders and that this could be abused; a court so found in *United States v. Dial.*[11]

The CFTC noted that there were already restrictions on government officials, and it stated that certain additional restrictions were warranted to ensure that employees of self-regulatory organizations do not seek to profit from the futures markets on the basis of information obtained from their employment. The CFTC stated that it would be proposing rules for that purpose. The CFTC did not find sufficient evidence to warrant the development of any recommendations to Congress with respect to persons issuing market-affecting reports or persons trading in cash markets who might possess some form of inside information (as for example, information concerning one's own cash position or trading and its effect on the market, or general market information, such as supply data that might not otherwise be available to the general public).

The CFTC reviewed past instances where it was claimed that inside information had played a role in affecting prices (such as the Soviet "Grain Robbery of 1972") but found no evidence that inside information was abused. In another instance, it was noted that Henry Kaufman, chief economist for Phibro-Salomon, had announced on August 17, 1982, that interest rates would fall. The market response was strong and rapid. Prior to the announcement, Phibro-Salomon had reportedly purchased several million dollars of futures contracts in financial instruments, but the CFTC report found that no connection between the announcement and the purchase had been demonstrated.

The CFTC thus limited its concern with inside information to a narrow range of persons. This is in stark contrast with the securities markets where the SEC, in recent years, has substantially focused its enforcement program on persons trading on inside information in the securities markets. Of course, there is a significant difference in the commodities markets. Information in the commodities market is generally "market" information. It is not information, as in the securities industry, that is specific to a single company.

This was a justification by the CFTC in not advocating a broader insider trading prohibition in the commodities industry. This approach, however, should be contrasted with that of the CFTC's first chairman, William Bagley, who stated a few months after the creation of the CFTC:

> Now, I recognize the vast difference between the securities market and the futures market in an approach to the "insider," but I'll bet you that the general public and the consumer want us to ask questions about the possibility of large cash traders and of employees and associates of large traders in the cash markets using their knowledge to play the futures market with perhaps an inordinate effect thereupon. I don't know the answers at this point, but I am going to ask the questions..... [12]

Nevertheless, the CFTC declined to adopt an antifraud standard for commodity options patterned after the antifraud provisions of the federal securities laws, because it was "particularly concerned with the possibility" that decisions reached on "commodity cases might misapply nondisclosure—of information standards taken from securities laws decisions, although it fully appreciates that a failure to disclose information may operate as a fraud or deceit with respect to commodity transactions in certain circumstances."[13]

SOYBEANS AGAIN

In 1983 the CFTC conducted a study of volatile soybean prices following a drought. The CFTC's study found no evidence of price manipulation but concluded that some traders with unusually large positions were associated with intra-day price fluctuations. The report stated that even if these traders did not intend to affect prices, they may have had that effect. Nevertheless, the CFTC believed that additional regulations or limitations on soybean trading were not necessary.

PART II

THE CFTC AND ITS OPERATIONS

9

THE CFTC AND
ITS OPERATIONS

THE CHAIRMAN'S OFFICE

The Commodity Futures Trading Commission is a "collegial" body composed of five commissioners. It is headed by a chairman, who is authorized by the Commodity Exchange Act to act as the Commission's chief administrative officer and to preside at hearings before the Commission. The functions of the chairman also include the authority to appoint and supervise personnel employed by the Commission, except for the heads of the principal administrative units, and the executive director and the general counsel, who are approved by the entire Commission. The chairman also determines what business shall be handled by which members or administrative units of the staff, and may expend funds in the manner and under the programs established by the Commission.

In fulfilling these functions, the chairman is called on to perform a strong leadership role at the Commission, to set its tone and to carry out its policies. The CFTC's first two chairmen, however, ran into difficulties in fulfilling that ideal. Its first chairman, William Bagley, prided himself in the fact that he was not an "expert" on commodity futures trading. Nor did he show any inclination to become one. Instead, he used his tenure as chairman to pursue various causes such as "open" government and changes in government-wide administrative procedures, as well as general self-promotion, none of which was useful to the development of the CFTC's principal role of establishing a workable and effective regulatory scheme over commodity futures trading.

In particular, Bagley sought to open CFTC meetings to the public, and he often complained of the federal administrative process, which allows an agency to bring charges against individuals for violations of the statutes they administer and then to sit in judgment on those charges, while the agency's staff prosecutes the case. Although the CFTC has been perennially short of funds, Bagley also granted a consulting contract to study the relationship of the California open meetings law and the Federal Sunshine Act, a matter that was hardly at the center of the CFTC's universe.

Bagley, a Phi Beta Kappa and the valedictorian of his college class at UCLA, had been the chairman of several important committees in the California Assembly, including its Revenue and Taxation Committee, Judiciary Committee, and the Joint Committee on National Tax Policy. He was even voted "most effective assemblyman" by the Sacramento capitol press corps. In 1974, however, his ambition led him to enter a tough election for the powerful position of state comptroller in California. He lost, but as a reward for his effort, Gerald Ford appointed him chairman of the CFTC in 1975.

Bagley, by anyone's light, was a colorful character. After touring Italy, he prominently displayed a souvenir poster in his CFTC office that he had "liberated," and which advocated support for the Italian Communist Party. He was also wont to call press conferences, including the one on Memorial Bridge over the Potomac River, into which he threw the agency's "confidential" rubber stamps, and his press conference describing the Hunts' soybean positions led Congress to amend the Commodity Exchange Act to prevent such disclosures in the future.

Bagley's name also had a way of finding its way into the papers without the aid of a formal press conference. For example, in a front page story, the *Washington Post* reported that columnist Joseph Kraft had mistakenly taken the raincoat of a fellow passenger when leaving the Eastern Airlines shuttle between Washington and New York. In a pocket of the coat, Kraft found a personal check for $24 million made out by Chairman Bagley to the coat's owner, Dr. Henry Jarecki, the head of Moccata Metals Corp., one of the largest precious metals dealers in the world. Apparently alerted to this story by Kraft, a *Washington Post* reporter confronted Bagley in his office at the CFTC and asked for an explanation. Bagley stated that Jarecki had complained that some rules adopted by the CFTC were going to cost Moccata some $24 million. Whereupon, Bagley pulled out his checkbook and wrote Jarecki a personal check for that amount.[1] This was not the only occasion of such generosity by Bagley. He also showed the *Washington Post* reporter another one of his checks that was framed on his office wall. It was made out in the amount of $4.6 billion to California Governor Pat Brown. Bagley had sent the check to cover the California budget after Brown complained that Bagley, then a Republican legislator, was delaying its passage.[2]

Bagley was a personable individual. But he refused to exercise strong administrative control at the CFTC. As one unnamed congressional source stated, "I'm sure he's a great guy to go drinking with . . . [b]ut he doesn't do his homework and he doesn't seem to take his job seriously."[3] His appointments of some of the senior staff were criticized as purely political, and it was stated that "rampant politicalization" was occurring at the CFTC.[4] The constant in-fighting between the executive director's office and the lawyers on the CFTC staff, and later between the various divisions, resulted in serious disruptions of the agency's activities. Bagley's refusal to become involved in the substantive aspects of the agency's operations was also damaging, since the staff had little guidance from the Commission.[5]

Congress' annoyance with Bagley made itself felt, as noted above, in the 1978 reauthorization process. Indeed, the Commodity Exchange Act was amended to ensure that he could be removed as chairman. The act as originally adopted in 1974 did not by its terms allow the president to remove a chairman from office or to appoint another one until the incumbent chairman's term expired. The 1978 amendments, however, allowed the president to appoint a new chairman, and Bagley quickly exited after this legislation became a reality.[6]

Bagley's successor as chairman was James M. Stone, then thirty-one years old. Like Bagley, Stone had impressive academic credentials. He received his doctorate in economics at Harvard in 1973 and was a lecturer on economics there. He also served as a commissioner of insurance for Massachusetts and had authored a number of publications on economics and finance. Unfortunately, Stone's administrative skills and leadership abilities did not match his intellectual powers.

Stone was a rigid administrator, inflexible in his views, and he bore a definite anti-industry bias.[7] He was not popular at all with the CFTC staff, and morale plummeted to an all-time low.[8] In addition, his attacks on the industry only exacerbated an already deteriorating situation. The industry was particularly incensed by his exaggerated charge, which followed the events in the silver futures markets in 1980, that commodity futures speculation threatened the financial structure of the entire U.S. economy.

Stone's abrasive personality and regulatory posture also led to conflict with other commissioners. As a result, the Commission was often deadlocked on all but the most routine of Commission business, and the agency nearly ground to a halt.[9] In an attempt to break that deadlock, Stone and the Carter administration named Hugh Cadden, a bright and well-qualified CFTC staff member, to an open commissioner's slot. It was thought that this would give Stone a majority. Cadden, however, was too close to Stone, and the industry successfully mobilized to stop his confirmation, an unfortunate loss.

Stone's intensity also led to his hospitalization for exhaustion while chairman, and this further removed him from the decision-making process. Finally, with the election of Ronald Reagan, Stone, seeing the handwriting on the wall, submitted his resignation to President Carter as chairman, although he retained his position as an individual commissioner.[10] But the damage had been done.[11] For almost the first six years of its existence, the CFTC had no effective full-time chairman. It suffered greatly as a result.

This situation was corrected with the subsequent appointment of Phillip Johnson, a partner in the well-known Chicago firm of Kirkland & Ellis. Johnson, a graduate of the Yale Law School and an editor of the *Yale Law Journal,* had been outside counsel for the Chicago Board of Trade for many years. He had also authored a two-volume treatise on the Commodity Exchange Act and had published several law review articles concerning commodities regulation. Johnson was well acquainted with the intricacies of the business and the pitfalls of regulation. He also proved to be an effective administrator, and his appointment to the CFTC rescued it from the abyss into which it had fallen. Johnson restored staff morale, as well as congressional and industry confidence, and the agency began operating as a cohesive unit.

To be sure, Johnson did run into trouble with the industry when he unexpectedly announced a large package of Commission-sponsored amendments to the Commodity Exchange Act during the 1982 reauthorization process. Included in this surprise package was a bombshell, the "user fee" that would have required the industry to pay transaction costs that would in turn be used to pay for the operations of the CFTC. The industry believed it was bad enough to be saddled with the CFTC; it should not also have to pay for it. Intensive lobbying by the industry resulted in the defeat of that measure. It also cost Johnson some prestige, but certainly his accomplishments were still significant.

Unfortunately, Johnson cut his tenure at the Commission short to return to private practice after only two years. His replacement was Susan M. Phillips, who had previously been appointed as commissioner on November 16, 1981. The holder of a doctorate in finance, Phillips had served in the administration and the faculty at the University of Iowa. She was also previously an Economic Fellow at the Securities Exchange Commission and a Brookings Institute Economic Policy Fellow. Phillips had published numerous articles and had written a book entitled *The SEC And The Public Interest.* President Reagan used Phillips' appointment to the chairmanship as a means of diffusing charges that he had made an insufficient number of appointments of women. Whatever the success of that effort, Phillips was a well-qualified administrator, and her reign at the CFTC (with the exception of the brouhaha over the concentration rules resulting from the Volume Investors default) has been a peaceful one.

THE COMMISSIONERS

The individual commissioners at the CFTC have been a disparate group. The initial commissioners included Vice-Chairman John Rainbolt, who had steeped himself in the regulation of commodities while serving as counsel to the House Committee investigating the need to amend the Commodity Exchange Act in 1974. Rainbolt also acted as an effective liaison with congressional committees, at a time when the CFTC desperately needed a credible and knowledgeable lobbyist. Another individual commissioner was Read Dunn, who was also knowledgeable about the industry,[12] as was Commissioner Martin, the former chairman of the Chicago Board of Trade.[13] Although it might be thought that his experience prejudiced him entirely against regulation, Martin was in fact a strong supporter of enforcement actions against individuals abusing the marketplace. In fact, Martin was the sole commissioner voting in favor of suspending commodity options transactions before the occurrence of scandals that so badly tarnished the CFTC's image.

Gary Seevers, a conservative economist, and another of the first group of CFTC commissioners, applied himself to understanding the mechanics operations of the commodities markets and quickly became a knowledgeable and able commissioner.[14] He later served as vice-chairman of the CFTC and, for a time, as acting chairman of the CFTC after Bagley's resignation. His tenure as acting chairman was a period of calm and stability for the agency. Unfortunately, it was all too brief. After the White House delayed action on his reappointment, Seevers resigned to become a senior executive at Goldman, Sachs & Co. His replacement was James Stone.

There were differences in viewpoints and some indecision among the first group of individual commissioners and the chairmen. Bagley's failure to provide effective leadership exacerbated that situation. In addition, each of the individual commissioners had strong personalities and had his or her own definite views on the manner and nature of regulation. This, of course, compounded an already difficult situation. At times, decisions were not made promptly, if at all, and the staff was given little guidance on regulatory goals. The staff simply generated their own proposals and ideas in many cases and hoped for the best when they were submitted to the Commission.

In fairness, the commissioners were faced with a difficult, almost impossible task. As a collegial body they were required to make decisions, often under impossible time constraints and on matters that would have long-range effects on their successors and the industry that could not even be conceived. The commissioners had little guidance from past precedent and could depend only on their own instincts to chart a proper and unknown course. At the same time, they met with strong industry opposition against any regulation, whatever its form or reasonableness. To their credit, despite those trying conditions, they did establish the fundamentals of the regulatory scheme that now exists. It should also be noted that, despite their differences in view, they engaged in remarkably few personal attacks on each other.

Later commissioners had it much easier. Much of the CFTC's policies and regulatory schemes were established by the first group of commissioners. Precedent and experience were gained. Mistakes in the past were learned from, and future actions were guided by, the actions of that first group. Moreover, the group was faced from its inception with an onslaught of problems of unimaginable proportions, particularly the options scandals. They were also faced with a burgeoning, indeed exploding, industry that was developing new products at an unprecedented rate. Trading volume was increasing at rates heretofore unknown, and the economy was uncertain, causing wide price fluctuations, accompanying problems, and speculative fever. Consequently, it is doubtful that any group of individuals could have done better. Indeed, those individuals are to be commended for the public service they rendered under those trying and impossible conditions.

This first group of commissioners began breaking up following Bagley's beheading. Rainbolt was the first to go. He was replaced by David Gartner, who had helped steer the 1974 amendments to the Commodity Exchange Act through the Senate. But he quickly became a political liability, after the controversy over the gifts to his children by a prominent industrial figure.[15] He also created another storm of controversy when, in a regulatory first, he sued his fellow commissioners in an unsuccessful attempt to keep them from turning tapes of closed Commission meetings over to congressional investigators. Gartner eventually left the Commission when his term expired.

By 1982 all of the original commissioners had left the CFTC. Their replacements included Kalo Hineman, a representative for agricultural interests who had served in the OSS during World War II. Hineman was a cattleman and wheat farmer in Kansas, as well as a member of the Kansas legislature. Fowler West was also appointed in 1982. He had worked on Capitol Hill as staff director of the House Committee on Agriculture. Consequently, he was well versed in the CFTC's operations. William Seale, a former member of the faculty of the Department of Agricultural Economics at the University of Kentucky, took office in 1983. He had previously served as legislative assistant to Walter D. Huddleston, who was on the Senate Committee having oversight responsibility for the CFTC. Seale had also worked for a futures exchange (Commodity Exchange Inc.) and had a doctorate in agricultural economics.

The remaining commissioner, Robert R. Davis, took office in 1984. He had been a vice-president at the Harris Trust and Savings Bank of Chicago, where he specialized in macroeconomic analysis, monetary policy, and financial markets. Davis had also served as senior economist for the Joint Economic Committee of Congress and on the Federal Deposit Insurance Corporation's staff. He holds a doctorate in economics from Virginia Polytechnic Institute and had served on the Vanderbilt faculty.

The present group of commissioners is, for the most part, cohesive. But none of them are lawyers, a significant handicap in view of the fact that much of the CFTC functions are of a legal nature. Consequently, the CFTC's general counsel plays a vital role in the Commission's deliberations, becoming in effect a sixth commissioner.

THE OFFICE OF GENERAL COUNSEL

The Commodity Exchange Act was amended in 1974 specifically to provide for a general counsel to advise the CFTC. This was an important administrative step because, for the first time, the agency administering the Commodity Exchange Act could seek its own legal counsel. This avoided the delay and uncertainty of using the Department of Agriculture counsel, who had other responsibilities. The 1974 amendments also allowed the CFTC to represent itself in court. This too was an important step because it allowed the CFTC to formulate its own litigation tactics and strategies and to present its own views in court, undiluted by the bureaucracies at the Department of Justice, Department of Agriculture, or other agencies.

The CFTC's first general counsel was Howard Schneider. Initially all attorneys in the agency reported to him, except for those on the staff of the individual commissioners and chairman. Later, the Division of Trading and Markets and the Division of Enforcement were spun out of the general counsel's office, and those divisions were given their own attorneys. The general counsel's role then became one of adviser to the Commission and defender of the Commission in court, particularly in appeals from Division of Enforcement cases or Commission actions. As a consequence, the Office of General Counsel does not now formulate regulatory policy in any broad sense. Rather, it generally will review and advise the Commission on the policies and recommendations developed by other divisions and their legal implications. The general counsel has also been the Commission's liaison with the states. The general counsel is thus the chairman of the CFTC's advisory committee on state jurisdiction and responsibility, which is composed primarily of state securities administrators. Under the guise of this Committee, the CFTC's general counsel has assumed authority for determining whether particular off-exchange instruments are subject to CFTC regulation.

Another important function of the Office of General Counsel is to advise the Commission with respect to its administrative proceedings and to prepare its opinions in those proceedings. These include reparation appeals from the initial decisions of the CFTC's administrative law judges in reparations, as well as disciplinary proceedings. Those decisions are the principal basis for the CFTC to interpret the provisions of the Commodity

Exchange Act and to create a body of law on which persons subject to the statute may rely.

Still another function of the Office of General Counsel is to participate as *amicus curiae* (friend of the court) in actions where provisions of the Commodity Exchange Act will be interpreted. This participation is important because it ensures that the courts will have the views of the CFTC in mind when they decide the appropriate scope and applicability of the statute.

The Office of General Counsel has traditionally been one of the best-managed units of the Commission.[16] Kenneth Raisler, the current CFTC General Counsel, has been a particularly outstanding appointment. The success of this office has been due to its small size and limited scope, as well as good management and the personnel that was recruited. But it has had its shortcomings as well. The general counsel's review process has traditionally been a prime factor in delaying agency operations. For example, Division of Enforcement actions are reviewed by the General Counsel's Office, and this inevitably resulted in nit-picking and delay, as well as tension between the Division and the Office of General Counsel, which has diverted an incalculable amount of staff time and resources.

In addition, the Office of General Counsel in its early years tended to be somewhat arrogant and pompous, as well as extremely conservative in its views. The latter created problems when the Office of General Counsel was issuing so-called no action letters in which it interpreted the provisions of the Commodity Exchange Act. Those opinions were often so conservative, or so limited in scope and couched with so many reservations, that they provided little help to the industry in seeking to comply with the provisions of the Commodity Exchange Act. They were also so negative in their tone and took so long to obtain that the industry was reluctant to seek advice from the agency. In recent years, however, that function has been transferred for the most part to the Division of Trading and Markets, which is much more flexible and realistic in its approach to the need for the industry to obtain workable interpretations of the statute. As a result, this problem has been much alleviated.

The Office of General Counsel, however, continues to issue occasional interpretations that still tend to be negative, heavily "legalistic," and do not provide effective guidance on what is permissible. The office also continues to be concerned that any loophole in its interpretations will allow abuses to arise. As a result, its interpretations often sweep with too broad a brush. Consequently, such interpretations may be sought by the industry only as a last resort. The net effect has been to discourage people from seeking advice from the CFTC staff and to prevent or restrict important commercial business.

On the other hand, the accomplishments of the Office of General Counsel have been many. It was successful in the CFTC's appeal in the

Hunt soybean decision, so that the Seventh Circuit reversed the district court's decision denying injunctive relief to the Commission, and the court of appeals stated that disgorgement of the Hunts' profits could be sought by the Commission. The Office of General Counsel was successful in defending the CFTC in several actions involving the exchanges, including the March 1979 wheat emergency. It fought off numerous challenges brought by individuals who were subjects of Commission investigations or proceedings and successfully defended numerous attacks against CFTC rules and decisions. The Office of General Counsel was successful in its amicus participation in seeking to establish a private right of action under the Commodity Exchange Act.

It also had its litigation setbacks. For example, in *Wiscope S.A. v. CFTC,*[17] *supra,* the court of appeals reversed a Commission "special call" to a foreign broker because it had been sent to the wrong company. The office lost another important appeal against Lloyd Carr and Co. that could have resulted in stopping that firm at an early date. In that case, the CFTC had denied Lloyd Carr's application for registration, which would have provided a basis on which to more immediately enjoin its operations. Lloyd Carr appealed, represented by Skadden, Arps, Slate, Meagher, & Flom, a prominent New York law firm (this was at the time when his identity as an escaped felon was still unknown), and his appeal was successful. The Second Circuit reversed the CFTC because the CFTC administrative law judge had not permitted certain defense witnesses to testify, because they were three minutes late for the hearing as the result of flight delays caused by a snowstorm.[18]

The Office of General Counsel also lost on the issue of whether the CFTC could subpoena a foreign national located outside the United States. In that case, *CFTC v. Nahas,*[19] the Court of Appeals held that the Commodity Exchange Act, by terms, did not extend such investigative authority to the CFTC. The CFTC has sought legislation to reverse this decision. On the other hand, the office was successful in appeals for the CFTC's crackdown on off-exchange instruments; it successfully fought in the Supreme Court to establish the CFTC's right to question the attorney of a bankrupt futures commission merchant;[20] and the Supreme Court upheld the CFTC's authority to allow counterclaims in reparations proceedings.[21]

10
THE EXECUTIVE
DIRECTOR'S OFFICE

In creating the CFTC in 1974, Congress had envisioned that the executive director would have overall control of the CFTC's staff and program responsibility. Indeed, the House Committee on Agriculture published, in its report recommending the creation of the CFTC, an organizational chart, with all principal divisions of the Commission except the general counsel reporting to the executive director.[1] This was the primacy that was unsuccessfully sought by the CFTC's first executive director, Beverly Splane.

Splane was ill-equipped for a bureaucratic war of any dimension, much less the storms of controversy she encountered at the CFTC. Splane "had not had any significant first-hand management or executive experience prior to assuming the position of CFTC executive director"; she came to the CFTC from the White House where she had been an executive recruiter.[2] She found formidable opposition from Thomas Russo, head of the Division of Trading and Markets, and a former SEC staff member well acquainted with guerrilla and set-piece warfare in government bureaucracies.

Howard Schneider, as the general counsel, and William Schief, another former SEC staff member who headed the Division of Enforcement, as well as Mark Powers, a former Chicago Mercantile official who headed the Division of Economics and Education, were also aligned against Splane and her successor, Anthony McDonald. They were all strong willed and adamant that they be permitted to report to the Commission directly, which they did. The result was that the executive director had authority only over the relatively low civil service grade employees inherited from the CEA. This also meant that nearly all policy was being decided and programs administered by the newly created Divisions of Enforcement, Trading and Markets, and Education and Economics. The executive director was effectively sidelined. Indeed, the executive director's hold over former CEA employees was tenuous because they too would eventually have to be incorporated into the operating divisions.

Splane gave up after only a few months of bitter warfare, resigning on November 7, 1975, to accept a position at the Chicago Mercantile Exchange. Her successor, Anthony McDonald, fared no better. His management experience was also virtually nonexistent. It was found that in his prior jobs he had supervised one person, a secretary. He had also been the rather unsuccessful director of public relations for Nixon's Committee to Reelect the President (CREEP).

McDonald expressed his dissatisfaction with the executive director's role in the CFTC, and largely because of his discontent the Commission agreed, in November 1976, to restructure the Commission staff and give the executive director overall authority over the operating divisions. The staff rebelled. As was noted in a Senate hearing:

> One division head (the Chief Economist) refused to submit to the authority of the Executive Director and as a result his Division (the Division of Economics and Education) had to be restructured completely, leaving him with a largely consultative and advisory role. Other operating division heads continued their former pattern of reporting directly to the Chairman thereby increasing the frustration of the Executive Director and further straining his relationship with these individuals.[3]

Because he was unable to implement the authority delegated to him, McDonald left the agency on August 1, 1977. The executive director slot stayed open for several months, after the principal candidate for the position became the target of a Jack Anderson column and a *Washington Post* article that disclosed he had been under the "scrutiny" of two grand juries over the handling of his expense accounts while president of the San Francisco Bay Area Rapid Transit System. No wrongdoing was charged, but this apparently was enough to squelch his appointment.[4] Finally, a former CEA staff member, Donald Tendick, was appointed to the executive director position, and he did a thoroughly professional job in establishing and carrying out its present responsibilities. Tendick served for several years, but was eventually replaced by Susan Wagner, a political appointee. The present executive director is Molly Bayley.

Another problem confronting the initial executive director was a provision in the 1974 amendments that required her confirmation by Congress. President Ford had objected that this provision was unconstitutional, and it was deleted from the Commodity Exchange Act in 1978. In the meantime, some individuals challenged CFTC proceedings, claiming that the CFTC was acting improperly because it had not met the confirmation requirement. Those claims were rejected by the courts.[5]

In any event, the Office of the Executive Director is today responsible for a broad range of CFTC management matters. This includes personnel issues, including handling all Commission job actions, job classifications, employee grievances, equal employment programs, and training approvals. The Executive Director's Office has also developed the Commission's automated data processing systems, and conducted internal CFTC audits. It has established training programs of varying levels of sophistication for CFTC employees and other regulators, including foreign governments having an interest in the commodity markets. The Executive Director's Office has also acted to coordinate responses to the Government Accounting Office and to congressional inquiries requesting information on the agency's activities.

Another important administrative function of the office has been its management of the CFTC's Complaints Section, a part of the "Office of Proceedings." The Complaints Section reviews complaintants from the public who seek to institute reparations proceedings. This section initially reviews the complaints to ensure that they properly claim damages for a violation of the Commodity Exchange Act by a commodity professional registered with the CFTC. The Hearings Section (the other section of the Office of Proceedings) conducts the CFTC's formal evidentiary hearings in reparations and CFTC disciplinary proceedings. It is staffed with administrative law judges and hearing officers and their support staff.[6]

REGIONAL OFFICES

A problem that has plagued the CFTC from its inception has been the management of the field offices it inherited from the CEA. Those offices had been managed by individuals who reported directly to the CEA's last administrator, Alex Caldwell. In 1974, the principal regional offices of the CFTC were Chicago, New York, and Kansas City. The New York and Chicago regional offices were quite large and handled the bulk of the CEA's regulatory functions. The staff in these offices was intimately familiar with the commodity futures industry. Unfortunately, those offices were held hostage in the war between the new divisions and the Executive Director's Office. As a consequence, it took several years to integrate them into the CFTC.

The executive director thus sought control of the regional offices by having the regional directors (former CEA personnel), report directly to her, and the regional directors were made responsible for enforcement of the Commodity Exchange Act and administration of the programs of the CFTC in their respective regions. To fulfill this mandate the regional directors had various units operating under them. But each of these units was fulfilling the programs and directives of the three operating divisions in Washington (Enforcement, Trading and Markets, and Economic Analysis), to whom they did not report. This proved to be completely unworkable, particularly in the enforcement area, because there were no attorneys to develop cases and no means of establishing priorities for prosecution. The result was a bureaucratic nightmare. An attempt was made to alleviate this situation by appointing regional counsel to act as the Enforcement Division's representatives in the regions, but this too proved unworkable because the regional directors still sought to exercise program control. Finally, the division directors in Washington were given program authority over their operations in all of the regional offices, which eliminated the confusion about lines of authority.

Today the CFTC has regional offices in New York, Chicago, Washington, D.C., Kansas City, and Los Angeles, with a sub-office in Minneapolis. The Los Angeles regional office was previously located in San Francisco. That office had been initially established by the Commission's first chairman, William Bagley, principally to reflect his California origins and to dispense patronage. The West Coast, however, has traditionally been, and continues to be, a primary source of CFTC problems, particularly off-exchange instruments. Consequently, the California office deserves to be an important regional center for CFTC enforcement. To date, that has not occurred, principally because the office has traditionally been understaffed. Although many of the CFTC's important cases have arisen in that area, they are often prosecuted by the headquarters staff in Washington, D.C.

In any event, to ensure that there is nationwide responsibility and that responsibilities do not overlap, the CFTC regional offices have responsibility over specified regions. The staff breakdown for the regional offices in 1984 were: 107 employees in Chicago; 6 in California; 2 in Minneapolis; 8 in Kansas City; and 70 in New York. There is also a Southern Region office located in the CFTC's Washington, D.C., headquarters.

OTHER OFFICES

The CFTC has a number of other administrative offices that fall within the domain of the chairman's office. This includes the secretariat, which is responsible for managing the Commission's paperwork, a significant task. It also schedules and monitors Commission meetings, as well as formal Commission hearings. It processes all rule proposals, recommendations to the Commission, comment letters on proposed rules, and it receives and tracks correspondence to the Commission. It also maintains the Commission's agenda calendar and makes certain that all necessary paperwork is done so that the Commission can consider it fully before its scheduled meetings.

The secretariat's work may not seem as glamorous as that of the operating division's, but it was, and continues to be, an important part of the agency. It reduced the chaos of paperwork that was present at the initial stages of the Commission, as much as any other organizational control—(initially every staff member was making recommendations, or attempting to do so, directly to the Commission). The Secretariat stopped much of that confusion, and it made sure the Commission had adequate time to review proposals and establish a businesslike agenda. It has been a significant contribution to the Commission. Its first secretariat, the late Jane K. Stuckey, is responsible for that successful operation. She has been succeeded by Jean Webb.[7]

An apparently defunct office maintained by the chairman was the Office of Policy Review. It was an obscure body, whose exact function is unclear. It once described its role as follows:

> The Office of Policy Review ensures the consistency and effectiveness of Commission policies. It reviews and analyzes policy aspects of all major regulatory actions, assesses agency performance and effectiveness in accomplishing objectives and analyzes all budget and planning materials.[8]

This is, of course, vague, and its role was not clarified in subsequent years. This office appears to have disappeared some time after 1978, but its passing went unrecorded.

The CFTC's first chairman, William Bagley, also created two additional offices as a part of the chairman's office. They were the Office of Congressional Affairs and the Office of Intergovernmental Affairs. A congressional investigation found that these offices were overstaffed and that their functions could be better handled by the operating divisions. It was also found that the function of the Office of Intergovernmental Affairs was largely one of public relations. But this did not deter the CFTC, and these offices continued in one form or another until they were merged into an Office of Congressional and Governmental Affairs. The functions of the present office is to carry out provisions of the Commodity Exchange Act that require the CFTC to maintain communications with the Departments of Agriculture and Treasury, the Federal Reserve Board, and the SEC. It maintains communications with numerous other federal agencies interested in CFTC operations, as well as foreign governments. The congressional liaison office in the Office of Congressional and Governmental Affairs also maintains "an information-sharing network" with Congress to "contribute to the understanding of CFTC positions and Congress' concerns."[9]

Still another office administered by the chairman is the Office of Communication and Education Services. It is the result of a merger of two other offices, the Education Unit, which was a part of the Division of

Economics and Education, and the Office of Public Information. The Office of Public Information was charged as being a personal publicist for the CFTC's first chairman, William Bagley. The Office of Public Information issued press releases or "media advisories" on actions taken by the CFTC and handled general public inquiries. It was also responsible for the CFTC consumer hotline set up in response to the numerous fraudulent commodity options firms that began operating before the CFTC's suspension of option trading in 1978. In its first ten months of operation, the hotline received nearly 11,000 calls, virtually all of them options related. It later added a hotline in California.

One of the more important activities of the Office of Public Information involved its role in preparing CFTC Commissioner John Rainbolt to face the cameras on the CBS television program, *60 Minutes*. That program was directed at the CFTC's failure to regulate options trading adequately. A second segment on *60 Minutes* detailed how option boiler room operators expanded into other areas after the CFTC's suspension of options trading.

The office also prepared a 20-minute documentary film showing an overview of the commodity futures industry and the CFTC, and developed booklets for general distribution to the public, with titles such as *Farmers, Futures and Grain Prices* and *Economic Purposes of Futures Trading*. It also conducted a survey of college and university professors in 1978 and found that forty-eight of them offered courses focused primarily on futures trading, and that another fourteen courses were planned.[10]

Today, the Office of Communication and Education Services answers public and media inquiries on matters concerning CFTC regulations. It still prepares and issues the CFTC's press releases, and it prepares a quarterly newsletter entitled the *Education Quarterly,* which analyzes current events in the futures industry and CFTC regulations. It distributes another quarterly report entitled *AgReport,* which is directed at CFTC activities in the agricultural markets. The CFTC Office of Communication and Education Services also prepares a daily news digest for the CFTC and its staff. These are articles taken from newspapers, magazines, and other sources across the country and around the world that relate to CFTC matters. This service ensures that the CFTC and its staff are kept up to date on current events affecting the commodity futures market.

THE DIVISION OF ECONOMIC ANALYSIS

The Division of Economic Analysis has had a tortured past. It initially was named the Division of Education and Economics, and was headed by Mark Powers.[11] In December 1976, however, the Division of Education and Economics was abolished because its head refused to report to the executive director and because Powers wished to devote his efforts to economic research and long-range planning, without the burden of day-to-day market surveillance and analysis. Accordingly, an Office of Chief Economist was created for Powers that reported directly to the Commission. This office had seven economists. In addition, a new Division of Surveillance and Analysis was created, and it was made responsible for the day-to-day surveillance of trading on the exchanges. It also conducted the economic analysis of contract applications. A separate Office of Education was also established.

In 1978, in still another power struggle, the CFTC's organizational structure "was improved" through a merger of the offices of Surveillance and Analysis, Education, and Chief Economist into the Division of Economics and Education. This new division initially reported to the executive director, but by 1983 the division was reporting directly to the Commission. In 1984 it was renamed the Division of Economic Analysis, and its Education Unit was moved into the Chairman's Office of Communication and Education Services.

Despite this tangled history, this division and the Office of the Chief Economist have played an important role at the CFTC. The Office of Chief Economist was responsible for revising the definition of bona fide hedging for purposes of CFTC speculative limits, a very important part of the CFTC's regulatory controls. That office also worked with other divisions in formulating the CFTC's policy for determining whether accounts should be aggregated for speculative limit purposes, and it revised the CFTC's reporting requirements.

The chief economist prepared a report on the "spot committees" used by various exchanges to establish spot price quotations. It recommended that these committees be balanced between commodity buyers and sellers and that the CFTC should establish record-keeping requirements that would allow committee decisions on spot quotations to be reviewed, an issue the Justice Department was also examining. The chief economist conducted a study to determine the rate of defaults on forward contracts by agricultural producers. The report generated by the Office of Chief Economist found that there have been a few defaults on cash forward contracts in the major grains and cotton, *i.e.,* less than 1% of all United States farmers with annual gross sales greater than $10,000 were involved in a default in 1976. Thereafter, through a special appropriation of Congress, the Office of Chief Economist conducted a further study of defaults on agricultural forward contracts. The study concluded that federal regulation would not be cost effective because there had been a low rate of default.

This office also conducted two nationwide surveys in order to determine the number of farmers who were using the futures market. The office discovered that approximately 5 percent of all farmers with annual commodity sales of more than $10,000 used the commodity markets in 1977, and that at least 70 percent of that participation involved some speculative trading. This confirmed the findings of its earlier study conducted in 1976. The study found that large farm operations were more likely to use the markets: 11 percent of all farmers with gross annual sales in excess of $100,000, 18 percent of those in excess of $200,000, and 33 percent of all farmers with sales of $500,000 or more participated in the futures markets. It was also found that a number of producers, who did not themselves trade futures, followed futures prices during their planting periods, and that 80 percent of farmers using forward contracts indicated that forward contract prices were in some way based on futures prices.

The Office of Chief Economist also conducted a survey of participants in the financial futures markets. It found that there was a considerable use of the financial futures markets for hedging, particularly the new interest rate futures. It found that the participants in these markets included mortgage bankers, mutual funds, securities dealers, commercial banks, savings and loan associations, real estate developers, builders, and institutional investors, such as life insurance companies and pension funds.

In 1979 another survey of the financial futures markets was conducted by the Division of Economics and Education. Among other things, it found that floor traders, commodity trading advisers, and futures commission merchants who were not securities dealers held a higher proportion of the open interest in interest rate futures than any other occupational group trading these futures. Commercial traders accounted for nearly one-third of each side of the open interest in the 90-day Treasury Bill market. It also was discovered that securities dealers were using interest rates futures in conjunction with their cash market trading activities. They were found to be the most active commercial group in many of the interest rate futures markets. Commercial banks were also found to be using the financial futures markets (they maintained their largest positions in the 90-day Treasury Bill futures contract), and savings and loan associations were found to be holding large portions of the open interest in the GNMA contract. On the other hand, pension funds, employee benefit funds, and insurance companies were represented by only four traders in the interest rate markets. Two of these four indicated that they used the market solely to lock in yields on anticipated purchases of fixed-income securities. It was also found that foreign traders did not hold significant positions in the market.

The Office of Surveillance and Analysis also played an important part in the CFTC's formative years. It was responsible for maintaining surveillance over the commodity markets nationwide, and it was charged with informing the CFTC of potential and actual problems in the markets. The office accomplished that function through analyses of reports filed by large traders and through direct contacts with the exchanges and traders. It encountered numerous market problems that required Commission attention, most of which were resolved without the necessity of formal CFTC action.

It was the Office of Surveillance and Analysis (spearheaded by Britt Lenz) that uncovered the large Hunt positions that led to the CFTC's action against them, and this office was deeply involved in the 1976 Maine potato debacle and the problems encountered by the CFTC in the coffee market. Another emergency, which did not require formal CFTC action, was occasioned by the jump in orange juice prices caused by a severe freeze in 1977.

Still other market problems were encountered in soybean oil. There it was discovered that one trader owned a substantial portion of deliverable March 1978 soybean oil stocks. The Surveillance and Analysis staff (renamed the Division of Economics and Education) contacted that trader, as well as major short traders and the Chicago Board of Trade. The long trader was called before the Business Conduct Committee of the Chicago Board of Trade and, as a result of that pressure, the trader liquidated part of his positions on the last day of trading, and the futures expired smoothly. In another instance, a large long position in GNMAs in March 1978 resulted in pressure being placed on the trader by the CFTC staff, and that trader liquidated part of his position, allowing a smooth delivery process.

The Division also discovered serious problems in the 1978 lumber market, where there was a lack of available supplies to meet contract delivery specifications. The Surveillance and Analysis staff also found that there were some large traders in the markets that presented potential liquidation problems. The Division's economists contacted lumber mills, wood product dealers, and large traders to obtain available supply estimates and determine the delivery capabilities and intentions of the large traders. It also issued warnings to traders. In December 1978, the Chicago Mercantile Exchange took emergency action on the lumber contract by reducing its speculative position limits, and the contract was later revised by that exchange.

This did not end the CFTC's concerns with the lumber contract. The Chicago Mercantile Exchange added a new contract for lumber that would have significantly increased the deliverable supply of lumber (it added British Columbia lumber). But a strike by the British Columbia woodworkers presented a potential delivery problem in the July 1980 contract. Nevertheless, the contract expired without incident when lumber produced in the Northwestern United States did become available for delivery.

The Division also encountered problems in the 1979, 90-day Treasury Bill futures contract traded on the Chicago Mercantile Exchange. The staff's concern was based on the large open interest in that contract as delivery date approached. The future expired, however, with no liquidation problems, although there was a record number of deliveries.

Several other market problems were encountered in 1981. This included concerns with the 1980 cotton crop, which was small and of lower-than-normal quality. The Commission closely monitored the market because the long positions in the market were collectively larger than the certified stocks for delivery. To alleviate market congestion, the Cotton Exchange raised margins and limited trading to liquidation only. As a result, liquidation went smoothly. Problems were also encountered in oats, which had its smallest crop since 1881, and stocks were the lowest since records were first kept on those supplies in 1942. The CFTC staff worked closely with the Chicago Board of Trade and with traders in the market, and the contracts expired without problem. Similar problems were encountered in oats in the following year, but once again serious problems were avoided.

The Division also monitored the liquidation of the Chicago Mercantile Exchange's three-month Treasury Bill contract, which had grown in open interest tremendously during fiscal year 1981. The CFTC staff became concerned that there would not be a sufficient deliverable supply, because of the contract's narrow specifications. The Division's staff worked with the Exchange and the Federal Reserve and Treasury, and no apparent liquidation problems were encountered, even though large deliveries were taken.

In 1981 problems were encountered in feeder cattle, because of a reduced number of feeder steers being marketed and because of increased demand. The Division's staff was particularly concerned with the November 1981 contract, which had an abnormally large open interest that was not being reduced. The staff was also concerned with concentration of long positions in this contract, and the Chicago Mercantile Exchange declared a market emergency, ordering trading for liquidation only and taking other actions. As a result there was no market disruption.

Problems in pork bellies were encountered in 1981 because of supply shortages; storage stocks were one-half of the previous year's level and hog production was reduced. Consequently, there was substantial price volatility. Once again, the CFTC staff worked closely with the Chicago Mercantile Exchange, and potential congestion problems were avoided. At the same time, the live hog contract was presenting problems, because declines in hog production had resulted in historically high prices. The open interest in this contract was at a record high level. Its price volatility had attracted a large number of speculative traders, and the Division's staff worked closely with the largest traders to be sure that there were no congestion problems. The Division noted, however, that the market had become important in allowing cash forward sales of farmers' live hogs.

Problems were encountered, once again, in pork bellies in the liquidation of the August 1983 pork belly contract, after the price of that contract increased more rapidly than the price of cash pork bellies. The contract traded at an unusual premium over the cash price. Various rumors were also circulating as to delivery demands (e.g., it was rumored that a large bacon-slicing company was going to use the August future as a major source of supply and that a possible squeeze was developing). The Chicago Mercantile Exchange initially "jawboned" its members to prevent a disruption, but then it took more forceful action, declaring a market emergency and ordering reductions of positions and increases in margins.

The July 1983 corn futures contract also raised potential problems because of low corn supplies. The Division found that the futures positions of the major long traders were substantially greater than deliverable supplies. The amount of corn marketed was low because of heavy participation by farmers in the Department of Agriculture's farmer-owned reserve and payment-in-kind (PIK) program. Traders and brokers with large positions were contacted, sometimes on a daily basis, to ensure that liquidation was orderly. As a consequence, no serious problems developed.

In 1985 large commercial positions in the cocoa market raised CFTC eyebrows, and grain trading on the Chicago Board of Trade was closely monitored because government price support programs had reduced deliverable supplies. The Division also encountered problems in price volitality on days in which stock index contracts were expiring. This was apparently due to a phenomenon known as the "triple witching hour." This occurs when stock index options and futures expire simultaneously and arbitrageurs unwind their positions in these instruments, and in the underlying equities, resulting in price volatility on the options, futures, and stock exchanges. The SEC and CFTC are addressing this problem.

The Division also conducted studies for the Commission in the soybean market in 1983 and 1984, and prepared the CFTC's study of large livestock hedgers, as required by the 1982 amendments to the Commodity Exchange Act. This report found that commercial traders had contributed to two problem liquidations in the livestock market by standing for delivery in situations that did appear to be economically warranted. The Division also played a large role in the development of the CFTC's inside information study.[12]

11
THE DIVISION OF
TRADING AND MARKETS

The Division of Trading and Markets is the creation of Thomas Russo, who sought to model it after a division with similar responsibilities at the Securities and Exchange Commission. Russo had started at the CFTC as its deputy general counsel, under Howard Schneider. An ambitious and able attorney, Russo quickly acted to set up his own division, the Division of Trading and Markets. He also acted quickly to preempt the areas over which he wanted control, which included the bulk of the CFTC's substantive regulation. This included oversight responsibility for the exchanges, futures commission merchants, floor brokers, commodity pool operators, commodity trading advisers, and associated persons. Russo was also responsible for the creation of much of the substantive regulations eventually adopted by the CFTC, including its rules establishing financial responsibility requirements for futures commission merchants, registration requirements, contract market disciplinary actions, and customer protection. After Russo's departure, the Division continued to play a central role in the CFTC's operations.[1]

A principal function of the Division has been its review or approval of contract market rules. Under the 1974 amendments, the CFTC was required to review the existing contract market rules by August 18, 1975, or notify the exchanges that a review of their rules could not be done within that period, which the CFTC did for the existing rules of the exchanges. The CFTC adopted a rule that required the exchanges to enforce the exchange's rules then in effect and advised them that it would review their rules at a later date, which has never occurred. The Division then proposed and adopted a rule allowing exchanges to adopt temporary emergency rules without prior CFTC approval. This provision, however, required the exchanges to file all of their rules with the CFTC, including margin rules. Rules of the exchanges' clearing houses were also required to be submitted to the approval process, which did not sit well with the exchanges. The Chicago Board of Trade, in its first real offense against the CFTC, unsuccessfully sued the CFTC, contending that this provision exceeded the CFTC's authority. The Board of Trade contended that the CFTC did not have authority to review the rules of clearing corporations that were incorporated separately from the exchanges. In any event, the CFTC attempted to avoid delays in the process by broadly exempting from the approval process operational and administrative rules. But this did not avoid delays. Consequently, as noted above, the Commodity Exchange Act was amended in 1982 to streamline this process.

The Division ran into similar delay problems in the registration process for commodity professionals. It was responsible for reviewing applications and carrying out background checks through the FBI and other agencies.[2] But the Division was soon overwhelmed with the sheer magnitude of this task and fell far behind in processing applications. Registrants were often kept waiting months for their licenses. The industry, of course, was incensed by the delays and innumerable foul-ups that were occurring in registrations. An effort to computerize and streamline the process did not alleviate the problem. As a result, the Commodity Exchange Act was amended to provide temporary registration and otherwise reduce delays in this process, as well as to allow the National Futures Association to take over most registration functions entirely. After initial start-up problems with its computers, the NFA now appears to be handling this function smoothly.

Another prime area of responsibility for the Division of Trading and Markets was that of conducting audits of registrants. This was essentially a carryover function from the CEA and was largely staffed by former CEA personnel. The Division's initial audits were directed principally at futures commission merchants to ensure that they were meeting segregation and financial requirements. Audits were also conducted of exchanges' clearing houses and of exchanges with approved minimum financial requirements—initially, the Chicago Mercantile Exchange and the Chicago Board of Trade. The latter audits were to determine if the exchanges were guaranteeing that their members met segregation and minimum financial responsibility requirements. The Division would also conduct periodic audits of the firms, subject to the exchanges' requirements, to be sure they were meeting customer fund segregation requirements. Until the creation of the NFA, the CFTC also had primary audit responsibility for firms that were not members of exchanges with financial responsibility rules approved by the CFTC. When violations were found, the Division would issue warning or compliance letters to the registrant or refer the matter in more serious cases to the Division of Enforcement. A comprehensive Audit Program Guide for CFTC auditors was also prepared and published by the Division.

In 1978, as noted above, the CFTC adopted amendments to its financial responsibility rules that effectively shifted much of its audit burden onto certified public accounts; that is, it required brokerage firms to submit audited financial statements to the CFTC setting forth their financial condition and net capital compliance. The Division also began moving further away from conducting direct audits of registrants and toward audit oversight of self-regulatory organizations. In that regard, by 1980, all eleven existing commodity exchanges had uniform minimum financial rules. The CFTC also approved two joint audit plans designed to eliminate the burden on firms that had to meet the financial responsibility requirements of more than one exchange. The CFTC staff noted that without the joint audit programs, some futures commission merchants could have been subject to as many as ten self-regulatory audits. This shift in responsibility allowed the CFTC audit program to focus on non-exchange member firms and special problem firms, and to review the exchanges' enforcement of their financial responsibility rules, as well as examine commodity pools that were then proliferating around the country without any oversight body. The advent of the NFA further relieved the Division of direct audit responsibility over firms that were not members of exchanges.

In 1980 a new audit function was also created by the Division of Trading and Markets for "Front Office" compliance. This unit has the responsibility for reviewing sales and marketing practices and the handling of customers' accounts by brokerage firms, commodity pool operators, and commodity trading advisers. Its principal responsibility is to ensure that sales material and "marketing techniques" provide a fair disclosure of the risks and costs associated with commodity trading, and that front office operations are in compliance with CFTC requirements. In that regard, it examines customer accounts for evidence of churning and improper allocation of trades. It also reviews disclosure documents of commodity pool operators and commodity trading advisers.

The Front Office unit initially focused most of its resources on commodity pool operators and commodity trading advisers. In 1981 that effort resulted in the issuance of fifty warning letters and fifteen referrals to the Enforcement Division. Later, in 1983, it shifted its focus to exchange rule enforcement programs for commodity option sales practices. Its report on those programs recommended improvements in exchange programs, but found that the exchanges were generally carrying out their responsibilities. The unit also interprets CFTC regulations governing commodity pool operators and commodity trading advisers. In addition, it conducted an industry-wide survey of market research programs and methods of disseminating such advice and reviewed the sales practice oversight program of the NFA.[3]

As noted, the Division of Trading and Markets also plays an important role in the formulation of CFTC substantive rules. Spearheaded by Fred White, a former SEC staff member, the Division was the proponent of the initial package of CFTC customer protection rules. As discussed above, those rules, however, ran into the shoals of industry opposition and only a few of the rules were eventually adopted. In proposing those rules, the Division had obtained the support of the Commission's Advisory Committee Commodity Futures Trading Professionals, which had several industry representatives. That effort at diplomacy, however, was unsuccessful when industry opposition arose after the full package of rules was exposed for public comment and only a few were adopted. More successfully, the Division played a central role in formulating the regulations adopted by the CFTC for "dual trading": that is, rules regulating the condition under which floor brokers can trade for their own accounts as well as customers, and standards for the handling of orders by futures commission merchants. Still another area of rulemaking by the Division was regulations for commodity trading advisers and commodity pool operators, which included various exclusions from registration requirements. More recently, the Division implemented a rule to allow investment companies registered with the Securities and Exchange Commission and certain other regulated entities to be excluded from registering as commodity pool operators, provided they meet various criteria. The Division was also instrumental in establishing regulations for the pilot program for exchange-traded options, "final" interim rules for leverage contracts, exchange-traded options on agricultural commodities, and bankruptcy rules for futures commission merchants.

The Commodity Exchange Act requires the exchanges to enforce their rules, and CFTC regulations require an "affirmative action" program to ensure such enforcement is effective and that due diligence is used by the exchanges. The Division of Trading and Markets in turn conducts periodic reviews of exchange rules enforcement programs to ensure their efficiency, and the Division prepares reports of those reviews. The first such rule review report concerned the five New York exchanges.[4] A number of serious deficiencies were found, and the exchanges were so notified. These included the lack of an adequate staff and record-keeping requirements. After the Division's report its director, Tom Russo, met with the exchanges, as did the Commission itself. It was found from these meetings that, while the situation had not been corrected after the first Division warning, the exchanges, on the whole, were taking measures they believed would lead to more effective rule enforcement.

Thereafter, the Kansas City Board of Trade was examined and deficiencies were found, and Division representatives met with exchange officials to correct those deficiencies. The Division stated that these reviews "confirmed a belief that an effective rule enforcement program is the product of the attitude of exchange governing bodies." The Division, therefore, began examining the governing boards of the exchanges "with a view toward broadening their base of representation."[5] Several exchanges, thereafter, did add public members to their board of directors. Nevertheless, even after he left office, Russo continued to call for still greater diversity in the representation on exchange boards, which are often effectively controlled by the traders on the floor, to the detriment of commission houses and the public. In an article in the *New York Times,* Russo pointed out that 50 percent of the board members of the major stock exchanges are composed of public members, while only 26 of 217 commodity exchange directors were public representatives.[6] A rule review of the Chicago Board of Trade also led the Division to conclude that the Board of Trade's "cavalier approach to rule enforcement makes a mockery of self-regulation."[7]

The Division's rule reviews also led to enforcement actions. A review of the Pacific Commodity Exchange, which principally traded palm oil, was directed to correct deficiencies in its rule enforcement program; it failed to do so, and a proceeding was commenced to revoke the exchange's designation as a contract market. As a result, the exchange terminated its operations. A review of the operations of the Mid-America Commodity Exchange disclosed conflicts of interest and differences in its enforcement program. An enforcement proceeding was brought and a $50,000 civil penalty was imposed against the exchange. The exchange was also required to have a new president, to add "public" (non-member) directors to its board of directors, to create an advisory committee (with at least three public members) to advise the exchange on its management, and to employ an adequate and trained enforcement staff.[8] In contrast, a rule review of the Chicago Mercantile Exchange in 1977 revealed that its enforcement program was the most effective reviewed to that date, and the staff made little criticism of its operations.

These and subsequent rule reviews led to a significant overall improvement in the exchanges' rule enforcement programs. Much credit is to be given for this to Donald R. Levine, now an attorney with E. F. Hutton, who headed the Rule Enforcement Unit in the Division of Trading and Markets for several years. The Division of Trading and Markets was allowed by this improvement to change the focus on its rule enforcement reviews in 1980 "from consideration of overall enforcement programs to review of selected program aspects . . . in greater depth."[9] Several such reviews are conducted each year. One was conducted of the two emergency actions ordered by the Commodity Exchange Inc. (Comex) during the rapid rise and fall of silver prices in 1980. This review resulted from charges by Nelson and Herbert Hunt that members of the Comex's board had market positions that improperly influenced their actions in imposing restrictions on the silver market, which the Hunts believed resulted in the collapse in prices. After examining the positions of various board members, the Division concluded that the exchanges' approaches to such problems could result in a perception of conflict of interest. No evidence was found, however, that the exchange's actions were taken in bad faith. A later, voluminous CFTC report, completed some six years after the events in the silver market, also determined that the exchanges and the members had acted properly.

A review of emergency actions ordered by the Chicago Board of Trade during the liquidation of the March 1979 wheat futures contracts also led the Division to conclude, once again, that, "at a minimum," there could be "a perception of conflicts of interest among individuals charged with decision making responsibility."[10] Specifically, it was charged by the *Washington Post,* and other newspapers, that the vice-chairman of the Chicago Board of Trade, Leslie Rosenthal, sat in on policymaking discussions by the exchanges' board of governors, where they considered what action should be taken in the March 1978 wheat contract. Rosenthal did not participate in the discussions, but he and one of his partners were two of the four persons controlling some 90 percent of the March wheat contracts, which "put the four in a position to corner the wheat market and drive up the price."[11] As a result of these concerns, the Division sought public comment on the adequacy of contract market rules governing procedures for board or committee members to follow when a potential conflict of interest exists.

Still other rule reviews found differences in the market surveillance program of the New York Coffee, Sugar and Cocoa Exchange, the New York Cotton Exchange, and the Commodity Exchange, Inc. A review in 1984 also led the Division to conclude, once again, that the Chicago Board of Trade was not in compliance with the Commodity Exchange Act. This led to a storm of protest by the Board of Trade, and a hurried follow-up report found that the exchange had adopted most of the Division's recommendations for improvement. In fact, the Division "commended" the Board of Trade for its "commitment toward implementation of an 'on-line' trade practice surveillance system and a computerized large trader reporting system."[12]

Reviews in 1984 of the Chicago Mercantile Exchange, the New York Mercantile Exchange, the Mid-American Commodity Exchange, the New York Futures Exchange, and the Kansas City Board of Trade found no significant problems. The Kansas City Board of Trade, however, was the target of an enforcement action brought by the CFTC's Division of Enforcement for failing to prevent wash trading that was being conducted for the purpose of "chumming"; that is, wash trades were conducted in order to increase the volume on the exchange in a new stock index contract. Such trading was done so that the contract would appear more liquid than a competing contract on the Chicago Mercantile Exchange. Without admitting or denying the allegations of the complaint, the Kansas City Board of Trade consented to a civil penalty of $60,000. Two actions were also brought against the Commodity Exchange, Inc. for failing to enforce its rules. In one, the exchange consented, without admitting or denying the allegations, to a civil penalty of $70,000. In 1985 the Comex was also the subject of a CFTC enforcement proceeding for its actions in connection with the Volume Investors default discussed *supra,* which the exchange is contesting. A civil penalty of $200,000 was imposed against the New York Mercantile Exchange in 1981 and its designation as a contract market for certain commodities was revoked as the result of its failure to prevent fictitious trading.

The Division of Trading and Markets took up the responsibility for trade practice investigations such as those conducted by the CEA. It too was criticized in Congress, in 1978, for conducting an inadequate number of such investigations. These investigations included a review of the Comex's "switch" session, which later resulted in the disapproval of the Comex rule allowing that practice. This was the first exchange rule ever disapproved formally by the CFTC. The switch sessions were trading sessions conducted after regular trading in gold and silver futures. During this session, spread trades could be conducted in a noncompetitive manner. This was convenient for persons engaging in so-called "tax straddles," because it allowed them to trade with little economic risk. Indeed, such straddles accounted for some 75 percent of the Comex's business at times. In disapproving this rule, the CFTC required all spread trading to be competitive during the Comex's regular trading hours.

The number of trade practice investigations by the Division has increased from six in 1978, to forty in 1980, and to seventy-five in 1982. These investigations resulted in various letters of referral to the exchanges or to the Division of Enforcement. For example, in 1983 the findings of sixty-five trade practice investigations were so referred. These referrals resulted in the issuance of several formal orders of investigation. Fifteen of these investigations involved more than 200 traders who were not properly registered as floor brokers. Action was brought and over $180,000 in fines was collected.[13] In another trade practice investigation, the Division examined exchange audit trail systems and compared them to those in the securities industry. After reviewing the report, the Commission directed the Division to prepare rules requiring the exchanges to implement a complete audit trail, including execution time.

The Division, in recent years, has also been more vigorous in altering and disapproving exchange rules. In addition to the Comex switch sessions disapproval, it altered the rules of the Chicago Board of Trade and Chicago Mercantile Exchange when they added trading cycles to their contracts without CFTC approval. It also initiated proceedings to disapprove rules governing the determination of settlement prices on the Chicago Board of Trade, the Chicago Mercantile Exchange, the Comex, and the New York Mercantile Exchange. Another disapproval and rule alteration proceeding was directed at the arbitration rules of the Chicago Board of Trade, which did not require exchange members to submit disputes with customers to arbitration. The exchange sought to enjoin the CFTC action, but the Seventh Circuit ruled that the issue was not "ripe" for adjudication.

In 1983 the Chicago Board of Trade was the target of still another disapproval proceeding. This action was the result of an effort to prevent the large brokerage houses from simply hiring floor brokers at a salary much less than what they were being paid on a per trade basis. This exchange rule typifies what has been endemic to futures exchanges—the floor members' concentrated numbers often allow them to control the exchange's government, and they pass rules for their own immediate benefit, even if it adversely affects the brokerage firms who provide their order flow.

The Division of Trading and Markets also performs an important function of answering questions from the public and persons regulated by the CFTC. They are the principal source of information and interpretations on the CFTC requirements. The staff is, almost inevitably, quite willing to discuss informally, or formally, proper methods for compliance and are invaluable to persons in need of interpretative advice. They are not in any way as rigid and formal as the Office of General Counsel. Although, of course, serious policy issues may delay responses and interpretation may not be forthcoming where policy is in flux. Nevertheless, to the extent possible, the Division staff is generally helpful. Much credit for this must be given to its present director, Andrea Corcoran. In 1984, for example, the Division of Trading and Markets responded to some 2,000 inquiries regarding commodity pool operators and commodity trading advisers alone. It also prepared eighty-five responses to formal requests for interpretation for exemption from rules governing those entities.

Still another important function of the Division of Trading and Market is the role it plays in the approval of futures contracts. Under the Commodity Exchange Act, such contracts must be approved by the CFTC before they can be traded. The responsibility for reviewing such contracts for approval is shared between the Division of Trading and Markets and the Division of Economic Analysis. The CFTC's extended review process has drawn much industry criticism in the past. These delays have been the result of CFTC concerns on the economic effect of new contracts, their susceptibility to manipulation and, in early stages, the proliferation of identical contracts that could cause liquidity problems when volume is split up between several exchanges. The CFTC broke this logjam by essentially adopting the view that the marketplace, not the CFTC, should judge the economic viability of futures contracts.

One of the highest-visibility contract market approvals was the CFTC's approval of the international link between the Chicago Mercantile Exchange and the Singapore International Monetary Exchange, a process in which the Division played a principal role. This link establishes a "mutual offset" system that effectively allows traders to conduct trading during extended trading hours when one of the other exchanges is open.[14]

12
THE DIVISION OF ENFORCEMENT

The Division of Enforcement was intended to be the CFTC's fighting arm. But in its first several years of existence, the Division was anything but that. Plagued with management problems, lack of resources, a tidal wave of problems in options and other off-exchange instruments, as well as the need to develop a body of case law virtually from scratch, the Division was stymied. Nevertheless, the Division, virtually from the outset, began to develop a far-reaching body of law and challenged widespread market abuses that had heretofore been unchecked by federal regulators. In so doing, the Division confronted some of the largest and most well-established market operators, and it established a body of law that will guide futures regulation in years to come. Substantial progress has been made in recent years, and it is now fast becoming an effective enforcement unit. Nevertheless, many problems, particularly the fairness of its procedures, remain to be resolved.

The Division's first director was William Schief, a former SEC regional administrator. Schief was an experienced and able litigator who was unafraid to do battle with the industry's stalwarts. He was not, however, an administrator capable of handling the multitude of administrative and "political" problems that were thrust upon him—nor was any other person, living or dead, so endowed. Nevertheless, with virtually no resources, Schief laid the groundwork for the Division's present structure. Among his first recruits were John Schobel, who was carrying much of the load in the Division of Trading and Markets, and a CFTC Commissioner's legal assistant. They did enforcement work on a temporary basis in their spare time, which was precious little. Their temporary assignments included prosecution of the first CFTC injunctive action, the American Options Corporation case. They even cornered Harold Goldstein, the notorious options dealer, for a deposition. Harold, fresh from jail, was an experience not to be forgotten.[1]

Also joining the Division from its inception, but as a full-time player, was Hugh Cadden. Cadden was an experienced and highly talented trial lawyer, and he became one of the bright stars on the CFTC staff. He, too, joined the options fray, as well as complicated manipulation and fraud cases. He later became the CFTC's regional attorney for California and still later deputy director of the Division.[2] Other early appointments included Donald Weiss, a former SEC staffer, Michael Koblenz from the Justice Department, Darryl Dandy from the Department of Agriculture, Nate Fishkin, Alan Freedman, and William O. Hoar.

One of the first problems encountered by Schief was the integration of the CEA Compliance Division staff into the Division's structure. None of the CEA staff were lawyers, yet they insisted on preparing their own cases, submitting them through the regional director, then to the executive director, and finally to the director of Enforcement for review, after which the Office of General Counsel would conduct still another review. This multilevel review process was simply too cumbersome and proved to be completely unworkable, since the cases would generally have to be reinvestigated by Division attorneys who would try the cases. Nevertheless, the CEA investigators were, almost without exception, totally resistant to working directly for Division attorneys in investigating cases, viewing this to be a usurpation of their roles.[3] They therefore commenced guerilla warfare against the Division, utilizing every opportunity to criticize the work and investigative techniques of the Division's attorneys, even testifying against the Division and supplying information to opposing parties. It was an unhappy and completely unworkable situation that Schief was powerless to correct under the division of authority that then existed.

There were also serious management problems in the CEA staff, particularly in the CFTC's Chicago office. There, it was charged, the Compliance staff had completely bogged down under bureaucratic restrictions, and Bagley directed an internal audit to be conducted of that operation. The audit team was headed by James South, a consultant on leave from the Department of State who was well versed in governmental operations and experienced in government management. This audit (the "South Report") was submitted to Bagley and later to Congress. The South Report painted a very unhappy picture of the Chicago regional office. It found conditions there were seriously hampering the enforcement efforts of the Division. The report found undue delays in the supervisory review of investigative reports, warning letters were being issued with little or no follow-up, training of personnel was inadequate, sworn testimony was not being obtained, the staff was being frustrated in obtaining information from brokerage firms, and subpoenas were not being used to obtain information. Morale was also poor.

Efforts were made to improve the situation, but the divided chain of reporting authority frustrated that effort. Later, regional counsel were added to the regional offices as Enforcement Division representatives. The regional counsel, at least initially, still faced a bifurcated command structure, but they eventually were able to organize the former CEA Compliance Unit's efforts and integrate those resources into the Division. Meanwhile, the Division had also continued its efforts to add seasoned litigators to its staff, including Lloyd Kadish and Robert Boraks, two excellent trial lawyers. Although these individuals were highly individualistic and unwilling to submit in the long term to the bureaucratic restrictions of a government agency, they did provide much-needed expertise and muscle. They also were responsible for litigation that became an important part of the "body of law" administered by the CFTC.

Another internal audit of the Division was conducted in 1976, and it was highly critical of the Division, although it noted that substantial improvements were being made. Among other things, it was found that training for Division personnel was inadequate, and the role of the investigators and lawyers had still not been articulated. Administrative procedures and investigative files were found to be especially poor. A still later review conducted by the Surveys and Investigations Staff of the House Appropriations Committee found little or no effort had been made to correct the deficiencies in the 1976 internal audit of the Division. It was also charged that inadequate delegation of authority by the Division director had reduced the Division's effectiveness.

In fact, the Division had made substantial efforts to organize itself effectively. Experienced attorneys such as Lloyd Kadish (Chicago) and Hugh Cadden (San Francisco) were appointed as regional counsels. A deputy director for the Division was hired from the SEC. He was Michael Stewart, a gravel-voiced, hard-driving, and very capable attorney, who had served as regional director of most, if not all, of the SEC regional offices and in its General Counsel's Office. He began immediately to bolster morale and provide needed credibility with the Commission. Stewart also took the lead role in the Hunt soybean litigation, but in the middle of the Hunt trial he quit the agency. Disgusted with the internal bickering at the CFTC, Stewart returned to the SEC. In doing so, he turned down numerous blandishments from Bagley designed to induce him to stay, including an around-the-world trip and his pick of any job in the agency. His loss was sorely felt by the Division.

Much of the blame for the Division's problems was visited unfairly on Schief. He, too, resigned, and was replaced by Jack Field, a former U.S. attorney.[4] He brought staff with him from West Virginia to the CFTC, who were promptly dubbed the "Highway Patrol." Hugh Cadden was appointed as the Division's deputy director, and Richard Levie was named the Division's new chief counsel. Three new assistant directors were also appointed, and a new associate director was hired.

Another internal review was then commenced by the Division. Administrative deficiencies were still found to be prevalent, but some progress was made in integrating the CEA investigators. A reorganization of the

Division was also undertaken in November 1977. Among other things, a new assistant director was given responsibility for training and development of investigator programs, as well as effecting coordination with the "Chief Regional Investigators." A new record-keeping system was created to catalog complaints. This reorganization also established functional units in Washington to handle different types of cases: Trading and Markets, Trade Practices, Options, and Manipulations/Special Investigation. The units were each staffed by at least three persons and operated under an assistant division director.

The Trading and Markets Unit was established to handle registration denial cases, financial responsibility requests, and record-keeping violations. It brought forty-six registration denial cases in its first year. The Trade Practice Unit, on the other hand, had responsibility for fraud cases and "abusive" trading practices. But this unit was diverted from its principal functions during its early years when it was thrown into the options wars.

The Options Unit was assigned the impossible task of fighting the spreading London options problems. A flavor of the type of boiler room operations discovered by the CFTC in the Miami area can be found in *CFTC v. Crown Colony Commodity Options, Ltd.*[5] There, options were sold in two evening shifts using the facilities of a wigs and chemical sales operation that operated during normal working hours. Sales personnel were given little or no training on the rules or mechanics of options trading. Rather, they were instructed on sales techniques designed to stimulate the greed of the "mooches" (prospective customers). The Option Unit's biggest operation was a "mini-strike" force sent to fight a wave of boiler shops in an area of Miami that became known as "Maggot Mile" as a result of the activities of these firms. Over twenty cases were brought by the task force. The suspension of Options Trading by the CFTC in 1978 led to the termination of the Options Unit.

The Division's Manipulation/Special Investigation Unit, as its name suggests, was responsible for manipulation cases. This unit took over the personnel of the Options Unit. It also assumed responsibility for off-exchange instruments, which resulted in several cases against options firms that continued to sell options illegally under the guise of "deferred delivery" contracts.

Still another reorganization occurred in 1980. The Division director was then given program and administrative control over enforcement operations in the regions. Two new sections were created, each headed by deputy division directors. One such section was the Market Integrity Section. This section handled exchange-related violations, and it included a Manipulation and Trade Practices Unit, supplanting the Manipulation/ Special Investigation Unit. This section also included a Rule Enforcement Unit. A Customer Protection Section was also created, principally to handle sales practice-type violations and off-exchange instrument problems.

In 1983 the Division's organization became somewhat fuzzy. Several units were operating, including a special unit to handle the investigation arising out of the events in the silver market in 1979-1980. In addition, in 1984, a State/Federal Liaison Unit was established to provide technical and legal assistance to federal and state law enforcement agencies in the investigation and presentation of commodity-related offenses. The other units included Manipulation and Special Operations, Multi-District Fraud, and Rule Enforcement.

The ever-changing structure of the Division is a reflection of the continuing changes in its leadership. Jack Fields' tenure was not an extended one. He was replaced by Thomas Loughran. Loughran, an aggressive attorney and a former SEC staff member, was also given too little resources to fight the fly-by-night commodity operations that seemed to spring up everywhere. To his credit, he continued the process of building the staff and stabilizing the Division's management, as well as the commencement of several important cases. He was responsible for several successful actions, including a settlement of the Hunt soybean litigation with a record $500,000 fine.

Loughran was a disciple of Stanley Sporkin (the fire-breathing enforcement chief at the Securities and Exchange Commission), and he was soon at odds with the Commission. His successor was Dennis Klejna, a Division staff attorney who had worked his way up through the ranks. He had previously headed the coffee investigation, drawing the ire of large segments of the industry. He also caused the near apoplexy of the State Department and a foreign government official he served with a CFTC subpoena while the official was visiting the United States. Klejna, a no-nonsense attorney, has had a remarkable acuity for avoiding the bureaucratic pitfalls at the CFTC. His tenure as Division director is setting longevity records. With legislation allowing the states to pursue the off-exchange operations, Klejna has also been permitted to pursue market abuses and fraudulent practices that have long been neglected. At the same time, the Division has accrued substantial resources, and its presence in the industry is now being felt.

THE OPTION WARS REVISITED

Much ink has already been spent on the CFTC's options battles, but their adverse effect on the Enforcement Division cannot be overstated. The CFTC's initial cases were settled by consent or were easy victories. But it then began to encounter serious opposition with firms selling so-called London commodity options. The first such instance was J. S. Love & Associates Options Ltd. A fast and furious investigation was conducted of this company, after the CFTC received numerous complaints concerning its operations. The investigation found wholesale fraud being committed.

For example, its marketing brochure displayed a picture of a yacht, in an attempt to suggest that fabulous profits could be made from options. But CFTC investigators dispatched to the scene discovered that the yacht was actually a rather broken-down tub that had been wrecked by one of the salesmen who, after a drunken outing, rammed it forward at top speed into its dock. This particular salesman operated out of his home. Tended there by an incredibly attractive wife, who he had obtained from a newspaper advertisement, this salesman successfully solicited hundreds of thousands of dollars from investors while reading hot news to them off a ticker tape he had fitted to roll across his bed.

The company agreed to an injunction and was placed in receivership. Nevertheless, a sales manager took the case to trial and was successful in escaping the CFTC's requested injunctive relief, even though violations were found. This gave added hope to other options entrepreneurs who began an all-out resistance to the CFTC.

One such firm was British American Commodity Options, which was headed by John Forma. The CFTC first tried to obtain an injunction to require it to stop business, until it was registered as a commodity trading adviser. The district court, in a decision reported jointly with the J. S. Love decision, declined to do so, stating that this was an unfair burden on the company. Much later, the Court of Appeals reversed the decision, and an antifraud injunction was also obtained by the CFTC. In the meantime, the expenditure of Division resources was enormous, and the company was able to operate without restraint.

No less frustrating was Lloyd Carr, the largest of the London options firms. The chronology is telling. In January 1977, Lloyd Carr's company applied for required registration as a futures commission merchant (it had previously been registered as a commodity trading adviser). Lloyd Carr's application for futures commission merchant registration was aggressively challenged by the Enforcement Division staff, because they had determined that the company was operating without being registered. The company then informed the CFTC that it would not submit to audit or allow its records to be inspected, rejecting all regulation. In February 1977, the CFTC instituted formal administrative proceedings to deny the required registration. It also brought an action in Boston to enjoin the company from violating CFTC registration requirements, which would have put it out of business, and to appoint a receiver. At this time the company was just starting its rapid expansion. The district court denied the requested relief, pending the CFTC's decision on whether to grant registration.

One month later, in March 1977, a CFTC administrative law judge held expedited hearings on the company's registration application, and in April 1977 rendered his decision, denying registration and imposing a civil penalty of $120,000. Lloyd Carr unsuccessfully sought to enjoin that action. It also appealed the administrative law judge's decision to the CFTC itself.

The CFTC affirmed the denial of registration in August 1977, and Lloyd Carr's attorneys appealed that decision to the Second Circuit. Lloyd Carr also brought an appeal in the Second Circuit to challenge the Commission's new options regulations and from there he went to the Supreme Court, all at a time when he was an escaped felon.

In August 1977, the CFTC returned to the district court in Boston to renew its request for injunctive relief. That request was denied. In September 1977 it made still another request, after a decision in the Second Circuit against British American that required an injunction against a commodity options firm operating without registration. That request was denied a third time by the Boston court. The CFTC then petitioned the First Circuit to require the Boston judge to enter injunctive relief. In November 1977 the First Circuit advised the CFTC that it declined to do so.

The Division of Enforcement, led by Robert Boraks, then joined with the Michigan state securities authorities to obtain an antifraud injunction against Lloyd Carr. The Michigan federal judge, Noel Fox, quickly granted that request and ordered that the CFTC be given access to Lloyd Carr's records. But this was not the end of the drama. In December 1977 the Massachusetts Division of Securities raided Lloyd Carr's headquarters and issued a cease-and-desist order against further Massachusetts securities law violations. Shortly afterward, however, the Second Circuit reversed the CFTC denial of Lloyd Carr's registration, remanding the case for a new hearing on the ground that the CFTC administrative law judge had refused to allow Lloyd Carr witnesses to testify because they were three minutes late for the hearing.

At about the same time, the CFTC sought to hold Carr and others in contempt of the Michigan federal district court because fraud violations were continuing. Carr was arrested and released over the CFTC's objection under a $100,000 cash bond, after being fingerprinted. The results of the fingerprint check came back a few days later. It disclosed that Carr was actually Alan Abrahams, a felon who had escaped from a New Jersey prison. His record was an illustrious one. It included convictions for forged checks; he was also wanted for federal parole violations and for passport fraud in Canada. In addition, Abrahams had previously been arrested on a fugitive warrant in Bermuda and had talked the U.S. Consul there into posting bail for him. Abrahams forfeited that bond and fled the island.

Abrahams fled once again after his arrest by the CFTC. A worldwide search was launched after it was learned that he had transferred $3 million out of the country and that he had some 50 bank accounts, many of them located outside the United States. Within a month, Abrahams was in custody once again as the result of dedicated efforts by the FBI. He was apprehended in a luxury hotel in Tarpon Springs, Florida, where he had taken refuge after dyeing his hair to conceal his identity. Despite the efforts of his attorney, F. Lee Bailey, Abrahams was returned to prison. It was only after the publicity following Abrahams' arrest that the District Court in Boston issued an injunction and placed the company in receivership. Customer losses were in the amount of some $50 million.

The Lloyd Carr case drained the Division of Enforcement's resources. But it was only the tip of the iceberg. An options case against Rosenthal and Co. in Chicago was also hotly contested. That firm, headed by Leslie Rosenthal, who was subsequently to become the chairman of the Chicago Board of Trade, spent almost $500,000 fighting the CFTC. The CFTC in turn spent some $1.5 million and 50 staff-years on options-related cases in 1977, 20 percent of the operating time and personnel of the agency. It was also receiving some 600 options-related reparations cases, which completely backlogged that procedure.

The Division did successfully obtain injunctions against some sixty options firms, and put some fourteen companies out of business in 1977. But by early 1978, when the CFTC decided to suspend options trading, there were still some thirty-eight firms selling options. Thirty of those were under active investigation for apparent violations of the Commodity Exchange Act. Those thirty firms and the ones sued by the CFTC, most of which were boiler room operations, had over 120 branch offices and some 4,000 salespersons.

The suspension of options trading stopped the spiraling growth of the options firms, but many simply renamed their products "deferred delivery" contracts. The Division had better success in curbing those subterfuges. In doing so, it initiated almost thirty cases involving sixty companies and over 100 individuals. In one options ban violation case brought against First Commodity Corp. of Boston, total civil penalties of $335,000 were imposed against individual respondents. In addition, the firm agreed to establish a fund of $600,000 to compensate customers and an injunction was obtained. A special counsel was also required to review the firm's operations and to prepare a report to the Commission. Despite those actions and subsequent legislation allowing the states to bring actions against firms dealing in off-exchange instruments, such operations continue to be a problem for the Division, although a much smaller one. The CFTC began cooperative efforts with the states to attack remaining off-exchange boiler rooms in 1984, including the states of Arizona, California, Kansas, and Missouri. In one action, the CFTC and the state of New York named sixty-six individuals and firms as defendants. Working with government authorities in California, it also led a concerted attack against off-exchange boiler room operations in Southern California.

TAX STRADDLES

The South Report on the Chicago office had uncovered serious problems. But the audit also found that some very serious investigations were under way. Leslie Jordan, a CEA investigator inherited by the CFTC, was conducting an investigation of what appeared to be bogus trades on the Chicago Mercantile Exchange. Her investigation was quickly broadened by two CFTC attorneys, Donald Weiss and Nate Fishkin, and their efforts led to a massive effort by the U.S. government to suppress tax evasion and avoidance schemes in commodity futures that were costing the government large amounts of tax revenues. The Internal Revenue Code was also amended in 1982 to prevent such abuses.

The first case to surface from Jordan's discovery involved the Siegel Trading Company and certain of its officers, including Joseph Siegel and Alvin Winograd, who had previously been the subject of various CEA administrative actions. The CFTC charged that Siegel had induced a wealthy customer, Harold Brady, to engage in commodity futures transactions in order to shelter some $500,000 in capital gains. This was done through a 1,000-contract "butterfly straddle" in Mexican peso futures contracts traded on the International Monetary Market. The CFTC, however, contended that the loss was not a real one. Thus the loss on one side of the straddle, caused by rising prices, was offset by gains that were experienced in the opposite "leg" of the straddle. Only the loss side was realized in one tax year. The gain was carried over by, in effect, establishing a new straddle to "lock" the gain in until the next tax year. As a consequence, only "paper" losses were being produced, without any real economic loss. In the next year, Siegel entered into transactions designed to obtain a $2 million paper loss for Brady.

Siegel's response to the CFTC's charges was vigorous and prolonged. Brady, a large shareholder in Bache & Co., also brought suit against Siegel, and Siegel attempted to use that case for obtaining discovery in the Commission's investigation. That effort was unsuccessful. Siegel also brought an action to stop the CFTC's investigation, charging that the investigation was improperly motivated by the desire of the CFTC chairman, William Bagley, to stop "tax dodges," rather than as an effort to enforce the Commodity Exchange Act. That effort was also unsuccessful.

The CFTC instituted administrative proceedings against Siegel, and a CFTC administrative law judge imposed a $100,000 civil penalty after the company failed to respond to the Division's request that it admit the Commission's allegations. The company refused to do so on Fifth Amendment grounds. On appeal the CFTC reversed, holding that there were unique circumstances that permitted the company to claim the privilege (although normally the Fifth Amendment is not available to a corporation).

The Fifth Amendment concerns asserted by Siegel were real ones. In the interim, the Division of Enforcement had realized that the Siegel case was the tip of a very large iceberg, and the Justice Department was brought in to conduct a criminal inquiry. A grand jury was empaneled and Siegel and others were indicted. The CFTC then stayed its administrative proceedings pending the outcome of the criminal action.

A massive criminal investigation was also launched into trading in several futures contracts for tax evasion or other futures purposes. A CFTC attorney, Michael Koblenz, was assigned to the Justice Department as a Special Assistant to the United States Attorney. He worked on the grand jury's investigation of trading in the soybean pit on the Chicago Board of Trade. IRS and Postal Service employees were also brought in to assist the criminal investigations, which spread to the silver and soybean pits on the Chicago Board of Trade. Other CFTC investigators involved in these futures trading cases included Charlotte Ohmiller, Martha Kozlowski, and Richard Fung.

Siegel and others launched a multifront attack against the grand jury investigation, charging the CFTC staff with abusing the grand jury process. In one case, a trader refused to testify before the grand jury on the ground that CFTC investigators had improperly been given access to grand jury materials. That and other challenges were unsuccessful. Several indictments were returned, including one against a blind trader, and convictions were obtained against several individuals. The federal district court in Chicago, however, dismissed an indictment against one defendant on the grounds that the prohibition against "fictitious" sales in the Commodity Exchange Act, which the defendant was charged with violating, was unconstitutionally vague.

In the meantime, the CFTC's efforts had alerted the federal establishment to the enormity of the situation. Through such trading some $1 billion in taxes was being evaded or avoided. The word was further spread by two CFTC staff members who had worked on the grand jury investigation for over two years and who had developed a training seminar and a manual for the Internal Revenue Service and the Justice Department.

A grand jury was also empaneled in New York to conduct investigations of trading abuses there. One case that resulted from the investigation involved Norman Turkish, the sales manager for the commodity department of Bear Stearns & Co. Turkish was a specialist in tax straddles for the purpose of deferring taxes for his customers on income in amounts of at least $50,000. Turkish was convicted of engaging in illegal futures transactions in the New York Mercantile Exchange futures petroleum contract. Turkish and others had fraudulently manipulated virtually the entire crude oil futures market so that tax losses could be assured. The CFTC also brought cases against him for that conduct and for engaging in prohibited trading practices for tax purposes in gold futures contracts on the New York Mercantile Exchange. Bear Stearns also consented to a civil penalty of $80,000 and to a cease-and-desist order.

The CFTC additionally brought administrative proceedings against forty-three floor brokers and brokerage firms, charging noncompetitive and fictitious trading in gold and silver futures contracts on the New York Mercantile Exchange. In addition, that exchange was charged with failing to enforce its rules. The exchange settled the proceeding by consenting to a civil penalty of $200,000, and its designation as a contract market in certain silver and gold futures contracts was revoked.

Similar charges of prearranged and fictitious trading were brought against two firms and six individuals in connection with futures trading in U.S. Treasury bill futures on the International Monetary Market of the Chicago Mercantile Exchange. Criminal and administrative proceedings were also brought as the result of such trading on the New York Cotton Exchange. Civil penalties totaling over $500,000 were imposed by the CFTC against several of these traders, as well as suspension and revocations of their licenses and trading privileges. Sanctions were also entered by a CFTC Administrative Law Judge in the Siegel case.

The order of battle expanded even further when the IRS began disallowing deduction and other tax benefits claimed through so-called tax straddles. One such case received national attention and became a subject of controversy in the confirmation hearings of Donald Regan for Secretary of Treasury. It was reported that the brokerage firm he headed had tried to settle a case brought against it by taxpayers whose tax straddles had been challenged by the Internal Revenue Service. The publicity and the Internal Revenue Service's denunciation of the firm's motivation aborted the settlement, but the Internal Revenue Service was to regret that passing victory. The Tax Court thus ruled that, while these taxpayers did not have the required profit motive to justify a deduction, the court would not adopt a per se rule against all tax straddles. Rather, it would consider them on a case-by-case basis. This was a disaster for the government because it would have to prove a lack of economic motivation in every case, a most difficult task, particularly in the complex futures market. The amounts at stake were also enormous, reportedly totaling some $300 million, and the IRS is seeking legislation to overturn this result.

In the meantime, the IRS had publicized various rulings against tax straddles, and legislation was adopted to eliminate these abuses. That legislation in effect eliminated the holding period for futures contracts and taxed them at a maximum effective rate of approximately 32 percent. In addition, all contracts were "marked to market" at year's end if the transactions were still open. Grandfather provisions were adopted allowing a delay of tax payment for traders who had been shifting their losses for years.

FRAUD CASES

The CFTC's first non-options-related fraud case involved the American International Trading Company (AITC), a Los Angeles-based company headed by Harold Berman. The company offered a managed account program for trading in commodity futures contracts and required an investment of as little as $2,000. AITC promised speculators profits and guaranteed customers that they would not lose more than they invested; that is, customers would not be subject to margin calls. The program was widely advertised in Los Angeles. Berman even conducted television shows on a Los Angeles financial broadcast station, where one of his guest stars was Jack Savage, who acted as an adviser to AITC.

Savage was somewhat of a legend in the commodity industry. Among other things, he was one of the first persons denied registration by the CFTC because of his past criminal convictions in connection with Securities and Exchange Commission statutes. But this did not remove Savage from the industry. Seizing on a loophole in the registration scheme, Savage began trading for his own account on the floor of the Mid-America Commodity Exchange in Chicago.

Savage also sought to take advantage of another apparent loophole in the CFTC's registration scheme, which does not require someone to register as a commodity trading adviser if they are advising less than fifteen people. Savage interpreted this to mean that he could advise AITC and count it as one "person," rather than the several hundred persons whose accounts were being managed by AITC and who were "benefiting" from the advice.

The CFTC charged that, through these loopholes, Savage and Berman operated a scheme to cheat and defraud AITC customers. One way this was carried out was by wash sales. Berman entered opposite buy and sell orders for AITC customers that had no effect except to generate commissions for AITC. In addition, it was charged that Berman and Savage entered into prearranged trades for customers on the floor of the Mid-America Exchange in a manner that allowed Savage to make large profits to the detriment of AITC customers. AITC was additionally charged with entering into a series of "Robin Hood" transactions where profitable sides of offsetting trades were allocated to customers whose equity had declined below zero, requiring AITC to meet their margin calls. The nonprofitable sides of those trades were placed in the accounts of AITC customers with positive equity balances. This trading effectively transferred funds from customers with positive equity balances to customers with negative balances. Although AITC's motives were not as pure as those of Robin Hood, it was in effect stealing from the rich to give to the poor.[6]

The CFTC obtained injunctive relief and administrative sanctions against AITC, Berman, Savage, and others. AITC was closed down and a civil penalty of $250,000 was imposed by consent, a penalty that was never collected. Savage appealed the injunction obtained by the CFTC. Although he was successful in some issues, the injunction was affirmed in other respects. Savage, however, continued to plague authorities in the United States and abroad.

Another early case with AITC overtones involved the Citadel Trading Company of St. Louis and Stewart Fason, the author of a book entitled *A License to Steal.* The book depicted the asserted trading successes of its author in the futures market, where he purportedly had made over a million dollars. Fason promoted his book by offering to trade the funds of persons attending seminars he gave and extolling his trading methods. In making that offer, Fason advised prospective investors that he would retain 20 percent of their net profits as the sole compensation for his successful trading of their accounts. He would, however, waive that fee for six months for persons who allowed him to trade their accounts and would then give him an affadavit certifying his trading success. Fason claimed that he wanted to use these affidavits to promote his book.

Fason placed the funds of a large number of customers who responded to the offer with the Citadel Trading Company. There the funds were traded in wash sales and other transactions designed simply to generate commissions that were secretly shared with Fason through deposits in an account he controlled. That account was designated as the "ALTS" account. It did not take CFTC attorneys long to conclude that this was simply an acronym for Fason's book, *A License to Steal,* as indeed it was. It was also discovered that Citadel was using customer funds to pay for an automobile, an apartment, and a "breast enhancement" operation for one of its more attractive employees. Administrative sanctions were entered against Citadel and Fason. A floor broker handling the Citadel wash sales was also barred from registration as a floor broker for a period of five years.

Other significant fraud cases involved charges of unauthorized trading. For example, in a case brought against Jeffrey Silverman, the respondent had entered unauthorized commodity futures trades for eggs and pork bellies and continued to do so even after at least one customer objected. The Seventh Circuit upheld the CFTC's order, prohibiting Silverman from trading futures contracts on U.S. exchanges for a period of two years. Similarly, in a case against Robert Haltmier, the account executive was sanctioned for entering several unauthorized transactions for a customer who was traveling abroad. The CFTC's action was upheld by the Second Circuit, but the Court criticized the CTFC for prohibiting Haltmier from trading on U.S. exchanges. The Second Circuit pointed out that Haltmier's conduct involved the illegal trading of customer accounts, for which he should have been sanctioned, and not his own personal trading, to which the prohibition applied.[7] A more sophisticated illegal form of unauthorized transactions arose involving Winchester-Hardin-Oppenheimer Trading Company. There it was charged that respondents had engaged in a fraudulent scheme to allocate profitable transactions to a nominee account of a respondent and losing trades to customer accounts.

The Division of Enforcement has also brought numerous registration denial and revocation cases, the first contested case being that of Jack Savage. In another case, involving Lambert J. Hagan, registration was granted to a respondent over the Division's objections. Hagan had previously been convicted of a felony for making a false application to the Federal Housing Administration, and he failed to report that conviction to the CFTC on his registration application. The CTFC found that the omission of that information was the result of a misunderstanding of the instructions on the CFTC's application. He was also found to be rehabilitated after his prior conviction.

Other applicants were not so lucky. Registration was thus denied for a bank robbery, false statements in a CFTC registration application, petty larceny, felony tax violations, a conviction for false statements to the Department of Housing and Urban Development, acting without required registration, federal securities law violations, and failure to disclose to the CFTC prior part-time employment as a real estate salesman. On the other hand, a convicted counterfeiter was allowed to register.

One of the Division's more highly publicized registration cases was against Larry Williams. The Division had sought to deny Williams registration as a commodity trading adviser on the grounds that he had previously been sanctioned by the SEC on the basis of a consent settlement and that he had misleadingly promoted his futures trading system and his book on futures trading, entitled *How I made $1,000,000 Trading Commodities Last Year*. Williams had promoted his futures system through seminars for which he charged $1,500 per participant and offering gains of 100 percent. Over 500 persons attended these seminars.

The Division's case against Williams suffered several weaknesses. The SEC had reinstated Williams' registration as an investment adviser, undercutting the suggestion that his prior securities activities were evidence of his continuing unfitness to deal with the public. The Division's claim that Williams had misrepresented his trading successes in his book were also nebulous. The Division asserted that, while he had made $1 million trading, not all of that profit was for his own account. But this was not found to be misleading, since customers were concerned about the trading results and not who benefited. A CFTC administrative law judge did find that Williams had been at least negligent with respect to misleading statements in announcements promoting his seminars because it portrayed his trading system as perfect when in fact it had serious flaws. The CFTC, however, concluded that because the conduct occurred before the creation of the CFTC, it would not be used to disqualify him from registration.

Williams' commodity experience later became political news when

Williams became the Republican candidate for the Senate race in Montana in 1978. Although the Division's charges did not seem to register with the voters, his opponent made effective use of pictures of Williams when he was a commodity trader, which showed him as a "modish resident of Southern California who wore beads, open shirts and long hair." This was in sharp contrast to the dark suits and shirts worn during his candidacy. Williams also had to contend with a 1976 front-page *Wall Street Journal* article about his commodity trading in which he admitted that he was a con artist. In any event, Williams lost this hotly contested Senate race to then Representative Max Baucus.

A continuing problem for the Division of Enforcement has been abuses by commodity pools and their advisers. The large amount of liquid funds that may be obtained from the public for the operation of these pools made them particularly susceptible to abuse. Perhaps the most famous commodity pool case brought by the Division (whose efforts were spear-headed by John Cotton, one of the Division's senior staff members) involved Chilcott Portfolio Management Inc., an Oklahoma firm that was the creation of Thomas D. Chilcott, and which was placed in receivership by the CFTC. Chilcott converted (i.e., stole) over $80 million of funds it had solicited from over 400 customers. The financial shenanigans of Chilcott also played a role in the collapse of the Penn Square Bank in Oklahoma.

In *CFTC v. Troyer*,[8] the Division successfully obtained an injunction against an unregistered commodity pool operator that had not made required disclosures to its customers. The assets of the firm were also frozen by the court and a receiver was appointed. Similarly, *In the Matter of Peabody Trading Co. of Boston*,[9] administrative sanctions were entered for violations of CFTC commodity pool operator requirements, including the failure to disclose commission charges and potential conflicts of interest. In *CFTC v. Falk*,[10] a district court held that a commodity pool operator had fraudulently reported increases in their net asset value in the pool at a time when the pool was actually suffering large losses. Daniel Falk, the operator of this pool, had referred Bruce Thompson, a CFTC investigator, to his accountant, who Falk stated held the pool's records. Thompson followed the directions given by Falk and arrived at a combination funeral home and cemetery. No accountant, at least no live ones, were in attendance. Injunctive and other relief was obtained.

In *CFTC v. Daskoski*,[11] the CFTC encountered another con man. In this case, an individual named Bernard Striar had successfully solicited several million dollars from Southern California investors that he had purportedly invested in commodity futures with his old friend "Buzz" at a major brokerage firm. Catching wind of the rapid growth of Striar's pools, the CFTC scheduled an audit. But, just before the audit date, Striar fled, leaving notes admitting that the entire operation was a fraud. It was also revealed that Striar had previously led four separate lives with different aliases and separate families in different cities. He was eventually captured and jailed.

Another pool case involved a Ponzi scheme. The operator of the pool, Barbara Skorupakas, solicited almost $3 million from members of the tightly knit Polish community in Detroit, Michigan, for investment in commodity futures. Many of those customers could ill afford a trading loss. Skorupakas portrayed herself as a latter-day "Joan of Arc from whom one could be assured of financial security." Drawn by word of mouth, she often addressed prospective customers in large meetings of 100 or more in rented halls. The CFTC was successful in obtaining an injunction against Skorupakas, but she continued her solicitations and was eventually held in contempt of court. Skorupakas convinced many investors that she was being unfairly prosecuted by the CFTC, and hundreds of cards were received by the court hearing the case from investors protesting the CFTC's action. Before contempt could be imposed, however, Skorupakas launched another series of pools through which she obtained some $700,000.

Criminal convictions were obtained against another commodity pool operator, Constantine Kepreos. There a defendant was convicted despite his claims that he was suffering from psychological deficiencies that precluded him from understanding the wrongfulness of his acts. Still another commodity pool scam involved the Big Red Commodity Corporation operated by Larry Pinckney. Pinckney diverted about $200,000 in customer funds, for which he was sentenced to four years in prison. The CFTC upheld the position of the Division of Enforcement that Pinckney was an agent of Rosenthal and Company, and that, as such, it was responsible for Pinckney's activities, even though it was unaware of his fraud.

MANIPULATION

The single most important goal of the Commodity Exchange has been, from its inception, to prevent the manipulation of commodity prices. The act does not define that term, however, nor is any other guidance given on what are the elements of this violation. The result has been fifty years of confusion, protracted litigation, and a virtual nullification of that statutory prohibition.

Under the CEA, it was not unusual for a case to take eight years or more to reach a conclusion. No better results have been achieved by the CFTC's Division of Enforcement. Indeed, the Division took five years just to investigate the events in the silver market between 1979 and 1980, before it filed manipulation charges against the Hunts and others. Undoubtedly, any final adjudication of these charges will take even longer.

The Division has also suffered a number of setbacks in its manipulation cases. Moreover, even when it has been successful, generally in settlements, the sanctions have not been particularly stringent. In all likelihood, this set of affairs will continue until Congress and the CFTC can establish some workable formula for the prosecution of these cases.

The difficulty under the present statute is that the Division of Enforcement must prove that the alleged manipulator was seeking to create an "artificial" price, that is, a price other than that determined by the forces of supply and demand. This requires a subjective determination of the trader's intent as well as a completely unreliable exchange of testimony by economists on what the market price should have been under the normal forces of supply and demand. Illustrative of the difficulty of proving such a standard is the Division of Enforcement's first contested manipulation case, which had been initiated by the CEA and involved Hohenberg Bros. Co., a cotton firm.

There it was charged that Hohenberg attempted to manipulate the price of December 1971 cotton futures downward by maintaining a short position equal to almost 50 percent of the December contract, by continuing to sell short until the delivery period, by promptly tendering a large number of notices for delivery, and by urging another large cotton firm not to take delivery. The CFTC, however, found no manipulation because it could find no manipulative intent on the part of the respondent. Rather, the tender of delivery notices was found simply to be an attempt to obtain the best price for cotton held by the firm. This decision effectively signaled that circumstantial evidence alone would not generally be sufficient to prove manipulation. Of course, direct evidence of the state of mind of an alleged manipulator is difficult, if not impossible, to obtain.

In another CEA-generated case, the CFTC's Division of Enforcement settled manipulation charges brought against a floor broker, Hugh P. King. He was accused of manipulating the July 1972 oats futures on the Chicago Board of Trade. Pursuant to the settlement, findings were made that the respondent, a floor broker, had held long futures contracts for some 1.2 million bushels of oats, which contributed 100 percent of the open interest in long July contracts. Thereafter, he stood for delivery on 310 thousand bushels, which constituted 95 percent of the oats available for delivery in Chicago. King demanded a price of as much as 4¢ per bushel over a later contract month for the long contracts he held for some 850 thousand bushels (the later contract month typically traded below the July contract). This came at a time when commodity prices were highly volatile. Notwithstanding these circumstances, the settlement required only a forty-five-day suspension of the floor broker.

A more serious sanction was imposed in another CEA-initiated manipulation case against the Plains Cotton Cooperative Association. In that case, a one-year suspension from trading was imposed as a part of a Division settlement. It was charged that the respondent increased its long positions in cotton futures on the New York Cotton Exchange to 95 percent of the open long interest, accepted large deliveries, and made cotton nondeliverable for other traders. It was claimed that this caused sellers to pay an artificially high price to settle their cotton contracts.

A much lighter sanction was imposed against Tysons Foods Inc., another CEA-generated case, in which it was charged that the respondents engaged in a long manipulation of September 1970 shell egg contracts on the Chicago Mercantile Exchange. The respondents held almost 100 percent of the open long interest at one point and accepted delivery of large amounts of eggs, which were sold at a loss and in a manner designed to make them unavailable for redelivery. It was also claimed that the respondent's aggregate position exceeded available supplies of eggs. The respondents were suspended from trading for periods ranging from two months to a year, and Tysons Foods was fined $10,000 and its trading privileges except for certain hedging transactions were suspended for one year. In accepting this settlement, the CFTC stated that it was doing so in the interest of conserving its resources and administrative economies. Yet, within a year, the trading bar against Tysons Foods was partially lifted because it had entered a new business (in hogs), where the price instability was such that the company wished to engage in expanded hedging operations, which the CFTC agreed to permit. A CEA carryover manipulation case against the Chicago Mercantile Exchange was also dismissed. There the exchange had taken a number of emergency actions after federal price controls were lifted on pork bellies in 1973. It was found that the exchange had not acted in bad faith.

The investigation and handling of these manipulation cases involved a large amount of CEA and CFTC resources, with little success. The cases were investigated and brought for the most part by the CEA, but the lack of success was not due to its investigative shortcomings. The problem lay with the difficulty of proving the elements of manipulation. Subsequent CFTC manipulation cases (or lack thereof) proved this to be the case.

For example, in the May 1976 Maine Potato manipulation case, the Division settled early on with some principal respondents by imposing trading suspension of two to eight years and civil penalties of $2,000 to $50,000. Although these were substantial penalties, they hardly seemed too harsh for the alleged manipulation that led to the largest default ever experienced in the commodities industry. The Division's coffee manipulation case against Compania de Salvadorana de Cafe also resulted in minimal sanctions: a trading bar and a civil penalty of $200,000 were imposed by default against the general manager, and a lesser sanction against the company's successor firm.

Similarly, in a case involving Clayton Brokerage Company of St. Louis, the Division charged that a brokerage firm and certain of its employees, including its former president, manipulated silver prices on the Chicago Board of Trade in 1978. The firm was also charged with cheating customers and with violations of the Commission's reporting and financial regulations. A civil penalty of $200,000 was imposed against the firm in a settlement with the Division. No trading bar was imposed.

In another case a brokerage firm and its president, Al S. Polonyi, settled a charge that they had manipulated the settlement price of the May 1980 wheat future contract on the Kansas City Board of Trade by paying a civil penalty of $15,000 and consenting to a trading bar of the president for thirty days. In another CEA-generated case against Edward A. Cox, Jr. and George F. Frey, Jr., two floor brokers, a manipulation of the May 1971 wheat futures contract on the Chicago Board of Trade was found to have occurred. The CFTC administrative law judge in this case revoked the floor broker registrations of the two respondents and barred them from trading for two years. That decision was rendered in 1983 (some twelve years after the event), and the decision is still not effective, since it is on appeal to the CFTC.

The most decisive blow to the Division of Enforcement's antimanipulative efforts came in a case against the Indiana Farm Bureau Cooperative Association. There a CFTC administrative law judge had found that, while the July 1973 corn futures contract on the Chicago Board of Trade was traded at artificial prices, the respondent was not shown to have the requisite intent of creating an artificial price. On appeal, the CFTC disagreed with the conclusion that there were artificial prices and affirmed the dismissal of the action, with the Commissioners filing multiple opinions and views. The majority opinion, while swaddled in cautionary words, asserted that it was permissible for a trader to exploit a "natural" corner caused by crop shortages. This, of course, places an impossible burden on the Division of Enforcement. Not only must it prove the artificiality of prices, it must show something more than the fact that a trader continued to trade in a manner that could exacerbate the situation. The decision is equally troubling for traders, because it is full of caveats and warnings that provide little specific guidance as to what is expected of a large trader involved in a legitimate market play. Consequently, neither the Division nor large traders have any useful guidance and will not likely be given any until Congress acts. In the meantime, the situation is unfair to the Division and traders and poses a worse danger to the public.

FOREIGN TRADERS AND OTHER CASES

One of the principal thrusts of the Division of Enforcement has been its efforts to curb market abuses by foreign traders. It has done this principally through the Commission's special call procedure, whereby it requests so-called foreign brokers to identify their customers. Such disclosure allows the CFTC to target potential market abusers operating behind the scenes of an omnibus foreign broker's account.

The first significant test of this authority was the Division's case against Wiscope, a foreign broker. The Division was seeking information about trading in coffee futures contracts from Wiscope. Wiscope, a Swiss firm, refused to identify its customers on the ground that such disclosure was prohibited by Swiss law. The CFTC rejected that defense on the ground that foreign customers trading in U.S. markets subject themselves to U.S. disclosure requirements. According to the CFTC, the foreign broker should have obtained waivers of foreign secrecy requirements before trading for its customers.

This decision created an international controversy, because the Swiss believed that it was an infringement on their sovereignty. The Swiss government also protested the fact that the CFTC had served its complaint on Wiscope without going through diplomatic channels. It was necessary for the CFTC to send a delegation to Switzerland to smooth over that breach of protocol. In any event, the case was appealed to the Second Circuit, which reversed the CFTC on the embarrassing grounds that the special call had been sent to the wrong Wiscope affiliate and because the CFTC had improperly considered evidence outside the record of proceedings in reaching its decision. Undaunted, the CFTC continued its use of the special call.

In an action against the Banque Populaire Suisse, the Division sought to enforce a special call against a large Swiss bank that was acting as a foreign broker in trading futures contracts. The CFTC was seeking in this case to obtain the identity of the bank's customers, who were trading silver futures contracts during 1979, a period of rapid price increases in silver. Once again, the CFTC rejected claims that Swiss bank secrecy laws precluded disclosure of the identity of the Banque's customers, and sanctions were imposed against the Banque.

In a case against Alan J. Ridge & Co., the stakes were raised. In this case, the respondent, a British company, had been taking large deliveries on coffee futures contracts in New York, and the CFTC was seeking to ascertain what it was doing with the coffee. The company refused to respond. The British government also issued an order that forbade Ridge & Co. from responding to the CFTC request. The order was issued pursuant to a statute that had been passed to block the CFTC's special call procedure in England. The CFTC ignored this imperial impertinence and imposed sanctions against the firm. It has also continued in other cases to impose sanctions when special calls are refused. In one such case, against Ralli Brothers (Bankers) S.A., a CFTC administrative law judge imposed a civil penalty of $100,000 and barred the foreign broker from trading on U.S. contract markets for a period of two years.

The Division has also brought cases against firms and individuals who fail to (or improperly) file required "large trader" reports used by the CFTC in its surveillance functions. In an early decision against the Pacific Trading Company, the Division successfully prosecuted a case brought against a futures commission merchant that had improperly filed reports of its customers' trading as the result of lax administration and poor supervision. The firm was suspended for seven days as a result of conduct. Other cases have resulted in fines. For example, the Virginia Trading Corporation was fined $30,000, while a civil penalty of $100,000 was imposed against ACLI International Inc. for reporting problems. In an action against E.D.P. Commodity Inc., a default proceeding, the respondent was barred from trading entirely and was fined $10,000.

Speculative limit cases are also prosecuted by the Division of Enforcement, the Hunt soybean case being the most noteworthy, with a civil penalty of $500,000 being imposed. In an action against Nassim Suleiman, a settlement was accepted pursuant to which the trader was suspended for twenty days, while Eddy Van Den Broeke, a potato trader, was suspended from trading for five years. Yet, in still another position limit proceeding the respondent, Anthony Spinale, was suspended for only thirty days.

In one of its most significant cases, which was brought against Refco Inc., the Division charged that Refco and its past president, Thomas Dittmer, had violated CFTC speculative position limits. Refco is now one of the largest commodity brokerage firms in the country, after conducting an acquisition binge that swept up several old-line firms, including ContiCommodity. Dittmer is also a well-known figure in the industry. The complaint was settled with a total civil penalty of $525,000, the largest penalty ever imposed by the CFTC. Most recently, a civil penalty of $425,000 was imposed against Commodities Corporation for position limit violations.

Another routine form of prosecution by the Division is record-keeping cases and failures to segregate customer funds. For example, in one of its first injunctive actions, the Division obtained injunctive relief against City Commodities Inc. for failing to keep records required by CFTC regulations. In an action against Prudential-Bache Securities, Inc., the brokerage firm was fined $15,000 in a consent settlement for failing to obtain and retain a required risk disclosure document from one of its thousands of customers, an apparent case of overkill. In numerous cases injunctions have been obtained for segregation violations, and the registration of a futures commission merchant, Donney Securities Ltd., was revoked for failing to segregate customer funds. Net capital violations are also targets for the Division of Enforcement. For example, the CFTC forced Premex Inc., a Southern California leverage dealer, out of business because it was not meeting net capital requirements, even though it was not acting as a futures commission merchant.

INJUNCTIVE ACTIONS

The principal enforcement tool of the SEC traditionally has been injunctive actions brought in the federal courts. The SEC also has the authority to institute administrative proceedings, but the wider availability and higher visibility of the injunctive action has made it the SEC's weapon of choice. Most SEC actions are settled by consent, without admission or denial of wrongdoing.[12]

The CFTC's Division of Enforcement has not followed the same pattern. It generally prefers to bring administrative proceedings rather than injunctive actions. This has been because many of its injunctive actions were contested, causing an enormous drain on the Division's resources; discovery, motion practice, and trial in federal court is an expensive and time-consuming process. In contrast, discovery is limited in CFTC administrative proceedings, the proceedings are more informal, and the Division enjoys a home court advantage (although the CFTC and its administrative law judges have frequently ruled against the Division). Civil penalties of up to $100,000 for each violation may also be imposed in administrative proceedings. Such penalties are not available in injunctive actions, although disgorgement of monies obtained illegally or other "ancillary" injunctive relief may be available.

Another factor discouraging the CFTC's use of the injunctive action has been the many frustrations it encountered in federal court. The British American, Lloyd Carr, J. S. Love & Associates Option Ltd., and the Hunt soybean cases were all unsuccessful or delayed in the federal district court, even though violations had occurred in each case. It took an enormous amount of resources to bring to trial and conclude these actions successfully (J. S. Love was not appealed), causing the Division to look more often to its administrative procedures for remedies. Nevertheless, the injunctive action remains a powerful and highly visible weapon when the CFTC determines to use it. For example, the Division has had considerable success with injunctive actions in stopping illegal off-board futures and options trading.

The requirements for injunctive relief for the CFTC are much the same as those for the SEC. The requirements for both have also been tightened in recent years. In brief, past violations alone are not sufficient for an injunction. Rather, there must be a reasonable likelihood of future violations. To be sure, past violations may suggest that possibility, but something more is needed. The factors that may be considered are the defendant's *scienter* (state of mind), the isolated or recurrent nature of violations, ongoing violations, the sincerity of assurances and efforts to prevent future violations, the defendant's recognition of his past wrongful conduct, contrition, and the nature of the defendant's profession or activities (i.e., if he is a professional trader he is more likely to violate the statute). The CFTC need not prove irreparable injury or other equitable requirements imposed on private parties seeking injunctions.

The CFTC may also seek "ancillary relief" in its injunctive actions. This may include disgorgement of profits obtained from illegal trading, as in the Hunt soybean case. In *CFTC v. Muller*,[13] the court also enjoined the defendant from concealing or disposing of his assets, except that he was allowed to withdraw $1,000 per month from his checking account for living expenses. In other cases, receivers have been appointed, business activities restricted, disclosure requirements imposed, return of attorneys fees required, accountings ordered, and the courts have directed that the CFTC be given access to books and records.

The courts continue to place restrictions on CFTC injunctive actions. For example, in an action involving Incomco, Inc., the Second Circuit held that a CFTC injunctive action could not be decided on the basis of affidavits where there were disputed issues of fact. The courts also continue on occasion to deny CFTC requested injunctions. For example, in a case against Lincolnwood, Inc., a district court required the CFTC to pay a defendant's attorney fees, concluding that the CFTC's injunctive action was not substantially justified. In *CFTC v. Commodities Fluctuations Systems, Inc.*,[14] after a week-long trial, injunctive relief was denied against a party found to have failed to supervise its agents properly. The court found there was no reasonable likelihood that violations would continue. But later problems resulted in an injunction.

A remedy inevitably sought by the Division of Enforcement in its administrative proceedings is a cease-and-desist order, which is in effect the same as an injunction. The CFTC, however, has held that cease-and-desist orders are not necessary unless there is, in effect, a reasonable likelihood of future violations. In an action against Dillon-Gage, Inc., the CFTC held that a cease-and-desist order was unnecessary where a brokerage firm had rectified the problems that had resulted in violations. Nevertheless, a mere cessation of violative activity will not always be a defense. In *Precious Metals Inc. v. CFTC*,[15] the Court of Appeals upheld the imposition of a CFTC cease-and-desist order, despite the respondent's claim that it had stopped selling illegal commodity options, which it had sold under the guise of "limited risk forward" contracts.

Another remedy sought by the Division in administrative proceedings is the imposition of a civil penalty of up to $100,000 per violation. The Division has increasingly sought stiffer civil penalties over the years, and the CFTC has increasingly sanctioned its use. The Commodity Exchange, however, establishes specific criteria that must be considered in deciding the size of the penalty, including the nature and size of the respondent's business or net worth, and the gravity of the violation. The CFTC has held that its administrative law judges must specifically address those factors and the collectability of any fine before imposing a monetary penalty.

CRIMINAL PROCEEDINGS

An important part of the Division's enforcement program has been its criminal referrals. In that regard the Division, apparently quoting William Bagley, has stated that the "only thing a big-time fraud operator can't factor into the cost of doing business is five years in a federal penitentiary."[16] Bluster aside, the number of criminal cases under the Commodity Exchange Act has been increasing each year. In 1980 the Division boasted of a few indictments and convictions obtained during that year, while the following year over fifty individuals were indicted and thirty-eight convicted. A comparable number of indictments and convictions were obtained in 1983, including some stiff sentences of up to fifteen years. Criminal contempt proceedings have also been brought against several individuals who violated CFTC injunctions.

ATTACKS AGAINST THE STAFF

Defense attorneys dealing with the Division of Enforcement often come away with the feeling that the Division is operating with a bunker or siege mentality. Their perceptions are not in error. The Division has been under attack from its inception. As a consequence, its attorneys still suffer from a deep-seated paranoia and often refuse to provide even the most innocuous information to attorneys seeking to determine the status of investigations before the Division. This is an unfortunate situation, both for the Division and individuals involved in CFTC enforcement proceedings.

The attacks against the Division came from every quarter. One of the more serious charges was that the Division was improperly given access to secret grand jury information in the investigations that led to the indictments for illegal tax straddles. As noted above, the Siegel Trading Company had charged that a CFTC investigation was improperly motivated as a tax collection case, rather than a matter of concern under the Commodity Exchange Act. It was also claimed, at about the same time, that the Division had illegally induced a Minnesota state security official to record his telephone conversation with a commodity option salesperson. The plaintiff claimed that this violated an Illinois eavesdropping statute. All of these actions were unsuccessful, but they engendered much concern on the part of the Enforcement staff, and created a deep-seated mistrust of defense counsel tactics. But these were not the only attacks against the staff.

In *Fairchild, Arabatzis & Smith Inc. v. Sackheim,*[17] it was charged that CFTC investigators had been rude in conducting an inspection of a brokerage firm. The rude conduct was described as "demanding information, interrupting a Christmas party, snatching documents from people, and screaming" at the firm's employees. It was also charged that a formal investigation was instituted by the Division in retaliation for the company's complaints concerning the staff's rude conduct. The case was dismissed, however, because no actionable misconduct was found to have existed.

In another case, *American International Trading Company v. Bagley*,[18] it was claimed that the Division had improperly used a customer list of the firm, obtained through its inspection authority, to question customers. It was stated that customers were asked such questions as:

1. Who was your account executive?
2. What did he promise you in the way of percentage of return?
3. He must have made some pitch to induce you to become a client.
4. Are you sure he did not give you a sales pitch?
5. How much money did you put into your account?

The district court enjoined the CFTC from further use of the customer lists. On appeal to the Seventh Circuit, however, the district court was reversed. Justice Tom Clark, sitting by designation, held for the Seventh Circuit panel that the CFTC's use of the customer list was legitimate. He stated that while perhaps "questions (3) and (4) smacked of the 'When did you stop beating your wife technique,'. . . . Fire sometimes has to be fought with fire."

The Division generally prevailed in the attacks against it. Nevertheless, it developed a deep distrust of the defense bar. It was particularly appalled at what it identified as the "Chicago screamers." This was a short-hand reference to a defense tactic of refusing to comply with CFTC subpoenas or providing any information at all to the CFTC staff, to resist every move by the CFTC staff regardless of its legitimacy, and to oppose and delay the staff whenever possible, even if the result is to prejudice the client. These tactics were particularly common in Chicago, where the financial and legal communities engaged in an all-out resistance to the CFTC.

These obstructionist and dilatory tactics did result in delay, but only rarely were they successful in the ultimate outcome and only then at great expense. Another unfortunate result was that the Division of Enforcement cut itself off from any meaningful exchanges with defense counsel, and it is now difficult, if not impossible, to obtain even basic information from the staff on the status of an investigation or their views on its outcome. This is unfair to the persons who are targets of CFTC investigations, and it is a substantial factor in undermining the Division's credibility with those it regulates and who seek to act responsibly.

SUBPOENAS AND INSPECTION AUTHORITY

The Division's principal means of obtaining information is by cooperation and through its inspection and subpoena authority. Cooperation has been rare. Consequently, the Division has been left to its mandatory devices for obtaining information. The inspection powers of the Division are contained in the provisions of the Commodity Exchange Act, which require registrants to make records available for inspection by the agency.

The Commission has also adopted a regulation requiring registrants to make copies of documents available upon request. The Division has read this provision to mean that it can direct registrants to conduct searches of their files and to supply copies to the Division of Enforcement. This is akin to the authority contained in a subpoena, but the protections available in a subpoena are lacking. Subpoenas are authorized by the CFTC itself, pursuant to a formal order of investigation that is not issued until after the Division provides a memorandum to the CFTC justifying the investigation. In contrast, the Division can initiate an inspection on its own initiative. Under the view adopted by the Division of Enforcement, a CFTC investigator at any one of its offices can demand that sweeping file searches be made under its inspection authority and that copies be made of documents, whatever the cost and without Commission review. Such demands can require thousands of hours of work and many thousands of dollars in employee and counsel time.

The Division will also take testimony pursuant to a *subpoena duces tecum*. This is conducted much in the manner of a deposition in a civil suit. A court reporter will be present or the testimony will otherwise be recorded, and it will be transcribed. Witnesses are entitled to have an attorney present, but the Division has taken a high-handed view as to the role of the attorney. It will allow a witness to consult with an attorney, but on occasion has refused to allow attorneys to make objections to assertions made by the Division on the record.

The Division has frequently brought subpoena enforcement proceedings where a recipient of a subpoena refuses to provide the requested information. In an early case, *United States v. Security State Bank and Trust Co.*,[19] the CEA had sought to enforce a *subpoena duces tecum* that had been issued under the Commodity Exchange Act. The court held that it would not "rubber stamp" subpoenas and that it would provide a meaningful day in court for someone resisting a subpoena. The court stated that the burden is on the government to show that the investigation is for a lawful purpose and that the evidence sought in the subpoena is relevant to the investigation. In that case, the CEA failed to establish that the information it was seeking was relevant to its investigation of possible manipulation in the trading of shell egg futures contracts.

The Division of Enforcement was equally unsuccessful in its first subpoena enforcement action, against the Hunt family of Dallas, Texas. There, the Division had sought to subpoena the Hunts' records and require them to testify in Chicago, even though they resided in Dallas, Texas. The district court held that the CFTC would be required to go to Texas to examine the respondents and their records. But it was more successful in *CFTC v. First National Bullion Corp.*,[20] where the court enforced the CFTC subpoena, finding that the requested records were sufficiently relevant to the CFTC's investigation of off-exchange futures contracts.

In *CFTC v. Bloch*,[21] the district court also enforced a CFTC administrative subpoena, rejecting the defendant's claim that the subpoena was issued in bad faith. It was found that the CFTC investigators had not improperly contacted customers and that there had not been any threats, as claimed, against employees of a defendant. In still another case, a district court refused to order an individual to testify in a CFTC investigation because the witness had claimed the Fifth Amendment. The court stated that the witness could be granted immunity in areas where he was vulnerable for criminal violations, but that he would be required to testify in areas where he was not connected.

In an action against Rosenthal & Co., however, the Division suffered a serious setback. There, although it later enforced the subpoena, the court allowed the targets of a subpoena enforcement action to question CFTC investigators on the purpose and scope of their investigation and whether the matter had been referred criminally, thereby providing broad-scale discovery to the targets of the investigation. Perhaps the biggest setback experienced by the Division of Enforcement in exercising its investigative authority came in *CFTC v. Nahas*.[22] There, the District of Columbia Court of Appeals held that the CFTC was without authority to subpoena a nonresident foreign national. Because many of the problems encountered in recent years by the CFTC have involved foreign traders, this effectively limited its ability to meet that threat. The CFTC has sought legislation to reverse this decision.

CFTC rules provide that witnesses at CFTC proceedings are entitled to obtain a copy of the transcript and to inspect it, except that upon good cause shown, the witness may be denied a copy of the transcript. In practice, the Division of Enforcement seeks to effectively deny copies of transcripts to virtually all persons testifying before it, with or without good cause. This is a direct violation of the CFTC's own rules, but to date the Division has not been directly challenged on this issue in court. Nevertheless, it is reflective of the Division's efforts to avoid any scrutiny of its investigative processes.

The Division has also been overly defensive in negotiating settlements with individuals to be charged with violations. In the past, it has filed cases without advising a respondent or its counsel before doing so. The defendant and counsel were simply left to read about it in the papers. As might be expected, this was somewhat of a shock to the individual or firm being charged. This practice is also unproductive, since a respondent may frequently wish to settle a case simultaneously with the filing of the complaint, thereby incurring only one burst of adverse publicity instead of two when a subsequent settlement is announced. The incentive to settle is much reduced if a case is filed before the settlement is negotiated. The Division has modified this practice recently and has been attempting to provide settlement opportunities.

Division procedures have been unfair in other respects. For example, in the past, the Division has not allowed a respondent or its counsel seeking a settlement to see a copy of the complaint prepared by the Division until after it is filed. This, of course, makes pre-filing settlement somewhat difficult since the respondent is given only a vague outline of what the charges are. This procedure presents the danger, a very real one, that the complaint will contain errors.

The Division has refused to reveal the proposed complaint on the ground that it could result in a negotiation of the charges in the complaint. The Division has asserted that it will not engage in such negotiations, even though the SEC and other agencies customarily do discuss and negotiate the terms of a complaint as a part of a settlement. Of course, even if such negotiations are not acceptable to the Division, logic does not support the use of that position for denying a respondent the right to see the complaint. The staff can simply refuse to negotiate. The Division on occasion also asserts, as an additional justification for withholding the complaint, that it cannot reveal it because the Commission has not approved the document. This appears to be nonsense, since the staff often reviews draft documents with persons to be affected by the contents before transmitting them to the Commission. Once again, this position is being modified to allow respondents in at least some cases to see the complaint before it is filed, and complaints are being negotiated.

The Division has also been inconsistent in its procedures. For example, it has allowed attorneys on many occasions to represent employees or former employees of a firm under investigation solely in their capacity as employees or former employees. Recently, however, the New York office of the CFTC has taken the position that it will allow attorneys to represent witnesses only in their personal capacity. This is unfair in that many witnesses are called simply to testify as employees or former employees of a company. Whatever the case, the Division's procedures should at least be uniform.

Finally, there is no "Wells submission" procedure at the CFTC. A Wells submission is an opportunity for a person about to be charged with violations by the staff of the SEC to submit to the Commission in writing the reasons why he should not be so charged. This procedure was adopted by the SEC after a report of one of its advisory committees in 1972, which recommended this procedure. It was correctly viewed that the most punitive sanction in most SEC cases (and in those of the CFTC) is the adverse publicity that results for the company or individual being charged. It was thought that before such publicity resulted from a charge, which may be ill-founded, a respondent should in fairness be given an opportunity to state his side of the case to the Commission.

The SEC adopted such a procedure, and as a matter of practice in almost every case affords such an opportunity. In fact, the Wells submission often works to the benefit of the SEC staff, because it requires respondents to take a position and to outline the theory of their case at an early point in time. If litigation results, the defendants are locked into that strategy, and the staff has an opportunity to attach it during subsequent discovery.

Gerald Fishman, a Chicago attorney, petitioned the CFTC to adopt rules permitting a Wells submission procedure. The CFTC's Office of General Counsel and the Division of Enforcement opposed that petition, and the CFTC therefore denied the request, on the grounds that the procedure would unduly burden the resources of the Commission and would serve to delay proceedings. But this claim does not withstand even a cursory examination. CFTC investigations often last years before a case is brought; an additional delay of a few weeks to allow a Wells submission would hardly constitute a material delay. Such a procedure would also pose little burden, except possibly to require the Division to respond to credible arguments raised in a Wells submission, which it would be required to do in any event in the subsequent litigation. Moreover, if the agency were to stop one improvident proceeding and thereby conserve the resources it would consume as a result of the Wells submission, any delays that would be caused by responding to Wells submissions would be more than justified. The protection of the rights of individuals and the overriding requirement of fairness in government proceedings far outweigh the disadvantages claimed by the Division. In 1986 Fishman resubmitted his Wells submission proposal. The CFTC, apparently over the objections of the Enforcement Division, recently adopted a Wells submission procedure.

The unfairness in the Division's investigative and settlement procedures and its refusal to permit a Wells submission have all served to develop a reputation for arrogance and high-handed action on the part of the Division. The SEC came under much criticism during the 1970s as a result of its sometimes overly aggressive enforcement procedures, and the CFTC's Division of Enforcement is now blindly and unnecessarily subjecting itself to that same type of criticism. By adopting rules and procedures designed to ensure fairness, such as the CFTC did for Wells submissions, it could alleviate much criticism with very little cost to itself.

CFTC ENFORCEMENT IN THE FUTURE

The Division of Enforcement was crippled during much of its existence by lack of resources and by the demands of the commodity options scandals and the off-exchange instruments. With the enactment of the 1982 amendments, which removed the CFTC's exclusive jurisdiction for off-exchange instruments, and with the suspension of off-exchange options trading, the Division was allowed to pursue trade practice problems in the mainstream of commodity futures trading. It acted swiftly by attacking commodity futures practices that have not been challenged in the past because of its lack of resources. This was confirmed in October 1985, when the CFTC announced settlements in several cases (including cases against major firms) that imposed civil penalties of almost $1 million. In making that announcement, the Division's head, Dennis Klejna, sought to assure reporters that the Division did indeed have "teeth."

The Division's recent efforts, coupled with pressures on the exchanges to enforce their surveillance procedures, has now made the CFTC's regulatory framework a stringent one. The question now becomes whether the CFTC will go too far. There is a very real concern that the CFTC will lose important support from the brokerage firms and members of the futures community who are now coming under attack by the Division of Enforcement. Of course, these firms are not insulated from the requirements of the Commodity Exchange Act, but there is concern that some of the CFTC's cases are being brought simply to pad statistics. For example, the Division has brought cases after an exchange has already reviewed and even sanctioned the conduct. One such case, In the Matter of Murphy,[23] involved "ginzy" trades, which are, simply stated, trading practices designed to allow one-half tick trading in a low-volume market. The administrative law judge imposed a smaller fine, concluding that, while there were violations, the practices had not defrauded customers and that the matter should have been left for exchange officials to handle. The CFTC, however, imposed additional sanctions, even though the exchange and the administrative law judge had found that such sanctions were not appropriate.

Whatever the merits of the CFTC's charges, the traders should not be subjected to punishment in circumstances where there is such a divergence of views. To be sure, the CFTC may want to send a message to the industry that sanctions must be stiff. But, participants in the marketplace should have a right to be shielded from double prosecutions and second guessing of the exchanges, unless the conduct is so serious that the respondent is being put out of the business by both regulators. If the CFTC is concerned that its administrative law judges or the exchanges are not imposing sufficient sanctions, they should do so by means other than punishing traders and brokers caught in the middle of disputes where there is a genuine difference of opinion.

The Division has also brought cases where a private right of action has already been brought to remedy the violation and where a firm has turned itself into the Division. Once again, a private right of action or a voluntary disclosure of violations should not insulate a respondent from prosecution. On the other hand, it should not automatically result in charges being brought against it by the Division. This will only forestall settlement and result in a lack of cooperation from the industry.

The Division's crackdown on supervisory personnel in large firms may also have serious adverse effects. Office managers are often charged with failing to supervise as a result of conduct of a single broker, based on hindsight determinations of what the office manager should have discovered concerning the employee's activity. In fact, office managers often supervise both securities and commodities employees in fast-moving markets, and no manager can be aware at all times of the activities of all of the brokers in the office. Supervisory cases should be reserved only for those instances where there is a real supervisory failure, not on the basis of hindsight or second guessing. Office manager positions are difficult ones to fill with capable people. Unreasonable standards imposed on such persons will only discourage qualified individuals from seeking those positions.

A delicate balancing process is at stake. On one hand, strong enforcement has been sorely needed in the commodity futures markets, particularly against manipulation. Yet, no effective enforcement will occur until changes are made in the law. Consequently, the Division has used its resources to attack other areas. This imbalance is forestalling truly effective regulation. It may also force the large retail brokerage firms, who have never posed any serious threat, to retract from the market, if they are to become the Division's principal targets. This is particularly a danger in handling smaller accounts that require the greatest supervision. The result may well be that the small "bandit" firms that have traditionally posed the most serious problems will remain in the industry or will be the only firms willing to serve smaller customers.

Certainly, the Division's task is a thankless one, and it will never be able to satisfy all sides. Nevertheless, its role is vital to the functioning of the CFTC and central to the continued effectiveness of the markets. Serious policy judgments must therefore be made as to the scope and nature of the Division's enforcement program. To date, it does not appear that such considerations have been addressed by the Commission.

PART III

INSTRUMENTS REGULATED

13

LEVERAGE TRANSACTIONS

BACKGROUND

Leverage contracts initially made their appearance on the West Coast, where they were sold by a company known as Monex International, which at one point did business under the name Pacific Coast Coin Exchange. Monex's founders started their company with a $10,000 initial investment. Monex developed into a $1 billion operation.

Initially, Monex sought to buy and sell silver coins and bullion to customers. To finance their purchases, Monex also arranged secured loans with banks that allowed customers to post the silver coins or bullion they were purchasing as collateral. Later, Monex began trading futures contracts in precious metals and forward contracts with large firms. This enabled Monex itself to sell coin obligations to customers and allowed customers to obtain leverage that was much greater than was available from a bank loan. This was done through what became known as a leverage contract.

The growth of Monex and other leverage dealers was due to the fact that by the fall of 1970, the effects of monetary expansion began to have serious effects on the gold and silver markets, causing prices to rise rapidly. The U.S. government had also lifted its ban on the melting of silver coins, and it had discontinued its sale of silver reserves in the open market, increasing speculative interest in the market. In addition, in 1969, the New York Mercantile Exchange began to trade futures contracts for silver coins, also increasing speculative interest.

The advent of domestic and worldwide economic concerns and accelerating inflation further increased the interest in gold and silver coins. Financial advisers began advocating gold and silver as investments, and public interest increased in these investments. A popular book by Harry Browne, *How You Can Profit from the Coming Devaluation,* warned of runaway inflation, and devaluation of the U.S. dollar, and depression. Its author advocated investments in silver, gold, and Swiss francs as a means to protect against this impending economic disorder. This book became a best seller and, when the United States later effectively devalued the dollar, it became even more popular. All of this helped develop a widespread interest on the part of the general public in gold and silver investments. But access to the bullion markets was limited for small investors, who wanted to finance their transactions, and futures contracts posed unacceptable risks for many such investors. It was that gap that Monex and other leverage merchants sought to fill.

Leverage contracts are essentially financing arrangements for the purchase of commodities. Another way of viewing a leverage contract is that of a "lay-away" plan used by retail stores in past years (a consumer picks out an item and makes a down payment, and the item is then set aside until complete payment is made, often through installments). Conceptually, a leverage contract is much the same. In reality, however, leverage contracts often operate much differently. In addition, unlike the lay-away plan, the leverage purchaser may have his commodity sold if he does not meet margin calls. The leverage contract is thus a combination of a margin arrangement and an installment sale. Further, unlike the retail store, the vendor of a leverage contract may not actually own the commodity being purchased. Instead, it may simply hedge its obligations on a futures exchange. It should also be noted that leverage contracts may involve the sale of a commodity as well as its purchase.

Shortly after it commenced operation, Monex became the subject of an action by the SEC, which sought an injunction as well as the appointment of a receiver and disgorgement of profits. The SEC charged that Monex's contract was in fact a security.[1] The SEC further charged that Monex had raised approximately $1 billion from some 25,000 investors through a nationwide marketing campaign directed at small and unsophisticated investors. None of these charges were ever proven. Instead, a settlement was reached with the SEC in 1974, after the CFTC was given exclusive jurisdiction over leverage contracts, thereby preempting the SEC's jurisdiction. Pursuant to this settlement, Monex was enjoined from violating the CFTC antifraud rule for leverage contracts as well as the no longer applicable SEC requirements. The settlement allowed Monex to continue its leverage operations, and it prevailed in at least two state court actions on the issue of whether a leverage contract was a security.

The 1974 amendments legislation granted the CFTC authority to regulate transactions for the delivery of silver bullion, gold bullion, or bulk silver and gold coins pursuant to a "standardized contract commonly known as a margin account, margin contract, leverage account, or leverage contract." The legislation further provided that, if the CFTC determined that such transactions were in fact contracts for futures delivery, such transactions were to be regulated as futures contracts. This would mean that they would have to be traded on contract markets, which would result in a virtual elimination of the industry.

On April 18, 1975, a CFTC study group issued a report to the CFTC on trading and leverage contracts for gold and silver. This report reviewed the background and history of trading in leverage contracts. It found that there were specialized "leverage" firms, but that broker-dealers in the securities industry and merchant metal firms also engaged in margin-type transactions that offered customers standardized contracts in precious metals. It also noted that the New York Stock Exchange, on December 12, 1974, amended its rules to facilitate such trading in gold and silver bullion by member firms, while providing self-regulatory controls over those firms. Among other things, the New York Stock Exchange rules required that the exchange approve such transactions, established minimum margin requirements, and required ownership of the metal to be delivered under the contracts.

The CFTC study group, as noted, also found so-called merchant firms dealing in the metal were selling margin contracts, but those firms did not sell to the general public. It also found, however, that coin exchange firms did traffic in leverage contracts with the public.

The study group noted that the SEC and state security officials had contended that leverage contracts were securities, and that one state had adopted a commodity law geared toward coin exchange firms. It also noted that there was a great deal of diversity in the leverage contract industry and that, contrary to the suggestion in the legislation adopted by Congress, there was no contract commonly known as a margin account, margin contract, leverage account, or leverage contract. Rather, leverage contracts were standardized only for each firm.

The study group found:

The early coin exchange margin or leverage operations were predicated on the customer paying the seller the difference between the value of the silver content and the face value of the coins in return for securing a $1,000 loan from a bank, who held the coins as security. The great influx of competitors came in 1972, when the firms eliminated the bank and covered their sales by purchasing futures and forward contracts from the merchant firm. Only small amounts of inventory were maintained, and the margin or leverage contract took on many characteristics of a futures contract. The only differences seemed to be the size and length of the contract, the lack of a need for a customer to demonstrate financial responsibility, and the insulation the firm's corporate status provided its customers against margin calls. The firms continued to promote their sales of the "actual" commodity, however, and discredit futures. Under the current margin or leverage arrangement, the customer pays about one-third of the sales price of the commodity, incurs interest charges on the balance of the sales price, and hopes that he can sell back to the firm and receive more than his initial "investment." When analyzed, the margin or leverage purchasers have acquired nothing of intrinsic value and their fortune depends on a 35 or 40 percent annual rise in the value of the commodity and the firm's ability to make good.[2]

The study group recommended that the CFTC adopt an antifraud rule, require leverage firms to submit operating plans to the CFTC for approval, adopt rules requiring the registration of leverage firms, and establish rules to ensure the financial solvency of those firms. In addition, it recommended that minimum margin requirements be adopted and that commodities subject to leverage contracts be required to be within the possession or control of the leverage dealer. Another study group, however, recommended that leverage contracts be regulated as futures contracts.

The CFTC did not immediately embrace this regulatory scheme; although it did propose an antifraud rule modeled after the antifraud provisions of the federal securities laws, rather than the antifraud provisions of the Commodity Exchange Act. This proposal was made at the same time that the CFTC proposed antifraud rules for commodity options and foreign futures contracts, which were also modeled after the antifraud provisions of the federal securities laws. Subsequently, the CFTC adopted antifraud rules for the latter two instruments, but changed the form of the rule for options and foreign futures contract so that it was designed after the antifraud provisions of the Commodity Exchange Act. The CFTC, however, retained the antifraud rule modeled after the federal securities laws for leverage contracts, stating that these transactions were of a special type to which the antifraud provisions of the federal securities laws had been sought to be applied by the SEC prior to the creation of the CFTC. The CFTC saw no reason to disturb the applicability of those antifraud criteria to those specific transactions. Of course, this logic is not completely symmetrical, since the same antifraud rules had also been sought to be applied by the SEC to commodity options.

In any event, the CFTC continued its efforts to establish an appropriate regulatory program for leverage transactions. On August 20, 1975, it announced rule proposals to establish a regulatory scheme for these transactions. Essentially, these proposals would have prohibited the offer and sale of leverage contracts by anyone, unless they did so in accordance with a plan of business that had been filed with the CFTC and had been declared effective by it (another proposal advocated by the study group). The CFTC viewed this as a temporary measure that would remain in effect until it determined the appropriate form of permanent regulation for leverage transactions.

The business plan envisioned by the CFTC would have contained the identity of the offeror of the leverage contract, its officers and directors, their background, the terms of the leverage contract, and the text of promotional materials. Further, the plan would have included a current balance sheet and statements of profit and loss for the most recent three years of the "leverage transaction merchant." The CFTC stated that it would review these financial statements to ensure that the leverage transaction merchant had adequate financial responsibility to meet its commitments. The degree of leverage would also have been required to be specified in the plan, (i.e., the amount of margin required). The nature of the "cover" for the leverage contracts would also have been described, (including location and identity of any depository), as well as the terms of deposit arrangements (whether the property was segregated or commingled and whether the positions were to be covered by futures contracts). All fees and charges were to be disclosed and risk disclosures to customers were to be identified. Further, the leverage merchant would have been required to make annual submissions of its balance sheets and profit and loss statements to the CFTC.

This proposal was not adopted. Instead, the CFTC's Office of General Counsel proposed an addition, which would have required that the business plans be filed with state securities administrators and that a disclosure statement be given to customers at least forty-eight hours before each transaction. It would have also required a disclosure to the CFTC of the leverage merchants' standards for customer suitability. Still another proposed revision would have required minimum net working capital of $25,000 for leverage merchants, which was later increased to $100,000.

The CFTC also appointed an advisory committee to review and report to it on appropriate regulations for leverage transactions. The advisory committee, which rendered its report on July 16, 1976, found substantial differences among futures contracts, forward contracts, and leverage contracts, and concluded that leverage contracts should not be regulated as futures contracts.

In comparing the differences between futures forwards and leverage contracts, the advisory committee charted its relative terms. They found that futures contracts were traded on exchanges while leverage contracts were not. Further, pricing was reached by an auction market on futures exchanges, while it was established by individual dealers in leverage transactions. There was no central clearing house for leverage transactions and very little participation by commercial traders. It also found contract terms were not standardized by any independent agency for leverage transactions, but were standardized by each leverage merchant. The same was true for the quality and quantity to be delivered. In contrast, futures exchanges established standardization for all contracts traded by persons using its facilities. The advisory committee further found that security deposits or partial payments were required for both futures and leverage contracts, but that the margin was held by the leverage dealer rather than an independent third party, such as a futures commission merchant. Margin was paid by only one party (the customer) in a leverage transaction, unlike a futures contract. Both leverage and futures required variation margin.

In fact, while leverage dealers believe otherwise, the principal differences between leverage contracts and futures contracts identified by the advisory committee were due largely to the fact that leverage transactions were not traded on an exchange. Had they been, their differences would have been minor (e.g., standardization and holding of margin funds). Such a conceptual difference has been rejected by the CFTC in determining whether other transactions were futures contracts.

The advisory committee concluded that trading in leverage contracts should not be prohibited because the committee did not believe they were inherently fraudulent, manipulative, or incapable of being regulated. It advised the CFTC that regulations should be adopted for leverage merchants, and it identified several regulatory requirements that should be imposed. These included registration requirements, minimum working capital and net worth requirements, segregation of customers' funds, and 100 percent coverage of leverage merchant obligations through a CFTC-determined formula of futures contracts and physical commodities.

The advisory committee also believed that leverage merchants should be free to determine initial sales prices and repurchase prices, but that appropriate disclosures should be made to customers. It recommended that repurchase should not be mandatory, and it stated that leverage merchants should be allowed to impose carrying charges and other fees for services actually rendered, subject to appropriate disclosures. The advisory committee also recommended various other disclosures be made to customers, including the existence of conflicts of interest and fundamental risks and major aspects of the leverage transaction. It would have required leverage merchants to submit financial statements to the CFTC, including annual audited and quarterly unaudited statements, and the committee would have imposed a "know your customer" rule on leverage merchants, which would include an affirmative duty to consider whether the transaction was suitable for a particular customer.

In addition to comparing them with futures, the advisory committee also focused on the nature of leverage transactions. It described a leverage transaction as a contract under which the purchaser pays a portion of the purchase price at the outset and agrees to buy a specified amount of the commodity at a given price at a stated time in the future. The purchase price is determined by the leverage merchant, as well as the amount of initial payment. It found that the terms of leverage contracts varied, but they could cover a period as long as ten years. The advisory committee also noted that early delivery could be obtained by payment of the balance of the deliverer's contract. It found that sales commissions were charged, as well as "maintenance," "interest," "finance," or "leverage" charges on the unpaid balance of the contract. These charges were ostensibly to defray the carrying costs incurred by the leverage merchant in covering its obligations, but the committee found that coverage in the actual commodity generally constituted only a small portion of the cover used by some leverage merchants. It noted that leverage merchants generally covered their obligations through positions in the futures markets and to a lesser extent by forward contracts and ownership for physical commodities, which usually were hypothecated to financial institutions.

The advisory committee also found that service fees were sometimes imposed, which were supposed to represent administrative and other service-related elements of the leverage merchant's cost, including the servicing of the customer's account. Additional charges were imposed, including taxes, freight, and similar charges. The advisory committee noted that when a leverage transaction merchant was required to meet margin calls on the futures positions, it often did so by making margin calls on its customers.

It was found that delivery was rare in leverage contracts, just as in the case of futures contracts, and most contracts were liquidated prior to maturity. Generally, liquidation was effected through a repurchase agreement with the leverage merchant, which the leverage merchant was not obligated to make, but often did so as an accommodation to its customers.

The advisory committee report focused substantial light on leverage transactions, but it did not result in any immediate regulatory action by the CFTC. Rather, the CFTC sought an amendment in Congress to incorporate the leverage provision of the CFTC Act of 1974 directly into the Commodity Exchange Act, to make clear that the CFTC's power under the latter statute also applied to leverage transactions (e.g., rulemaking and injunctive authority). The CFTC also concluded, on October 12, 1976, that leverage transactions were *not* futures contracts, and it directed its staff to prepare guidelines for interim regulations. But no action was taken on that directive. Instead, on November 8, 1977, the CFTC directed a task force to be established to study the leverage transaction industry.

Once again, there was no immediate result. But, in February 1978, the CFTC recommended to Congress during the CFTC's reauthorization hearings that Section 217 of the CFTC Act of 1974 be repealed. The CFTC made this recommendation because of its concern that option firms that had engaged in fraudulent practices might transfer their operations into the leverage area. This recommendation was made by the CFTC as a result of the nationwide scandals it was facing in commodity options, and it was concerned that those scandals would be renewed in the leverage business. The CFTC suggested that if these transactions were not regulated as futures, they could be better regulated under state and federal securities laws. It was clear, however, from the testimony of the CFTC commissioners that this was a controversial subject; each commissioner expressed different views.

While Congress was considering these issues, the CFTC, on June 1, 1978, proposed a moratorium on the entry of new firms into the leverage contract business, grandfathering leverage firms already in existence. The CFTC stated that it had studied the leverage industry and had conducted an in-depth survey, in which it reviewed the operation of firms that were known to be currently marketing leverage contracts. From that survey, it found that leverage contracts in the amount of at least $100 million were outstanding, and that the size of the business was increasing. The CFTC also concluded that principal characteristics of leverage contracts appeared to be similar, "if not identical," to futures contracts, but without the advantages of an auction-style futures market. It found that léverage market prices and trade information were not generally or widely disseminated and that leverage contracts were entered into solely for the purpose of speculating and not for hedging. The CFTC also found that some eleven firms engaged in leverage business had experienced financial failure since 1973.

The CFTC adopted its moratorium on December 5, 1978. In doing so, the CFTC noted that in April 1978, it had conducted a survey in which it determined that there were only seven firms actively engaged in selling leverage transactions. When it proposed its moratorium in June 1978, that number had risen to approximately twenty. Thereafter, at the time of adoption of the moratorium, the CFTC had identified nearly eighty firms claiming to be engaged in leverage transactions. The CFTC noted that, as in the case of commodity options, it was witnessing an explosive growth in the marketing of speculative instruments to the public, and it had found that a number of leverage dealers were in fact former options dealers who were using the same boiler-room techniques that led to the debacle in commodity options.

In the midst of all this, Congress enacted the Futures Trading Act of 1978. In brief, those amendments prohibited leverage transactions on the previously regulated commodities, required the CFTC to regulate leverage transactions involving gold or silver bullion or bulk coins, and authorized the CFTC to prohibit or regulate leverage transactions in all other commodities. It continued the authorization for the CFTC to regulate any leverage transactions as a futures contract if it were determined to be such. But the Congress cautioned the CFTC not to determine that leverage contracts were futures contracts as a means simply to avoid adopting a regulatory scheme. The Conference Committee noted that the CFTC's Office of General Counsel had recommended that the CFTC determine that leverage contracts be regulated as futures contracts, and that the CFTC had advised Congress of its intention to publish that determination for comment. The Conference Committee, however, stated that it had not contemplated such action, and that it expected that the Commission would not take any final action on that recommendation until appropriate congressional committees had an opportunity to receive testimony on that issue.

After adoption of this legislation, the CFTC directed its staff to draft rules expanding its antifraud rule and a rule to prohibit all leverage transactions except those involving gold and silver as well as proposals for either a prohibition of leverage transactions or the establishment of a regulatory program for them.

On November 14, 1978, the CFTC announced a proposed revision of its leverage transaction antifraud rule. This proposal sought to extend the antifraud rule to leverage transactions in commodities in addition to silver or gold bullion or bulk coins. This included platinum, diamonds, and other precious gems, which were starting to experience options-type boiler-room problems. The CFTC stated, in proposing this rule, that it was given exclusive jurisdiction over leverage transactions, but that the states could enforce their own criminal or antifraud and other statutes of general applicability. The CFTC noted that the proposed rule, like its predecessor, was modeled after Securities and Exchange Commission rule 10b-5, and that it intended that the broad remedial interpretations that had been accorded to rule 10b-5 also apply with respect to leverage transactions. The CFTC stated, however, that it intended *scienter* not be required to establish violation of this antifraud rule, rejecting the Supreme Court's interpretation of rule 10b-5 in *Ernst & Ernst v. Hochfelder*.[3] This antifraud rule was adopted on December 15, 1978, by the CFTC without substantial revision or comment.

The next step by the CFTC occurred on February 2, 1979, when it proposed a suspension of all leverage contracts except for gold and silver. In proposing this ban, the CFTC asked for information on whether leverage contracts, other than silver and gold, had an economic purpose and whether there were particularized contracts that were distinguishable from leverage contracts previously regulated by the CFTC. The CFTC stated that it was seeking to ban such leverage transactions because it was concerned that options dealers now subject to the CFTC's commodity option ban would move into this industry and renew the abuses that led to the options suspension. Among other things, the CFTC noted that the marketing of leverage contracts in diamonds was being used as a medium for abusive sales practices, and it found that other precious gems, copper, and platinum were the subject of such sales abuses.

This moratorium was adopted and made effective as of June 1, 1978. In so doing, the CFTC noted that little information had been supplied to it in response to its request as to whether leverage contracts in other than silver and gold served an economic purpose. In light of the lack of any evidence to suggest a commercial need for such transactions, and in view of the potential for abuse, the CFTC determined that a moratorium would be appropriate. It noted that an additional investigation by its Division of Enforcement had found that some seventy-three firms were selling off-exchange instruments, some of which appeared to be leverage contracts. The staff had also found a likelihood of high-pressure boiler-room sales techniques such as those found in the options area.

In the interim, on March 12, 1979, the CFTC had also sought comment on two possible regulatory approaches to regulating leverage transactions. The first was to determine whether leverage contracts should be regulated as futures contracts. The second approach would be to adopt a comprehensive regulatory scheme for leverage contracts, separate from the regulatory scheme for other instruments regulated by the CFTC. This would include registration, minimum net capital, segregation of customer funds, disclosure, and record-keeping requirements.

In reference to the first of these proposals, the CFTC noted its Office of General Counsel had concluded that leverage contracts were in fact futures contracts and that the CFTC's chief economist had also concluded that such transactions were essentially contracts for future delivery. The CFTC noted, however, that the conference committee on the 1978 amendments to the Commodity Exchange Act had asked that, before the CFTC take final action on the recommendation of its general counsel, the appropriate House and Senate committees be given an opportunity to receive testimony on the issue.

With respect to its second alternative, a separate regulatory scheme, the CFTC stated that it was being guided by the recommendations, discussed above, from its Advisory Committee on Market Instruments on Futures, Forward and Leverage Contracts and Transactions. The CFTC requested comment on whether registration with the CFTC should be required and whether sales personnel and persons supervising salespersons should register as associated persons. Financial reporting requirements were being considered as well as net capital, including annual audited and quarterly unaudited financial statements. A requirement for the retention of promotional material and detailed disclosures was also proposed, including a boldfaced warning concerning the high degree of risk inherent in such transactions, as well as the essential terms of the transactions. Customer funds would be required to be segregated, and "cover" requirements would have been imposed, including record-keeping requirements.

On July 27, 1979, the CFTC announced that it was following the first of the above regulatory approaches, that leverage contracts should be regulated as futures contracts. The CFTC stated that it advised Congress of this determination and that it expected to take final action on its determination sometime before January 1, 1980. On December 3, 1979, however, the CFTC announced that it was postponing the effective date of this determination until June 30, 1980. Although that date passed, the CFTC did not take action. Instead, it delayed action at the request of Congress until its reauthorization hearings in 1982. There the CFTC had proposed that Congress ratify and extend its moratorium on leverage transactions, but Congress declined to do so. Rather, it directed the CFTC "quickly" to adopt a comprehensive regulatory scheme for leverage transactions. Congress concluded that, to impose the moratorium by statute, particularly in light of its grandfather provisions, was inherently anticompetitive and thereby contrary to the "fundamental objectives of economic competition and the free market place." Congress further directed the CFTC to regulate leverage transactions and not to ban them. In doing so it repealed the provision in the Commodity Exchange Act that authorizes the CFTC to determine that leverage contracts could be treated as futures contracts. It directed the CFTC to issue comprehensive regulations governing leverage transactions as expeditiously as possible. It also allowed the CFTC to prohibit leverage contracts in any commodity that was not the subject of leverage transactions on or before December 9, 1982, if the CFTC determined that such trading was contrary to public interest.

On June 23, 1983, the CFTC proposed a set of regulations to regulate leverage contracts in gold and silver bullion or bulk coins and other commodities; the previously regulated commodities still could not be subject to leverage transactions. The CFTC stated that it was its intention to limit leverage contracts trading to gold and silver bullion or bulk coins, platinum, and copper, and currency. The CFTC also asserted that, as far as Congress indicated would be appropriate, it intended to continue its regulatory moratorium on the entry of new firms into the business of offering or selling such leverage transactions.

The proposed regulations defined the term *leverage contract,* specified registration requirements, required that the registrant be designated by the CFTC to trade in the particular leverage transaction, and imposed minimum financial requirements, segregation requirements, and record-keeping and other reporting. In addition, disclosure statements were proposed, and a "cooling off" period of three days during which a first-time customer could rescind the transaction was advocated. The CFTC noted that its rules were similar to requirements imposed by the Federal Trade Commission for door-to-door salespersons and the Department of Housing and Urban Development providing for revocation rights under the Interstate Land Sales Full Disclosure Act. These proposals would also have required leverage merchants to repurchase leverage contracts.

Thereafter, the CFTC adopted "interim final rules" governing the regulation of leverage transactions for firms operating under the grandfather provisions of its moratorium. The CFTC characterized its rules as "interim" because it intended to adopt more permanent rules at a later date. These rules applied only to firms operating under its moratorium; that is, the CFTC did not lift the moratorium for the firms that were not operating under the CFTC's grandfather provisions. The CFTC, among other things, established a definition for leverage contracts. In so doing, it stated that the transactions that did not fall within that definition were not subject to its jurisdiction. As a consequence, such transactions may now be open to regulation and enforcement by the states.

The CFTC's rules set forth the distinguishing characteristics of a leverage commodity and defines a leverage contract as having a duration of ten years or more. In defining a leverage contract in this way, the CFTC was excluding recently popular forms of the contracts that were of a lesser duration.

The CFTC's rules imposed a registration requirement on leverage commodities. It required each leveraged commodity upon which a leverage contract is offered for sale by a leverage transaction merchant to be separately registered with the CFTC. The rules further provide that registration would be granted only when the person seeking registration is registered as an authorized "leverage transaction merchant." Associated persons of leverage transaction merchants were also required to be registered.

The rules impose minimum financial coverage. In brief, each leverage transaction merchant is required to maintain cover of at least 90 percent of the amount of the physical commodity subject to open leverage contracts. At least 25 percent of the amount of physical commodities subject to open leverage contracts must be covered by "permissible" coverage e.g., warehouse receipts. The remaining cover (65 percent of the amount of physical commodity subject to open leverage contracts) could be covered by futures contracts. Daily computations of cover are required and other record-keeping requirements were imposed.

In addition, as noted, net capital requirements were imposed in the amount of at least $2.5 million. Specific computation provisions were established for determining net capital, in light of the peculiarities of the leverage transaction business. The CFTC interim regulations also establish requirements for the repurchase of leverage contracts. In brief, the leverage transaction merchant is required to repurchase any such contracts.

Disclosure requirements are also imposed, including boldfaced risk warnings and customer rights. For example:

> Because of the unpredictable nature of the prices of precious and other metals and foreign currencies, leverage contracts involve a high degree of risk and are not suitable for many members of the public.[4]

In addition, disclosure is required concerning the provisions of the leverage contract, its duration, any costs including initial charges, carrying charges, termination charges, a description of the bid and asked prices, an explanation of margin, a description of the leverage customer's responsibilities with respect to margin calls, and other pertinent information such as calculation of the break-even point. The CFTC also adopted the earlier proposal for a cooling-off period. Segregation requirements for customer funds were also imposed. This required a separate accounting and a provision against commingling or removing the funds from the United States.

As noted above, these rules are only "interim," although doubtless they will be of some duration and have already been amended by the CFTC to further strengthen their requirements. In January 1985, the CFTC's chairman indicated that lifting the leverage moratorium would not be a CFTC priority. The CFTC, however, subsequently conducted a study to determine what resources would be required if the moratorium were lifted, and the leverage transaction struggle continued in the CFTC 1986 reauthorization that was the subject of congressional hearings in 1986. In fact, the exchanges mounted a concerted campaign to have Congress require leverage contracts to be traded on exchanges only, thereby eliminating their competition.

The CFTC proposed to Congress in the 1986 reauthorization that its jurisdiction over leverage contracts be eliminated. Under the CFTC's interpretation, this would have the effect of making leverage contracts futures contracts. The Senate committee responsible for the CFTC's reauthorization adopted the CFTC proposal but its counterpart committee in the House declined to do so. The House committee determined that the CFTC should retain jurisdiction and that it should lift its moratorium on gold, silver, and copper leverage contracts. As of this writing, this impasse is yet to be broken by Congress, and it has delayed the CFTC reauthorization process.

CASES

The CFTC has brought a host of cases against firms selling leverage contracts in violation of its moratorium. It has also brought actions against the grandfathered leverage dealers, variously charging that they were engaged in the sale of futures contracts that would be required to be traded on exchanges, or that they had violated other CFTC regulations. In one such action against First National Monetary Corp. and Monex, two of the largest leverage dealers, the CFTC charged that these firms were selling futures contracts, which they were denominating as cash forwards. The respondents defended this action on the ground, among other things, that these were leverage transactions. The administrative law judge heard testimony from various experts and closely examined the terms of each of these contracts. He also examined the various characteristics of forward and futures contracts and concluded that these were futures contracts, rather than leverage or "deferred delivery" contracts that are not subject to the CFTC's regulation.

The administrative law judge noted that the Commodity Exchange Act does not define a leverage contract. Rather, it states that it is a contract commonly known to the trade as such. He therefore concluded that the determination that an instrument is a leverage contract hinged on the understanding of the members of the trade as to whether the instruments in question were, in fact, leverage contracts. On this issue, the judge rejected the expert testimony offered by respondents on the ground that either the witnesses were interested or were not a part of the trade. Accordingly, he found insufficient evidence to establish that these were contracts commonly known to the trade as leverage contracts, and therefore rejected the respondent's defenses. The judge noted, however, that he was not addressing the other forms of contracts offered by the respondents in which they themselves had been denominated as leverage contracts in their promotional materials. On appeal the CFTC reversed. In an almost incomprehensible decision, it held that the contracts were futures contracts under the CFTC's new rules, but that the evidence established they were actually leverage contracts at the time they were being sold. Therefore, it dismissed the action.

Another principal enforcement effort by the CFTC was against Premex, a former leader in the sale of leverage contracts. Although not required to do so, Premex had registered as a futures commission merchant with the CFTC. At one point, however, it failed to meet the minimum net capital requirements for a futures commission merchant, which the CFTC required to be met, even though it had no "futures" customers. The CFTC sought injunctive relief in the Northern District of Illinois, and Premex consented to injunctive relief. The CFTC also later brought a contempt proceeding when Premex once again failed to meet net capital requirements, but the court concluded that the undercapitalization was a technical violation only and allowed Premex to continue its futures business.

Previously, the Seventh Circuit had held that Premex had violated a consent decree against antifraudulent conduct. Thereafter, the CFTC revoked Premex's registration as a futures commission merchant and commodity trading adviser, imposed a large civil penalty, and effectively barred it from further leverage business. Among other things, the CFTC rejected the claim that its net capital and other violations were harmless; the leverage merchant had argued that its registration as a futures commission merchant was not required, because it was in the leverage business and was allowed to offer leverage contracts under the grandfather provisions of the moratorium. The CFTC denied the stay of its order and sought injunctive relief to require Premex to cease business. The district court required Premex to close down, and later a temporary equity receiver was appointed by the court.

14

COMMODITY OPTIONS

A commodity option contract entitles the purchaser, in the case of a "call" option, to elect to purchase a commodity at an agreed price at any time before the expiration date of the option contract. Conversely, the seller is obligated to deliver the commodity at the agreed price if the buyer exercises his option. A "put" option entitles the purchaser to sell a commodity, to "put" it to the writer of the option, at a given price, at any time before the expiration date of the option.

The purchaser of a put or call option pays a "premium" for the right to purchase (or to sell in the case of a put) the underlying commodity at the agreed price (the "strike" price). The purchaser of a call option will not receive a profit until the commodity price has increased in an amount sufficient to exceed the amount of the premium and transaction costs. This is the purchaser's "break-even" point.

Options may also be traded on futures contracts. An option on a futures contract grants the purchaser the right to enter into a position in the underlying futures contract. If exercise of the option occurs, initial margin in connection with the underlying futures contract must be posted and, unless the futures position is liquidated, variation margin payments must be made as the value of the futures contracts fluctuates.

A form of option contract is a so-called London option. These are simply options traded on or off exchanges in London, England. These contracts are subject to clearing house guarantees for performance, if they are traded through the London Commodity Exchange or through other exchanges guaranteed by the International Commodity Clearing House in London. Other contracts, such as those on the London Metals Exchange, are not so guaranteed. Rather, performance on those contracts is ensured only by the financial integrity of the member firm granting the option. It should be noted, however, that defaults have been rare in these markets, at least until 1985, when a default in tin threatened the entire London Metal Exchange.

Another form of option is a "naked" or "uncovered" option. These options are not traded on an exchange, and the grantor of the option does not own the underlying commodity. In such cases, the grantor is betting that the purchaser of the option will be wrong or that his resources will be sufficient to allow him to purchase the commodity to "cover" in the event the option is exercised. Naked options are extremely dangerous financial instruments. Thus, while a purchaser of an option has a limited risk in the event of adverse market moves, the seller does not. As a result, grantors of naked options often are unable to perform on their obligations as the result of adverse market moves. In such event, the purchaser of the option loses his investment (the premium) and any opportunity to profit from his investment.

"Mocatta" or "dealer" options are options granted by a commercial firm owning the underlying commodity. "Commercial" options are options sold to a purchaser who has a commercial need for the commodity underlying the option, rather than a speculator or a member of the public. A "European" option is an option that may be exercised on only one date, in contrast to other options that may be exercised at any time before their expiration date.

The problems encountered by the CFTC principally concerned firms selling London options. In fact, these firms often did not execute the transactions in London. Further, even if they did, when profits were claimed by some customers, those customers often could not be paid because the London firms would offset the losses of other customers against the profitable positions that were held in the U.S. dealer's omnibus account. Sales abuses were also prevalent among these commodity option firms. Many of the firms were simply boiler shops where untrained salesmen made thousands of phone calls each day promising large profits with limited risks, using high-pressure sales techniques in nationwide cold call selling campaigns. Options were sold to customers without any regard to their suitability or their knowledge or sophistication in commodity transactions. Enormous mark-ups were charged over the London option calls, thereby effectively restricting the ability of customers to profit (i.e., their break-even point was a point well over the premium thought by market specialists as being the market value of the contract). Even when profits were made, customers often encountered difficulty in withdrawing their profits, either because the options were not purchased, or because customers were pressured into reinvesting into equally speculative transactions that most frequently did not result in further profits. To the contrary, the customer's entire investment was frequently lost.

Initially, the CFTC's regulatory efforts were limited to the adoption of an antifraud rule for commodity options. It also sought to require firms selling options to register as commodity trading advisers. This is because in their marketing efforts, the option firms were necessarily advising on the value of the underlying commodities or related futures.

As a result of continued abuses, the CFTC subsequently adopted a new series of rules designed to provide greater regulatory control over commodity options transactions. The CFTC rules required option dealers to be registered as futures commission merchants and to comply with minimum net capital requirements, so that the dealer maintains adjusted working capital in excess of $50,000. Additionally, disclosure rules were adopted requiring a summary disclosure statement to be provided to customers that contained specific disclosures of risk and which described the mechanics of options trading. Firms dealing in options were further required to segregate 90 percent of the payments received from customers in a bank account until expiration or exercise of the option. Record-keeping requirements were also imposed.

These rules were immediately challenged.[1] Among other things, options firms contended that the segregation requirement resulted in double segregation for London options, such that premiums had to be paid to the London firms for execution of the customer's options on the London markets, while at the same time the U.S. firm was required to segregate funds in the United States. Indeed, one firm claimed that this double segregation requirement would require it to raise several million dollars in capital and would strangle the industry. The CFTC, however, wanted to be sure that there were sufficient funds on hand to meet all customer obligations, if they exercised their options. This was especially needed, because many options firms were thinly capitalized and often did not execute an option in the London market.

The district court hearing the challenge to the CFTC's rules concluded that the double segregation requirement was inappropriate, but upon appeal the Second Circuit upheld the requirement, as well as the other provisions of the CFTC's regulations.

The CFTC, nevertheless, shortly thereafter concluded that even these rules were not sufficient to stop fraud in the industry. The Lloyd Carr and other commodity option scandals led the CFTC to suspend all commodity options trading in the United States, with certain limited exceptions.

EXCEPTIONS TO THE OPTIONS BAN

Dealer Options

"Mocotta" or "dealer" options were sold in the United States for several years prior to the CFTC ban, without any of the problems that attended London options and the naked options that were sold by Lloyd Carr &

Co. and Goldstein. The CFTC, nevertheless, initially included such options in its trading suspension because it did not want to create a loophole that would allow a new options industry and its attending problems to develop, but the CFTC did delay the effective date of its options suspension in order to ameliorate the hardship of its suspension for dealer options. Before the effective date, however, Mocatta Metals Corp. and another firm petitioned the CFTC to exempt dealer options from the ban. In its petition, Mocatta noted that Congress was considering bills with respect to the CFTC reauthorization that would permit the CFTC to allow the continuation of dealer options. After receiving comment on this petition, and in light of the legislation then pending in Congress which appeared likely to be adopted, the CFTC determined to exempt dealer options from the options suspension under certain limited circumstances; that is, it permitted the continuing sales of dealer options, but only by those firms that were already in the business. It also imposed strict requirements on these dealers. This included a minimum net worth requirement of several million dollars; joint and several liability of the grantor with persons selling its options; segregation, record-keeping, and other requirements. The CFTC is now considering whether to allow dealer options to be sold to the public by persons who were not in that business at the time of the options suspension in 1978.

Commercial Options

In banning commodity option transactions in the United States, the CFTC also exempted from that ban so-called commercial or trade options. This exemption applies to options that are "offered by a person who has a reasonable basis to believe that the option is offered to a producer, processor, or commercial user of, or a merchant handling, the commodity which is the subject of the commodity option transaction . . . and that such producer, processor, commercial user, or merchant is offered or enters into the commodity option transaction solely for purposes related to its business as such."[2]

This exemption does not require a commercial purpose on the part of the seller. Rather, the determination is made on the part of the person purchasing the option. That purpose must be for a nonspeculative purpose by a commercial enterprise engaged in transactions in physical commodities.

The CFTC staff has issued interpretations of this commercial option exemption. In one, the CFTC staff stated that, while the commodity or "trade" option exemption as originally conceived may have pertained primarily to off-exchange sales of nonstandardized option contracts to commercial interests, the exemption does permit the purchase of foreign exchange traded commodity options by qualifying offerees. This, once again, allows London and other foreign options to be bought in the United States, but only by commercial purchasers who are "producers, processors or commercial users of, or a merchant handling, the commodity which is the subject of the commodity option transaction, or the products or by-products thereof... [and who] enter the transaction solely for non-speculative purposes related to a business as such."[3]

In this interpretation, the Commission staff was specifically asked to apply the exemption to commodity options being offered and sold by a foreign exchange to banks in the United States. The staff concluded that the *purchase* of an option by a bank would be permissible if the purchase was for a purpose that bore a direct nonspeculative relationship to the bank's transactions in the currency. The CFTC stated that this would include transactions that were conducted for bona fide hedging purposes. A bona fide hedging transaction in the CFTC regulations is a concept that is applied to exempt hedgers from CFTC speculative limits; that is, CFTC rules limit the amount of futures transactions that a speculator may engage in particular contracts. This definition, however, is very restrictive and does not encompass many commercial operations. In a second interpretation, however, the CFTC staff indicated that a commercial purpose could be broader than the bona fide hedging exemption for speculative limits.

In the first interpretive letter, the CFTC staff stated that banks could not write options through the foreign exchange because it would not know the purpose for which the options were being purchased; that is, the clearing house would be interjected and the ultimate purchaser could be purchasing for speculative reasons. Accordingly, without information on the commercial purpose of the purchaser, sale transactions in options would not be permitted through the exchange. In this regard, the staff stated that the writer of a commercial option must take affirmative steps to ensure that the purchasing institution qualifies under the CFTC commercial option exception. This would mean that mere reliance on the undocumented representations of the purchaser would not be sufficient.

The CFTC's staff interpretation that the trade option exemption does not permit the sale of options through an exchange appeared to be in conflict with the views of the CFTC itself, when it readopted this exemption after the 1978 amendments to the Commodity Exchange Act that authorized the CFTC suspension. The CFTC thus stated:

> The question has also arisen whether a producer, processor, commercial user, or merchant handling a physical commodity may grant an option on that commodity through the facilities of a foreign exchange for purposes solely related to its business as such.
> The Commission is not purporting to regulate the business affairs of commercial enterprises within the United States, but only to regulate the offer and sale of options in this country. Nor does the Commission in-

terpret the general prohibition on option transactions imposed by . . . the Act to prevent commercial enterprises from granting options through foreign boards of trade. Accordingly, in the Commission's view, the grant of an option through a foreign board of trade by a domestic commercial enterprise would not contravene the purpose of the general prohibition on option transactions . . . so long as it is not part of a scheme to offer, sell, or resell the option to a member of the public in the United States.[4]

In the second interpretation referred to above, the CFTC staff issued an opinion stating that option contracts on silver, which were traded on a foreign exchange, could be purchased in the United States if the purchaser had a commercial purpose for the option. It was indicated in this interpretation by the staff that the commercial purpose could be broader than bona fide hedging transactions. The CFTC staff also stressed, once again, that the trade option exemption did not authorize the offer and sale of options to the general public.

More recently, the CFTC announced that it was considering whether to require that grantors of options be a commercial enterprise, as well as the purchaser. It stated that it did not believe that that persons engaged in the occasional sale of commodities or their by-products, who may be unsophisticated in the use of options, should be able to take advantage of the exemption. Presently, the purchaser of an option would not violate the rule even if it did not have a commercial purpose. Rather, the seller would be in violation, if the seller did not have a reasonable basis to believe that the purchaser had a commercial purpose. The proposed amendment would also place the purchaser in violation. In addition, the proposed rule would clarify that a seller of dealer options could use the commercial option exemption to hedge its transactions. The CFTC had previously asserted that this would be permissible.

The trade options exemption does not apply to options on the "previously regulated" agricultural commodities, that is, those commodities regulated before the creation of the CFTC. An intrepretation rendered by the CFTC's Office of General Counsel concluded that the following was an illegal "trade" option because it involved a previously regulated commodity:

> The contract establishes a minimum contract price determined when the contract is written, and a premium is collected, either at the initiation of the contract, during the life of the contract or, together with interest accumulated over the life of the contract, at the time of settlement. In return for the premium, the producer has the right to require the merchant to accept delivery of and pay a minimum contract price for the crop. However, the producer may forfeit the premium and seek a higher price for, and deliver, the crop elsewhere.[5]

On the other hand, the Office of General Counsel allowed an insurance company to sell price protection insurance to farmers for their crops, including the previously nonregulated commodities.

Exchange-Traded Options

Prior to the adoption of its options suspension, the CFTC had considered proposals to permit exchange-traded options trading, which would permit self-regulatory control and clearing house protections to customers that were unavailable for naked options and even London options that were being sold by U.S. dealers. On April 5, 1977, the CFTC proposed to implement a comprehensive and rigidly controlled three-year test program for exchange-traded commodity options. It stated that it intended to adopt final regulations for this part of the program by July 31, 1977. That was not to be the case. Instead, on October 17, 1977, the CFTC announced a revised proposal for commodity options transactions to be conducted on exchanges. But a final rule was not adopted until November 3, 1981.

The implementation of the options suspension thus delayed that program, but did not stop efforts to permit such trading under rigidly controlled conditions. On June 29, 1981, the CFTC announced proposed regulations for a pilot program under which commodity options on a limited number of commodity futures contracts would be permitted on contract markets under a pilot program. Thereafter, on November 3, 1981, the CFTC adopted rules permitting a pilot program for options trading on domestic contract markets, but permitted each contract market to trade only one such option on a futures contract, excluding options on physical commodities. The CFTC pilot program was almost immediately challenged by the American Stock Exchange because it did not permit the trading of options on a physical commodity. That effort was unsuccessful, but the CFTC had proposed and did subsequently adopt rules that permitted options trading on physical commodities. The options pilot program has also been expanded to allow expanded trading in commodity options.

The CFTC pilot program for options has imposed an elaborate set of regulatory controls to ensure that abuses do not recur in commodity options trading. For example, firms conducting transactions in exchange-traded options are required to register as futures commission merchants with the CFTC, and such firms are required to be a member of the contract market where the option is traded or a member of the National Futures Association, thereby ensuring self-regulatory control over these firms. In addition, firms dealing in options are required to collect the full amount of premiums paid by customers for commodity options, and contract markets are required to establish rules and procedures to ensure that futures contracts or physical commodities on which options are traded are sufficiently liquid to diminish the possibility of manipulation. Further, exchanges are required to adopt rules governing "deep-out-of-the-money" options (whose exercise prices were so far removed from the strike price as to make their profitability unlikely), and contract markets are required to establish rules requiring their members to maintain records of customer complaints and supply copies to the contract market. In addition, firms dealing in options are required to submit their promotional material to the contract market for its review and to establish specific procedures for supervising options accounts in which the customer gives up discretion to the broker. Other sales practices are required to be regulated, including prohibitions against fraudulent or high-pressure sales communications, and contract markets are required to conduct audits of member firm sales practices and maintain a list of occupation or business categories of commercial users of the commodity, in order to assist the CFTC in its determination of the appropriateness of continuing the options program.

The CFTC also required brokerage firms to maintain copies of their promotional material, as well as the true source of the authority for the information contained in such material. Specific disclosures were required to be given to customers in a form of an "Options Disclosure Statement," in which specified information was required to be contained. The required disclosures include descriptions of the mechanics of the options trading and warnings as to the possibility of loss:

> A person should not purchase any commodity option unless he is able to sustain a total loss of the premium and transaction costs of purchasing the option. A person should not grant any commodity option unless he is able to meet additional calls for margin when the market moves against his position and, in such circumstances, to sustain a very large financial loss.[6]

The CFTC has also imposed requirements on margins for options trading, unlike futures contracts over which it has little authority to exercise control, and it amended its reporting requirements to ensure that it could obtain information on individuals trading in the options markets.

Finally, as noted above, the 1982 amendments to the Commodity Exchange Act authorized the CFTC to permit trading on a trial basis in options contracts on the previously regulated agricultural commodities, transactions that had been prohibited since 1936, and the CFTC has acted to permit trading on such agricultural options. To date, the option program has been very successful and has worked well. The Volume Investors default in gold options did throw a cloud over the whole exchange-traded options program, and the CFTC's initial response may well have crippled options trading, had it been implemented. Hopefully, a more workable solution will be adopted.

15
CASH CONTRACTS

Cash, physical, or *actual transactions* are terms basic to commodity markets. They are simply a reference to the commodity itself. A person who buys grain from a farmer and takes immediate delivery of the grain has engaged in a "physical," "actual," or "cash" commodity transaction, whichever you may wish to term it.

Cash transactions are subject only to very limited regulation by the CFTC and the exchanges; the Commodity Exchange Act does not impose the elaborate regulatory scheme utilized for other transactions falling within its ambit, such as futures contracts and commodity options. There are, for example, no restrictions placed on the amount of price fluctuations that will be permitted in the cash price during any given day, as is common for many futures contracts. Also, unlike futures contracts, cash transactions need not be traded on a contract market that is licensed by the CFTC. The CFTC's principal regulatory oversight is limited to ensuring that cash prices are not manipulated. A CFTC Advisory Committee Report, however, recommended that even the CFTC's surveillance of cash markets should be limited:

> The Commission should undertake an affirmative monitoring or surveillance effort in connection with a cash market only in those extraordinary circumstances where (i) a danger to the public is clear and present; (ii) where that imminent danger threatens the Commission's primary areas of responsibility such as futures markets, commodity options or leverage contracts; (iii) adequate resources are available for commitment to the program without dissipating the Commission's ability to perform its primary functions, and (iv) only for such period of time as the benefits decisively outweigh the many negative consequences of the program.[1]

Indeed, the predecessor to the CFTC, the CEA, had advocated the removal of all cash market jurisdiction from the Commodity Exchange Act, including manipulation, unless it was related to a futures market.

Initially, the CFTC had also required persons rendering advice with respect to the value of commodities, even where commodity futures contracts were not involved, to register as commodity trading advisers under the Commodity Exchange Act. Later, the CFTC adopted a rule excluding cash commodity advice from this registration requirement, where the advice was incidental to the person's cash commodity business. Still later, in 1982, the Commodity Exchange Act was amended to require commodity trading adviser registration only for persons rendering advice with respect to futures contracts, unless the CFTC determined otherwise, which it has not done.

The scandals in recent years involving cash transactions in precious metals and other cash commodities, particularly silver and gold bullion, was the result of a regulatory hiatus between the Commodity Exchange Act and the federal securities laws, none of which specifically applied to cash transactions. These scandals included the International Gold Bullion Exchange in Florida, which failed, leaving some 25,000 creditors claiming more than $75 million in losses. Another highly publicized case involved the Bullion Reserve of North America, which also failed, leaving millions of dollars in customer claims and nothing in its vault but some old typewriters and wooden bars painted to look like gold. In response to these scandals, the Senate Permanent Subcommittee on Investigations conducted hearings on legislation needed to fill this regulatory gap. As yet, however, no legislation has been adopted.

Transactions in bullion have been conducted in various forms, including the purchase and sale of certificates representing gold held for the purchaser by the seller. Provision is often made for repurchase of the gold, at the seller's option. Numerous such programs have been adopted by brokerage firms and precious metals dealers.

FORWARD OR DEFERRED DELIVERY CONTRACTS

A *forward* or *deferred delivery* contract closely resembles a cash transaction, except that delivery is made at a date in the future. To illustrate, if you were to agree to buy 1,000 bushels of soybeans from a farmer with delivery to be made by the farmer in two months, you would have engaged in a "forward" or "deferred" delivery transaction. Like cash transactions, forward contracts are not subject to the elaborate regulatory scheme imposed on futures and options contracts.

The price in forward contracts may be agreed on in advance, or there may be agreement that the price will be determined at the time of delivery.

Similarly, payment terms may vary (e.g., payment may be immediate or delayed). In the case of deferred payment, down payment deposits may be required to ensure performance.

As will be discussed below, contracts for forward delivery are also "personalized"; that is, the delivery time and amount are determined between the seller and the customer individually and are not standardized, thereby limiting their ability to be traded in secondary markets. Further, unlike futures contracts, actual delivery of the commodity is contemplated in most instances and the parties have the capacity to make and take delivery. Contracts are offset or cancelled only for commercial purposes and not for speculation.

COMMODITY FUTURES CONTRACTS

A *commodity futures contract* is an obligation on the part of the purchaser (the "long") to buy a stated amount of a commodity of a given grade or specification, with delivery to be made at a stated time in the future. The seller (the "short") in this bilateral executory agreement incurs a reciprocal obligation to deliver the commodity at an agreed-upon date. Commodity futures contracts are standardized (e.g., they have standard delivery dates and specifications for the quantity and quality of the commodity). The only term that is not standardized is the price of the commodity, which is negotiated in pits or rings on a contract market.

The concept of futures contract has changed in recent years. As Charles Robinson, an official of the Futures Industry Association, had noted with respect to a futures contract:

> Traditionally, it is defined as a type of forward or delayed delivery contract in which the parties agree to the purchase and sale of a specified property during a specified period some time in the future at a price established in the present. The key feature of a futures contract is standardized, uniform, terms which make individual contracts fungible, permitting an offset process for settlement rather than settlement by performance.
>
> In today's world the definition I have just given you is troublesome. There are a number of cash settlement contracts—the eurodollar time deposit contract, the index contracts, and others. Where is the purchase and sale of a "specified property"?
>
> From an economic point of view, a futures contract is a standardized, tradeable device to enable enterprises engaged in production, merchandising or finance to shift to others certain commercial or financial risks associated with the conduct of such enterprises, thereby facilitating their risk management and the assumption of such risks by other risk managers and by speculators. Inasmuch as a futures contract is a separate risk package, it can be traded freely among speculators as well as risk shifters.[2]

In any event, futures contracts must be traded on a *contract market,* a statutory term for exchanges or *boards of trade* that are licensed by the CFTC for each contract traded. A typical futures exchange is, therefore, several contract markets, one for each commodity traded. A contract market is composed of the exchange itself and a *clearing house.* The exchange and the clearing house are generally separate corporations or otherwise separate entities that operate autonomously. The CFTC, as already noted, has treated the clearing houses and exchanges as a single entity for purposes of regulatory controls.

The clearing house guarantees performance of a futures contract. It does this by interceding itself between the ultimate buyer and seller; customers purchasing and selling futures contracts do so directly from the clearing house. The clearing house must perform even if a customer with a reciprocal obligation defaults. The clearing house guarantee is backed by a clearing fund or member guarantees, as well as the guarantees of the contract market member(s) executing and clearing the transaction.

An individual wishing to trade in the futures market must utilize the services of a futures commission merchant (FCM). FCMs engage in the solicitation and acceptance of orders for the purchase or sale of futures contracts and are registered with the CFTC as such. When an FCM receives a customer order, it transmits the order to a broker on the floor of an exchange, who then executes the order with other "floor brokers" in the "pit" or "ring" on the floor of the exchange. When two traders have reached an agreement on the floor of the exchange, the transactions are reported to the clearing house to clear. The FCMs are treated as principals by the clearing house. If an FCM is not a clearing house member, it must deal through an FCM that is.[3]

In addition to the clearing house guarantee, as a means to further ensure performance on the futures contracts, the exchanges and brokerage firms establish margin requirements. This concept should not be confused with margin in the securities industry. Margin for commodities futures is not an extension of credit, as in the case of securities, but is a good faith deposit of money to ensure that the purchaser and seller will perform their obligations. Margin requirements for commodity futures contain two distinctive elements. First, "initial" margin is required for each contract when it is initially executed. This amount can be as little as 5 percent of the value of the commodity. Second, "variation" margin requirements are also imposed. This is an additional deposit of money required to reflect market losses by the purchaser or seller on the commodity futures contract after it is entered into by the parties.

Variation margin requirements are computed daily through a "mark to market" system, that is, the market value of the commodity is computed daily to determine if its value has changed. If so, the purchaser or seller experiencing a loss is required to post an additional amount equivalent to that loss. Conversely, the seller or purchaser receiving a profit is paid that amount of money each day.

To illustrate, a purchaser of gold futures contracts on the Commodity Exchange Inc. (the "Comex") agrees to purchase 100 troy ounces of gold at a negotiated price for delivery on a date in the future. If the purchaser agreed to pay $400 an ounce for the gold with delivery and payment to be effected in the December delivery month, and if the price of gold were to rise by $10, the purchaser would have a profit of $1000. Conversely, the seller would have had a loss of that amount, that is, the seller would be required to deliver for $400 an ounce a commodity now costing the seller $410 an ounce. Of course, if the seller owned the gold, there would be no out-of-pocket loss but rather an opportunity loss. Many futures traders, however, do not own the underlying commodity; if they are a speculator (as will be discussed below), other traders (hedgers) do own the commodity. In any event, in the event of a price increase of $10, the seller would have been issued a variation margin call of at least $1000 to reflect this market loss. The exchange or the broker could issue other margin calls if there was concern that the customer's ability to pay future margin calls was affected by that loss.

Because of the standardized nature of the terms of the commodity futures contract, these contracts are interchangeable; only the price varies. Delivery dates are also standardized, although there are various options available as to delivery. The effect of this standardization and interchangeability is that a secondary market can be conducted in these contracts. As a result, a holder of a long position in a futures contract who wishes to liquidate that position can simply buy an offsetting sell position to the marketplace. Because the clearing house is interceded between all buyers and sellers, these transactions are simply matched off with the clearing house and cancel each other out. Conversely, the seller can liquidate his position by entering into an offsetting purchase contract. It is this flexibility that permitted the growth and development of exchanges and allowed futures trading to occur in the United States.

The advantage of offsetting contracts is that a speculator or hedger can remove themselves from the market should they wish to discontinue the hedge or should their speculative strategy change or be of only a short-term duration.

The standardization of futures contracts, therefore, allows futures contracts to be satisfied either by the acceptance or making of delivery, as called for in the contract. This, however, occurs in only some 3 percent of all futures contracts. Instead, most futures contracts are settled by offsetting transactions in the marketplace.

A party may also discharge an obligation to deliver or accept delivery by engaging in a transaction known as an *exchange of futures for physical* (EFP). To effect an EFP, parties with opposite futures positions negotiate a private transaction covering the commodity involved. Through such a transaction the long trader may avoid his contractual commitment to deliver by, in effect, delivering his long futures contracts to the opposite party, the short seller, through an off-exchange negotiation. The short seller in return may deliver the actual commodity to the parties. EFP transactions are done for the commercial purposes of the parties.

Trading in commodities futures contracts is subject to some unique restrictions that are not generally found in the securities industry. For example, the CFTC and the exchanges impose limitations on the amount of commodity futures contracts that may be held by any one speculator or speculators acting together. There are also price limits set by exchanges on commodity prices. These limits, which are subject to variation by the exchange, restrict the amount of price fluctuation that may occur in a given commodity on a given day. For example, silver has, at times, been limited from increasing or decreasing in price more than $1 per ounce per day, while at other times limits in silver have been as low as 50¢. Because of these restrictions, traders may not be able to liquidate their contracts in a "locked limit" market, and a trader in an adverse position can be subject to continuing losses for several days, until the price limits catch up with the actual losses suffered in the market.

There are essentially two broad categories of traders in the commodities markets. First, there are hedgers. These traders are seeking to protect themselves against commercial risk by purchasing or selling commodity futures contracts. To illustrate, a grain merchant may contract to sell to a foreign government large amounts of an agricultural product, such as soybeans or wheat, at a fixed price. In so doing, the grain company has exposed itself to a large risk if it does not already have that amount of grain in inventory, which it often does not. Thus, if after contracting with a foreign country, the price of the product were to increase by one dollar, the grain company would have its profits reduced or incur losses by that amount per bushel (i.e., the grain company would have to push the grain at the much higher price but sell it at the fixed price agreed to with the foreign country). Because the grain markets are highly volatile, such an event is not at all unlikely.

To insure against this risk, the grain company will buy futures contracts. If the price goes up, the grain company will still be forced to purchase grain at the higher price and sell it at the fixed price to the foreign country. But the futures contracts purchased by the grain company will sustain a profit sufficient, if properly hedged, to offset the price increase paid by it for the actual commodity to be delivered. As a consequence, the grain company has protected itself against the price increase, with the futures contracts acting as an insurance policy against the increase. Of course, the grain company also gave up the opportunity to profit; if grain prices had fallen, it could have purchased the grain at an even lower price and resold it to the foreign country at an increase. The risk of a price increase, however, is generally a sufficient deterrent to preclude a company from incurring that kind of risk.[4]

With the advent of financial futures contracts, even more sophisticated hedging strategies were permitted. For example, futures contracts allowing the purchase and sale of debt instruments for future delivery allow commercial entities to hedge against changes in interest rates. Similarly, stock index contracts allow portfolio managers to hedge against decreases in their portfolios. Another important aspect of futures trading is that it permits price "discovery"; speculators bring information to the market that more rapidly allows the discovery of the appropriate price of a commodity. It also provides a basis for pricing similar goods that are not traded on exchanges. It is these beneficial aspects of commodity futures trading that have led Congress and regulatory authorities to seek the continuance of commodities futures trading and to protect it from unnecessary regulation and from fraudulent or manipulative conduct that could impair its free functioning.

A second category of traders is the speculators. Generally, speculation is not thought to be a desirable product in the financial community. Nevertheless, speculation plays a vital role in the commodity futures industry. It is the speculators who absorb the risk being displaced by the hedgers. Without speculators, commodities futures markets could not function; its important hedging aspects would not be available to commercial firms. Speculators appear in many forms. They may be "chartists" or "technical" analysts who trade on the basis of empirical data that is based on prior price movements in the commodity markets or complex mathematical formulas, extrapolating data into what they believe will be futures price movements. Other speculators are "fundamentalists" who base their trading on fundamental factors in the marketplace such as crop reports, freezes, political events, federal borrowing, or other information that could have a fundamental effect on prices. There are also "day traders." These are individuals who move quickly in and out of the market, seeking to take advantage of rapid price changes. In order to profit, however, their gains must exceed their losses and the commissions they pay. Consequently, day traders are often found trading on the floor of the exchange as members (and who are called "scalpers"), where they obtain lower commission rates and more instant access to market changes. There are also "position" traders who hold futures contracts overnight or longer in order to take advantage of longer-term movements in the price. Of course, commodity futures traders do not hold their contracts for years, because futures are short-lived, in comparison to securities.

There are also numerous other trading strategies in the futures markets. For example, there are "straddle" or "spread" traders. Simply stated, a straddle is a long and short position in the same commodity but with different delivery dates. If the prices of the two delivery dates move in tandem, there will be no gain or loss. On the other hand, if one delivery month has price changes that vary, then there will be a gain or loss depending on the nature of the straddle. To understand a spread or straddle, it is necessary to understand the term *contango*. In brief, and as a general rule only, it can be expected that a futures contract with a more distant delivery date will trade at a higher price than a futures contract with a nearer-term delivery date. This is because there is a theoretical storage charge and interest cost for the commodity that is subject to delivery. For example, a silver contract with a December delivery date can be expected to trade at a lower price than a silver contract with a delivery date in the following March.

A spread trader will seek to take advantages when these differences do not move in tandem as the price of the underlying commodity change. For example, soybeans are divided into old and new crops. The "old crop" would be, if we are now in January 1986, the contract months for delivery up to September. (September is an "intercrop month.") The following delivery months are the "new crop" months. This is because in November, the crops harvested at the end of the 1986 summer will be available for delivery. Prior to that only the old crop (the 1985 crop) would be available.

A straddle trader in January 1986 could reason that even though there is now a shortage of old crop soybeans, a surplus will be available with the advent of the new crop. Such a trader could thereby go "long" the nearby, old crop contracts, expecting them to increase in price as current supplies grow tighter, and "short" the new crop months, expecting their price to decrease as favorable crop reports come in for the new crop. In such an event, the trader could profit in both "legs" or sides of the straddle as prices change. On the other hand, the trader could compound his losses if his predictions are not correct.

Generally, straddles are designed to limit losses. The above example would not do so; in fact, it could compound them. In many cases, however, it can be expected that each month will move somewhat in tandem, so that there is no new or old crop for silver and other nonagricultural commodities. If that is the case, the speculator will be expecting events to affect one leg of the straddle less so or more so than the other because of their long- or short-term effect. On the other hand, if major events occur that dramatically affect the price of the commodity, then the trader will be protected against the large loss that could be sustained in a straight forward long or short position (e.g., if the news is bearish, the trader will gain on the short side while losing on the long side; or if the news is bullish, the trader will gain on the long side but lose on the short side).

At the same time, however, there would be an opportunity for profit for any variances in contract months. For example, if a trader were in long for a March delivery silver contract and short for the following December, and if there was some near-term event causing disorder in the world (which precious metal prices generally respond to), it is possible that the more near-term contract will increase or decrease in value more so than the December contract (e.g., in the belief that the effect of the event will have abated in the longer term). By taking advantage of those price disparities between those different contract months, the trader could profit, or at least limit losses, to an amount much smaller than what would be experienced by a trader who was on the wrong side of the market and who was only long or short.

It should be noted that with respect to the contango, "backwardation" can occur. This is a phenomenon in which nearby contract deliver months have values increased over that of more distant months. This can occur in a number of instances, as, for example, with respect to the soybean situation described above.

LEGISLATION

In 1982, Sections 4 and 4h were consolidated into Section 4 of the CEA, insofar as they prohibited commodity futures transactions except through a member of a contract market and through a contract market. In the House Report on the 1982 Amendments to the Commodity Exchange Act, it was stated that the consolidation of sections 4 and 4h was intended to result in a single simplified provision that would require that all transactions in commodity futures contracts in the United States be effected on boards of trade that have been designated as contract markets. No change in the existing law was intended.

The prohibitions in Section 4 of the CEA thus preclude anyone from executing any transactions in contracts for the purchase or sale of any "commodity for future delivery," except through a contract market and its members. Unfortunately, the CEA does not define the term "commodity for futures delivery" (a futures contract). Rather, the act simply states that the term "future delivery" does not include "any sale of any cash commodity for deferred shipment or delivery," and defines the term "contract of sale" to include "sales and agreements of sales, and agreements to sell." Neither of these terms, however, is too helpful in identifying whether a particular transaction is a commodity futures contract.

The legislative history of the CEA also offers little helpful guidance. The "deferred delivery" exclusion originated in the Futures Trading Act of 1921 which, while declared unconstitutional, was later incorporated in its successor, the Grain Futures Act of 1922, the predecessor of the Commodity Exchange Act. The scant legislative history available suggests that this provision was included to make clear that the act was not intended to interfere with cash transactions in grain, the only commodities then being considered for regulation. As one witness stated, the deferred delivery exclusion would exclude the farmer in selling his wheat to the mill; in other words, it was to apply to actual grain sales.

To limit the exclusion to actual contracts, however, is at odds with the historical parallel of the commodity futures industry, specifically the securities industry. The Securities Exchange Act of 1934 extended regulation specifically to exchanges and transactions on those exchanges, and the Securities Act of 1933 imposed disclosure requirements. Neither of these statutes, however, restricted trading to exchanges. Indeed, over-the-counter transactions were allowed to proceed pretty much unhindered, since the Securities and Exchange Act of 1934 did not require all securities transactions to be conducted on exchanges. It was not until 1938 that Congress decided that legislation was needed for the regulation of over-the-counter trading in the United States, when it adopted the Maloney Act. Even then, over-the-counter trading was permitted to continue.

The CFTC has reviewed the CEA's legislative history and concluded that an opposite result was intended by Congress for futures contracts. The CFTC noted that the Futures Trading Act of 1921 allowed futures trading, but imposed a prohibitive tax applicable to all futures contracts except those exempted by the act. By its terms, that act exempted only contracts traded by or through members of boards of trade designated as contract markets. From this, the CFTC concluded that the subsequent enactment of the Grain Futures Act and the Commodity Exchange Act in 1936 intended a similar result, that trading would not be permitted except through a board of trade, designated as a "contract market."

The CFTC's scrutiny of the legislative history also noted that the House of Representatives had passed and sent to the Senate the bill that ultimately became the Futures Trading Act of 1921. It contained language exempting transactions "made at, on, or in, an exchange, board of trade or similar institutional place of business." The Senate changed this and added the "deferred delivery" exemption. The Senate Agriculture Committee explained that this change was necessary because the House provision may have inadvertently exempted from the tax private exchanges or bucket shops (businesses that accepted customer orders for execution on the exchange but simply failed to execute them). The Senate Committee's report stated that it did not want private exchanges or bucket shops to be permitted. In other words, in the CFTC's view, the Senate wanted to discourage the creation of private institutions trading in commodity futures transactions in order to escape the tax that was being imposed.

This analysis is of more than historical interest, because numerous cases have been brought by the CFTC against firms marketing futures-type contracts by asserting that, since they were not traded on a contract market, they could not be futures contracts. The CFTC rejected that thesis, asserting that if it had the element of a futures contract then it was illegal *unless* it was traded on a contract market. As will be discussed in Chapter 17, the difficult part is identifying the elements of a futures contract, particularly since many commodity contracts are of a "hybrid" nature.

CFTC AND JUDICIAL PRONOUNCEMENTS CONCERNING FUTURES CONTRACTS

The CFTC Office of General Counsel has stated, in an interpretative letter concerning the scope of the prohibition against off-exchange futures contracts, that it should not be construed so literally as to include within its proscriptions bona fide, commercial transactions that are not designed for, or have the effect of, circumventing the requirements and policies set forth in the Commodity Exchange Act. In that instance, the staff expressed the view that the security interest of a bank in futures contracts used to hedge inventory financed by the bank for a customer was not a commodity for future delivery.

In a more recent interpretation, the Office of General Counsel asserted that the exemption for deferred delivery contracts requires that the contract's terms, and the parties' practice under the contract, make clear that both parties to the contracts deal in and contemplate delivery of the actual commodity. It also noted that forward contracts are often not standardized or, if standardized, various terms may be left open for negotiation. The interpretation noted an instrument called a *deferred pricing contract* had evolved from agricultural commodities which did not establish a price until a later closing date, often using a futures contract as the mechanism for setting the price at a later date. Such contracts also specify a period of time in which the producer may fix the final price. The interpretation concluded that this contract was an exempt deferred delivery contract if delivery of the actual commodity was required. The Office of General Counsel further asserted that contracts of this nature, which also contain a minimum price guarantee, were not futures contracts or options, if delivery was required.

The preeminent CFTC case on this issue is *In re Stovall.*[5] There, the respondent was charged with illegally engaging in off-exchange futures transactions, rather than cash commodities for "deferred delivery." The CFTC concluded that the exclusion for deferred delivery applied only to contracts for sale that were entered into with the expectation that the delivery of the actual commodity would eventually occur. This would mean that the seller would necessarily have the ability to deliver, and the buyer would have the ability to accept delivery, unlike a futures contract, where delivery is taken only on a small percentage of cases. On that basis, the CFTC concluded that the contracts at issue were not deferred delivery contracts because they generally were not fulfilled by delivery. It was also found that the respondent's operations were directed at the general public and not to persons with a specific interest in acquiring or disposing of commodities. The CFTC found that delivery had been taken by only one customer. Other customers simply offset their obligations. The contracts were also standardized in the same manner as commodity futures contracts.

The CFTC identified what it believed were four "classic elements" common to a futures contract: (1) the existence of standardized contracts for the purchase or sale of commodities that provide for futures as opposed to immediate delivery; (2) such transactions are directly or indirectly offered to the general public; (3) the transactions are generally secured by earnest money or "margin"; and (4) the transactions are entered into primarily for the purpose of assuming or shifting the risk of change of value of commodities, rather than for transferring ownership of the actual commodities. With respect to the last element, the CFTC noted that most parties to a commodity futures contract extinguish their legal obligations to make or take delivery by offsetting prior to the date on which delivery is called for, accepting a profit or loss for any difference in price between initial and offsetting transactions.

The CFTC found that Stovall's transactions had all the classic elements of a commodity contract for sale with future delivery. The CFTC asserted, however, that commodity futures contracts need not have all of these elements or that those elements were exhaustive. Rather, it stated it would look at transactions on a case-by-case basis to determine whether a futures contract was present. The CFTC also warned that it would not be governed by the label the parties attached to the instrument.

The courts have also spoken in this area. In the CFTC's action against Harold Goldstein's CoPetro Company, a district court entered an injunction against the continued sale of commodity futures contracts, despite the defendant's claims that they were selling cash commodities for deferred delivery. The court noted that this was a distinct and novel issue, which had not previously been addressed by other courts. It examined the legislative history of the exclusion for deferred delivery contracts and concluded, as did the CFTC in the *Stovall* case, that the exclusion was intended solely to enable a farmer to sell his grain to an elevator without routing such a transaction through a contract market.

On appeal, the Ninth Circuit upheld the district court in CoPetro. It was stressed by the court of appeals that CoPetro marketed these contracts extensively to the general public through newspaper advertisements, private seminars, commission telephone solicitors, and various other sales agents. The court of appeals noted that the statutory language provided little guidance as to the distinction between regulated futures contracts and excluded cash forward contracts, but the court looked to the legislative history for guidance and concluded that CoPetro's agreements were futures contracts. Like the district court, the court of appeals concluded that legislative history evidenced that Congress intended that the exclusion for deferred delivery contracts to apply to commercial transactions where the parties dealt in commodity and contemplated future delivery of the commodity in question. Here, the court of appeals noted that CoPetro's public customers had no intention of taking delivery or the capacity to do so. Rather, it was to the general public that the sales pitches were made.

The court of appeals also noted that, while CoPetro's agreements were not as rigidly standardized as most futures contracts, they were not individualized; tables furnished to the sales agents evidenced that there was a basic size for the contracts, and relevant dates in the agreements were uniform. The court noted that the reason for standardization of futures contracts was to facilitate the ability to offset the contracts. Here, CoPetro was acting as a market maker and thereby facilitated the offset of the contracts, allowing customers to deal in the contracts without being forced to take delivery. Accordingly, the standardized element was not determinative.

Like the CFTC, the court of appeals asserted that, in determining whether a commodity futures contract is present, there is no single definition or list of characterizing elements that is determinative. Instead, the transaction must be viewed as a whole, with a critical eye to its underlying purpose. Here the contracts were found to represent speculative ventures in commodity futures that were marketed to individuals for whom delivery was not an expectation.

In a CFTC action against the National Coal Exchange, the district court concluded that the defendants were selling illegal futures contracts. The transactions there were "coal purchase contracts" which purported to obligate the purchaser to take delivery of a specified amount of coal at a future date. The contract forms were standardized quantities and qualities of coal and payment terms; there was a requirement of an initial down payment of a percentage of the total purchase price and there were non-refundable commission fees. It was further found by the district court that the purchase agreement was promoted, not as an opportunity to acquire coal, but as a speculative investment vehicle, often through misleading sales presentations by telephone and mail to the members of the investing public who were unsophisticated and unknowledgeable about coal or the coal market. It was also found that customers invested to speculate on the price, not to take possession of the coal, and that they had no intent or means to accept delivery of large quantities of coal.

The district court concluded that a commodity futures contract had the following elements:

1. A standardized form of contract;
2. Specified future delivery provision;
3. Price determination at time of agreement;

4. Opportunity for offset or extinguishment of delivery obligations;
5. Transferability of risk;
6. Some form of price quotation system and competitive market trading.

The court noted that the contract before it had some elements of both futures contracts and deferred delivery contracts, but the court concluded that the overall effect was to make them futures contracts.

16
FOREIGN FUTURES
AND OPTIONS

Commodity futures trading has been conducted throughout the world, as well as in the United States. There are now exchanges in England, Hong Kong, Japan, Brazil, France, Indonesia, Kuala Lumpur, New Zealand, and Australia. Canada has also had futures exchanges for a number of years, including the Winnipeg Grain Exchange, and Bermuda has a new computerized futures exchange. South Korea and Switzerland are also proposing exchanges.

Futures contracts on foreign exchanges may be offered and sold in the United States. Unlike domestic futures contracts, foreign futures sold here need not be traded on a contract market. The same is not true of foreign options contracts. They may be offered and sold in the United States only pursuant to limited exemptions in the CFTC's option ban.

THE LONDON EXCHANGES

As in the United States, cash and forward transactions abroad evolved into futures trading on organized exchanges with standardized contract terms that permitted offsetting transactions for speculation and hedging. The Baltic Exchange in London, for example, was formed as a result of England's expansion of its overseas trade in all types of commodities, including coffee, tobacco, sugar, cotton, and tallow. Trading also developed, by 1744, in ocean rates, and cargo space in ships was sold. By 1812 the Baltic Exchange formed itself into a club with limited membership and a sales room to permit the chartering of vessels and selling of cargo space. Later, this exchange developed into a world center for establishing ocean freight rates, and more recently it proposed the adoption of a futures contract in ocean freight rates. Air freight charters are traded at the Baltic Exchange, as well as ocean rates.

There are numerous markets in Britain that deal in different commodities. One such market, the Liverpool Exchange, played an important role in the U.S. cotton market during the earlier part of this century. Indeed, its role was a subject of discussion in the debates that led to the Commodity Exchange Act of 1936 (discussed below). Congress recognized that its adoption of the Commodity Exchange Act would not impose U.S. government controls over trading on the Liverpool Exchange.

Other exchanges developed in Britain as well. The London Commodity Exchange had its origin in the middle of the sixteenth century, as the result of trade with the Antwerp markets for woolen cloth, silver, silks, spices, drugs, sugar, tapestries, oriental carpets, and other goods. The London Commodity Exchange's facilities (the Royal Exchange) were destroyed in the Great Fire of 1666, but were rebuilt and open for business again by 1670. The rebuilt Royal Exchange was once again destroyed in 1941 during an air raid and was moved to the Plantation House in Mincing Lane. It was there that the London Commodity Exchange developed into a world market for futures trading in cocoa, sugar, and coffee (the "soft" commodities). The London Commodity Exchange is often used by traders in the United States to arbitrage where there are price disparities between United States and London markets. It also offers opportunities for hedging by traders who deal in these world markets.[1]

Transactions on the London Commodity Exchange are guaranteed by the International Commodity Clearinghouse (ICCH), in a manner similar to clearing houses in the United States. Nevertheless, the London commodity markets are distinct from the U.S. exchanges in several respects. First, at least for U.S. traders, there is a foreign currency risk should the British pound fluctuate adversely to the trader. Second, there are no trading limits or "locked limit" markets as in the United States. Commodity prices are allowed to fluctuate freely in futures as well as spot months.

London has also several other exchanges, including the London Metal Exchange (LME). The LME traces its history back to the middle of the nineteenth century, but it was not formally constituted until 1876. Early metals traders had conducted their business at the Royal Exchange and later at the Lombard Exchange, but these facilities were inadequate, and it was for that reason that the LME was established. It was during the early formative stages of this new exchange that "ring" trading began, "when a member would chalk a large circle on the floor of the room, and at the cry 'Ring, ring,' those wishing to trade would take up their accustomed places around it." There are two trading sessions on the LME, morning and afternoon sessions where "ring" trading is conducted. During these sessions all members are allowed to participate in an auction-style trading such as that in the United States. There also are periods of fifteen minutes at the end of each regular ring session where all metals are traded simultaneously around the ring.

Trading on the LME is conducted in copper, tin, lead, zinc, silver, aluminum, and other metals. It, too, is a world center for trading, and its prices often set the price for these metals throughout the world. The LME differs somewhat from the U.S. exchanges. For example, transactions here may be conducted off the exchange at any hours. This interoffice or pre-market trading (trading outside the exchange's regular hours) is extensive. There are also "kerb" trading sessions. The latter term comes from the early history of commodity trading that was literally conducted on the kerb, or curb, of the street.[2]

Trading is also different from that in the United States in that there is no clearing house on the LME such as that found in the United States. Rather, the transactions are "principal" trades, and the parties to the agreements are dependent on the financial resources of the opposite party. There have been few failures at the LME in its long history, but in October 1985 a default by the International Tin Council on its LME tin contracts threatened the viability of the exchange and several of its members.

The LME deals in so-called prompts. These are forward contracts that are not closed out automatically by an offsetting position, as in the case of futures contracts in the United States. Nevertheless, offsetting transactions can be entered into that effectively allow traders to liquidate their positions. The positions are in effect liquidated by offsetting prompt transactions, but price settlement for profits and losses must await the maturity of the contracts (the prompt date).

Another popular exchange in England is the London Gold Market, which sets the London fix for gold. A futures market in gold was also opened in April 1982, the London Gold Futures Market, which conducted trading in gold options and futures and cleared its transactions through the ICCH. Unfortunately, this exchange was not a success, and its operations were discontinued. Another defunct futures exchange in London is the London Rubber Futures Exchange. There are efforts under way, however, to revitalize this exchange.

A new London exchange is the London International Financial Futures Exchange (LIFFE). LIFFE has brought renewed attention to the London markets, allowing the financial communities on both sides of the Atlantic to trade in financial futures. Still another relatively new futures exchange in London is the International Petroleum Exchange. This market, together with the New York Mercantile Exchange, has experienced rapid growth with the destabilization of oil prices. It trades a gas-oil futures contract, and its trades are cleared by the ICCH. There are also other futures exchanges in London of recent origin, including the London Potato Futures

Market, the London Meat Futures Exchange, and the Soybean Meal Futures Exchange. The London Grain Futures Market, which trades EEC wheat and barley, has also operated in London since 1929.

Trading volume on the London markets is small, for the most part, in comparison to that in the United States. Nevertheless, it is substantial. For example, on January 30, 1985, total volume on LIFFE was almost 24,000 contracts. But this should be contrasted with the over 80,000 contracts traded in a single futures contract on the Chicago Board of Trade on January 24, 1985. It should also be noted that options are traded on London exchanges. The options ban, however, imposed by the CFTC presently precludes the offer and sale of those instruments in the United States, except when pursuant to limited exemptions.

These markets have worldwide breadth and depth, and must be considered formidable forces in the commodity futures industry. They are also the subject of increased regulatory concern on the part of the British government. A new investor protection agency for the commodity and financial futures markets in London has also been formed recently. It is the Association of Futures Brokers and Dealers.

FRANCE

For some 100 years, futures trading in sugar was conducted on the Paris bourse. In the 1970s, however, the sugar market in Paris collapsed after a speculative binge and was closed for two years. Only recently, over ten years after the event, the head of the Paris futures brokers association was sentenced to four years in prison as a result of the collapse. The French government also tightened its regulatory procedures, and futures trading is once again being developed in France. The Paris Futures Exchange now trades white sugar, cocoa, coffee, soybean meal, and sugar. The ICCH in London provides reciprocal clearing facilities for trading on the London and Paris futures markets. The Paris exchange was sought to broaden its appeal by offering free "currency translation" services to foreign traders. This service allows a foreign trader there to hold his trading position denominated in U.S. dollars, rather than French francs. Paris has also linked its reporting services to the London markets, and plans a new cocoa butter contract.

A potato futures exchange is scheduled to open outside Paris, and the Paris bourse is planning a futures market in bond trading.

ITALY

A coffee futures contract is being planned in Trieste.

SWITZERLAND

Switzerland does not as yet have a futures market. Nevertheless, the Swiss banking community is active in the bullion market. Swiss banks also frequently use the U.S. futures markets. As noted in earlier chapters, this sometimes results in conflicts with Swiss bank secrecy and CFTC disclosure requirements. The Swiss are also considering a Zurich exchange to trade a Swiss-based stock index. In addition, European banks are proposing the creation of a forward or futures market that would trade an index contract and permit the hedging of interest rate risks. There is also an active over-the-counter, currency options market.

CANADA

The Winnipeg Grain Exchange has long been a center for trading in grain futures. It traces its origins back to the development of wheat farming in Canada in the late nineteenth century. By 1928, Canada was accounting for almost half of the world trade in wheat. The principal commodity traded on the Winnipeg exchange has long been wheat, but rapeseed has also become a popular futures contract; Winnipeg also opened a gold futures market in 1972 and later an options market in gold. The exchange also created a new division in 1981, the Canadian Financial Futures Market, which offers futures in Canadian interest rates and silver. Today the Winnipeg exchange has over 300 members and its membership includes residents of the United States, England, Germany, Switzerland, France, Cyprus, Japan, and Hong Kong. It should be noted that, while the Winnipeg exchange has branched off into financial futures, it still remains an important futures market in grains including barley, flaxseed, wheat, rapeseed, oats, and rye.

The Montreal Stock Exchange also has had a longstanding connection to commodity trading. It was first organized as the Montreal Board of Produce Brokers in 1849 and was used to establish prices in farm produce, as well as stocks and bonds. Stock trading soon become its specialty and it was chartered as the Montreal Stock Exchange in 1874. The explosive growth of options and futures trading in the United States in the 1970s and 1980s, however, caused Montreal once again to return to commodity transactions. The Montreal Exchange has now developed a futures exchange to trade various futures contracts, including lumber. It has options contracts on gold and currencies, as well as index contracts.

Toronto also has a futures exchange. Its present and planned contracts include futures on bonds, treasury bills, and stock indexes. The Toronto Exchange is also planning an options market.

THE EUROPEAN OPTIONS EXCHANGE—AMSTERDAM

The European Options Exchange trades options contracts on gold and silver certificates, Canadian bonds, gold, and currencies, including the British pound sterling, the Deutsch mark, the Swiss franc, the Japanese yen, and the Canadian dollar. This exchange is in fact a combination of three exchanges, the Amsterdam exchange in the Netherlands, the International Options Market in Montreal, and the Vancouver exchange. These exchanges jointly own a clearing facility, and the European Options Exchange is one of many international exchange linkages that have been or are now being developed to allow extended trading hours. Recently, it was reported that the Sydney Exchange in Australia is joining the European Options Exchange. The Amsterdam exchange is also planning a gold futures market.

THE BERMUDA EXCHANGE—INTEX

A recent newcomer to the futures industry is the International Futures Exchange Ltd. in Bermuda. (INTEX). This exchange, which has no trading floor, conducts computerized trading in "Dry Bulk Index." The Dry Bulk Index is a cash settlement contract that is based on an index of dry bulk commodity charters. INTEX also traded a gold contract but it was discontinued for lack of interest. Transactions on INTEX are guaranteed and cleared by the ICCH in London.

BRAZIL

São Paulo conducts trading in gold and has a futures market for individual securities. Rio de Janiero recently opened a Brazilian futures market that trades futures contracts on gold. It plans in the future to offer interest rate futures contracts, as well as stock index futures based on an index of stocks traded on the Rio de Janiero stock exchange. Gold futures exchanges have also opened in Brasilia and São Paulo. The Brazilian government, however, now prohibits foreigners from speculating in the domestic gold market.

NEW ZEALAND

The New Zealand Commodities Market trades wool futures, and it is trading or planning additional financial futures contracts. It is also planning to become a completely automated futures exchange. Its contracts will be cleared by the ICCH.

AUSTRALIA

The Sydney Exchange has recently expanded and is seeking to become a world center for trading commodity futures. The Australian government has assisted this effort by easing its currency restrictions to permit foreign participation. The Sydney Exchange conducts futures trading in interest rate instruments, cattle, currencies, gold, lamb, silver, and wool. It also has a stock index future.

The Sydney Exchange is linked to the ICCH in London, which clears its transactions through a branch office in Australia. It is also, as noted above, joining the European Options Exchange, and is seeking a link with the Comex in New York. The Australia Financial Futures Market has also been formed by its parent company, the Melbourne Stock Exchange, to trade indexes of stocks listed on that exchange.

KUALA LUMPUR AND DJAKARTA

The Kuala Lumpur Futures Exchange trades in palm oil and rubber, and is planning a tin contract. The ICCH had a partial interest in the clearing house for this exchange. In 1984, however, a large default occurred in the palm oil market on the exchange, resulting in large losses. The government of Malaysia is now seeking to revitalize the exchange.

Djakarta has established the Djakarta Commodities Exchange, and it plans to trade coffee, rubber, plywood, palm oil, tin, and tobacco.

HONG KONG

The Hong Kong Commodities Exchange was established in May 1977 and has been growing rapidly. It trades cotton, sugar, soybeans, and gold and is considering a futures contract on local stocks. The ICCH also provides clearing services for this exchange. Hong Kong has sought to develop a more modern futures exchange but has had difficulty in that effort.

JAPAN

Historians have credited Japan as the innovator of modern futures trading, tracing the establishment of the rice exchange in Japan to approximately 1650. A Commodity Exchange Act was adopted there in 1893, as a result of abuses, but this did not slow the growth of commodity exchanges in Japan. By 1898, there were 128 commodity exchanges in Japan. Futures trading was renewed in Japan after the war, in 1949, and a new Commodity

Exchange Act was passed in 1950, which was based on the U.S. Commodity Exchange Act. There are now some sixteen commodity exchanges in Japan. The Tokyo futures exchange is now seeking to expand its operations worldwide and is conducting trading in platinum, gold, and silver. It too is planning to expand, including a possible new contract for bond futures, and it has been flirting with the Chicago Board of Trade for a possible link.

SOUTH KOREA

The South Korean government has proposed the creation of a futures exchange that would permit it to become a part of the international futures community.

SOME BACKGROUND ON CFTC REGULATION OF FOREIGN FUTURES

The Commodity Exchange Authority, the CFTC's predecessor, did not assert any regulatory control over foreign futures contracts offered and sold in the United States. In 1974, however, when the CFTC was created by the CFTC Act, Congress expanded the application of the Commodity Exchange Act, not only to contracts traded on United States contract markets, but also to "any other board of trade exchange or market." This language was intended to give the CFTC jurisdiction on futures contracts purchased and sold in the United States that are executed on a foreign board of trade, exchange, or market.

Thereafter, the CFTC adopted an antifraud rule for foreign futures transactions, but it did not construe the expansion of its jurisdiction to preclude the trading of foreign futures contracts in the United States; that is, it did not require them to be traded on a contract market registered with the CFTC. As a practical matter, had such a requirement been applied, foreign futures contracts would have been effectively banned in the United States, because it is doubtful that foreign exchanges would have submitted to the regulatory control that the CFTC exerts over United States contract markets.

This creates a regulatory disparity, and a competitive advantage for foreign futures contracts. Most foreign exchanges, for example, are subject to much lower levels of regulation, and attending expense, than are U.S. contract markets. Nevertheless, a large market in foreign futures contracts did not develop in the United States. Nor were there abuses or scandals that merited greater regulatory control.

The creation of LIFFE, however, and increased domestic interest in foreign futures, as well as proposals for the linkage of domestic and foreign exchange, resulted in a call for greater regulatory control. Accordingly, in 1982, Congress amended the Commodity Exchange Act to expand the CFTC's jurisdiction over foreign futures contracts. The 1982 amendments authorized the CFTC to impose books and record requirements on firms selling foreign futures in the United States, as well as minimum financial requirements. The amendment also permits the CFTC to require customer funds to be segregated and specific risk disclosures to be given. Congress, however, prohibited the CFTC from requiring foreign exchanges to submit their contract terms to the CFTC for approval. Similarly, the CFTC was prohibited from regulating the rules of foreign exchange.

In a House Report on the 1982 Amendments to the Commodity Exchange Act, it was also stated that foreign exchanges could seek a "certification" from the CFTC that their futures contracts conform with the requirements of the Commodity Exchange Act. Thereafter, the Toronto Futures Exchange asked the CFTC staff whether it could market an index futures contract in the United States that was based on an index of stocks that included U.S. securities. The CFTC's Office of General Counsel responded that the CFTC had no criteria for a "certification" of the contract, but that it would use the same requirements it applies to approve domestic contracts before certifying such contracts. On that basis, the staff stated that the Toronto stock index futures contract could be offered and sold in the United States. This letter is somewhat anomalous, since there does not appear to be any statutory requirement for such certification, because the House report's suggestion for a certification was not contained in the legislation that was enacted in 1982. In any event, the INTEX exchange in Bermuda has also sought and obtained such a clearance for its index contract.[3]

In order to implement the 1982 amendments, the CFTC sought public comment on what rules it should adopt. The CFTC stated that the need for such rules was in recognition of the growing volume of foreign futures contracts and their increasing attractiveness to American investors. The CFTC asked for comment on several issues, including information on who is engaging in foreign futures transactions, how extensive public participation is, and where foreign futures contracts of interest are trading.

The CFTC noted that its staff had conducted an informal survey of futures commission merchants. Of the 357 futures commission merchants responding, approximately 10 percent stated they handled business on foreign markets. Another survey conducted in 1981 indicated that some thirteen futures commission merchants held in excess of $67,000,000 in customer funds in connection with foreign futures transactions. The Commission stated that it believed that this amount had increased even further in recent years, and that it was particularly interested in finding which futures commission merchants handled foreign futures contracts and whether other persons, who were not registered as futures commission merchants, were soliciting and accepting orders for foreign futures contracts. The CFTC also stated that it was seeking comment on whether to adopt a rule requiring reporting of foreign futures activities by firms handling such transactions. Rules have been proposed by the CFTC under the additional authority granted by the 1982 amendments. These proposals would require foreign futures to be conducted for the most part through entities registered with the CFTC. Further, foreign futures could be traded here only under a regulatory framework similar to that for domestic futures contracts, except that the foreign market upon which the futures are traded would not be regulated by the CFTC. As of this writing, these proposals have not been adopted.

FOREIGN FUTURES—INTERPRETATIONS

The CFTC's Office of General Counsel has issued interpretive letters discussing the requirements of the Commodity Exchange Act and their application to foreign futures contracts. In one, it was stated that it was clear from the legislative history of the Commodity Exchange Act, when adopted in 1936, that it was not intended to affect foreign futures transactions. The letter quoted the following testimony:

> *Mr. Sabath:* Is there any provision in this proposed bill to regulate those men who may operate on the Liverpool and Winnipeg grain exchange?
> *Mr. Jones:* No. I do not know whether we could make such a provision; but there is none in this [act].[4]

The CFTC staff stated that the prohibitions in Section 4h (now Section 4) of the Commodity Exchange Act were intended to provide a statutory prohibition against the operation of bucket shops that were prevalent prior to 1936. The staff further stated that a firm trading in foreign futures need not register as a futures commission merchant or as a commodity pool operator.

In another interpretative letter issued by the CFTC Office of General Counsel, it was stated that individual states could bring antifraud charges based on CFTC regulations or under state general civil or criminal antifraud provisions against persons dealing in the sale of foreign futures contracts in the United States. The letter stated, however, that a state authority could not bring an action under other state law provisions (such as, presumably, state security laws), because such state provisions were preempted by the Commodity Exchange Act.

On June 28, 1976, the CFTC issued an advisory notice concerning transactions occurring in the United States in options on foreign futures contracts in wool. Specifically, the CFTC was concerned with the sale in the United States of options on greasy wool and on Sydney wool futures contracts traded on exchanges in London and Sydney. The Commodity Exchange Act did not permit options trading in the United States on the "previously regulated" commodities (those commodities that were regulated prior to the creation of the CFTC). The CFTC stated that the options prohibition was

> unaffected by whether or not some activity related to the carrying out of an option transaction occurs outside the United States. Therefore, the fact that an option transaction may involve a foreign futures contract does not remove it from the purview of, or prohibitions contained in, . . . [the Commodity Exchange Act]. A contrary interpretation would emasculate the decision of Congress to ban trading in the United States in options in those commodities. . . . [previously regulated].[5]

FOREIGN OPTION RESTRICTIONS

The CFTC's suspension of options trading in the United States, with its limited exceptions, applies equally to foreign options contracts offered and sold in the United States. Indeed, it was the trading abuses in connection with London option contracts that led to the suspension. Consequently, unless foreign options transactions fall within a CFTC exemption, they will not be permitted in the United States. The broadest exemption available is for commercial options. Nevertheless, as noted above, it must be shown that the purchaser had a commercial purpose in buying the option. The CFTC staff has also concluded that this would not permit the sale of options from the United States on a foreign exchange, since the seller would be unable to determine if the purchaser had a valid commercial purpose.

U. S. firms may, nevertheless, offer and sell options abroad. In several early CEA administrative determinations it was concluded that United States brokerage firms could use their foreign offices to solicit orders for options transactions on the Winnipeg Grain Exchange in Canada for Canadian customers, as long as the offer, sale execution, and confirmation of the trade was done outside the United States. More recently, the CFTC's Office of General Counsel has issued an interpretive letter, which concluded that a multinational financial institution incorporated in the United States could grant options on commodities through its foreign offices although such transactions were to be entered into solely with foreign investors; all of the contracts would be executed outside the United States. In this instance, the only contacts that the option sales would have with the United States were that the firm's United States offices would supply support services, maintain duplicate books and records, and conduct cover or hedging transactions for the options being sold on domestic exchanges. The Office of General Counsel ruled that these limited contacts would not bring such option transactions within the prohibition against options trading in the United States.

Most recently, the CFTC has proposed rules to establish a system of regulation for the offer and the sale of commodity options traded on foreign boards of trade. This would allow the renewed sale of so-called London commodity options as well as options on the European Options Exchange and its worldwide affiliates. It is hoped that the regulatory scheme, if adopted, will prevent the types of abuses previously associated in this country with London options. In brief, the proposal seeks to establish a regulatory scheme similar to that for domestic futures contract, except the operations of foreign markets would not be regulated.

17

HYBRID INSTRUMENTS

The CFTC has established elaborate regulatory structures for trading in futures, commodity options, and leverage contracts. Under CFTC rules, these instruments may be traded only in limited circumstances. For example, as described above, domestic futures contracts may be traded only through an exchange designated as a contract market; commodity options may be traded only on contract markets or pursuant to certain other limited exemptions; and leverage contracts may be traded only by licensed dealers who fall within the grandfather provisions of the CFTC's rules.

There are other commodity-related transactions, in seemingly endless variations, that have elements of futures options or leverage contracts but do not fit into the common perception of one or the other of these instruments. In creating and entering into such "hybrid" transactions, examination should be made to determine whether they are in reality futures, options, or leverage contracts that may be traded only under the CFTC's strict regulatory controls. The CFTC is now actively examining many of these contracts, and that review may have broad ramifications for many businesses if the CFTC determines that their transactions are futures contracts (e.g., if particular contracts are futures contracts, they could be traded only on an exchange and not through private transactions).

SUNSHINE MINING COMPANY BONDS

In 1980 the Sunshine Mining Company, which operates the largest silver mine in the United States, offered to the public what it described as silver indexed bonds.[1] The company had subsequent offerings for these types of securities, each of which it registered with the Securities and Exchange Commission as a public offering.

In brief, these bonds were redeemable at an "index principal amount." The index principal amount for each $1,000 face amount bond was the greater of $1,000 or the market value of 50 ounces of silver. If the index principal amount was greater than $1,000, the company could deliver, in lieu of the index principal amount, 50 ounces of silver for each $1,000 face amount of outstanding bonds.

To illustrate, in Sunshine's 1983 offering, the bonds had a face amount of $1,000 each, which was payable at maturity or redemption at the greater of $1,000 or an average market price of 50 ounces of silver (the indexed principal amount). If the indexed principal amount was greater than $1,000, the company could, at its option, deliver 50 ounces of silver to holders. It was noted in the prospectus that as of the closing of trading on February 10, 1983, the spot settlement price of silver on the Comex was $14.125 per ounce; at this price, 50 ounces of silver would be valued at $706.25. This would require an increase in the value of the silver of $293.75 before the purchaser would receive any added benefit from this unique feature of a $1,000 face amount bond.

The index feature is in fact a "sweetener" for purchasers of the bond. Like investors in the shares of the company, it indirectly allows purchasers of the bonds to receive the benefits of increases in the value of the silver owned by the company. But, unlike purchasers of the company's stock, bondholders are not subject to a diminution of their investment in the event that silver prices fall. At a minimum, assuming no default, they will receive $1,000 for each bond, or more if silver prices increase.

The Sunshine bond has elements of futures and commodities options in that purchasers are allowed to speculate, to some extent, in the price of silver, and the seller has the option of delivering silver. Yet, at the same time, they are assured of a minimum return on their investment in the event that silver prices do not accelerate.

In the *In re Stovall* case,[2] the CFTC specified the elements of a futures contract. These included:

1. The existence of standardized contracts for the purchase or sale of commodities which provide for futures as opposed to immediate delivery.
2. Such transactions are directly or indirectly offered to the general public.
3. The transactions are generally secured by owner's money or margin, and;
4. The transactions are entered into primarily for the purpose of assuming or shifting the risk of change in value of the commodities, rather than for transferring ownership of the actual commodities.

The Sunshine bonds are standardized, and it could be argued that they provide for the future delivery of a commodity, subject to the contingency of increased value. These transactions are also directly offered to the general public, but are not secured by earnest money or margin. Rather, they represent an actual investment in a loan obligation. It is also questionable whether the fourth element is met (i.e., that the transactions are entered into primarily for the purpose of assuming or shifting the risk of change in value of the commodity). Rather, the silver feature is simply a "sweetener" to the terms of the bond. On the other hand, it does provide a limited tool for speculating in silver prices.

Similarly, there is an option element. The company is given the option of delivering silver, and the buyer accepting, in the event that the value of the silver increases beyond the face amount of the bond. For example, the 1983 offering of the silver index bonds was redeemable in whole on or after February 15, 1988, at the option of the company at the index principal amount together with accrued interest, if the principal amount equaled or exceeded $2,000 for a period of thirty consecutive calendar days. The holders of the bonds could elect to receive silver in lieu of cash.

Nevertheless, it can hardly be construed to be anything approaching a futures contract or as an option. Consequently, these transactions would appear to fall outside the jurisdiction of the CFTC. In any event, the bonds are subject to regulation as securities under the federal securities laws. Accordingly, there is no lack of regulation or customer protection available.

A bond offering similar to the Sunshine issue was also made by the Texas International Company. This offering had an index feature based on oil prices. Other offerings have also been cleared informally by the CFTC staff where the "bond-like" elements of the instrument outweigh any futures or options features.

The CFTC has taken a more restrictive view, however, with respect to other instruments, even though they constitute part of a securities offering. In an interpretive letter dated March 6, 1985, the CFTC staff considered whether gold warrants sold as a part of a securities offering, which had been filed with the Securities and Exchange Commission on a Form S-1 registration statement and which covered 1.3 million shares of common stock, were options subject to the CFTC's jurisdiction. Each share of stock had two warrants attached: one for the purchase of common stock and one to purchase .01 troy ounces of gold from the company at an initial price of $6.00. The gold and stock warrants were detachable and transferable.

The CFTC staff noted that the gold warrants gave the holder the conditional right, but not the obligation, to purchase physical gold. It further noted that part of the purchase price of the offer was directly attributable to the value of the gold warrant, and would thus serve the same economic purpose as a premium in an option transaction. The CFTC staff concluded that "these instruments constitute options on a physical commodity and . . . are subject to the general prohibition on options in the [Commodity Exchange Act]." The staff concluded that these warrants could not be offered unless they were subject to an options exemption under the Commodity Exchange Act; none of them were available for the public offering envisioned by the company.[3] This interpretation was rendered despite an amendment to the Commodity Exchange in 1974 (the "Treasury Amendment") which states that the Commodity Exchange Act shall not apply to security warrants unless traded on a board of trade.

Subsequently, however, the CFTC staff allowed Quadrex Securities to place with a U.S. investor $3 million of a $25 million Eurodollar convertible instrument offering by Pegasus Gold Corp. The bonds were convertible into gold, and this was permitted by the CFTC because the U.S. investor waived his conversion rights. The U.S. investor could only hold the bonds to maturity or sell them overseas. Nevertheless, the sale abroad would allow the investor to profit from gold prices. He would simply receive his conversion premium in cash in such an event.

In another interpretation, the CFTC staff considered whether "commodity certificates" offered to the public were futures contracts that had to be traded on a contract market. The commodity certificates were in denominations of $1,000 and were to be of 60 to 180 days' duration. At the expiration of the certificate, the holder was to receive, for each $1,000 certificate, cash equal to the prevailing price of a "commodity unit" or $1,000, whichever was greater. The commodity unit was a specified quantity of an underlying commodity. The commodity certificate did not pay interest.

The CFTC staff concluded that the commodity certificates were futures contracts, and possibly commodity options. The staff stated:

> Because the anticipated returns to Holders of Commodity Certificates are referenced to the prevailing prices of commodities traded on designated contract markets, the sales of those certificates appear to constitute "dealings in commodities for future delivery that are or may be used for . . . determining the price basis of any such transaction in interstate commerce." Such dealings are unlawful unless executed by or through a member of a board of trade which . . . has been designated as a contract market with respect to the proposed Commodity Certificates.[4]

AMERICAN STOCK EXCHANGE "BULLION VALUE DEMAND PROMISSORY NOTE"

In 1981 the American Stock Exchange announced a proposal to trade put and call options on "bullion value demand promissory notes" (BVNs). It submitted this proposal to the SEC for approval (the Commission exercises jurisdiction over stock options exchanges) rather than to the CFTC, which has jurisdiction over commodity options. The American Stock Exchange (Amex) described a BVN:

A promissory note issued by an Amex-approved issuer. It is a non-interest bearing obligation of the issuer to pay an amount in U.S. currency, equal to the market value of the number of fine troy ounces of gold or silver bullion described in note, based upon the price at which the bullion is fixed at the A.M. London fixing for the particular bullion on the business day immediately following the date of demand. . . . [5]

The Amex proposed to trade options on these BVNs with $25 to $50 exercise intervals for gold and 50¢ exercise intervals for silver BVNs. The Amex stated that the proposed new option "would make it possible to shift risks associated with bullion ownership, while at the same time providing opportunities for investment and trading of options on securities whose prices would be closely related to those of gold and silver bullion." With respect to the jurisdiction of the CFTC, the Amex proposal stated that the creation of the BVN "makes possible a program for trading such options in the well-monitored, regulated environment of the securities markets subject to the jurisdiction of the Securities and Exchange Commission, since the BVN is a 'security' within the meaning of . . . the Exchange Act, and is not a 'commodity' within the meaning of . . . the Commodity Exchange Act."[6]

In effect, what the Amex has done is to convert an investment in bullion into a security (a promissory note). It then sought to trade options on the security, which meant that the jurisdiction of the SEC (over options on securities) would apply, rather than that of the CFTC, which has jurisdiction over the underlying commodity in this case.

All in all, this was an artful way of avoiding CFTC regulation. As a practical matter, however, the options would be of no different nature than an option on the underlying commodity or an option on the underlying futures contract. This is because, as the Amex stated in its proposal, "BVNs would provide investors with means of obtaining 'the store-of-value' benefits inherent in the physical ownership of gold or silver bullion (through debt instruments valued at the price of the bullion), while eliminating concerns associated with the actual ownership of bullion such as transportation, storage, insurance, and resale."[7] Exchange-traded commodity options and futures contracts provide the same benefits.

The BVN proposal was never effectuated by the Amex. Rather, the Amex commodities corporation subsequently began trading options on gold bullion under the CFTC's pilot program for exchange-listed options. The option is traded on the physical commodity, but gold bullion option exercises are settled in cash, rather than by transfer of the physical gold. Cash settlement is based on the afternoon gold fixing price of the London gold market. Interestingly, trading in this option is conducted through a "board broker," a concept developed by the Chicago Board of Options Exchange for security options. A designated "board broker" maintains the book of limit orders rather than floor brokers, as in the case of the commodities industry. This, however, has met opposition from the commodity futures industry.

Specifically, the Chicago Board of Trade contended that the board broker system is a "carefully disguised and renamed system for a specialist."[8] Under the specialist system, the specialist is in effect given a monopoly on customer orders but at the same time has an obligation to maintain a fair and orderly market by bidding adversely to reduce the effects of market swings. In fact, the board broker only holds customer limit orders and does not trade for its own account, unlike the specialist.

It should be noted that a complicating factor is that in 1977 both the Senate and the House passed a bill that permitted individuals to make loan agreements requiring monetary repayment in gold or currency backed by gold.[9] It may be claimed that this legalizes off-exchange trading of BVNs and other gold-clause promissory notes.

INTEREST RATE "SWAPS"

In recent years, a popular phenomenon for hedging or displacing interest rate risks has been so-called swap transactions. In effect, one company is swapping its fixed interest rate obligations for the variable–rate obligations of another. For example, a company with a large variable-rate loan may be concerned that interest rates will rise and thereby increase its operating costs, spending greater amounts to pay the interest on the principal as the variable rate increases.

In order to prevent this from occurring, by "hedging" that obligation, it may seek to swap the variable rate for a fixed rate. It could do this by seeking out another company with a fixed-rate loan that it wishes to convert into a variable-rate portfolio (i.e., the second company may believe interest rates will, instead, decline and would prefer a variable rate that would let it take advantage of such a decline). The first company would then "swap" its variable-rate portfolio for the fixed-rate portfolio of the second company. In fact, the loan obligations are not exchanged. Rather, a cash settlement is made at various times from the differences between the fixed rate and the variable rate.

Initially these swaps were conducted party to party, and were often arranged by banks. Later, double swaps were developed whereby banks were interceded between the two swapping parties so as to reduce the credit risks to the parties. Still later, banks and other institutions began experimenting with the use of financial futures contracts that allowed them to transform a customer's portfolio into either a fixed rate or adjustable rate. As one author stated:

Several banks, brokers say, are also experimenting with the use of futures in interest rate swaps, exchanging for example a . . . fixed-rate loan for a customer's . . . variable-rate loan of the same term period. The bank then hedges . . . using futures contracts instruments. . . . "Basically the bank is hedging . . . in financial futures but calling it a swap and charging a swap fee," explains a futures expert. "It's a palatable way to sell people who have a fear of the financial futures market."[10]

In effect, these transactions provide many of the same benefits as the futures markets. The futures markets could be used by the holder of a fixed-rate portfolio to hedge that portfolio. The company could engage in a futures transaction that would result in profit in the event interest rates increased, which would offset the increased costs effected by an increase in the adjustable rate of the loan. Conversely, the holder of a fixed rate could benefit from a decline in rates by entering into a futures transaction that would allow it to profit in the event of a decline. Of course, if interest rates were to go up after the transaction, there would be a loss in the futures contract, but this would be offset by the lower-than-market-rate borrowing charges made possible by the fixed-rate portfolio loan (i.e., the fixed rate mortgage will not go up as would a variable rate, but the futures contract would cause increased costs, effectively converting this into a variable-rate loan).

On the other hand, essential elements of a futures contract are missing. First, these transactions are individually negotiated for term, amount, and other items, although standardized terms may be used on other essential features of the contract. Most such transactions do not involve margin, although security in various forms may be required to ensure performance. Third, these transactions are not generally offered directly or indirectly to the general public. To the contrary, they are conducted between large financial institutions that are well able to protect themselves. Finally, as noted above, it is true that the transactions are entered for the purpose of assuming or shifting the risk of change in the value of interest rates, just as in a futures contract. There is, however, no effective secondary market in these transactions that would allow individuals to speculate or to otherwise operate as a futures exchange in any traditional sense. Accordingly, on balance, such transactions should not be, and have not been, treated as futures contracts.[11]

INTEREST RATE OBLIGATIONS

Another popular method for hedging interest rate risks is the use of interest rate obligation agreements that set a ceiling or floor on interest rate charges. For example, a customer with a variable-rate loan may enter into an agreement with a bank or a brokerage firm whereby they agree to pay the customer an amount equivalent to any increase in interest charges over the index rate upon which the customer's variable-rate loan is based. Under such agreements, these differences are periodically computed and payments made to the customer, if any are due. These agreements may set a ceiling (pay increases over the rate) or they may establish floors (pay the amount of decreases in variable loan rates). In such a case, the latter would be used by a firm that makes a variable-rate loan. The interest rate obligation agreement ensures that its return will be fixed. A variation of these transactions is for the brokerage firm or bank to provide a customer, for a fee, with a commitment to make a loan in the future at an agreed-upon rate or to receive a fixed rate of return on funds to be deposited in the future.

All of these transactions are distinguishable from swaps. First, only the bank would make payments to a customer. The two parties do not settle any differences; if the variable rate in fact dropped from a ceiling rate agreement, the customer would not owe the bank anything. Instead, the bank is paid a fee for this transaction.

These programs have been offered only to large commercial customers and only for substantial amounts, thereby excluding the public from participation and eliminating one element of what is traditionally viewed as a futures contract. Further, while some terms of the agreements may be standardized, the essential terms of the contract such as price, settlement date, size, and interest rates are individually negotiated according to each customer's particular needs and circumstances. There are also generally no margin requirements associated with these transactions; only a fee is paid.

It can be argued that these transactions are entered into for the purpose of assuming or shifting the risk of change in value of commodities, rather than for transferring ownership of the commodities, the last element in the *Stovall* test. Nevertheless, unlike a futures contract, neither party's obligation under an interest rate agreement can be settled through the execution of offsetting transactions. Rather, the customer will pay a stated fee and the bank becomes absolutely obligated to make a payment, which is simply contingent on changes in a stated rate. Both parties' obligations are therefore unqualified and cannot be avoided or offset, as in the case of a futures contract. Further, because of their individualized nature, no large trafficking or secondary market can develop in these types of transactions; therefore the general public would not be involved.[12]

CROP PRICE INSURANCE PROGRAM

A transaction similar to interest rate obligations has been given approval by the CFTC Office of General Counsel. Under this program, upon payment of a premium, farmers would be allowed to select a guaranteed price per bushel of a grain they were about to plant. The price guarantee level would be similar to the price the farmer could obtain from the local elevator if the farmer were to enter into a forward contract for delivery of the crop at harvest time. The farmer would elect whether to guarantee the price of 50 to 90 percent of his projected crop.

The Office of General Counsel concluded that it would not recommend an enforcement action against this program even though it contained elements of an option contract, such as the payment of a premium and a form of price protection. That conclusion is clearly an appropriate one since there is no "option" element. The company offering the program must, in all events, pay the price difference; there is no delivery option, which is the key aspect of an option transaction.

In issuing this no-action letter, however, the CFTC placed reliance on the fact that the company was planning to offer the program only to existing customers, at least initially and that it had assured the CFTC that it would comply with any applicable state insurance laws. In fact, these factors should not distinguish any similar program. The company in question was an insurance company offering crop insurance to farmers in the United States. Presumably that company and other insurance companies that would rely on the CFTC's interpretation letter serve most farmers. Therefore, this factor is no real limitation on the size or nature of the program. Similarly, the assurance that the company would comply with applicable insurance laws merely states the obvious—everyone must comply with applicable laws—and does not distinguish this transaction's elements from any other program with similar elements.

FOREIGN CURRENCY MARKETS

Foreign currency markets have long functioned as mechanisms to displace risk. For example, a domestic company receiving a payment on a contract in a foreign currency has a foreign currency exposure, so that it may suffer a loss that could wipe out its profits, and even cause losses, should the foreign currency in which it is paid be devalued in relation to the dollars for which the company is paying for the services or goods it is delivering under the contract. To obviate this risk, the company could simply sell forward the foreign currency and thereby be assured that it would receive the current price of that currency.

Multinational corporation banks and other entities exposed to such risks have long conducted these "FX" or "Forex" transactions through the so-called interbank currency market. This is an informal network of banks, brokerage firms, and traders worldwide that buy and sell currencies. This market was specifically exempted from the Commodity Exchange Act. The reason for this exemption is that bank regulatory authorities had long maintained controls over the principal institutions engaging in these transactions.

To provide greater access to the benefits of currency trading, a futures market in currency was developed in Chicago in the 1970s. The Chicago Mercantile Exchange, supported by Milton Friedman, the economist whose monetary theories have now gained some acceptance, thus foresaw large fluctuations in currency values and saw an opportunity to speculate in them. That exchange therefore developed a futures contract. A contract market for foreign currencies was developed and futures trading evolved. This is the International Monetary Market in Chicago. It allows access to the general public for speculation and even hedging in futures transactions involving currencies.

The Philadelphia Stock Exchange also conducts options transactions in foreign currency. Such transactions, however, are subject to the jurisdiction of the Securities and Exchange Commission, because that trading on the Philadelphia Stock Exchange is conducted under its license as a "national securities exchange," rather than a contract market regulated by the CFTC.

Traders and corporations also buy and sell foreign currencies in the interbank currency market. Here the customer may be required only to make an initial down payment or may be provided a line of credit to secure the transaction. In the latter instance, collateral may be required to secure the line of credit. A customer may also be required to post additional security in the event that the value of the currency is impaired.

Many transactions in the interbank market are, in effect, forward contracts calling for delivery at some later date. But even "spot" transactions in the interbank market generally provide for two-day settlement. Transactions are generally individually negotiated for amount, time, and price. Such transactions can also be offset by purchasing or selling an offsetting contract from the bank or other dealer. The proceeds from offsetting transactions deliverable on the same day may then be paid against each other or netted out, the difference being the profit or loss to the customer.

There is a specific exemption from the provisions of the Commodity Exchange Act for transactions in foreign currency. The act states that nothing in the Commodity Exchange Act shall be deemed to govern or in any way be applicable to transactions in foreign currency unless such transactions involve a sale for future delivery conducted on a board of trade. This is the "Treasury Amendment" to the statute.[13]

The foreign currency exemption was created as a part of the 1974 amendments to the Commodity Exchange Act in order to permit the large and established over-the-counter markets in foreign currencies to continue to operate without CFTC control or regulation. This exemption is by its terms broader than a simple exemption for cash or forward transactions where delivery always occurs. Indeed, there is already a provision in the statute exempting spot and forward transactions; to limit the foreign currency exemption in the same matter would simply be redundant.

Consequently, off-exchange foreign currency transactions should not be held to constitute futures contracts that must be traded on a contract market (and thus are not governed by the Commodity Exchange Act) unless they are futures contracts traded on a board of trade. In this regard, the legislative history of the 1974 amendments stated that its provisions were not to be applicable to trading in foreign currencies unless they were traded on a formally organized futures exchange.

In *Abrams v. Oppenheimer Government Securities Inc.*,[14] the court of appeals held that forward contracts in Government National Mortgage Association (GNMA) mortgage-backed certificates were beyond the scope of CFTC regulation, based on the same provision of the Commodity Exchange Act which exempts GNMAs as well as foreign currency transactions. In that instance, the court found that because GNMA certificates were excluded from the Commodity Exchange Act, contracts for the purchase and sale thereof also are not subject to the statute unless traded on an organized exchange.

It should be noted that the CFTC's Office of General Counsel had previously asserted that a loosely defined network of dealers in GNMA certificates could constitute a board of trade, although not formally organized as such. In that letter, however, the CFTC's Office of General Counsel concluded that the offer and sale of GNMA forward contracts would not violate the Commodity Exchange Act if such instruments were not marketed to the general public.

This is somewhat confusing, since an analysis would have to be made, at least under the CFTC staff opinion, to determine whether the exchange or marketplace for the transactions was sufficiently formal to constitute a "board of trade." The *Abrams* decision seemed to have eschewed such an analysis. It concluded that since the GNMA "forwards" were not traded on a formally designated contract market, then, by terms, the act exempts the transaction. The CFTC and other courts, however, have not adapted a similar analysis in determining whether futures contracts are present that must be traded on the contract market. Indeed, on October 23, 1985, the CFTC issued a statement concerning the exemption for interbank currency. There it stated that the exemption did not apply to off-exchange futures-type transactions in currency when such involved members of the general public. The CFTC sought comment on whether it would be appropriate to identify the permissible activities and participants within the exemption. It specifically asked for comment on who the participants were in the market when the Treasury Amendment was adopted in 1974 and who the participants are today.[15]

Prior to this release, the CFTC's Office of General Counsel had proposed to issue an interpretation that *all* transactions by individuals were excluded from the interbank exemption. But the major Wall Street brokerage firms and several banks revolted. The CFTC statement and the request for comment were the result.

The comment letters filed in opposition to the CFTC's attempt to narrow the interbank exemption were vociferous. On the basis of a comment letter submitted by Merrill Lynch, the CFTC staff conceded that individuals had in fact been in the interbank market since its inception. As the Merrill Lynch comment letter pointed out, popular magazine articles had made this fact clear at the time Congress was considering the interbank exemption. Opposition by the Federal Reserve Board (which suggested setting minimum transaction or other requirements), by the Comptroller of the Currency, and by the Treasury Department also surfaced, and the CFTC is now re-examining its position.

At least two courts have also held that options on foreign currency are not included with the interbank exception, since they constitute transactions "involving," but not "in," foreign currency. Those holdings apply only to options on currency, not to forward or other forms of delayed delivery contracts. In fact, the court in one of those decisions noted that a "contract to buy a specified amount of Swiss francs for future delivery is also a transaction *in* that currency: when one pays the purchase price all that remains is for the currency to be delivered (unless, as in the usual case, the purchaser liquidates his position prior to delivery)."[16]

Foreign exchange transactions may also be exempt from CFTC regulations if they are *foreign* futures contracts. Thus, even if, under the above analysis, it is concluded that the CFTC has regulatory jurisdiction over foreign currency futures contracts traded on a market that is not a formally organized board of trade, a further analysis is necessary to determine the location of that market. If the market is located abroad, then the CFTC would have only limited jurisdiction over the futures contract. For example, it has no authority to approve the contract or the terms and conditions of the contract. Further, the Commodity Exchange Act prohibits the trading of off-exchange futures contracts unless the contract is made on or subject to the rules of a board of trade, exchange, or market located outside the United States, its territories, or possessions.[17]

Under the CFTC General Counsel Office analysis, this exemption could be available even to a loosely structured group or nonformal market located abroad.[18] Nevertheless, the CFTC would undoubtedly require that the transactions be executed abroad before they could constitute foreign futures contracts. It should be noted, however, that there is no similar exemption for foreign options. Consequently, options on foreign currency could be traded only under the commercial option exemption or other limited exemption provisions of the CFTC's suspension of over-the-counter commodity options trading.

MORE ON EXEMPTED TRANSACTIONS

The Commodity Exchange Act, as noted, specifically exempts certain types of transactions from its provisions. These include deferred delivery, and cash and foreign currency transactions, all described elsewhere. In addition, certain other types of transactions are specifically exempt. The Treasury Amendment thus states:

> Nothing in this [Act] shall be deemed to govern or in any way be applicable to transactions in . . . security warrants, security rights, resales of installment loan contracts, repurchase options, government securities, or mortgages and mortgage purchase commitments, unless such transactions involve the sale thereof for future delivery conducted on a board of trade.[19]

These exempted transactions are not further defined by the Commodity Exchange Act. But the wording of this provision seems to specifically exempt all transactions in these instruments, unless they are conducted on a board of trade in the form of futures contracts. As discussed above, this creates some confusion. Apparently Congress envisioned that these transactions would have aspects of futures contracts, as is the case in the foreign currency market. Congress apparently did not intend to exempt only forward or cash transactions in these instruments. If that were the case, as in the case of foreign currency, the exemption would be redundant, because forward delivery and cash transactions are already exempted. Congress chose these specific exemptions because they occur in markets with sophisticated investors and because they were already regulated to some extent. The single identifying theme for these exemptions appears to be that they are commercial transactions that could not generally lend themselves to abuses such as those sometimes found in futures and options.

As also discussed above with respect to foreign currency transactions, these exemptions are not available for futures transactions conducted on a board of trade. The act defines a board of trade to include "any exchange or association, whether incorporated or unincorporated, of persons who shall be engaged in the business of buying or selling any commodity or receiving the same for sale or on consignment." The CFTC has stated that this term need not apply only to contract markets that describe themselves as a futures exchange. Rather, it could apply to other groups or associations conducting transactions on futures, even inadvertently.

Specifically, the CFTC General Counsel has stated that, while the term, *contract for sale of a commodity for future delivery* is not defined in the Commodity Exchange Act, its plain meaning would encompass forward contracts, even if they were privately negotiated between the buyer and the seller. The CFTC General Counsel stated, however, that Congress did not intend to regulate such contracts. Rather, Congress was focusing on the nature of the marketplace in which the buyer and seller entered into the contract, and that Congress therefore intended by the "deferred delivery" exception to exclude "essentially private transactions conducted off a board of trade."[20]

In sum, the CFTC General Counsel concluded that the thrust of the jurisdictional provisions of the Commodity Exchange Act was toward the marketplace in which the transaction occurred, rather than the element of deferred shipment. It was further of the view that, when forward contracts are traded by a group of persons acting as a board of trade, the contract could lose its essentially private nature and come within the category of contracts for future delivery to which the Commodity Exchange Act would apply. In this regard, the CFTC General Counsel stated that regulation by the CFTC was

> Unnecessary where there exists an informal market among institutional participants in transactions for future delivery in the specified financial instruments only so long as it is supervised by those agencies having regulatory responsibility over those participants. However, where that market is not supervised and where those transactions are conducted with participation by members of the general public, we do not understand the committee [of Congress] to have intended that a regulatory gap should exist. In these circumstances, we believe the Commodity Exchange Act should be construed broadly to assure that the public interest will be protected by Commission regulation of those transactions.[21]

The CFTC's general counsel thereby took the approach that the determinative test is whether the transactions involve members of the public and not whether there is a forward element or deferred shipment element that could constitute a characterization of the transaction as being one for future delivery. This is the same approach taken by the CFTC on the foreign currency exemption discussed above.

In *Stovall,* which was a case rendered some three months after the above opinion was expressed, the CFTC rejected a claim that the transactions in issue were not commodity futures because they were conducted off an exchange (i.e., the futures transactions were not conducted through a board of trade and therefore *ipso facto* were not subject to the Commodity Exchange Act). The CFTC took the view that Congress intended all futures contracts to be traded on the exchanges so as to ensure regulatory control. Again, however, the CFTC included as one of its elements of futures contracts the fact that there was public participation. This then may be the determinative element. It should also be noted, as discussed above, that at least one court has taken the view that exemptions from the Commodity Exchange Act are to apply broadly and not to be subject to a subjective test of their elements. Thus, in *Abrams v. Oppenheimer Government Securities, Inc.,*[22] the court of appeals held that, because GNMA certificates are excluded from the Commodity Exchange Act, contracts for the purchase and sale thereof are also not subject to the statute, unless traded on an organized exchange.

In this connection, the Treasury Department, in a letter to the CFTC concerning its interbank currency interpretation, stated that the Treasury amendment is a transactional one that places outside the coverage of the Commodity Exchange Act all off-exchange futures transactions in the financial instruments listed in the Treasury amendment. The Treasury Department further noted the Treasury Amendment contains no language limiting its coverage to the characteristics of participants in a transaction.

In sum, the best that can be said for transactions set forth in the exemptive provision (indeed other transactions with futures elements) is that public participation would lead to heightened concern that the Commodity Exchange Act should be applied. This is bolstered by the legislative history, which indicates Congress believes that the ability of the large participants in these markets to protect themselves and the loose regulatory authority already available were sufficient. On the other hand, it may also be argued on the basis of the *Oppenheimer* decision that these exemptions should be taken more literally and that the Commodity Exchange Act would not apply, unless they are in fact traded on a formally organized exchange. This would shift the focus from the terms of the contract and its investors to the circumstances under which it is traded.

REPURCHASE ARRANGEMENTS

Another commercial arrangement that results in the displacement of price risks in commodity transactions involves numerous types of repurchase arrangements. To illustrate, a commercial firm that consumes sugar would like to have its sugar prices fixed; otherwise an increase in prices could reduce its expected profits on items previously contracted for at a fixed price. In order to displace this risk, the sugar-consuming firm could seek out a sugar dealer who would be willing to set prices in advance for specified periods of time. That dealer, however, may not be readily accessible to the consumer and therefore could not itself supply the actual delivery at the fixed price. They may still, however, contract with each other in order to establish a fixed price. Under this arrangement, just as in the case of swap or interest rate obligations, the two parties could simply agree that the sugar producer would periodically pay any increases in sugar prices to the consumer for a fixed fee, or they could in effect swap their purchases and sales prices. The net result is that the sugar-consuming firm will be able to buy its sugar, directly or indirectly, at a previously agreed price, and the seller will have sold its sugar at that price. This fixes the price for both participants, even though they do not sell sugar to each other.

Once again, this arrangement would not appear to be the type of arrangement sought to be regulated by Congress through the Commodity Exchange Act. First, the essential terms are not standardized. There is generally no margin arrangement, or if there is, it is a commercial credit (collateral) arrangement. Third, there is no public participation because the two contracting parties are commercial entities who are well able to fend for themselves in determining credit and other risks that they may encounter. Finally, it is a mechanism for displacing risk but, as in the case of swaps and the interest rate obligations, does not permit the opportunity for a secondary market because the agreement is for a fixed period of time, and both parties are fully obligated to perform under the terms of the contract, subject only to certain contingencies.

There are numerous variations of these arrangements. For example, "cotton on call" contracts were used before the turn of the century to allow the purchasers of cotton to fix their price at any time. Essentially, the system worked as follows. Cotton millers seeking to cover their production requirements in advance, without assuming market risk, would contract with a dealer to buy cotton in an agreed amount, but the mill would be allowed to select the time of fixing the price of the cotton, based on a price of a designated future market at the time of the price selection. This permitted the mill to set the price of cotton at the time it sold its product, allowing it to fix the amount of its resale mark-up based on current market conditions, while assuring itself a quantity of cotton. Without the cotton-on-call system, the mill could have bought the cotton at inflated prices and would have had to sell it under cost if the market dropped before it resold the cotton. Alternatively, if the mill did not contract for the contract, it could find itself short of product when it needed it.

The CEA discovered, as early as 1939, that this cotton-on-call system was subject to abuse, where dealers manipulated futures prices to cause the mills to fix prices arbitrarily. It was also charged that this off-exchange system was threatening to replace futures trading. To protect against abuses, the CEA began a reporting system for cotton-on-call transactions. Since that time, this type of pricing program has spread widely in the commodities industry as futures trading expanded into different commodities. This has been made possible in part by futures trading, because the seller can displace the price risk by futures trading. The growth of these commercial arrangements underscores the importance of the markets to commerce. Further, since these are commercial activities for hedging prices, they should be encouraged rather then discouraged as illegal off-exchange trading. After all, the justification for futures trading is pricing and hedging, which is what is occurring in these transactions.

REPOS AND STANDBY COMMITMENTS

Another form of commodity-type transactions is "standby" commitments. Simply put, these are option contracts and are frequently used by banks and other dealers in U.S. government securities. Under the standby commitment, the purchaser of the put has the right to sell the securities or other commodities to the other party at a stated price prior to a set date. The seller or writer of the standby commitment is required to purchase the securities or the commodity at the other party's option.

To the extent that a standby commitment involves only an option on a U.S. government security, it would not be within the jurisdiction of the CFTC. Further, to the extent put options are used in other commercial settings in connection with commodity transactions, they would appear to fall within the CFTC's exemption for commercial options. Such commercial option exemption, however, applies only if the purchaser has a commercial purpose in purchasing the transaction. This will exclude the public in general from engaging in standby commitments within the jurisdiction of the CFTC.

Another popular form of commodity-type transaction is repo agreements. Simply stated, a repo agreement is an agreement by the owner of, for example, Treasury bills, to pass possession of the Treasury bills to another party. The purchasing party agrees to resell the securities to the original owner at a fixed date in the future. This in effect assures the owner of the Treasury bills that it will receive its securities back at a later date at a fixed price that is profitable. On the other hand, the purchasing party has access to Treasury bills that it may use to meet its operational or other requirements.

Because of these features of the repo agreement, it too has some elements of futures and options. It is not, however, generally sold to the public; it is not generally margined; and its terms are not generally standardized. Further, it does not in reality provide for the transfer of ownership, as in the case of futures.

The CFTC has not sought to include repo agreements within its regulatory structure. Indeed, at least tacitly, it had recognized that these transactions are not within its regulatory jurisdiction, except to the extent they are used in connection with other futures transactions, as in the investment of customer-segregated funds for futures contracts.

COMMODITY FINANCING PROGRAMS

Banks have also traditionally extended credit to customers for purposes of financing the acquisition of commodities. Indeed, many banks have internal departments devoted principally to these types of activities. In the most simplistic of these programs, the bank simply loans money sufficient to allow the customer to purchase the commodity, and the bank is then given a security interest in the commodity. This security interest may be secured by many methods, including Uniform Commercial Code filings, where applicable, or the possession of warehouse receipts for the collateral.

Generally, the bank will loan a percentage of the current market value of a commodity, for example, 80 percent of its market value. It may require that this percentage be maintained. In such event, the customer will be required to post additional collateral if the value of the collateral diminishes as the result of market fluctuations. For example: a customer is loaned $800,000 to buy a commodity worth $1 million and the value of the commodity later drops to $700,000. The customer would be required to post additional funds to bring the value of the collateral back to the 80 percent figure (i.e., the customer would be required to post an additional $300,000 in this example).

These transactions do not readily lend themselves to speculation or to abuses controlled by the Commodity Exchange Act. This is because leverage in such transactions is extremely limited, as compared to the 5 percent margins available in the commodity futures business. In any event, this type of transaction should not be construed as a futures contract if it is in fact a loan. First, under a precious metal purchase program, the metal is purchased on behalf of the customer, and held for his account (i.e., delivery is taken on the metal). The customer has title to the metal, subject only to the security interest of the bank or broker. Such a transaction is a loan program, not a futures contract. Nor is it a leverage contract. The essential difference is that the broker or bank actually purchases the metal from the customer, while a leverage merchant hedges its obligation on the futures markets.

This was confirmed in an interpretive letter from the CFTC's Office of General Counsel concerning the metal-trading activities of a bank. The bank bought and sold metal to traders, who sold it to the public. Settlement on the purchases and sales were settled within two days by payment and delivery or segregation of the metal. When resold to the public, the metal was placed in the public customer's name, and the purchase could be financed at up to 80 percent of its value. The Office of General Counsel concluded that these transactions were not leverage or futures contracts unless there was a provision for offsetting purchases and sales before full payment and transfer of ownership. This would require that the metal be placed in the customer's name and paid for or financed. Apparently, the metal could be sold later, but the customer would sell the metal and pay off the loan by changing ownership once again and completing the transaction by payment of the loan.[23]

A firm lending money should also be permitted to rehypothecate the collateral given as security. CFTC regulations allow futures commission merchants to hypothecate customer securities and property if the customer so permits. Consequently, such rehypothecation in a cash lending transaction (which the CFTC does not regulate) should not be precluded. Nor does the rehypothecation appear to lend any element of "futurity" that would change the nature of the transaction to a futures or leverage contract.

Banks and their customers may also use the futures markets as a means to secure loans. For example, the bank may require the borrower to hedge the inventory that forms the collateral for a loan by entering into an offsetting short transaction on the futures markets. In the event the value of the collateral declines, the value of the futures contract would increase, offsetting the diminution of value. Conversely, if the value of the collateral increases, the gain would be offset by the futures contract, but the bank would still be secured for the amount of money lent.[24]

In such instances, customers are often required to assign their interest in the futures contract to the bank or other lender, so that in the event of a default the bank may exercise the customer's rights under the futures contract. With respect to such assignments, the CFTC staff has stated that in the event a bank does take over a futures contract under such an assignment, the transfer of rights would not constitute an illegal off-exchange transaction, so that the bank would not have to liquidate the futures contracts and then reestablish a new position.

LEASES, "CASH AND CARRYS," AND OTHER DEALS

Another form of commodity transactions involves lease arrangements that provide for the transfer of commodities. For example, the owner of silver may lease it to a chemical company, which uses the silver as a catalyst and returns the silver at the end of the lease period. This allows the owner of the silver to obtain a return on his investment while it is being held for capital appreciation.

This type of arrangement does not fall within any accepted definition of futures trading. It does not generally involve margin, it is not generally involved with the public, its terms are not generally standardized, and there is no real provision for offset. Rather, the terms of the lease are carried out to their completion in most instances.

Still another, more sophisticated lease arrangement involves a play on futures prices. For example an astute trader may lease or "rent" silver from a silver producer or other owner for a stated period of time at an agreed-upon price. It will then sell the silver in the cash market and at the same time enter into a futures contract for delivery of the contract at a future period (the time when it is to return the silver to the owner).

In the meantime, the party renting the silver will take the cash proceeds from the sale and invest it in an interest-bearing account or other investment. The renter seeks to profit by obtaining a return greater than the rental payments and the cost of the money necessary to margin the contract.

This type of transaction does not meet the definition of a futures contract. Again, the terms are not generally standardized, there is no provision for margin, the general public is not generally involved, and there is no provision for offset. Rather, the terms of the rental agreement or lease are carried out to their conclusion.

Another form of commodity transaction is the "cash and carry." There are numerous derivatives to this transaction, but a common form involves a play, once again, on differences in prices between futures months. For example, a "spread" trader who is both short and long on the same commodity futures contracts, but with different delivery months, may take delivery on the long month and use the commodity delivered to satisfy his short obligation by redelivering the commodity. A trader would do this when, for example, prices are substantially higher than the price on the long contract for which delivery was taken (i.e., principal, storage, insurance, and interest costs are less than the price of his short contract).

Previously, there were also numerous other types of commodities transactions designed to defer or avoid income taxes, indeed in some cases to evade them. Many, but not all of these transactions have been curtailed as a result of changes in the tax laws in 1982 that basically provide for an effective 32 percent rate of taxation for "regulated futures contracts" without any holding period. Nevertheless, there are still quirks in the law that may lend themselves to structured commodity arrangements designed with tax effects in mind.

HYBRIDS IN GENERAL

The CFTC's Office of General Counsel is now devoting a substantial effort to examining a variety of commercial arrangements to determine whether they may be characterized as options or futures contracts that are barred or otherwise subject to CFTC regulations. An advisory committee (the Financial Products Advisory Committee) has also been formed by the CFTC to review this area. Hopefully, the result will be to allow commercially viable transactions while stopping pricing speculative transactions that are designed and used solely to fleece the public.

DOMESTIC AND FOREIGN EXCHANGE LINKAGES

The increased interest in commodity futures trading worldwide has developed a demand for extended trading hours, so that traders can respond to worldwide developments that may affect commodity prices, without awaiting the opening of their own domestic exchange. The availability of a 24-hour exchange would also diminish the risks inherent in commodity futures trading. For example, as noted above, a trader could respond immediately to worldwide developments occurring after normal trading hours by changing his position in the market immediately upon notice of the event, rather than awaiting the full market effect of the development, which may be exacerbated over the several-hour period between the time of closing of an exchange and its opening on the following day. Further, since many futures markets are international in scope, their linkage with each other is a natural development that is being made both possible and desirable as a result of increased sophistication in communications and computer technology.

One exchange that provides extended trading hours (although not 24 hours) is the INTEX Exchange in Bermuda. It is linked with the ICCH (the International Commodity Clearing House) in London which clears its trades, and it is fully computerized. This exchange does not, however, combine a domestic U.S. market with a foreign market. Rather, it is strictly a foreign futures exchange. Similarly, other exchange linkages abroad, such as the European Options Exchange, are not combined with a U.S. market yet, and the relationships enjoyed by the ICCH with the Hong Kong and other foreign exchanges are not combined with a U.S. market.

As a means of establishing a de facto link with some exchanges, several trading practices were also designed to allow extended trading hours and a linkage with exchanges. One such development involved precious metals trading between London and New York. The London market engaged in cash forward transactions in gold and silver during the normal working hours there. Customers wishing to continue to trade, however, could in effect roll over those positions into the Commodity Exchange Inc. in New York. This was done through exchange of physicals for cash transactions (EFPs). This allowed a means for offsetting risks in both the London and U.S. markets for an extended period, from the opening of business in London to the close of business on the Comex. But this was a complicated procedure. It was not generally understood or even available to the public. Consequently, the desire for more formal linkages between United States and foreign markets on a more simplified basis continued. The CFTC, however, in reviewing the Volume Investors default has questioned this practice because of its concern that this could result in abuses.

In any event, in 1984, a foreign and domestic exchange linkage was approved by the CFTC.[25] This was a link between the Chicago Mercantile

Exchange and the Simex, the Singapore International Monetary Exchange. Other exchanges have also been seeking to develop such linkages. Recently, for example, the Sydney Futures Exchange and the Comex announced that they had agreed in principle on such a linkage. This proposal has just been approved by the CFTC.

This hybrid arrangement creates numerous regulatory issues and concerns. First, regulation here is disparate. Domestic futures contracts must be traded through a contract market designated as such by the CFTC. A contract market is strictly regulated by the CFTC, its rules are approved by the CFTC, and trading in contracts through a contract market may not be conducted unless the CFTC approves such trading and approves the terms and conditions of the contract. The contrary is true with respect to foreign futures contracts. The CFTC has only limited jurisdiction with respect to such transactions. It is specifically excluded from regulating the terms and conditions of the contracts or even approving the offer and sale of the contracts. This creates a competitive difference, since regulations would be more expensive for contract markets and any new product development will be slowed by CFTC review and approval. On the other hand, the present time and place advantages of domestic contracts markets more than offset any actual perceived regulatory advantage. With the advent of the exchange linkages, however, this condition could change, and time will tell whether this advantage is significant.

The linkages also raise other concerns. For example, jurisdictional disputes arising from such transactions raise delicate questions of international law. The Simex and Chicago Mercantile Exchange linkage has attempted to reduce these to a minimum. They did so by maintaining separate clearing houses and separate exchange functions. A customer using the link, therefore, is subject to the rules of the exchange on which the transaction is conducted. It operates in the following manner. If a U.S. customer wanted to execute a contract on the Simex at a time when the Chicago Mercantile Exchange was closed, it would simply enter the order through its broker, and the broker would in turn transmit it for execution on the Simex. The trade is cleared through and guaranteed by the Simex clearing house. In the event that the customer wants to close the transaction on the Chicago Mercantile Exchange, the separateness is still maintained. What occurs is that the Simex becomes the customer of the Chicago Mercantile Exchange and vice versa for purposes of offsetting the transaction. In that way, the trade is effectively closed out and liquidated.

Nevertheless, concerns still remain. For example, a U.S. customer affected by conduct on the Simex will have to pursue those remedies through Simex and not through the Chicago Mercantile Exchange. This raises tough questions as to whether an action may be brought in the United States and whether U.S. or Singapore law will apply, as well as questions of the appropriate remedies and standards for determining whether a violation of the law has occurred.[26]

In addition, there are regulatory concerns. The CFTC maintains strict surveillance and regulatory controls over domestic contract markets in commodity trading. As noted, it does not have similar authority for foreign futures. In the event of manipulation, or indeed as a means to facilitate manipulation, the linkage could be used by a foreign trader to screen itself from CFTC scrutiny. This could be done by manipulating the market on the Singapore side and having its effects trail over to the Chicago Mercantile Exchange side on the following day. In order to carry out its surveillance activities fully, the CFTC predictably would want information concerning the Singapore trades as well as those on the Chicago Mercantile Exchange. If, however, Singapore were unwilling to allow this intrusion of the U.S. government into its internal affairs, the trader would be effectively screened.

This was a particular concern of the CFTC in approving the Simex proposal. Its concern was obviated somewhat, however, by the fact that the Singapore government agreed fully to cooperate with the CFTC in maintaining surveillance over the exchange. Other governments, however, may not be so willing to give up their sovereignty in such circumstances. Accordingly, until these issues are resolved, exchange linkages may be limited to only those countries willing to allow the CFTC an insight into their citizens' and residents' trading activities.

It is uncertain how these conflicts, if they should arise, will be resolved. But until the courts and the CFTC have had experience with these linkages, a degree of uncertainty remains. As the systems gain more experience and traders become aware of what they can expect in dispute resolutions and in surveillance areas, this uncertainty should diminish.

In the meantime, the CFTC may face difficult issues. For example, should it declare a market emergency on the Chicago Mercantile Exchange, it is unclear what effect this will have on the Singapore Exchange. The CFTC itself has stated that its own emergency powers may be limited to suspending or terminating the agreement between CME and Simex. In fact, the existence of the Simex could effectively obviate the CFTC's emergency powers. For example, the traders could simply transfer their activities to the Singapore side and continue whatever inappropriate conduct has caused the CFTC's concern. In such a case, the CFTC would be dependent on the good will of the Singapore government and the hope that the Singapore government viewed the conduct similarly. Otherwise, the CFTC's emergency action may do no more than impair trading by legitimate traders in the marketplace.

18
CONCLUSION

THE CFTC: ITS FIRST TEN YEARS

In October 1985, the CFTC celebrated its tenth anniversary with a conference and a gala dinner for members of the industry, as well as present and former CFTC commissioners and staff. It was a proud occassion for all those present. The CFTC also received a surprisingly warm letter from President Reagan:

> Because of your devoted efforts during the past decade, CFTC has established itself as an efficient and effective regulator of the nation's commodity futures exchanges.... "This Commission is one of my favorites because it proves that government can do a good job without soaking up taxpayers' money or over-regulating the marketplace." Today, I extend that praise to all of you and applaud the diligence and creativity with which you have fulfilled your responsibilities.[1]

In fact, the CFTC had come a long way since 1974. Although it had many setbacks, it could rightfully claim that it had established a broad and effective regulatory framework over the futures markets. The industry had also seen dramatic changes in its business. It was no longer the "anything goes" creature of yesterday. In the years following the CFTC's creation, it had changed from principally an agriculture enterprise to more of a well-disciplined Wall Street operation, trading financial futures, foreign currency, petroleum, precious metals, and other exotic "commodities." Indeed, the volume of these financial futures is as great, or greater, than the trading volume in the agricultural commodities.

The industry had also changed in other ways. A broad shake-up occurred in the 1980s that resulted in the consolidation or elimination of many established brokerage firms such as ContiCommodity Services and ACLI International Commodity Services Inc. Other traditional securities firms, such as Oppenheimer and Donaldson and Lufkin & Jenrette, cut short their entry into the highly competitive futures business. On the other hand, Goldman/Sachs, Salomon Brothers, and other financial institutions had become new forces in these markets. The banks also began creating their own futures commission merchant subsidiaries to compete with the traditional brokerage firms for commercial business, all of which has led to a highly competitive environment.

Despite the problems encountered by some firms, trading volume in futures contracts remains high. This has been due to the increased interest in financial futures, which has offset a declining trading interest in agricultural products.[2] But it is unlikely, under current economic conditions, that the expansion and attending regulatory problems experienced in the 1970s will recur in the near future. Nevertheless, as the CFTC begins to mature, it will confront the same problems that have been encountered by other "old-line" agencies. The foremost such concern is that of "overregulation." There is a very real danger that the CFTC's newly established preeminence may lead it to ignore or overcome industry opposition to regulations that are unduly burdensome or even unnecessary, and thereby stifle one of the most creative of the financial service industries.

Another serious concern is that of fairness and overreaching in CFTC proceedings and regulations. The Securities and Exchange Commission has long been the target of charges that it is arrogant in its regulation and unfair to individuals under investigation. Over-expansive interpretation of the statutes it administers has also led that agency to receive several rebuffs by the Supreme Court. The CFTC will be facing those types of issues in future years. Hopefully, it will avoid the pitfalls encountered by the SEC.

THE CFTC IN THE FUTURE

The commodity markets and the securities markets, as evidenced by their continual collisions with each other, are also fast becoming competitors on very broad fronts. The products they offer, at least to much of the public, do not often differ in material respects. Indeed, the New York Stock Exchange has entered the futures industry and is planning to jointly clear its futures trading with the Option Clearing Corporation, which clears trading for the securities options industry and which is regulated by the SEC. Yet, there are two sets of regulatory requirements for the two industries. For example, risk disclosure statements must be given to futures and options traders with terms specifically mandated by the CFTC. On the securities side, a more lengthy options disclosure document is given, but it is drafted by the exchanges. Margin requirements are set for the securities industry by the Federal Reserve Board, while, in futures, they are set by the exchanges. This, of course, creates a maze of conflicting and sometimes noncompetitive requirements for the various instruments. Indeed, the New York Futures Exchange is expected to seek, and the SEC to allow, cross-margining of securities and futures products to relieve some of this burden. Institutional trading is also hampered in the commodities industry by restrictions on trading that the CFTC and some commodity exchanges are seeking to impose.

"Upstairs" trading negotiations are being challenged by the CFTC and the commodity exchanges, even when they are sent to the floor for execution. Such anticompetitive regulatory actions will only encourage businesses to move their trading to securities-regulated products. There are also different and uncertain standards and remedies available to customers when they are injured by violations of the statutes. The Commodity Exchange Act has a provision for private rights of action, while the securities laws have very broad rights in some areas and none at all in still others. The right and access to arbitration is also regulated differently. Arbitration cannot be compelled under certain securities law provisions, while it is mandatory in other instances where an agreement has been signed. In contrast, the CFTC requires arbitration to be voluntary, allowing an election for reparations, which is not available at the SEC.

This all gives rise to periodic calls for the consolidation of the regulatory requirements for commodities and securities. Of course, competing regulators may result in more effective regulations; the inevitable bureaucratic competition between the two agencies may further that purpose. A monolithic agency would not be expected to do this. But a particular concern of the commodities industry has been that a merger would result in the commodity side being given short shrift by a combined agency. It concerned that it would not be managed by persons knowledgeable about the industry. In such an event, the securities side would gain dominance and the commodities' interest would be relegated to a subsidiary role, thus stifling the industry as it met regulatory roadblocks by an uncaring and uninformed agency.

There is much to be said for this argument. A combined merger of the SEC and the CFTC would inevitably result in the securities portion of the merged Commission (even if some seats are allocated for commodity representatives) being given predominance. This would happen because of the larger role the SEC plays in regulating equity securities. The securities staff would also be much larger, even if the CFTC staff is moved over, which would be required in any event, if any effective regulatory scheme is to continue forward.

Indeed, a merger could be a regulatory nightmare for the commodities industry. It has taken ten years for the CFTC and the industry to accommodate themselves to each other, and it is still an uneasy relationship. The

CFTC's institutional knowledge, particularly on policy levels, was at a very low level with respect to these markets. Today, the CFTC has gained much knowledge and experience. To lose that expertise and the present ability to regulate the industry would be a serious setback for the industry and the public.

A more pragmatic concern is that the two agencies are regulated by different committees of Congress. Although the agricultural committees, which regulate the CFTC, may not have particular interest in the financial products regulated by the CFTC, they do have a deep and abiding interest in agricultural futures trading, which is periodically blamed for all agricultural ills. It is unlikely that these committees would want that interest subsumed in a regulatory agency such as the SEC, whose sole interest is financial matters. It would also make little sense for the agricultural aspects of futures trading to be spun off into a separate agency, since the two separate agencies would have to develop the same expertise in any event. These roadblocks, therefore, make the merger path a difficult and uncertain one. Even the institutional savings that presumably would result (e.g., elimination of duplicative numbers of Commissioners, aides, congressional liaison and public relations personnel) would, in large measure, be offset by the loss of policymaking expertise and the detrimental effect on the industry of being relegated to a secondary role in the operations of another agency.

It should also be noted that stock options trading is a derivative of futures trading, which has been traditionally regulated by the CFTC and its predecessor, the Commodity Exchange Authority. The Chicago Board Options Exchange (CBOE), the initial stock option exchange, was developed by the Chicago Board of Trade as a part of a project designed to apply futures trading principles to securities trading. That effort was successful. At the time of its development, however, there was no CFTC, and the regulatory role of the Commodity Exchange Authority was extremely limited (to agricultural options). Perceiving this regulatory gap, the SEC required the CBOE to register its options with it as securities. But, as the Seventh Circuit subsequently noted, it was a mere historical accident that the SEC was able to take that position. Had the CBOE been developed a few years later, after the amendment of the Commodity Exchange Act in 1974, it would have been regulated by the CFTC. Therefore, either a historical or an "instrument" type analysis of whether a single agency should be given jurisdiction, would support, if anything, granting of jurisdiction over the regulation of stock options as well as futures to the CFTC, an agency familiar with these instruments and their dangers. Such an event is not likely to happen if the SEC has its way. Whatever the case, the issue will continue to reappear as the two industries continue to merge in these trading practices and products.

The merger issue was not raised in the 1986 reauthorization process before Congress. After some initial skirmishes with the exchanges, the CFTC diffused much of the exchanges' opposition in Congress by withdrawing the net capital proposal that it issued after the Volume Investors collapse and by assuring some flexibility on the time-stamping issue. It did, however, allow its reauthorization to become bogged down, as of this writing, on the issue of how leverage contracts are to be regulated. Whatever the outcome of that battle, the CFTC's existence appears to be asured for some years to come.

HISTORY REPEATS ITSELF

As we saw in Chapters 1 and 2, the populist revolt of the 1880s and the agrarian movement of that period had charged that short selling in the futures market was depressing grain prices. Those charges resulted in the first federal efforts to regulate the grain exchanges. History has a way of repeating itself. In 1978 and 1982, the American Agricultural Movement protested that the Chicago Board of Trade was depressing agricultural prices and creating crisis conditions in the American agricultural community. As was also reported in January 1985:

> Some 200 farmers from several states staged a protest Monday outside the Chicago Board of Trade over farm conditions. They charged that speculators inside were running down their prices below their costs of production. Some 12 farmers were arrested when they tried to enter the building to stop commodity trading.[3]

> Later, about 40 farmers marched to the local office of the Commodity Futures Trading Commission. The protesters demanded that regulations on futures trading be revised to prohibit trading by speculators, which they said drives prices down to levels that do not cover the cost of production.[4]

NOTES

CHAPTER 1

1. Futures Industry Association, *An Introduction to the Futures Markets* (Washington, D.C., 1984), p. 2; Bakken, Henry H., *Futures Trading—Origin, Development and Present Economic Status,* 3 Futures Trading Seminar (Madison, WI: Mimir Publishers, 1966), pp. 1-35; Chicago Board of Trade, *Commodity Trading Manual* (Chicago IL: Chicago Board of Trade, 1973), p. 2. The Chicago Board of Trade notes that the concept of a central marketplace in which to trade commodities began in the Greco-Roman era, survived the Dark Ages, and emerged during the feudal period in the fairs arranged by the *pieds poudres* ("men of dusty feet"). *Ibid.,* pp. 1-2.

2. A Professor Dumbell asserted that the creators of the "to arrive" contracts were speculators whose practices "were frowned upon by the more reputable merchants and brokers." Dumbell, Stanley, "The Origin of Cotton Futures," *Economic History* (May 1927):193-201, noted in Williams, Jeffery C., "The Origins of Futures Markets." *Agricultural History* (Berkeley, CA: University of California Press), 56 (January 1982):306-307. The "to arrive" were sometimes settled by paying differences between the contract price and the fair market price of a commodity under the contract. Short selling was also conducted in these contracts. See generally, Gregory, Owen, "Futures Markets: Comment." *Agricultural History* (Berkeley, CA: University of California Press) 56 (January 1982):317-20.

3. Initially, the Chicago Board of Trade had difficulty in attracting members. Indeed, by "1853 Board attendance was so poor that it had to be encouraged by free lunches." Lurie, Jonathan, *The Chicago Board of Trade, 1859-1905* (Urbana, II: University of Illinois Press, 1979), p. 25.

The disciplinary authority of the exchange sought to assure high standards of mercantile conduct, as well as decorum on the floor. With respect to the latter, problems ran from cursing to insults directed against the King of Hawaii, who was visiting the floor of the Chicago Board of Trade in 1875. *Ibid.,* pp. 30-31.

4. The Chicago Board of Trade's historian states that

The trade in futures began in a perfectly natural way. The storage capacity of Chicago was limited. It frequently happened that a northeast wind brought in a large fleet of vessels when there was little grain in Chicago, but plenty of corn and oats in storehouses along the line of the canal or Illinois River, and in later years along the railroads. Under these circumstances it was a convenience to the vessel owner, and to the Chicago grain merchant as well, if some holder of grain in the country, or some Chicago agent of such country owner, would agree to deliver it in Chicago within a specified time, i.e., "to arrive in 5 days," or "to arrive in 10 days." Sometimes the local market was unduly stimulated by a demand to complete cargoes of vessels under charter, and country holders who could not ship their grain in time to sell on such a "bulge" might be glad to accept something less for shipment the next week or the next month.

Taylor, Charles, *The History of the Board of Trade of the City of Chicago,* quoted in Vol. 2 Federal Trade Commission, *Report on the Grain Trade* (Washington, D.C.: U.S. Government Printing Office, September 15, 1920), p. 107.

5. The federal system, however, prohibits off-exchange transactions in futures contracts. 7 U.S.C. § 6. In contrast, the Chicago Board of Trade rule adopted in 1873 simply made such contracts unenforceable. Lurie, Jonathan, *The Chicago Board of Trade,* pp. 42-43 (see note 3).

6. As might be expected, there was some competition between the Open Board and the Chicago Board of Trade. In fact, the Chicago Board of Trade viewed the Chicago Open Board of Trade as "a small affair, a sort of blood-sucker on this association." Vol. 2 Federal Trade Commission, *Report on the Grain Trade,* pp. 128-29 (see note 4).

7. Hoffman, G. Wright, *Future Trading upon Organized Commodity Markets in the United States* (Philadelphia, PA: University of Pennsylvania Press, 1932), p. 18.

8. In 1903 Frank Norris published his novel entitled *The Pit,* which was based on the real life character of Leiter, and portrayed the evils of speculation on the Chicago Board of Trade. Norris, Frank, *The Pit* (Columbus, OH: Charles E. Merrill, 1970; reprint). See O'Connor, William, *Stock, Wheat and Pharaohs* (New York: Wener Books, 1961), p. 9.

9. In 1913 the Supreme Court upheld an indictment of Patten under the federal antitrust laws for his corner in 1909. See *United States v. Patten,* 226 U.S. 525 (1913).

10. Miller, Richard L., *Truman, The Rise to Power* (New York: McGraw-Hill, 1985), pp. 41, 47.

11. Dies, Edward J., *The Plunger, A Tale of the Wheat Pit* (New York: Covici-Friede, 1929), p. 63.

12. U.S. Department of Agriculture, *Trading in Privileges on the Chicago Board of Trade,* circular no. 323 (Washington, D.C.: U.S. Government Printing Office, December 1934), pp. 7-9.

13. One author had noted that

The term "bucketshop," as now applied in the United States, was first used in the late [18] '70s, but it is very evident that it was coined in London as many as fifty years ago, when it had absolutely no reference to any species of speculation or gambling. It appears that beer swillers from the East Side (London) went from street to street with a bucket, draining every keg they came across and picking up cast-off cigar butts. Arriving at a den, they gathered for social amusement around a table and passed the bucket as a loving cup, each taking a 'pull' as it came his way. In the interval there were smoking and rough jokes. The den soon came to be called a bucketshop. Later on the term was applied, both in England and the United States, as a byword of reproach, to small places where grain and stock deals were counterfeited.

Hill, John Jr., *Gold Bricks of Speculation* (Chicago, IL: Lincoln Book Concern, 1904), p. 39.

14. Van Smith, M., "The Commodity Futures Trading Commission and the Return of the Bucketeers: A Lesson in Regulatory Failure." *North Dakota Law Review* 57, no. 26

(1981):13. The Chicago Open Board of Trade later became the Mid-America Commodity Exchange, which traded smaller versions of contracts traded on the Chicago Board of Trade. The Mid-America Commodity Exchange joined with the Chicago Board of Trade in 1985, coming full circle after over a hundred years of independence.

15.   *Board of Trade v. Christie Grain and Stock Co.,* 198 U.S. 236 (1905).

16.   During the thirty-year period from 1866 to 1896, the country experienced one of the longest periods of continuous decline in agricultural prices in its history. See Guither, Harold D., "Commodities Exchanges, Agrarian 'Political Power,' and the Anti-Option Battle: Comment." *Agricultural History* (Berkeley, CA: University of California Press) 48 (January 1974):126-27.

17.   *Chicago Board of Trade v. Christie Grain and Stock Co.,* 198 U.S. 236, 247-48 (1905).

18.   These limitations are to allow traders to assess the market factors that have caused large price swings and to permit the exchanges and brokerage firms to make and collect margin calls, as well as to allow traders to meet such calls. Campbell, Donald, "Trading in Futures under the Commodity Exchange Act," *George Washington Law Review* 26 (1958):215, 226.

19.   Hurt, Harry, III, *Texas Rich* (New York: W. W. Norton & Co., 1981), pp. 28, 47-48.

20.   U.S. Congress, House, *Congressional Record,* 67th Cong., 1st Sess., May 11, 1921, p. 1318.

21.   U.S. Congress, Senate, *Congressional Record,* 67th Cong., 1st Sess., August 9, 1921, p. 4762.

22.   U.S. Congress, Senate, *Taxing Contracts for Sale of Grain for Future Delivery, and Options for Such Contracts, and Providing for Regulation of Boards of Trade etc.,* 67th Cong., 1st Sess., 1921, Senate Report 212, p. 5.

23.   U.S. Congress, Senate, *Congressional Record,* 67th Cong., 1st Sess., August 9, 1921, p. 4763.

24.   Stassen, John, "Propaganda as Positive Law: Section 3 of the Commodity Exchange Act," *Chicago Kent Law Review* 58 (1982):635, 641. The Chicago Board of Trade also had its supporters in the 1920s. It was noted in the hearings that "Herbert C. Hoover says the Chicago Board of Trade is the most economical and efficient agency for the marketing of foodstuffs found anywhere in the world." U.S. Congress, House, *Future Trading, Hearings Before the House Committee on Agriculture,* 66th Cong., 3d Sess., 1921, p. 583. It was also stated in this report on p. 125 by Representative Thaddeus Caraway of Arkansas (125) that

> I never have believed that someone who sits here in the basement of some Government building with his hair parted in the middle can run this country better than all the people can run their own private business. I have no patience with that. I never went to a department in my life I did not come away thoroughly angry and half ashamed of my government. . . .

25.   259 U.S. 44 (1922). The litigation in *Hill v. Wallace* was brought by eight members of the Chicago Board of Trade, who contended that the board of directors of the Board of Trade had refused to take any step to challenge the statute because "they feared to antagonize the public officials whose duty it was to construe and enforce the act. . . . " 259 U.S. at 46. Justice Taft concluded that the refusal of the board of directors to bring such an action was a failure of their duty. Justice Brandeis, in a concurring opinion, however, asserted that the Board of Trade should not be required "to play the knight-errant and tilt at every statute affecting it, which he believes to be invalid." 259 U.S. at 74, noted in Stassen, "Propaganda as Positive Law, p. 642 (see note 24).

26.   U.S. Congress, House, *Prevention and Removal of Obstructions and Burdens upon*

Interstate Commerce in Grain, by Regulating Transactions on Grain Futures Exchanges, 67th Cong., 2nd Sess., H.R. Rep. 1095, 1922, p. 2.

27. The changes made in 1982 were largely the result of efforts by the Chicago Board of Trade and a searing law review article by its counsel. Stassen, "Propaganda as Positive Law," p. 635 (see note 24).

28. The Grain Futures Act was upheld as constitutional by the Supreme Court in *Chicago Board of Trade v. Olsen,* 262 U.S. 1 (1923).

29. U.S. Department of Agriculture, *Report of the Chief of the Grain Futures Administration* (Washington, D.C.: U.S. Government Printing Office, September 1, 1931), p. 7.

30. U.S. Congress, House, *Agricultural Appropriations Bill, 1927, Hearings before a House Subcommittee of the Committee on Appropriations,* 69th Cong., 1st Sess., 1926, p. 727.

31. U.S. Department of Agriculture, *Report of the Chief of the Grain Futures Administration* (Washington, D.C.: U.S. Government Printing Office, September 23, 1930), p. 11.

32. 269 U.S. 475 (1926).

33. U.S. Department of Agriculture, *Trading in Privileges* (see note 12).

34. The House Committee on Agriculture later recommended the passing of a bill that would prohibit the selling of futures in the U.S. markets by foreign interests above a "short selling limit" unless it involved the hedging of commodities owned by the foreign interest within the United States. U.S. Congress, House, *Commodity Short Selling,* 72nd Cong., 1st Sess., 1932, H.R. Rep. 1551.

CHAPTER 2

1. U.S. Department of Agriculture, *Report of the Chief of the Grain Futures Administration* (Washington, D.C.: U.S. Government Printing Office, 1935), p. 4; Tamarkin, Bob, *The New Gatsbys* (New York: William Morrow & Co., 1985), p. 280.

2. Cutten, Arthur W., with Boyd Sparkes, "The Story of a Speculator," *Saturday Evening Post,* November 19, 1932; November 26, 1932; December 3, 1932; December 10, 1932; and March 25, 1933. In these articles Cutten gave the following account of his problems with the Grain Futures Administration:

> "Look," began the spokesman [for the Chicago Board of Trade] when the door had closed, "the Grain Futures Administration has made complaint that you are carrying too much open stuff."
> It would be hard for me to make anyone other than a LaSalle Street trader understand how I felt then, unless it might be some Russian farmer who had tasted the bitter flavor of government interference in matters which should not concern it.

3. 298 U.S. 229 (1936).

4. U.S. Congress, House, *Commodity Exchange Act,* 74th Cong., 1st Sess., 1935, H. R. Rept. 421, p. 2.

5. *Ibid.*

6. *Ibid.*

7. U.S. Congress, Senate, *Congressional Record,* 74th Cong., 2d Sess., May 25, 1936, pp. 7857-58; U.S. Congress, House, *Congressional Record,* 73d Cong., 2d Sess., June 4, 1934, p. 10,449.

8. U.S. Congress, House, *Congressional Record,* 73d Cong., 2d Sess., June 4, 1934, p. 10,448.

9. U.S. Congress, Senate, *Congressional Record,* 74th Cong., 2d Sess., April 27, 1936, p. 6160.

10. U.S. Congress, House, *Congressional Record,* 73d Cong., 2d Sess., May 25, 1936, p. 7863, and May 27, 1936, p. 8014. It was stated in the House debates:

The Chicago Grain Exchange is responsible for more ruined fortunes, more bankrupt grain merchants, than any other one agency. Man is a natural gambler; he wants to take a chance. By law we have sought to curb that tendency by prohibiting all lotteries, but we have allowed the grain exchange to run wild, luring its victims into nets by the most dishonest of methods, and the result has been the bankruptcy of thousands of farmers, millers, bankers, and business men of every kind.

U.S. Congress, House, *Congressional Record,* 73d Cong., 2d Sess., June 4, 1934, p. 10,449.

11. U.S. Congress, House, *Amend Grain Futures Act,* 73d Cong., 2d Sess., H.R. Rept. 1522, pt. 2, p. 3.

12. U.S. Congress, House, *Amend Grain Futures Act,* 73d Cong., 2d Sess., 1934, H.R. Rept. 1637, p. 1. It was stated in this report at page 3 that the exchanges had "failed utterly" in their efforts to achieve self-regulation in the commodity markets.

13. By 1939, the CEA consisted of:

Seven divisions as follows: Division of Business Administration, Division of Analytical Survey, Division of Designations and Registrations, Division of Information and Education, Division of Record Examination, Division of Statistics, and Division of Violations and Complaints. In addition to its central organization, it has established nine field offices located at Chicago, New York, New Orleans, Minneapolis, Kansas City, Seattle, San Francisco, Boston, and Houston.

U.S. Department of Agriculture, *Administrative Procedures and Practice in the Department of Agriculture under the Commodity Exchange Act* (Washington, D.C.: U.S. Government Printing Office, 1939), p. 17.

14. U.S. Department of Agriculture, *Report of the Secretary of Agriculture* (Washington, D.C.: U.S. Government Printing Office, 1937), p. 75.

15. *Ibid.*

16. U.S. Department of Agriculture, *Report of the Chief of the Commodity Exchange Administration* (Washington, D.C.: U.S. Government Printing Office, 1938), p. 14.

17. *Ibid.,* p. 15.

18. U.S. Department of Agriculture, *Report of the Chief of the Commodity Exchange Administration* (Washington, D.C.: U.S. Government Printing Office, 1939), pp. 35-36.

19. *Ibid.,* p. 40.

20. *Ibid.,* p. 45.

CHAPTER 3

1. U.S. Department of Agriculture, *Report of the Chief of the Commodity Exchange Administration, 1940* (Washington, D.C.: U.S. Government Printing Office, 1940), p. 3.

2. U.S. Department of Agriculture, *Report of the Chief of the Commodity Exchange Administration* (Washington, D.C.: U.S. Government Printing Office, 1941), p. 8.

3. U.S. Department of Agriculture, *Collapse in Cotton Prices October, 1946* (Washington, D.C.: Department of Agriculture, Commodity Exchange Authority, 1947), p. 1.

4. U.S. Department of Agriculture, *Report of the Administrator of the Commodity Exchange Authority* (Washington, D.C.: U.S. Government Printing Office, 1953), p. 6.

5. In *the matter of Murphy,* 2 Comm. Fut. L. Rep. (CCH) ¶22,798 (1985), it was held

that a similar practice of "ginzy" trading (i.e., split tick trading by noncompetitive transactions) violated the Commodity Exchange Act.

6. U.S. Department of Agriculture, *Report of the Administrator of the Commodity Exchange Authority* (Washington, D.C.: U.S. Government Printing Office, 1949), p. 4.

7. U.S. Department of Agriculture, *An analysis of Speculative Trading in Grain Futures,* technical bulletin no. 1001 (Washington, D.C.: U.S. Government Printing Office, 1949), pp. 129-30. These findings were confirmed in later studies. See Hudson, Robert A., "Customer Protection In the Commodity Futures Market," *Boston University Law Review* 58 (1978):1, 2, n. 14.

8. U.S. Department of Agriculture, *Current Speculation in Commodity Futures* (Washington, D.C.: Department of Agriculture, Commodity Exchange Authority, July 31, 1950), pp. 4-5.

9. Donovan, Robert J., *Conflict and Crisis* (New York: W. W. Norton & Co., 1977), pp. 349-50. In a radio address on July 19, 1950, President Truman also urged Congress to curb speculation in the agricultural commodities. Note "Federal Regulation of Commodity Futures Trading." *Yale Law Journal* 60, no. 2: 822 (1951).

10. "Federal Regulation of Commodity Futures Trading," ibid.

11. U.S. Department of Agriculture, *"Speculation in Soybeans"* (Washington, D.C.: Department of Agriculture, Commodity Exchange Authority, August 10, 1950), p. 5.

12. *Ibid.,* pp. 5-7.

13. U.S. Department of Agriculture, *Report of the Administrator of the Commodity Exchange Authority* (Washington, D.C.: U.S. Government Printing Office, 1950), pp. 15-16.

14. *Ibid.,* p. 17.

15. Hieronymus, Thomas A., "Survival And Change: Post World War II At the Chicago Board of Trade," Proceedings of the History of Futures Seminar, *Review of Research in Futures Markets* (Chicago, IL: Chicago Board of Trade) 2 (1983):226. See also *General Foods Corporation v. Brannan,* 170 F.2d 220 (7th Cir., 1948).

16. In 1974 it was stated in Congress:

> Twenty years ago, Mr. Speaker, during my first term in the House, rumors of a crop disaster for coffee producers in Brazil set off an orgy of futures trading in coffee in this country which in turn doubled and tripled the cost of a pound of coffee to the American consumer. When I called to the attention of the Eisenhower administration that the alleged coffee shortage appeared to be a hoax, the Federal Trade Commission undertook an investigation which confirmed that suspicion and pointed to excessive speculation and irregularities in coffee futures trading as a major factor in the incredible rise in actual coffee prices in the United States.
>
> That bubble burst when the FTC issued its report, leaving in its debris many lost fortunes and millions of dollars of lost consumer purchasing power from 6 months of artificially high retail coffee prices. Nevertheless, up to now futures trading in coffee has never been brought under any form of Federal regulation.

U.S. Congress, House, *Congressional Record,* 93rd Cong., 2d Sess., April 10, 1974, p. 2849.

17. The CEA stated that

> Regulation under the Commodity Exchange Act, especially the speculative limits, has made it more and more difficult for an individual large trader or "market leader" to manipulate prices singlehanded. Another means of manipulating prices and evading the statutory requirements may be described as the group-action technique.
>
> Manipulative activity by the group technique involves a number of closely associated speculators whose combined activities are large enough to manipulate price, although no one of the group may have holdings large enough to exert an apparent

price effect. The complexity of the trading operations involved requires a large amount of detailed time consuming enforcement work, both in investigations and in the presentation of evidence.

U.S. Department of Agriculture, *Futures Trading Under the Commodity Exchange Act, 1946-1954* (Washington, D.C.: Department of Agriculture, Commodity Exchange Authority, December 1954), p. 36.

18. The impetus for the onion legislation arose from wide price swings in the March 1953 onion contract on the Chicago Mercantile Exchange. "It seems to be the opinion within the trade that an abortive attempt to corner that contract was responsible." Comment, "Manipulation of Commodity Futures Prices—The Great Western Case," *University of Chicago Law Review* 21 (1953):94, 113. Indeed, as one author states, "[h]ardly a day passed, it seemed, without somebody trying to corner the onion market or squeeze prices higher or push them lower." Tamarkin, Bob, *The New Gatsbys* (New York: William Morrow & Co., 1985), p. 29.

CHAPTER 4

1. Miller, Norman C., *The Great Salad Oil Swindle* (New York: Coward, McCann, 1965), p. 24.

2. *Ibid.,* p. 80. Three years later, when this tank was drained, it was found to contain salt water underneath a floating roof upon which a few hundred pounds of soybean oil had been placed.

3. *Ibid.,* pp. 116-117, 129, 223. A New York court later found that the CEA had no advance knowledge of the fraudulent wrongdoings of DeAngelis, and that it had urged the New York Produce Exchange to take prompt action to liquidate DeAngelis' large positions. *Seligson v. New York Produce Exchange,* 378 F. Supp. 1076, 1097-98 (S.D.N.Y. 1974). See also *Miller v. New York Produce Exchange,* 550 F. 2d 762, 766 (2d Cir. 1977), *cert. denied,* 434 U.S. 823 (1977).

4. The assistant secretary further stated:

More recently, a corporation without assets applied for registration as a futures commission merchant. It was registered by CEA mainly because we had no authority to deny the application. It filed a financial statement showing substantial cash in the bank and an equivalent amount in capital and surplus. It appears that the financial statement was false. This firm also obtained membership on a leading exchange. It went bankrupt as a result of the firm's activities. The customers of the firm will lose more than $22,000 because the firm diverted customers' funds to finance the general operations of the business. The corporation and its principal officers have been indicted by a Federal grand Jury and are currently awaiting trial.

In the public interest, neither of the firms should have been registered and permitted to handle customer trades.

U.S. Congress, House, *Congressional Record,* 90th Cong., 1st Sess., August 22, 1967, pp. 23,650-52.

5. *Ibid.,* p. 23,653.

6. *Ibid.,* p. 23,650

7. U.S. Congress, House, *Amend the Commodity Exchange Act, Hearings before the House Committee on Agriculture on H.R. 11930 and H.R. 12317,* 90th Cong., 1st Sess., 1967, pp. 109-10.

8. It was stated on the floor of Congress that the House Agricultural Committee

dropped the provision for handling of violations through the issuance of injunctions. This provision was vigorously opposed by the exchanges and the committee felt that at least part of the enforcement advantages sought through the injunctive process might be achieved by other and less controversial methods. Any delays or difficulties in enforcement procedures which the Commodity Exchange Authority encounters because of the lack of injunctive authority should be at least partially overcome if the contract markets utilize fully their own more flexible and less formal regulatory powers. This, of course, will not apply when the violators are not members of a contract market, but there are likely to be instances where prompt action by an exchange backed up where necessary by the application of administrative and judicial proceedings, can result in stopping the development of abusive situations. It is highly desirable that the exchanges recognize and accept a special obligation to do all in their power to facilitate and expedite correction of disruptive operations.

U.S. Congress, House, *Congressional Record,* 90th Cong., 1st Sess., November 30, 1967, p. 34,403.

9.   Carrington, Tim, *The Year They Sold Wall Street* (Boston, MA: Houghton Mifflin, 1985), p. 57.

10.   "The 'grain robbery' of 1972 was one of those economic events that, like the OPEC oil embargo . . . can truly be said to have changed the world." Morgan, Dan, *Merchants of Grain* (New York: Viking Press, 1979), pp. 120-121.

11.   Greenstone, Wayne D., "The CFTC and Government Reorganization: Preserving Independence," *Business Lawyer* 33 (1977):163, 177-78.

12.   Meeting Panel, "The Commodity Futures Trading Commission," Introduction by John A. Knebel, *Administrative Law Review* 29 (1975):367.

13.   U.S. Congress, House, 93rd Cong., 2d Sess., 1974, H. Rep. 975, pp. 46-47.

CHAPTER 5

1.   U.S. Congress, House, *Hearings before the Subcommittee on Special Business Problems of the Permanent Select Committee on Small Business Problems Involved in the Marketing of Grain and Other Commodities,* 93rd Cong., 1st Sess., 1973, p. 113.

2.   U.S. Congress, Senate, 93rd Cong., 2d Sess., 1974, Senate Report 1131, pp. 1, 18.

3.   *Ibid.,* p. 19.

4.   U.S. Congress, House, 93rd Cong., 2d Sess., 1974, House Report 975, p. 37. The General Accounting Office had also recommended that the regulation of futures trading be placed in the hands of an independent regulatory agency. See Commodity Futures Trading Commission, *Commodity Futures Trading Commission—The First Ten Years* (Washington, D.C., 1985), p. 2.

5.   U.S. Congress, *Congressional Record,* 93rd Cong., 1st Sess., April 11, 1974, p. 2928.

6.   *Ibid.,* p. 2938.

7.   House Report 975, pp. 47-48 (see note 4).

8.   The Attorney General, however, opposed granting the CEA, or any other separate agency, the authority to conduct its own injunctive actions or to represent itself in court. See U.S. Congress, *Congressional Record,* 93rd Cong., 1st Sess., Oct. 9, 1974, p. 10,264.

9.   House Report 975, p. 79 (see note 4).

10.   U.S. Congress, House, *Congressional Record,* 93rd Cong., 1st Sess., April 10, 1974, p. 2850.

11.   U.S. Congress, House, 93rd Cong., 2d Sess., 1974, Senate Report 1194, pp. 35-36.

12. U.S. Congress, Pub. L. no. 93-463, 88 Stat. 1395, October 23, 1974.

13. Senate Report 1194, p. 36 (see note 11).

14. Originally the House Agriculture Committee had drafted a bill that would have created a Federal Commodity Account Insurance Corporation to insure individual customer accounts. Later, the Committee suggested that this would be better accomplished by the existing Securities Investors Protection Corporation. See House Report 975, p. 84 (see note 4). Neither provision was adopted.

CHAPTER 6

1. When these reports were first presented to the CFTC, "they received a less than enthusiastic reception; for all practical purposes, they were ignored by the incoming staff." Some of these reports, however, were later "resurrected" and used by the CFTC. U.S. Congress, House, *Investigative Study on the CFTC, Report to the Committee on Appropriations by Mr. Whitten for Use by the Subcommittee on Agriculture, Rural Development and Related Agencies* (committee print), 95th Cong., 2d Sess., 1978, p. i, 17. (hereinafter the *Whitten Report*).

2. On July 16, 1975, the CFTC also "requested" that the major grain firms report cash grain sales to foreign governments on the date of agreement to the CFTC rather than the date the contract was formally signed. U.S. Commodity Futures Trading Commission, *Annual Report* (Washington, D.C.: CFTC, 1975), p. 21. This action was taken to close a loophole in grain export sales reports. The CFTC was thus concerned that another "Russian grain robbery" could occur.

3. *Whitten Report,* p. i (see note 1).

4. As was stated in the *Whitten Report,* p. 23:

While the schism between the former CEA employees and the newly hired CFTC group may have contributed to some of the early organizational problems of the Commission, the [Subcommittee's] Investigative Staff was advised that of even greater significance were the rivalries between the new senior-level staff appointees.

The senior staff involved included primarily the Executive Director, the General Counsel, the Directors of the three major operating divisions (Economics and Education, Enforcement, and Trading and Markets), the Executive Assistant to the Chairman, and the Director of the Office of Hearings and Appeals. None of these individuals is now employed by CFTC. The Investigative Staff has been advised that these individuals were, for the most part, very capable, strong-willed, and highly motivated persons. While some of the disagreements were described as personality conflicts, the major points of contention were "turf battles," with each of the individuals jealously guarding his or her own prerogatives and sphere of authority and trying to expand his or her own jurisdiction and influence. The arguments ranged from such technical areas as the role of the respective divisions in writing regulations and supervising the activities of the market, to chain of command jealousies as to the line of authority and access to the Commission, to competition for number of personnel spaces to be assigned to each function, down to such minutiae as size and location of office space.

Two specific areas of contention described to the Investigative Staff involved the roles of the Executive Director and of the General Counsel. With respect to the Executive Director, the heads of the operating divisions felt that they should not be required to report to or through the Executive Director or to be subject to supervision by the Executive Director. With respect to the General Counsel, the heads of the operating divisions and the Executive Director felt that the Office of the General Counsel should limit its activities to being legal advisor to the Commission and not become involved in day-to-day operations and decisions of the agency.

The bickering among the upper-echelon personnel was bound to have an adverse effect upon the subordinate staff, as there was no clear delineation of authority or responsibility.

5. See generally, Bagley, William, *Address Before the National Press Club* [1975-77 Transfer Binder], Comm. Fut. L. Rep. (CCH) ¶20,067, August, 5, 1975.

6. U.S. Commodity Futures Trading Commission, *The Commodity Futures Trading Commission—The First Ten Years* (Washington, D.C., 1985), p. 15.

7. *Chicago Board of Trade v. SEC*, 677 F.2d 1137 (7th Cir. 1982), *vacated as moot*, 459 U.S. 1026 (1982).

8. *Chicago Mercantile Exchange v. Deaktor*, 414 U.S. 113 (1973); and *Ricci v. Chicago Mercantile Exchange*, 409 U.S. 289 (1973).

9. This was not the first problem encountered by the CFTC in potatoes. In 1975, after numerous customer complaints, the CFTC investigated trading in over 28,000 potato futures contracts. U.S. Commodity Futures Trading Commission, *Annual Report* (Washington, D.C.: CFTC, 1975), p. 23.

10. This was the "largest default in the history of commodity futures trading." *Strobl v. New York Mercantile Exchange*, [1984-86 Transfer Binder] Comm. Fut. L. Rep. (CCH) ¶22,647 (2d Cir. 1985), p. 30,733.

11. The Supreme Court considered the default in the context of whether there was a private right of action under the Commodity Exchange Act, concluding that there was. See *Merrill Lynch, Pierce, Fenner & Smith, Inc. v. Curran*, 456 U.S. 353 (1982), *aff'g.; Leist v. Simplot*, 638 F.2d 283 (2d Cir. 1980).

12. At one point, Senator Frank Church introduced a bill to ban all trading in potato futures. Jones, William H., "Church Introduces Plan to Ban Trading All Potato Futures, 1977," *Washington Post*, February 3, § D., p. 11.

13. Jensen, Michael C., "U.S. Studying Whether 2 Nations Acted to Keep Coffee Prices High of 1977," *New York Times*, December 30, § A, pp. 1, 7.

CHAPTER 7

1. Rustin, Richard E., "Troubled Incomco's President is Accused of Fraud by Firm's Bankruptcy Trustee," *Wall Street Journal*, September 10, 1980, p. 5.

2. A CFTC task force was established to study the feasibility of bracketing trades. Under the direction of Commissioner Gary Seevers, that task force visited all of the exchanges and advised the Commission that some method of time sequencing by bracketing "or better" was feasible on all exchanges. U.S. Commodity Futures Trading Commission, *Annual Report* (Washington, D.C.: U.S. Government Printing Office, 1976), p. 81.

3. [1984-86 Transfer Binder] Comm. Fut. L. Rep. (CCH) ¶22,450 (1984).

4. The CFTC's customer protection rules are set forth at 17 C.F.R. 1.55 and § 166.1 *et seq*. The rules consist of the risk disclosure requirement, definitions, the unauthorized trading rule, a supervisory requirement, and a provision limiting a branch office of a firm from using a name other than the name of the firm for which it is a branch, a very limited range of customer protection.

5. Huey, John and Jonathan Laing, "Battered Bettor: How Cook Industries Speculated and Lost Millions on Soybeans," *Wall Street Journal*, July 14, 1977, p. 1. These were not the only problems encountered by Cook Grain Company. That company and other large grain companies had been the subject of a scandal involving short-weighting and selling

adulterated grain. See generally, Morgan, Dan, *Merchants of Grain* (New York: Viking Press, 1979), pp. 317-60.

6. Congressman Frederick Richmond, the chairman of the House Agriculture Subcommittee on Domestic Marketing, Consumer Relations and Nutrition, had conducted an investigation of coffee prices for over one year and was not at all pleased by the CFTC regulation of the coffee market. See U.S. Congress, House, *Extend Commodity Exchange Act, Hearings Before the Subcommittee on Conservation and Credit of the Committee on Agriculture on H.R. 10285,* 95th Cong., 2d Sess., 1978, pp. 5-6.

7. Knight, Jerry, "Another Federal Regulator Resigns to Become a Lobbyist in His Field," *Washington Post,* November 4, 1978, § A, p. 1.

8. U.S. Congress, Senate, *Congressional Record,* 95th Cong., 2d Sess., July 12, 1978, p. 10,540-10,541. It was also stated in this report that the CFTC was the "biggest stumble bums in the world," and that it was the "worst agency in the Federal Government."

9. U.S. Congress, House, *Investigative Study on the Commodity Futures Trading Commission; Report to The Committee on Appropriations by Mr. Whitten for Use by the Subcommittee on Agriculture, Rural Development and Related Agencies,* 95th Cong. 2d Sess., 1978, pp. 51, 64-66, 72.

10. As one congressman noted:

I listened to the arguments of the Securities and Exchange Commission and the Department of the Treasury as they tried to make bureaucratic power grabs on the jurisdiction of the CFTC. Quickly it was apparent that they were using their well deserved prestige in efforts to usurp the jurisdiction of a new and controversial agency.

U.S. Congress, House, *Congressional Record,* 95th Cong., 2d Sess., July 24, 1978, p. 7,207.

11. The General Accounting Office had conducted a study of the CFTC and was highly critical of its operations. See *Extend the Commodity Exchange Act, Hearings Before the House Subcommittee on Conservation and Credit of the Committee on Agriculture on H. R. 10285,* p. 365 (see note 6). The industry was also critical of the CFTC. For example, Robert Wilmouth, president of the Chicago Board of Trade, and later the head of the National Futures Association, stated in these hearings on p. 279:

In the three years of the CFTC's existence, the consequences of actions taken by an inexperienced and undertrained staff have not produced effective regulation but have consumed time and money on the part of the agency and the industry to no avail.

12. It was stated:

The Commodity Futures Trading Commission has not worked well. It is leaderless and demoralized. . . . The CFTC has been pompous, self-righteous, brazen, and ill-informed. It does not deserve a vote of confidence. Its leadership has faltered from the beginning—and within that indictment I include the cozy appointments of senior staff by a "liberal" Republican Chairman who proudly proclaimed that he was no expert. Indeed, we all found out that he has not been. It is believed that he never knew what he was doing. He does not enjoy the confidence of staff, press, or Congress—and up to now he will not leave.

A new Commissioner, a political spear carrier who grasped for office, and now clings to it against all reason and prudent judgment, will also not depart. So long as he remains, an important regulatory agency labors under a cloud of suspicion. And all I can add is that the fat lady has not yet sung.

U.S. Congress, Senate, *Congressional Record,* 95th Cong., 2d Sess., July 12, 1978, p. 10,548.

13. This was not, of course, true in all instances. The Chicago Board of Trade thus charged that there was

> a tendency on the part of the CFTC to propose first and learn later. Numerous actions have been taken and rules have been proposed which reflect an alarming lack of understanding of futures trading and market economics.

Extend the Commodity Exchange Act, Hearings before the House Subcommittee on Conservation and Credit of the Committee on Agriculture on H. R. 10285, p. 280 (see note 6).

14. The Department of Agriculture and the CEA had opposed the provision in the 1974 legislation, which allowed the creation of voluntary self-regulatory futures associations, stating:

> Such associations would create an unnecessary layer of regulation, would tend to become pressure organizations forcing all in the commodity industry to join, and could make effective regulation by the Commission more difficult.

U.S. Congress, House, 93rd Cong., 2d Sess., 1974, House Report 975, p. 79.

CHAPTER 8

1. The CFTC has described its large trader reporting system as its "basic tool for market surveillance in the detection and prevention of market congestion and price manipulation and distortion." 1 Comm. Fut. L. Rep. (CCH) ¶8,001.

2. 604 F.2d 764 (2d Cir. 1979), *reversing* [1977-80 Transfer Binder] Comm. Fut. L. Rep. (CCH) ¶20,785 (CFTC 1979).

3. *Board of Trade v. CFTC* [1977-80 Transfer Binder] Comm. Fut. L. Rep. (CCH) ¶20,887 (7th Cir. 1979).

4. Goldstein's hijinks are detailed in Henderson, Bruce, "L. A.'s Ultimate Bunco Artist," *Los Angeles Magazine,* April 1981, p. 181.

5. The Hunts were forced to obtain a 1.1 billion dollar loan to bail out their trading accounts, an amount Chrysler Corporation did not have the assets to obtain, without a government guarantee. This caused a great amount of consternation in Congress and the press. The Hunt supporters, in response, simply pointed out that they had the assets to cover the loan, while Chrysler did not.

6. Commodity Futures Trading Commission, *Commodity Futures Trading Commission—The First Ten Years* (Washington, D.C., 1985), pp. 35-36.

7. The 1982 amendments did not immediately resolve all of the tension between the CFTC and the Securities and Exchange Commission concerning the approval of stock index contracts. They clashed over this issue once more, before reaching an agreement establishing minimum criteria for such indexes. The Securities and Exchange Commission also suggested to Vice-President Bush's task force on regulatory reform that the two agencies be merged.

8. It was argued in Congress that the industry would not finance the National Futures Association if it also had to pay user fees to the CFTC. This was the basis on which the user fee was voted down.

9. This proposal was supported by the Department of Agriculture, even though it had opposed options trading when the CEA was in existence.

10. The criticism of the CFTC that was so prevalent in the 1978 reauthorization process was for the most part lacking in 1982. Its new chairman, Philip Johnson, had given the agency a new aura of respectability, and the number of scandals were much reduced. Nevertheless,

the General Accounting Office filed a report criticizing the CFTC in a number of areas, albeit somewhat mildly.

11. [1984-1986 Transfer Binder] Comm. Fut., L. Rep. (CCH) ¶22,549 (7th Cir. 1985).

12. [1975-77 Transfer Binder] Comm. Fut., L. Rep. (CCH) ¶20,067 (1975).

13. [1975-77 Transfer Binder] Comm. Fut. L. Rep. (CCH) ¶20,049 (1975).

CHAPTER 9

1. Berry, John F., "The Case of the Mixed-Up Coats and the Check for $24 million," *Washington Post*, May 13, 1978, § 1, p. 1.

2. *Ibid.*

3. Sullivan, Colleen, "Difficulties at CFTC: Both Style and "Substance: CFTC Chief Bagley Draws Wrath of Nearly All," *Washington Post*, October 26, 1977, § E, p. 1. As another congressional critic stated: "Certainly his major desire in life seems to be liked by everybody. His job isn't to be liked, it's to get on with the day-to-day tough regulation of an industry." *Ibid.*

4. Sullivan, Colleen, "CRTC Becomes Target of Disparate Criticism" *Washington Post*, October 25, 1977, § D, p. 7.

5. Bagley conceded many of these charges, but asserted that they were simply "understandable start-up problems." See U.S. Commodity Futures Trading Commission, *Commodity Futures Trading Commission—The First Ten Years* (Washington, D.C., 1985), p. 25.

6. In a parting blast, Bagley made public a memorandum to the CFTC's executive director which reprimanded the staff for withholding documents from the public until they were discussed at Commission meetings. He also announced that he would be making an around-the-world trip on "official business" before leaving.

7. Before coming to the CFTC, Stone had published a book suggesting that stock exchanges should be replaced by computers, a thesis that did not endear him to the commodity exchanges. See Beckman, Aldo, "Carter Finds A Hot Commodity," *Chicago Tribune*, December 3, 1978. Interestingly, although Stone had been commissioner of insurance in Massachusetts, his appointment had not been supported by House Speaker Tip O'Neil. Instead, the Carter administration had pushed Stone because of his reputation gained as a consumer advocate while commissioner of insurance.

8. Jack Anderson reported that shortly after Stone took office, he "made unannounced visits to various staff offices, then ordered that all posters, commercial calendars and pinups be taken down. He also dismantled the private bar that Bagley had installed in the Chairman's office." Anderson, Jack, *Oklahoma City Journal*, August 22, 1979. See also, Edwards, John, "Profile: James Stone: Chairman with a Sense of Stern Purpose," *London Financial Times*, January 16, 1981. It was noted that Stone refused to have social contacts with the industry and required the CFTC staff to address him formally as "Commissioner" or "Dr. Stone."

9. It was reported that the commissioners, "as one member put it," could not "agree even on the day of the week" and that

> [t]he blame for what is apparently an impossible condition must be traced directly to the C.F.T.C. Chairman, James M. Stone. Mr. Stone, presented as an able and intelligent man by his proponents, is obviously so lacking in chairman-like skills that he has been unable to do anything to ease a terrible condition, even delighting in fanning the flames of discord.

"Peregrinations: A Sorry State at C.F.T.C.," *Milling & Baking News*, June 3, 1980.

10. Stone remained as chairman until January 1981, and he remained on the Commission as a commissioner until January 31, 1983.

11. Stone did have his defenders. One of his supporters, Tom Russo, stated that he was a success

> because, if nothing else, he put the fear of the law and public outrage into many industry people who had never been concerned with such matters.

Maidenberg, H. J., "Naysayer at C.F.T.C. Is Leaving," *New York Times,* December 27, 1982.

12. Dunn, a graduate of Millsaps College, had served for nine years as executive director of the International Institute for Cotton in Brussels, Belgium. Before that, he had served for many years as Washington representative and director of foreign trade for the National Cotton Council and as assistant to the president of the Commodity Credit Corporation. In addition, he had served on the National Defense Advisory Commission.

13. Commissioner Martin had served in almost every phase of the commodity futures industry, including positions as clerk, floor manager, pit broker, hedger, and speculator. He was an executive with various commercial and brokerage firms, including Goodbody & Co., a director of commodities and a partner of Walston & Co. in Chicago; and vice-president of Cook Grain Company. Martin's tenure at Cook Grain became a point of controversy during the Hunt Soybean suit brought by the CFTC. A Cook official had attempted to contact Martin before the CFTC's action against the Hunts, a matter of serious importance to Cook, since it had a large position opposite the Hunts. Nothing, however, ever became of this episode.

14. As noted above, Seevers had served as a member of the President's Council of Economic Advisers. He held B.S, M.A., and Ph.D. degrees from Michigan State University, where he graduated Phi Beta Kappa. He had previously taught agricultural economics at Oregon State University.

15. It was noted that Gartner who had been an administrative assistant to the late Senator Hubert Humphrey before coming to the CFTC, had "the unique if dubious distinction of being the only man in the federal bureacracy to say no to both President Carter and Vice President Mondale when they suggested he resign his post at the CFTC because of an apparent conflict of interest" from the gifts to his children. "CFTC Member Shuns Past to Concentrate on Futures," *Kansas City Star,* September 19, 1978.

16. Howard Schneider's staff included, to name a few, Pat Nicolette, Richard Nathan, Fred Santo, and Frederic Spindel. Schneider was succeeded in the general counsel's position by Jack Gaines, Dennis Dutterer, and Kenneth Raisler.

17. 604 F.2d 764 (2d Cir. 1979).

18. *Lloyd Carr & Co. v. Commodity Futures Trading Commission,* 567 F.2d 1193 (2d Cir. 1977). In fairness to the CFTC administrative law judge, he had warned the respondents that the witnesses absolutely had to be on time and that they should be brought into Washington the night before to ensure they would be present. That warning was issued after various delays had occurred in the proceeding.

19. 738 F.2d 487 (D.C. Cir. 1984).

20. *CFTC v. Wientraub,* [1985-86 Transfer Binder] Comm. Fut. L. Rep. (CCH) ¶22,563 (U.S. 1985).

21. *ContiCommodities Services Inc. v. Schor,* 473 U.S. (1985). On remand, however, the court of appeals ruled against the CFTC once again. See *Schor v. CFTC,* [1984-86 Transfer Binder] Comm. Fut. L. Rep. (CCH) ¶22,667 (D.C. Cir. 1985), and the Supreme Court once again granted *certiorari.*

CHAPTER 10

1. The role of the executive director would have been especially strong under the House Agricultural Committee's schematic diagram, because the bill it reported had envi-

sioned a five-man commission composed of the Secretary of Agriculture and four public members who would serve on a part-time basis. The executive director would thus have carried out the day-to-day regulations of the Commission.

2. U.S. Congress, Senate, *Reauthorization of the Commodity Futures Trading Commission: Hearing Before the Subcommittee on Agricultural Research and General Legislation of the Committee on Agriculture, Nutrition and Forestry*, 95th Cong., 2d Sess. (Part I), 1978, p. 29. *Ibid.* Splane had interviewed most of the CFTC commissioners prior to their appointments. Apparently this was her only connection with the commodity futures industry. Prior to joining the White House staff, she had worked as a management consultant at Harvard University, and she held a MBA from the University of Chicago.

3. *Ibid.*, pp. 29-30. The division heads and the general counsel also had difficulty in getting along with each other. One particularly memorable battle was over who would retain the CFTC staff's old telephone number in the Bender Building when the agency moved to its present location. The general counsel prevailed and that office, as of this writing, may still be reached on that number: (202) 254-9880.

4. Sullivan, Colleen, "Controversy Brews over CFTC Post," *Washington Post*, September 27, 1977, Section D, p. 8.

5. President Ford had objected to this feature of the statute because it required senatorial confirmation of a non-presidential appointment, usurping the president's authority to make such appointments. A research memorandum prepared by the American Law Division of the Congressional Research Service at the Library of Congress could find no other provision allowing Senate confirmation of a non-presidential appointment, and concluded that the weight of the authority indicated that such a requirement was not constitutional.

6. The Complaints Section had previously been a part of a Reparation Unit in the Division of Enforcement. The Reparations Unit was abolished in 1980, however, and the Complaints Section was placed under the administrative supervision of the executive director.

7. The Secretariat also supervises the CFTC's compliance with the Freedom of Information, Privacy, and Sunshine acts. It processes and responds to requests and carries out reporting and other obligations under those statutes, which are substantial. For example, the Secretariat reported in 1982 that some 11,300 hours of CFTC staff time was spent in complying with those statutes.

8. Commodity Futures Trading Commission, *Annual Report*, 1977, p. 106.

9. Commodity Futures Trading Commission, *Annual Report*, 1984, p. 121.

10. In addition, the Office of Communication and Education Services, in cooperation with the United States Office of Consumer Affairs, published brochures warning of the dangers of commodity trading. They were entitled: *Get the Facts* and *A Spotter's Guide To Commodity Fraud*, both of which warned of dangers in commodity trading. It also prepared a brochure on reparations: *Questions and Answers about How You Can Resolve a Commodity-Market Related Dispute.*

11. Powers, together with the economist Milton Friedman and Chicago trader Leo Melamed, was a moving force behind the creation of the International Monetary Market on the Chicago Mercantile Exchange. Subsequent heads of the Division have included James Culver, Vern Pherson, and Paula Tosini. The backbone of this division has been John Mielke, Lamont Reese, and Blake Imel.

12. The Division of Economics and Education was also heavily involved in the March 1979 wheat futures crisis on the Chicago Board of Trade and the sharp rise and fall of silver and gold prices during 1979 and 1980, as well as the jump in coffee prices which are discussed above. In 1982, for example, coffee stocks had fallen to their lowest level in more than ten years as a result of the quota system of the International Coffee Agreement. Accordingly, each coffee contract had to be monitored closely as it expired.

CHAPTER 11

1. Russo's principal lieutenants at the CFTC were John Schobel, John Manley, and Sandra Sturges. Schobel did much of the drafting of the substantive rules proposed by the Division during its initial stages and was in charge of several policy functions. Manley was a former staff member at the SEC, and he had previously worked for two large public accounting firms. Manley became the chief accountant for the Division, when he joined the CFTC and later became the Division's director. Another attorney who handled a large portion of the Division's work load in its early stages was Charles Hord, an apparently indefatigable worker. Russo's successors as head of the Division of Trading and Markets, in addition to Manley, were Terry Claassen, Hugh Cadden, and Andrea Corcoran.

2. In 1976 there were some 26,000 registrants. By 1983 the number of registrants had grown to almost 64,000.

3. The Front Office Audit Unit also reviews and processes disclosure documents required to be submitted by commodity pool operators and commodity trading advisors. In so doing, it will issue warning letters regarding deficiencies it finds in those documents. The unit additionally reviewed the dealer option and leverage programs offered by various firms in the industry, and it developed a direct audit program for leverage merchants, which are not subject to the review of self-regulatory organizations.

4. In fact, an informal rule enforcement review had been conducted of the operations of the Chicago Board of Trade at an earlier point. As a result of that review, the Division of Trading and Markets proposed a set of regulations governing contract market rule enforcement procedures and disciplinary proceedings. See 17 C.F.R. § 8.01 *et seq.*

5. U.S. Commodity Futures Trading Commission, *Annual Report* (Washington, D.C.: U.S. Government Printing Office, 1976), p. 76.

6. Russo, Thomas A., and Dan A. Glickman, "Business Forum: Look Beyond the "Pits" for Directors," *New York Times,* October 28, 1984, § 3, p. 3.

7. U.S. Congress, House, *Extend the Commodity Exchange Act, Hearings Before the Subcommittee on Conservation and Credit of the Committee on Agriculture on H. R. 10285,* 95th Cong., 2d Sess., 1978, p. 370.

8. Various requirements were also imposed on the exchange concerning the manner in which investigations and prosecutions were carried out for exchange rule violations. The CFTC staff also focused on a "changer" operation on the exchange. In brief, the exchange listed "mini" contracts, that is, smaller contracts than were available on the Chicago Board of Trade, that were designed to appeal to smaller investors. The changer operation was essentially an arbitrage mechanism using a direct line between the Mid-America Commodity Exchange and the Chicago Board of Trade. The mechanism had been subject to abuse because it allowed floor traders at the Mid-America to take advantage of customer orders by locking in their profits immediately through an offsetting transaction on the Chicago Board of Trade. The changer operation was still a matter of concern to the CFTC in 1985.

9. Commodity Futures Trading Commission, *Annual Report* (Washington, D.C.: U.S. Government Printing Office, 1979), pp. 98-99.

10. Commodity Futures Trading Commission, *Annual Report* (Washington D.C.: U.S. Government Printing Office, 1982), p. 77.

11. Knight, Jerry, "Wheat Probe Calls Witnesses," *Washington Post,* March 23, 1979, § F, p. 1.

12. Commodity Futures Trading Commission, *Annual Report* (Washington, D.C.: U.S. Government Printing Office, 1984), p. 79. The Division of Trading and Markets was severely criticized by the General Accounting Office during the 1982 CFTC reauthorization process, because it had not conducted a rule review of either the Chicago Board of Trade or the Chicago Mercantile Exchange for four years; those two exchanges handle most of the nation's commodities futures business. That criticism led to a speed-up in the Division's rule review process.

13. In 1984 the Division of Trading and Markets implemented a rule requiring contract markets to adopt rules requiring floor brokers to be registered properly with the CFTC before executing orders for customer accounts. 17 C.F.R., § 1.62.

14. The CFTC and its staff spent more than 1,500 hours on this proposal. According to the Division of Trading and Markets director, Andrea M. Corcoran, the review of this proposal exceeded by 200 times the amount of time spent reviewing typical exchange rules.

CHAPTER 12

1. In trying to locate Goldstein, who was rumored to be in the California area, a CFTC attorney sent subpoenas to every Harold Goldstein listed with the California Department of Motor Vehicle Administration as being located in the Los Angeles area. Several Harold Goldsteins showed up to testify, as well as an irate woman whose husband, Harold Goldstein, was recuperating from open heart surgery. None of these Harold Goldsteins was the one sought by the CFTC. After working through several sources, however, the CFTC finally located the real Harold Goldstein, who happily appeared to testify. He was a gregarious and likable individual. John Schobel, who took his deposition, was also shocked to find that he and Goldstein were exact look-alikes.

2. Cadden later became director of the Division of Trading and Markets. As noted above, he was later selected by the White House to become a commissioner in order to support Chairman James Stone's program. Cadden, however, withdrew from contention when his closeness to Stone emerged as an issue in Congress. It was an unfortunate loss for the CFTC.

3. A notable exception was Addie Blitzer, an accountant who worked as an investigator in the CEA's New York regional office. Blitzer had traded commodity futures herself and worked for commodity futures firms. Consequently, she was very knowledgeable about the business. She also relished the opportunity to work with Division attorneys, and she rapidly became the agency's chief investigator.

4. Field was brought to the CFTC as a consultant for two months while the Commission awaited Schief's resignation. *Whitten Report* (see Chapter 6, note 1).

5. 434 F. Supp. 911 (S.D. N.Y. 1977)

6. The CFTC's investigation of AITC was intensive and was conducted virtually around the clock. One exhausted witness was led weeping by her attorney from a deposition in Los Angeles at almost midnight. She and her attorney were somewhat startled to see another witness being brought in to begin his deposition as midnight approached.

7. The complaints in these cases had been filed originally by the CEA prior to the creation of the CFTC, but the CFTC rendered the decisions that were appealed and affirmed by the Second and Seventh Circuits.

8. [1982-84 Transfer Binder] Comm. Fut. L. Rep. (CCH) ¶21,779 (N.D. Ohio 1983).

9. [1982-84 Transfer Binder] Comm. Fut. L. Rep. (CCH) ¶21,725 (1983).

10. [1982-84 Transfer Binder] Comm. Fut. L. Rep. (CCH) ¶21,971 (W.D. Tex. 1983).

11. [1984-1986 Transfer Binder] Comm. Fut. L. Rep. (CCH) ¶22,230 (S.D. Cal. 1984).

12. The SEC has been severely criticized for using its injunctive authority to, in effect, promulgate rules and to implement substantive law beyond its fundamental role; thereby by-passing normal policy channels for the adoption of such requirements. See generally, Karmel, Roberta, *Regulation By Prosecution* (New York: Simon and Schuster, 1982).

13. 570 F.2d 1296 (5th Cir. 1978).

14. 583 F. Supp. 1382 (S.D.N.Y. 1984).

15. 620 F.2d 900 (1st Cir. 1980).

16. U.S. Commodity Futures Trading Commission, *Annual Report* (Washington, D.C.: U.S. Government Printing Office, 1978), p. 107.

17. 451 F. Supp. 1189 (S.D.N.Y. 1978).
18. 536 F.2d 1196 (7th Cir. 1976).
19. 473 F.2d 638 (5th Cir. 1973).
20. 461 F. Supp. 659 (S.D.N.Y. 1978), *aff'd*, 598 F.2d 609 (2d Cir. 1979).
21. [1980-82 Transfer Binder] Comm. Fut. L. Rep. (CCH) ¶21,321 (S.D. Fla. 1981).
22. 738 F.2d 487 (D.C. Cir. 1984).
23. [1984-86 Transfer Binder] Comm. Fut. L. Rep. (CCH) ¶22,798 (1985).

CHAPTER 13

1. *Securities and Exchange Commission v. Monex International Ltd., dba Pacific Coast Coin Exchange, et al.* (C.D. Cal. 1974), described in Securities and Exchange Commission Litigation Release no. 6638 (December 12, 1974).
2. U.S. Commodity Futures Trading Commission, *Report For the Commodity Futures Trading Commission, Trading In Leverage Contracts For Gold and Silver,* Project 217 (Washington, D.C.: CFTC Project Study Group, April 18, 1975), p. 4.
3. 425 U.S. 185 (1976).
4. 17 C.F.R., § 31.11.

CHAPTER 14

1. Two separate challenges were made to the Commission's rules. One, *British American Commodity Options Corp. v. Bagley,* no. 76-Civ. 5124 (S.D.N.Y. Nov. 15, 1976), was consolidated with an action brought in another district, *National Association of Commodity Option Dealers v. Bagley,* no. 76-Civ.-2250 (D.D.C.). The plaintiffs in the District of Columbia action appeared in the New York action and argued the motions in the district court that ultimately led to an appeal in the Second Circuit challenging the Commission's rules. See *British American Commodity Options Corp. v. Bagley,* 552 F.2d 482, 484 n.1 (2d Cir. 1977), *cert. denied,* 434 U.S. 938 (1977).
2   17 Code of Federal Register ("CFR") § 32.4
3. CFTC Interpretive Letter no. 84-7 [1982-84 Transfer Binder] Comm. Fut. L. Rep. (CCH) ¶22,025 (February 22, 1984).
4. 43 Fed. Reg. 54, 220, 54,222 (November 21, 1978).
5. [1984-86 Transfer Binder] Comm. Fut. L. Rep. (CCH) ¶22,718 (September 30, 1985).
6. 17 C.F.R., § 33.7.

CHAPTER 15

1. U.S. Commodity Futures Trading Commission, *Report of the Advisory Committee on Definition and Regulation of Market Instruments, Recommended Policies on the Cash Market Regulatory Authority and Cash Data Needs of the Commodity Futures Trading Commission* [1975-77 Transfer Binder] Comm. Fut. L. Rep. (CCH) ¶20,225 (October 18, 1976).
2. Robinson, Charles, *Address Before the Business Seminar Series, 1984-1985,* Graduate School of Business, University of Pittsburgh, Pittsburgh, PA, May 3, 1985.
3. A somewhat more vivid description of trading on a commodity exchange is contained in Frank Norris's *The Pit,* published in 1903:

Ah, this drama of the "Provision Pits," where the rush of millions of bushels of grain, and the clatter of millions of dollars, and the tramping and the wild shouting of thousands of men filled all the air with the noise of battle! Yes, here was drama in deadly earnest—drama and tragedy and death, and the jar of mortal fighting.

4. This is not to say that hedgers are always deterred from speculating. As we have seen already, in 1978, the Cook Grain Co., one of the world's largest trading companies, was nearly destroyed as a result of speculation in soybeans by some of its traders. Those traders took positions opposite to the Hunt family of Dallas, Texas.

5. In *the matter of Stovall* [1977-80 Transfer Binder] Comm. Fut. L. Rep. (CCH) ¶20,941 (1979).

CHAPTER 16

1. The London Commodity Exchange is composed of several terminal markets, which in effect operate as separate exchanges. These markets include: the Coffee Terminal Market Association of London, Limited; the London Cocoa Terminal Market Association, Limited; the International Petroleum Exchange of London, Limited; the GASTA Soya Bean Meal Futures Association, Limited; the London and New Zealand Futures Association, Limited; the London Vegetable Oil Terminal Market Association, Limited; the London Railroad Terminal Market Association, Limited; and the United Terminal Sugar Market Association, Limited.

2. Rudolf Wolff & Co., Ltd., *Wolff's Guide to the London Metal Exchange* (London: Metal Bulletin Books Ltd., 1980), p. 15.

3. The House Report stated that nothing in the 1982 Amendments "prevents a foreign board of trade from applying to the Commission for certification that its futures contracts conform with requirements of this Act where, by its terms, the Act establishes minimum requirements for a specifically identified contract." U.S. Congress, House, *Futures Trading Act of 1982*, 97th Cong., 2nd Sess., 1982, H. Rept. 565 (Part 1), p. 85. In that connection, the House Report noted (as did the CFTC's Office of General Counsel's letter cited in text) that the Commodity Exchange Act contains specific provisions establishing minimum requirements for stock index futures contracts.

4. U.S. Commodity Futures Trading Commission, Interpretive Letter no. 81-1 [1980-82 Transfer Binder] Comm. Fut. L. Rep. (CCH) ¶21,244 (1981).

5. [1975-77 Transfer Binder] Comm. Fut. L. Rep. (CCH) ¶20,175 (June 28, 1976).

CHAPTER 17

1. The Sunshine Mine was closed in 1982 due to depressed silver prices, but was reopened in 1983.

2. [1977-80 Transfer Binder] Comm. Fut. L. Rep. (CCH) ¶20,941 (1979).

3. Letter from Andrea M. Corcoran, director, CFTC Division of Trading and Markets, re: *"Gold Warrants" As Prohibited Off-Exchange Commodity Options*, March 6, 1985. A subsequent interpretation by the CFTC's Office of General Counsel was to the same effect in a similar case involving "Gold Purchase Warrants" that were sought to be listed on the American Stock Exchange. Letter from Kenneth M. Raisler, CFTC general counsel, dated September 17, 1985.

4. Letter from John L. Manley, director, CFTC Division of Trading and Markets, re: *Proposed Offering of Commodity Certificates*, August 10, 1982.

5. *Federal Register* 46 (November 5, 1981): 55,044.

6. *Ibid.*, p. 55,047.

7. *Ibid.*

8. *Securities Week,* February 4, 1985: pp. 7-8.

9. This legislation states that

> no provision of any law in effect on the date of enactment of this Act, and no rule, regulation, or order in effect . . . may be construed to prohibit any person from purchasing, holding, selling, or otherwise dealing with gold in the United States or abroad.

Public Law no. 93-373, 88 Stat. 445 (1974).

10. Andrews, "Can Banks Succeed in Futures?" *Institutional Investor,* February 1984, p. 174.

11. Swap transactions are not limited to interest rate obligations. They may also be used for currency.

12. If the interest rate obligations are in the form of a security, however, the federal securities laws may apply. This would require registration with the SEC or an exemption before they could be sold. Care should also be taken to ensure that such transactions are not conducted in the form of insurance. But see "The Unsurest Insurance," *Euromoney,* November 1984.

It has also been asserted that interest rate obligations may, in effect, be put options. But their commercial nature would exempt them from CFTC option restrictions. See 17 Code of Federal Register (C.F.R.), § 32.4.

13. 7 United States Code (U.S.C.), § 2.

14. 737 F.2d 582 (7th Cir. 1984).

15. 2 Comm. Fut.L. Rep. (CCH) ¶22,750 (October 23, 1985). The release did not address whether pools with public participants, which commonly trade in the international market, were precluded from such trading.

16. *CFTC v. The American Board of Trade,* 473 F. Supp. 1177, 1182 (S.D.N.Y. 1979).

17. 7 U.S.C., § 6(b).

18. CFTC Office of General Counsel Interpretive Letter no. 77-12 [1977-80 Transfer Binder] Comm. Fut. L. Rep. (CCH) ¶20,467 (August 17, 1977).

19. 7 U.S.C. § 2.

20. CFTC Office of General Counsel, Interpretive Letter no. 77-12 [1977-80 Transfer Binder] Comm. Fut. L. Rep. (CCH) ¶20,467 (Aug. 17, 1977).

21. *Ibid.*

22. 737 F.2d 582 (7th Cir. 1984).

23. Compare *CFTC v. Rose,* Civ. no. 84-6717 (S.D. Fla. 1984), where the defendants were selling "extended delivery" contracts in precious metals that allowed investors, on the "maturity date" of the contract, to accept ownership and delivery, to offset the contract, or to "roll over" the contract for an additional period. In addition, ownership did not pass automatically to the customer, and there was a provision for offset.

24. It was noted in one Senate report that banks "are increasingly reluctant to provide loans to producers, merchandizers and processors on unhedged production or inventories." U.S. Congress, Senate, Commodity Futures Trading Commission Act of 1974, 93d Cong., 2d Sess., 18 1974, Senate Report 1131, p. 18.

25. The approval of the CFTC was required because the Chicago Mercantile Exchange futures transactions are subject to the overall regulation of the CFTC, and it could theoretically deny approval of the trading of a contract that was linked to a foreign futures contract. On the other hand, the Commodity Exchange Act prohibits the CFTC from regulating the terms and conditions of foreign futures contracts.

26. The Singapore government has agreed that any disputes arising out of the plan

between the Chicago Mercantile Exchange and the Simex will be adjudicated by a U.S. federal district court.

CHAPTER 18

1. Letter from Ronald Reagan to Susan Phillips, chairman, CFTC, October 18, 1984.
2. In 1968 some 15.4 million futures contracts were traded with a value of over $60 billion. By 1977 this contract value had exceeded $1 trillion, and by 1980 the number of contracts traded exceeded 82 million. By 1984, this number had increased to almost 150 million; over half of that amount were contracts for nonagricultural products.
3. "News In Brief," *Christian Science Monitor,* January 22, 1985, p. 2.
4. "Around the Nation," *Washington Post,* January 23, 1985, §A, p. 8.

BIBLIOGRAPHY

Aroni, Julius. *Futures* (New Orleans, LA: James A. Gresham, 1882).

Atwood, Albert W. "The Exchanges and Speculation." *Modern Business* (New York: Alexander Hamilton Institute) 20 (1919).

Aulletta, Ken. *Greed and Glory on Wall Street: The Fall of the House of Lehman* (New York: Random House, 1985).

Baer, Julius B. and George P. Woodruff. *Commodity Exchanges* (New York: Harper & Brothers, 1935).

Bagley, William. "Introduction: A New Body of Law in an Era of Industry Growth." *Emory Law Journal* 27 (1978):849.

Baker, Rachel. "Federal Regulation of Discretionary Accounts." *Hastings Law Journal* 32 (1981):871.

Bakken, Henry H. *Futures Trading—Origin, Development and Present Economic Status,* Futures Trading Seminar, Vol. 3 (Madison, WI: Mimir Publishers, 1966).

———. *Historical Evaluation, Theory and Legal Status of Futures Trading in American Agricultural Commodities,* Futures Trading Seminar History and Development (Madison, WI: Mimir Publishers, 1960), p. 3.

Baltic International Freight and Futures Exchange. *Biffex* (London, 1985).

Bianco, Joseph J. "The Mechanics of Futures Trading: Speculation and Manipulation." *Hofstra Law Review* 6 (1977):27.

Bor, Robert M. "Some Issues Arising in Consideration of the Futures Trading Act of 1978." *Record of the Association of the Bar of the City of New York* 24 (April 1979):278.

Boureau and Evans. *The Chicago Board of Trade and Its Operations* (Philadelphia, PA: Boureau & Evans, undated).

Boyle, James E. *Speculation and the Chicago Board of Trade* (New York: Macmillan, 1920).

Brown, George. *A Study of Futures and Speculation* (Little Rock, AR: Little Rock Board of Trade, circa 1900).

Christie, C. C. *Shall the Chicago Board of Trade Aided by the Kansas City Board of Trade, the Minneapolis Chamber of Commerce and the New York Cotton Exchange, Be Allowed to Form a Trust in the Great Agricultural Staples of the United States—An Answer to Merrill A. Teague's Denunciation of Bucket Shops,* published in Everybody's Magazine (Kansas City, Mo, 1906).

Clark, Glenn Willett. "Genealogy and Genetics of 'Contract of Sale of a Commodity Future Delivery' in the Commodity Exchange Act." *Emory Law Journal* 27 (1978):1175.

Committee on Commodities Regulation. "40 Acts Applicability to Commodity Pools and Trading Advisors." *Record of the Association of the Bar of the City of New York* 37 (November 1982):611.

Cowing, Cederic B. *Populists, Plungers and Progressives* (Princeton, NJ: Princeton University Press, 1965).

Dewey, T. Henry. *A Treatise on Contracts for Future Delivery and Commercial Wagers Including Options, Futures and Short Sales* (New York: Baker, Voorhis & Co., 1886).

———. *Legislation Against Speculation and Gambling in the Forms of Trade Including "Futures," "Options," and "Shortsales"* (New York: Baker, Voorhis & Company, 1905).

Emery, Henry C. *Speculation on the Stock and Produce Exchanges of the United States* (New York: Greenwood Press, 1969).

Feldman, Franklin and Judah Sommer. "The Special Commodity Provisions of the New Bankruptcy Code." *Business Lawyer* 37 (1982):1487.

Ferrara, Ralph and Richard T. Chase. "SEC/CFTC Accord: One Year Later, An Uneasy Peace. *"Legal Times,* January 30, 1984, p. 15.

Futures and Options World (London: Metal Bulletin Journals Ltd.), monthly issues, 1985.

Gaine, John G. "The 1978 Sunset Review of the CFTC: Analysis and Comment." *The Record of the Association of the Bar of the City of New York* 34 (April 1979):290.

Gilberg, David J. "Precious Metals Trading—The Last Frontier of Unregulated Investment." *Washington & Lee Law Review* 41 (1984):943.

Greenstone, Wayne D. "Leverage Transactions on Creating a Regulatory Theme." *Emory Law Journal* 27 (1978):909.

Gregroy, Owen K. "Banking and Commodity Market Structure: The Early Chicago Board of Trade." *Proceedings of the History of the Futures Seminar* (Chicago, IL: Chicago Board of Trade) 2 (1983):169.

Hieronymus, Thomas A. "Survival and Change: Post-World War II at the Chicago Board of Trade." Review of Research of Futures Markets. *Proceedings of the History of Futures Seminar* 2 (Chicago, IL: Chicago Board of Trade) (1983):22.

———. "Manipulation in Commodity Futures Trading: Toward a Definition." *Hofstra Law Review* 6 (1977):41.

Hoffman, G. Wright. *Hedging by Dealing In Grain Futures* (Philadelphia, PA: University of PA. Press, 1925).

Horwitz, Don and David J. Gilberg. "Introducing Brokers under the Commodity Exchange Act: A New Category of Commodity Professionals." *Washington & Lee Law Review* 40 (1983):907.

Horwitz, Don and Jerry Markham. "Sunset on the Commodity Futures Trading Commission: Scene II." *Business Lawyer* 39 (1983):67.

International Futures Exchange Limited. *Intex, the Fastest, the Most Accurate, the Only Automated Futures Exchange in the World* (Bermuda: Intex, 1985).

International Petroleum Exchange. *International Petroleum Exchange* (London, 1985).

Kaiser, Robert G. "Montana Senate Race Pits 'Nice Guy' and 'Con Artists.' " *Washington Post,* November 4, 1978, § A, p. 2.

Kane, Edward J. "Regulatory Structure in Futures Markets: Jurisdictional Competition Between the SEC, the CFTC and Other Agencies." *Journal of Futures Markets* 4 (1984):367, 375.

Kwitny, Jonathan. "Confidence Man: How To Fleece Friends and Influence People and Be Loved Besides." *Wall Street Journal,* December 20, 1984, p. 1.

London International Financial Futures Exchange. *The London International Financial Futures Exchange: An Introduction* (London, 1985).

London Meat Futures Exchange. *Pig Meat Futures Non-Traded Options* (London, 1985).

London Metal Exchange. *London Metal Exchange* (London, 1985).

Lurie, Jonathan. "Commodities Exchanges as Self-Regulating Organizations in the Late 19th Century: Some Perimeters in the History of American Administrative Law." *Rutgers Law Review* 28 (1975):1107.

———. "Private Associations, Internal Regulation and Progressivism: the Chicago Board of Trade, 1880-1923." *American Journal of Legal History* (Philadelphia, PA: Temple University School of Law) 16 (1972):215.

———. "Speculation, Risk, and Profits: The Ambivalent Agrarian in the Late 19th Century." *Agricultural History* (Berkeley CA: University of California Press) 48 (1972):269.

———. *The Chicago Board of Trade, 1859-1905: The Dynamics of Self-Regulation* (Urbana, IL: University of Illinois Press, 1979).

———. *The Chicago Board of Trade, 1874-1905, and the Development of Certain Rules and Regulations Governing its Operations, a Study in the Effectiveness of Internal Regulation.* Ph.D. dissertation, University of Wisconsin, 1970.

Markham, Jerry. "Commodity Litigation Update—1984." *Review of Securities and Commodities Regulation* 18, no. 21 (1985):20.

———. "Commodity Litigation Update—1983." *Review of Securities and Commodities Regulation* 17 (1984):945.

———. "Commodity Litigation Update—1982." *Review of Securities and Commodities Regulation* 15 (1982):795.

———. "The Seventh Amendment and CFTC Reparation Proceedings." *Iowa Law Review* 68 (1982):87.

―――. "Developments in Commodities Litigation—1981." *Review of Securities Regulation* 14 (1981):843.

―――. "Developments in Commodities Litigation." *Review of Securities Regulation* 13 (1980):813.

―――. "CFTC Emergency Powers." *Review of Securities Regulation* 12 (1979).

―――. "Injunctive Actions under the Commodity Exchange Act." Bureau of National Affairs (BNA), *Securities and Regulation and Law Reporter* B-1 (1979).

―――. "Investigations under the Commodity Exchange Act." *Administrative Law Review* 31 (1979):285.

―――. "Regulation of International Transactions under the Commodity Exchange Act." *Fordham Law Review* 48 (1979):129.

―――. "Restrictions on Shared Decision-Making Authority in American Business." *California Western Law Review* 11 (1975):217.

Markham, Jerry and Kyra K. Bergin. "The Role of the Commodity Futures Trading Commission in International Commodity Transactions." *George Washington Journal of International Law and Economics* 18 (1985):301; reprinted in part in *Resources Policy* (Surrey, England: Butterworth Scientific Ltd., 1985).

―――. "Customer Rights under the Commodity Exchange Act." *Vanderbilt Law Review* 37 (1984):1299.

―――. "Problems with Futures Trading." *International Financial Law Review* (1984):23.

Markham, Jerry and David J. Gilberg. "Federal Regulation of Bank Activities in the Commodities Markets." *Business Lawyer* 39 (1984):1719.

―――. "Stock and Commodity Options—Two Regulatory Approaches and Their Conflicts." *Albany Law Review* 47 (1983):741.

―――. "Washington Watch—Stock Index Futures." *Corporation Law Review* 6 (1982):59.

Markham, Jerry and Ellen R. Meltzer. "Secondary Liability under the Commodity Exchange Act—Respondeat Superior, Aiding and Abetting, Supervision and Scienter." *Emory Law Journal* 27 (1978):1115.

Markham, Jerry and John M. Schobel. "Commodity Exchange Rule Approval—Procedural Mishmash or Anti-Trust Umbrella?" Special Supplement, BNA, *Anti-Trust and Trade Regulation Reporter*, January 14, 1976; and BNA, Special Supplement, *Securities Regulation and Law Reporter,.* January 15, 1976.

―――. "Self-Regulation under the Commodity Exchange Act—Can the CFTC Make It Work?" Special Supplement, BNA, *Securities Regulation and Law Reporter,* 1976.

McDonnell, William E., Jr., and Susan K. Freund. "The CFTC's Large Trader Reporting System: History and Development." *Business Lawyer* 38 (1983):917.

Meeting Panel. "The Commodity Futures Trading Commission." *Administrative Law Review* 27 (1975):367.

Melamed, Leo. "The Mechanics of a Commodity Futures Exchange: A Critique of Automation of the Transaction Process." *Hofstra Law Review* 6 (1977):149.

Mitchell, Mark H. "The Regulation of Commodity Trading Advisors." *Emory Law Journal* 27 (1978):957.

Note. "Federal Regulation of Commodity Futures Trading." *Yale Law Journal* 60
(1951):822.

Note. "Federal Regulatory Legislation: The Federal Grain Futures Act." *George
Washington Law Review* 2 (1934):457.

Note. "Legislation: The Commodity Exchange of 1936." *University of Pennsylvania
Law Review* 85 (1937):614.

Note. "The Coffee Exchange Debacle: Highlighting the Need for Further Regulation of Futures Trading Through the Sherman and Commodity Exchange
Acts." *Yale Law Journal* 64 (1955):906.

Note. "The Exchanges of Minneapolis, Duluth, Kansas City, Mo., Omaha, Buffalo,
Philadelphia, Milwaukee and Toledo." *Annals of the American Academy of
Political and Social Sciences,* (Philadelphia, PA: American Academy of Po-
litical and Social Sciences) 38 (1911):545.

Paul, Allen B. "The Past and Future of the Commodities Exchanges." *Agricultural
History* (Berkeley, CA: University of California Press) 56, no. 287 (1982).

Peterson, Arthur G. "Futures Trading with Particular Reference to Agricultural
Commodities." *Agricultural History* (Berkeley, CA: University of California
Press) 7 (1933), p. 68.

Pitt, Harvey and Jerry Markham. "SEC Civil Injunctive Actions: A Reply." *Review
of Securities Regulation* 6 (1973); reprinted, Securities Law Review, (1973):955;
and "Defending SEC Enforcement Actions—How to Litigate Securities Problems." *New York Law Journal* (1974).

Rainbolt, John V. II. "Regulating the Grain Gambler and His Successors." *Hofstra
Law Review* 6 (1977):1.

Rosen, Jeffrey S. "Reparations Proceedings under the Commodity Exchange Act."
Emory Law Journal 27 (1978):1005.

Rothstein, Morton. *American Wheat and the British Market, 1860-1905.* Ph. D.
dissertation, Cornell University, 1960.

Russo, Thomas A., and Edwin L. Lion. "The Exclusive Jurisdiction of the Commodity Futures Trading Commission." *Hofstra Law Review* 6 (1977):57.

Schief, William R. and Jerry Markham. "The Nation's 'Commodity Cops'—Efforts
by the Commodity Futures Trading Commission to Enforce the Commodity
Exchange Act." *Business Lawyer* 34 (1978):19.

Schneider, Howard. "Commodities Law and Predispute Arbitration Clauses." *Hofstra Law Review* 6 (1977):129.

Schneider, Howard and Fred Santo. "Commodity Futures Trading Commission:
A Review of the 1978 Legislation." *Business Lawyer* 34 (1979):1755.

Schobel, John M. and Jerry Markham. "Commodity Options—A New Industry or
Another Debacle?" Special Supplement, BNA, *Securities Regulation and Law
Reporter* (1976).

Singapore International Monetary Exchange. *Simex Financial Futures* (Singapore,
1985).

Sydney Futures Exchange Limited. *Annual Report* (Sydney, Australia, 1983).

Tamarkin, Bob. *The New Gatsbys* (New York: William Morrow and Company,
1985).

Taylor. "Trading in Commodity Futures—a New Standard of Legality?" *Yale Law Journal* 43 (1933):63.

Tokyo Grain Exchange. *The Tokyo Grain Exchange* (Tokyo, 1985).

U.S. Board of Governors of the Federal Reserve System, Commodity Futures Trading Commission and Securities and Exchange Commission. *A Study of the Effects on the Economy of Trading in Futures and Options* (Washington, D.C.: U.S. Government Printing Office, December 1984).

U.S. Commodity Futures Trading Commission. *A Study of The Nature, Extent and Effects of Futures Trading by Persons Possessing Material Non-Public Information* (Washington D.C., 1985).

———. *The Silver Market of 1979/80, Actions of the Chicago Board of Trade and the Commodity Exchange, Inc., Investigative Report of the Division of Trading and Markets* (Washington, D.C., 1985).

———. *Commodity Futures Trading Commission—The First Ten Years* (Washington, D.C., 1985).

———. *Addendum to 1984 Annual Report Uses of Live Stock Futures Markets by Large Hedgers* (Washington, D.C.: U.S. Government Printing Office, 1984).

———. *Report to Congress and Response to Section 21 of the Commodity Exchange Act, Pub. L. no. 96-276, 2d Sess., § 7, 94 Stat. 542* (Washington, D.C., June 1, 1980).

———. *Annual Reports* (Washington, D.C.: U.S. Government Printing Office, 1976-1984).

———. *Report of the Advisory Committee on the Market Instruments to the CFTC on Recommended Policies on Futures, Forward and Leverage Contracts and Transactions* (Washington, D.C., July 16, 1976).

———. *Report for the Commodity Futures Trading Commission: Trading in Leverage Contracts in Gold and Silver, Project no. 217* (Washington, D.C.: CFTC Program Study Group, April 18, 1975).

———. *Annual Report* (Washington, D.C., 1975).

U.S. Comptroller General. *Report to the Congress of the United States, Commodity Futures Regulations—Current Status and Unresolved Problems* (Washington, D.C.: U.S. Government Printing Office, July 15, 1982).

U.S. Congress. *Commodity Futures Trading Commission Act of 1974.* 93rd Cong., 2d Sess., 1974, H. Rept. 975.

———. *Congressional Record.* Senate, pp. 4760-71, August 9, 1921; House, pp. 1312-41, May 11, 1921; House, pp. 1366-99, May 12, 1921; House, p. 4888, August 11, 1921; Senate, pp. 4646-56, August 4, 1921; House, pp. 5555-60, August 23, 1921.

———. *Congressional Record.* House, pp. 9403-50, June 26, 1922.

———. *Congressional Record.* House, pp. 12,720-25, September 15, 1922.

———. *Congressional Record.* 74th Cong., 2d Sess: Senate, May 29, 1936, pp. 8288-93; Senate, April 27, 1936, pp. 6159-64; House, June 4, 1934, pp. 10,443-52; Senate, May 25, 1936, pp. 7845-73; House, June 3, 1935, pp. 8585-95; Senate, May 4, 1936, pp. 6612-13; Senate, May 26, 1936, pp. 7905-12; Senate, May 26, 1936, pp. 7916-23; Senate, May 27, 1936, pp. 8010-90.

———. *Congressional Record.* 90th Cong., 2d Sess., House, August 22, 1967, pp.

23,650-53; House, October 30, 1967, p. 30,496; House, November 29, 1967, pp. 34,206-207; House, November 30, 1967, p. 34,439, 34,391-34,403.

————. *Congressional Record.* 93rd Cong., 2d Sess., House, April 10, 1974, pp. 2846-51; House, April 11, 1974, p. 2923-55; House, October 9, 1974, pp. 10,247-66; Senate, September 9, 1974, pp. 16,127-37; Senate, October 10, 1974, pp. 18,864-72.

————. House. 97th Cong., 2d Sess., 1982, H. Rept. 565.

————. House. *Agriculture Appropriation Bills, Hearings Conducted Before a Sub-committee of the House Committee on Appropriations* (Washington, D.C.: U.S. Government Printing Office, 1924, 1926, 1928, 1930, 1934, 1936-38, 1943-46, 1954-1974).

————. House. *Amend Grain Futures Act.* 73rd Cong., 2d Sess., 1934, H. Rept. 1637.

————. House. *Amend the Commodity Exchange Act, Hearings Before the Committee on Agriculture on H.R. 11930 and H.R. 12317.* 90th Cong., 1st Sess., 1967.

————. House. *Amendment of Commodity Exchange Act.* 90th Cong., 1st Sess., 1967, H. Rept. 743.

————. House. *Clarifying the Jurisdiction of the Securities and Exchange Commission and the Definition of Securities.* 97th Cong., 2d Sess., June 24, 1982, H. Rept. 626, Part I.

————. House. *Commodity Exchange Act Extension and Amendments.* 95th Cong., 2d Sess., 1978, H. Rept. 1181.

————. House. *Commodity Futures Trading Commission Act of 1974, Hearings Before the Committee on Agriculture on H.R. 11955.* 93rd Cong., 2d Sess., 1974.

————. House. *Commodity Shortselling.* 72nd Cong., 1st Sess., 1932, H. Rept. 1551.

————. House. *Extend Commodity Exchange Act, Hearings Before the Subcommittee on Conservation and Credit of the Committee on Agriculture on H.R. 10285.* 95th Cong., 2d Sess., 1978.

————. House. *Futures Trading Act of 1982.* 97th Cong. 2d Sess., 1982, H.Rept. 565.

————. House. *Hearings Before the Committee on Agriculture on Bills for the Prevention of Dealing in Futures on Boards of Trade, etc..* 61st Cong., 2d Sess, 1910.

————. House. *Hearings Before the Subcommittee on Special Business Problems of the Permanent Select Committee on Small Business Problems Involved in the Marketing of Grain and Other Commodities.* 93rd Cong., 1st Sess., 1973.

————. House. *Investigative Study on the CFTC, Report to the Committee on Appropriations by Mr. Whitten for Use by the Subcommittee on Agriculture, Rural Development and Related Agencies.* 95th Cong., 2d Sess., 1978.

————. House. *Prevention and Removal of Obstructions and Burdens Upon Interstate Commerce and Grain by Regulating Transactions on Grain-Futures Exchanges.* 67th Cong., 2d Sess., 1922, H. Rept. 1095.

————. House. *Silver Prices and the Adequacy of Federal Actions in the Marketplace, 1979-80.* 97th Cong., 1st Sess., 1981, H. Rept. 395.

————. Senate. 67th Cong., 2d Sess., 1922, S. Rept. 871.

———. Senate. *Amendment of Commodity Exchange Act.* 90th Cong., 2d Sess., 1968, S. Rept. 947.

———. Senate. *Commodity Futures Trading Commission Act of 1974.* 93rd Cong., 2d Sess., 1974, S. Rept. 1131.

———. Senate. *Commodity Futures Trading Commission Act of 1974.* 93rd Cong., 2d Sess., 1974, S. Rept. 1194.

———. Senate. *Commodity Futures Trading Commission Act, Hearings Before the Committee on Agriculture and Forestry on S. 2485, S. 2578, S. 2837, and H.R. 13113.* 93rd Cong., 2d Sess., 1974.

———. *Commodity Investment Fraud.* 97th Cong., 2d Sess., 1982, S. Rept. 495.

———. Senate. *Fluctuations in Wheat Futures.* 69th Cong., 1st Sess. 1926, S. Doc. 135.

———. Senate. *Futures Trading Act of 1982.* 97th Cong., 2d Sess., 1982, S. Rept. 384.

———. Senate. *Futures Trading Act of 1978.* 95th Cong., 2d Sess., 1978, S. Rept. 1239.

———. Senate. *Future Trading in Grain, Hearings Before the Committee on Agriculture and Forestry on H.R. 5676.* 67th Cong., 1st Sess., 1921.

———. Senate. *Reauthorization of the Commodity Futures Trading Commission.* 95th Cong., 2d Sess., 1978, S. Rept. 850.

———. Senate. *Reauthorization of the Commodity Futures Trading Commission, Hearings Before the Subcommittee on Agricultural Research and General Legislation of the Committee on Agriculture, Nutrition and Forestry.* 95th Cong., 2d Sess., 1978.

———. Senate. *Study of Coffee Prices, Report of the Special Subcommittee on Coffee Prices of the Senate Committee on Banking and Currency,* subcommittee print. 83rd Cong., 2d Sess., 1955.

———. Senate. *Suspension of Reports of Large Speculative Accounts in Grain Futures.* Senate Doc. no. 61, 73rd Cong., 1st Sess., 1933.

———. Senate. *Trading in Grain Futures.* 68th Cong., 1st Sess., 1924, S. Doc. 110.

———. Senate and House Reports. 67 Cong., 1st Sess., 1921: H. R. Rep. 44; S. Rep. 212; H. R. Rep. 345; H. R. Rep. 362.

U.S. Department of Agriculture. *Annual Reports of the Department of Agriculture* (Washington, D.C.: U.S. Government Printing Office, 1922-1923).

———. *Collapse in Cotton Prices* (Washington, D.C.: Department of Agriculture, Commodity Exchange Authority, March 1947).

———. *Current Speculation in Commodity Futures* (Washington, D.C.: Department of Agriculture, Commodity Exchange Authority, July 31, 1950).

———. *Delivery Notices in Cotton Futures Markets,* Circular no. 794 (Washington, D.C.: U.S. Government Printing Office, July 1948).

———. *Futures Trading Under the Commodity Exchange, 1946-1954* (Washington, D.C.: Department of Agriculture, Commodity Exchange Authority, December 1954).

———. *Hearings Before the Commodity Exchange Authority, Trading in Puts and Calls on Non-Regulated Commodities* (Washington, D.C.: Commodity Exchange Authority, February 14, 1973).

————. *Report of the Secretary of Agriculture of 1937* (Washington, D.C.: U.S. Government Printing Office, 1937), p. 74.

————. *Reports of the Chief of the Commodity Exchange Administration* (Washington, D.C.: U.S. Government Printing Office, 1937-42, 1947-53).

————. *Reports of the Grain Futures Administration* (Washington, D.C.: U.S. Government Printing Office, 1925, 1930-36).

————. *Speculation in Soybeans* (Washington, D.C.: Department of Agriculture, Commodity Exchange Authority, August 10, 1950).

————. *Trading in Commodity Futures.* S. Doc. 110, 68th Cong., 1st Sess. (Washington, D.C.: U.S. Government Printing Office, 1924).

————. *Trading in Commodity Futures* (Washington, D.C.: Department of Agriculture, Commodity Exchange Authority, 1940).

————. *Trading for Others in Commodity Futures,* Circular no. 539 (Washington, D.C.: U.S. Government Printing Office, October 1935).

U.S. Federal Trade Commission. *Report on the Grain Trade,* vols. 1-7 (Washington, D.C.: U.S. Government Printing Office, 1920-1926).

U.S. President. *Presidential Documents: Gerald R. Ford,* vol. 10 Washington D.C.: U.S. Government Printing Office. (1974), p. 1366.

U.S. Securities and Exchange Commission. *Report of the SEC, the Silver Crisis of 1980* (Washington, D.C.: Securities and Exchange Commission, October 1983).

U.S. Treasury Department. *Treasury/Federal Reserve Study of Treasury Futures Markets,* vols. 1-2 (Washington, D.C., May, 1979).

White, Frederick L. "The Commodity-Related Provisions of the Bankruptcy Acts of 1978." *Record of the Association of the Bar of the City of New York* 34 (April 1979):262.

Winnipeg Grain Exchange. *The Winnipeg Grain Exchange* (Winnipeg, Canada, 1985).

Young, Mark D. "A Test of Federal Sunset: Congressional Reauthorization of the Commodity Futures Trading Commission." *Emory Law Journal* 27 (1978):853.

Zweig, Phillip L. *Belly Up: The Collapse of the Penn Square Bank* (New York: Crown Publishers, 1985).

CASES

Abrams v. Oppenheimer Government Securities Inc. 737 F. 2d 582 (7th Cir. 1984).
American International Trading Company v. Bagley. 536 F. 2d 1196 (7th Cir. 1976).

Board of Trade v. CFTC. [1977-80 Transfer Binder] Comm. Fut. L. Rep. (CCH) ¶20,887 (7th Cir. 1979).
Board of Trade v. Christie Grain and Stock Co. 198 U.S. 236 (1905).
British American Commodity Options Corp. v. Bagley. 552 F. 2d 482, 484 N.1 (2d Cir. 1977), *cert. denied,* 434 U.S. 938 (1977).

CFTC v. Bloch. [1980-82 Transfer Binder] Comm. Fut. L. Rep. (CCH) ¶21,321 (S.D. Fla. 1981).
CFTC v. Commodities Fluctuations Systems, Inc. 583 F. Supp. 1382 (S.D.N.Y. 1984).
CFTC v. Crown Colony Commodity Options, Ltd. 434 F. Supp. 911 (S.D.N.Y. 1977).
CFTC v. Daskoski. [1984-86 Transfer Binder] Comm. Fut. L. Rep. (CCH) ¶22,230 (S.D. Cal. 1984).
CFTC v. Falk. [1982-84 Transfer Binder] Comm. Fut. L. Rep. (CCH) ¶21,971 (W.D. Tex. 1983).
CFTC v. First National Bullion Corp. 461 F. Supp. 659 (S.D.N.Y. 1978), *aff'd,* 598 F. 2d 609 (2d Cir. 1979).
CFTC v. Muller. 570 F. 2d 1296 (5th Cir. 1978).
CFTC v. Nahas. 738 F. 2d 487 (D.C. Cir. 1984).
CFTC v. Rose. Civ. no. 84-6717 (S.D. Fla. 1984).
CFTC v. The American Board of Trade. 473 F. Supp. 1177, 1182 (S.D.N.Y. 1979).
CFTC v. Troyer. [1982-84 Transfer Binder] Comm. Fut. L. Rep. (CCH) ¶21,779 (N.D. Ohio 1983).
CFTC v. Wientraub. [1984-86 Transfer Binder] Comm. Fut. L. Rep. (CCH) ¶22,563 (U.S. 1985).
Cargill, Incorporated v. Hardin. 452 F. 2d, 1154, (8th Cir. 1971), *cert. denied, Cargill, Inc. v. Butz,* 406 U.S. 932, 1972.

Chicago Board of Trade v. SEC. 677 F. 2d 1137 (7th Cir. 1982), *vacated as moot,* 459 U.S. 1026 (1982).
Chicago Mercantile Exchange v. Deaktor. 414 U.S. 113 (1973).
ContiCommodities Services Inc. v. Schor. 473 U.S. (1985).

Ernst & Ernst v. Hochfelder. 425 U.S. 185 (1976).

Fairchild, Arabatzis, & Smith Inc. v. Sackheim. 451 F. Supp. 1189 (S.D.N.Y. 1978).

General Foods Corporation v. Brannan. 170 F. 2d 220 (7th Cir. 1948).
Great Western Food Distributors, Inc. v. Brannan. 201 F. 2d 476 (7th Cir. 1953), cert. denied; *Great Western Food Distributors, Inc. v. Benson.* 345 US 997 (1953).

Hill v. Wallace. 259 U.S. 46 (1922).

In the Matter of Murphy. 2 Comm. Fut. L. Rep. (CCH) ¶22,798 (1985).
In the Matter of Peabody Trading Co. of Boston. [1982-84 Transfer Binder] Comm. Fut. L. Rep. (CCH) ¶21,725 (1983).
In the Matter of Stovall [1977-80 Transfer Binder] Comm. Fut. L. Rep. (CCH) ¶20,941 (1978).

Leist v. Simplot. 638 F. 2d 283 (2d Cir. 1980), *affirmed Sub Nom., Merrill Lynch, Pierce, Fenner, & Smith, Inc. v. Curran,* 456 U.S. 353 (1982).
Lloyd Carr & Co. v. Commodity Futures Trading Commission. 567 F. 2d 1193 (2d Cir. 1977).

Merrill Lynch, Pierce, Fenner & Smith, Inc. v. Curran. 456 U.S. 353 (1982).
Miller v. New York Produce Exchange. 550 F. 2d 762, 766 (2d Cir. 1977), *cert. denied,* 434 U.S. 823 (1975).

Peto v. Howell. 101 F. 2d 353 (7th Cir. 1938) and 117 F. 2d 249 (7th Cir. 1941), *cert. denied,* 313 U.S. 583 (1941).
Precious Metals Associates Inc. v. CFTC. 620 F. 2d 900 (1st Cir. 1980).

Ricci v. Chicago Mercantile Exchange. 409 U.S. 289 (1973).

Schor v. CFTC. [1984-86 Transfer Binder] Comm. Fut. L. Rep. (CCH) ¶22,667 (D.C.Cir. 1985).
Seligson v. New York Produce Exchange. 378 F. Supp. 1076, 1097-1098 (S.D.N.Y. 1974).
Strobl v. New York Mercantile Exchange. [1984-86 Transfer Binder] Comm. Fut. L. Rep. (CCH) ¶22,647 (2d Cir. 1985), p. 30,733.

United States v. Dial. [1984-86 Transfer Binder] Comm. Fut. L. Rep. (CCH) ¶22,549 (7th Cir. 1985).
United States v. Patten. 226 U.S. 525 (1913).
United States v. Security State Bank and Trust Co. 473 F. 2d 638 (5th Cir. 1973).

Volkart Brothers, Inc. v. Freeman. 311 F. 2d 52, (5th Cir. 1962).

Wallace v. Cutten. 298 U.S. 229 (1936).
Wiscope S.A. v. CFTC 604 F. 2d 764 (2d Cir. 1979), *reversing* [1977-80 Transfer Binder] Comm. Fut. L. Rep. (CCH) ¶20,785 (1979).

INDEX

INDEX

ABOUT THE AUTHOR

Jerry W. Markham is a partner in the Washington, D.C., office of Rogers & Wells, specializing in commodities law and litigation. Mr. Markham is also an Adjunct Professor of Law at Georgetown University in Washington, D.C. He was previously Chief Counsel of the Division of Enforcement of the United States Commodity Futures Trading Commission, Secretary and Counsel of the Chicago Board Options Exchange, Inc., and an Attorney with the United States Securities and Exchange Commission.

Mr. Markham has published widely in the area of commodities futures regulations. His articles have appeared in the *Review of Securities and Commodities Regulation,* the *Fordham Law Review, The Business Lawyer,* and other legal publications. Mr. Markham holds law degrees from Georgetown University (LL.M.) and from the University of Kentucky (J.D.). He is a member of the bars of New York, District of Columbia, Illinois, and other jurisdictions.